Celtic

CROSSROADS

THE ART OF VAN MORRISON

Design: David Houghton
Printed by: Unwin Brothers Limited

Published by: Sanctuary Publishing Limited, The Colonnades,
82 Bishops Bridge Road, London W2 6BB

Photographs: Michael Ochs Archives/Redferns (cover),
Colin Moore for Wavelength, Retna Pictures and Redferns

While the publishers have made every reasonable effort to trace the
copyright owners for any or all of the photographs in this book,
there may be some omissions of credits for which we apologise.

ISBN: 1-86074-169-X

Celtic
CROSSROADS

THE ART OF VAN MORRISON

Brian Hinton

ABOUT THE AUTHOR

"The trip to the lighthouse became an important aspect of the show. Elton John's legendary percussionist Ray Cooper (last seen, photographed on the foreshore at Limehouse, modelling designer tat with his old mucker Steve Berkoff) offered a lift in his limo to a rain-drenched Dr Brian Hinton, poet, hedge scholar, and apologist for that great lost guitarist (and bibliophile), Martin Stone."
Iain Sinclair: Lights Out For The Territory (1997)

Brian Hinton co-edits *Tears In The Fence*, a literary and ecological magazine, and has recently co-ordinated a conference devoted to visionaries and outsiders in the arts. He read English at Magdalen College, Oxford, and went on to take his PhD in the uses of myth and legend in contemporary British poetry.

Sanctuary have already published Brian Hinton's *Message To Love: The Isle Of Wight Festival* and *Both Sides Now*, his recent and widely acclaimed study of Joni Mitchell. In *Celtic Crossroads* – a title which indicates the singer's immersion both in the spooked mythos of the blues and the rich brew of Western folklore – Hinton proves conclusively, and entertainingly, that Van Morrison is one of the major artists of our time.

ACKNOWLEDGMENTS

I would like to thank the following: Penny, Jeff, Michelle and Eddy at Sanctuary Publishing, Julian Bell, Emma Bradford, Ken Brooks, David and Monique Caddy – fellow poets and purveyors of fine homemade wines – Alan Clayson, Mike Cunliffe for keeping me sane (ish), (rock poet) Andy Darlington, Alan and Caroline Dawson at Replays, Jean Foister for having faith, Angela Hampton for the photographs and lots of lovely food, Happy Daze, David Harris for his generosity, Amanda Hemingway for her support and beauty, Sally, Scott and Dave Henderson, Jeff Lewis for sniffing out rare vinyl like a truffle hound, Carl Major for his deep knowledge of contemporary poetry, Eli McCarthy for her personal reminiscences, Eileen McManus for just about everything, Phil McMullen of the *Ptolemaic Terrascope*, Neil Philip for setting me on the right path, James Sale for guiding me through the Internet, Don Saul for the tapes, Oliver Scott (the rock sage of New Zealand), Iain Sinclair, Ron and Audrey Smith, Dick Taylor, Vic and the other two wise men of the Isle of Wight Rock Archives (thanks for the Robyn Hitchcock tapes), the long suffering staff at Dimbola, and the mysterious couple at the Southampton Record Fair.

Particular thanks to Geoff Wall who has helped way beyond the cause of duty with rare cassettes and videos, information and support, and to Ben Cunliffe for his hard work.

Clive Whichelow of Backnumbers has been invaluable in finding rare rock magazines missing from my own vast archive of memorabilia. I have listed my main sources of printed information in the bibliography.

CONTENTS

INTRODUCTION

Did Ye Get Healed?

It is early 1996, and Van Morrison and band headline *Later*, BBC2's mix and match of live music at its best, minted fresh in the studio. Van is dressed in black, from stetson to dark glasses to boots, like a reject from the film *Blues Brothers*. His stumpy frame is taut with intensity as he delivers his lyrics with a mixture of passion and bad temper, then steps back, his arms rigid at his sides, while his instrumentalists solo in turn. Van nods his head in time to the music, as if lost to it. Almost hidden in his clothes, he is coming on as a jazz singer, strict tempo and clipped back emotions, but to any viewer alive to Van's past, a whole cavalcade of images stretch behind him. The surly and long haired hard man of Them, all Irish snarls and sexual menace, the adopted Californian hippie – cool in a kaftan – of the early seventies, the mystical voyager of *Veedon Fleece*. All cohere into this highly private individual, whose image now repels any attempt to personalise or penetrate its armour. Propped up against Georgie Fame, whose affability and musical skill are upfront, and publicly acceptable, the singer remains an enigma, an empty space, a holy fool, his very lack of personality somehow directed into that wonderful voice, both passionate and threatening, mellifluous and spiky, all at the same time.

In his otherwise fine study of Van Morrison, John Collis opens by wrong footing his readers with the following statement of intent: "One false approach to Morrison's work is to regard him as a poet working within the rock framework." As this is the common perception of Van by his huge and deeply loyal audience, one asks for a little elucidation on this point. "Poetry should be language in its most polished form, and as a distillation of the poet's experience." Collis immediately wrong foots himself by admitting that Morrison often succeeds at doing exactly this. He then spoils things by adding that Van is more likely to repeat a phrase, mantra-like, or descend into scat singing. "The words may often be prosaic, and so can hardly be poetry."

To which one could retort that the distinguished poet and mystic Kathleen Raine once described poetry as "language organised for speaking aloud". Van Morrison's lyrics are spine tingling for exactly this reason; like any great poet from Blake to Seamus Heaney he takes words back to their origins in magic. By twisting and chanting and repeating and taking the prosaic to pieces, and building it into new structures, digging deep into the underlying rhythms of language and sound, he can transform both himself and his audience into a different reality. Indeed, Morrison is returning poetry to its earliest roots – as in Homer or Old English epics like *Beowulf* or the Psalms or folk song – in all of which words and music combine to form a new reality.

In this respect, Collis gives a useful warning, for any attempt to study Morrison's lyrics apart from the music that gives them life is doomed to failure, and the worst kind of academic drivel. As Greil Marcus once pointed out, too many rock critics attach far too much importance to lyrics alone. It is Morrison's flexible and highly rhythmic voice, and the musical patterns he and his carefully chosen sidemen (and women) weave around the words he extemporises, which transform them into a wider utterance. *Astral Weeks* is perhaps the finest example in all of rock of how everything can cohere into a highly emotional, charged whole. In an interview with the Irish fanzine *Into The Music*, David Hayes declares that Van is the only person he has met in the music business who "if all the elements are right and everything is in place, can take the music into a totally different realm, where you kind of melt into it". The guitarist Arty McGlynn told Joe Jackson of the *Irish Times* that working with Morrison was like "hanging on by your fingertips, eighty-five stories up".

Like any true poet, Van functions as a kind of shaman or high priest, heightening our senses. A rare recording by one of his great mentors, WB Yeats, brings through the crackle the sound of a voice which is singing, incantatory, strongly rhythmic. Morrison draws into his work all kinds of influences, from blues shouters to the hellfire preachers of pentecostal Christianity, from jazz and R&B and country and rock 'n' roll music to the English mystical tradition. The title of this book, *Celtic Crossroads*, reflects exactly this dichotomy between Van's literal and wished-for heritage, the blues and Irish traditional music, from which he has forged a new alchemy, "Caledonian soul".

It has long been my contention that the very greatest rock music has attempted similarly to forge a unity out of sensuality and mystical awareness. This is not something confined to rock music. Dante's *Divine Comedy* translates the poet's platonic love for Beatrice into a quest for paradise, just as Yeats' work abandons, conversely, its mystical enquiries to lie down in the "rag and bone shop of the heart". Nearer to the present day, John Coltrane's music can be viewed as a mystical quest, leading from post-bop and heroin addiction to a search for spiritual meaning, while Marvin Gaye's sad and tragic life was lit up by his search for "sexual healing". In rock terms, Tim Buckley's extraordinary album *Greetings From LA* abandons the singer's journey through psychedelic folk and free-form jazz for a kind of brutal Philly soul, in which "I talk in tongues" functions both as oral sex and the kind of pentecostal wordlessness which came to Christ's apostles after the Resurrection.

Much the same insight flickers briefly on the opening track of Lou Reed's masterful *New York*. A similar act of love offers a brief moment of illumination, doomed in that particular Romeo and Juliet conjunction, which returns as the album's one moment of real hope. In 'Beginning Of A Great Adventure', the man who once sailed darkened seas under the influence of heroin, and made the third Velvet album a cross-section of forbidden pleasures, surrenders himself to simple, heterosexual love, and the possibility of having children.

Van Morrison's greatest music inhabits this charmed space, where it is difficult to disentangle sacred and profane love. His favourite image of a garden all misty wet with rain could be Eden, or Paradise, or his own back garden. Only someone who has celebrated the bodily simplicities of 'Gloria', or the adult sex of *Moondance*, one of the great albums to which to make love, which can also voyage truly "into the mystic", can then take his audience with him into the complex truths of, say, *No Guru, No Method, No Teacher*. There is a kind of trust involved in such a venture which, once broken, is lost forever.

Morrison's particular muse is close to the charged beauty of Dylan's 'Sad Eyed Lady Of The Lowland', at once lover and goddess whom the singer both worships and fears, or a later song where (presumably) Sara is now both wife and Egyptian deity. "I married Isis on the fourth day of June." The particularity of the date is all important. It anchors a mysterious story in some kind of imagined fact. Richard Thompson at his greatest can touch the same world, in the holy terror of 'Devonside', or his album *Pour Down Like Silver* where songs of human love could just as well be addressed to Allah, or vice versa.

To be too precious about this sort of thing would be a disaster. The Top Ten is full of examples of music which works both on the dance floor and in the head. Prince's work seems to skate on the point between extreme and often deviant sex and religious abandon. Even Madonna, whose appropriation of Catholicism to secular couplings has provoked charges of blasphemy – her very name! – can also sing of the finest sex making her feel just "like a virgin, for the very first time". Good alliteration, by the way. In my own recent book on Joni Mitchell, I tried to show how the finest of Joni's music addressed just such a dichotomy, tied in with her own personal quest for freedom: Coyote smelling her scent on his fingers, the singer's hopeless yearning for 'Blue', the consolations of domestic love in *Wild Things Run Fast.*

Back in the hit parade, The Beach Boys' 'God Only Knows' is half love song, half hymn, while Alison Moyet's 'Love Resurrection' is both astoundingly filthy and genuinely moving. It is no coincidence that the author of, to date, probably the best biography of Van Morrison, Steve Turner, has also written brilliantly about these matters in *Hungry For Heaven: Rock And Roll And The Search For Redemption*, albeit from a strictly Christian perspective that I myself cannot fully share.

It is the beauty of Van Morrison's endless questioning of such matters that he has never settled long on any one faith or religion, taking what he can from each, and moving on. Those present at his greatest concerts all attest to the special atmosphere that he can weave between performer and audience, a communal joyousness, which they have only elsewhere experienced in the highest forms of – no marketing ploy intended – "world music", the Sufic chanting of Nusrat Fateh Khan, or the yearning soliloquies of Salif Keita. Perhaps it comes down to the power of the human voice, beyond that of any instrument, to express and channel such longings and such assurance.

In an earlier, and bad tempered, study of Morrison's music, John Rogan declares that "while some writers have attempted to present Van as the misunderstood, sensitive artist, I find such views conceptually naive". Well, I find, in turn, such cynicism conceptually null and void. Rather than trying to inflict some kind of amateur psychoanalysis on the singer – or the reader – I intend to look at the odd twists and turns of Morrison's career, from which a far clearer picture will emerge of a complex and fascinating character.

Van Morrison has followed a unique, sometimes perverse musical path, and along the way he has produced some of the most enduring and emotionally charged records of the last thirty years, from 'Gloria' to *The Healing Game*. His songs have acted as the soundtrack of a generation. Van's career has been both rich and strange, from apprentice days with an Irish showband to the rough R&B of Them, with whom he shared 1967 club appearances with The Doors, and onto the self-revelation of *Astral Weeks* and spellbinding live appearances with his Caledonia Soul Orchestra.

Since a mysterious three year disappearance at the height of his fame, Morrison has issued a series of increasingly profound albums – laced with his own peculiar wit – taking on board Celtic mysteries, his search for some kind of spiritual epiphany, and the simple joys of being alive. Sung with total passion, straight from his soul.

Musically, his work has grown to encompass pop, rock, jazz, R&B, blues, soul, folk, classical and ambient elements, fusing them into one. He has enjoyed fruitful collaborations with Bob Dylan, The Chieftains, Cliff Richard, The Band, the Irish poet Paul Durcan, Tom Jones, The Crusaders, Mose Allison, Georgie Fame, Frank Zappa and John Lee Hooker. Lyrically, he has namechecked everyone from William Blake to snooker player Alex Higgins, John Donne to Spike Milligan, William Wordsworth to George Best. Van in turn has influenced everybody from his near namesake Jim Morrison to Bruce Springsteen, Elvis Costello to U2, Robyn Hitchcock to Lisa Stansfield. Meanwhile, live appearances have remained wildly unpredictable. At his best, Morrison can transfix an audience like no other living performer, briefly taking them out of space and time, and truly "into the mystic". All this from someone recently awarded the Order of the British Empire.

At one and the same time Morrison can be highly comic and Mr Grumpy, a mystic and a misfit, by turns naive and majestic. Just like you and me, really, except that he has also slowly crafted a catalogue of songs and performances which will outlast the Millennium. Where better to start than with the opening lines to 'Astral Weeks', great poetry by any computation.

> *"If I ventured in the slipstream*
> *Between the viaducts of your dreams*
> *Where the mobile steel rims crack*
> *And the ditch and the back roads stop*
> *Could you find me...?"*

CHAPTER ONE

On Hyndford Street

In *Myths, Dreams And Mysteries*, Mircea Eliade describes our lingering sense of being at one with the natural world as a "profound feeling of having come from the soil, of having been born of Earth in the same way that the Earth, with her inexhaustible fecundity, gives birth to the rocks, rivers, trees and flowers". For Jeremy Hooker, all poets since Wordsworth "have identified themselves with places with an intensity born of loss". The landscapes they celebrate have been an expression of their isolation, and "have been with fellow poets…rather than with a 'people'".

Van Morrison's celebration of his own native ground is also a curiously isolated one. Written about largely in exile, it comprises the Belfast suburb of his childhood and landscapes drawn from his imagination: summertime in England, the fields of Avalon. For all of us, the landscape in which we grew up evokes an obscure, elegiac sadness. For Jeremy Hooker, it is "the original country that can never be re-entered, a condition of complete being…a locus of the sacred, a 'centre' where wholeness of being may be found".

As George Eliot wrote, "we could never have loved the earth so well if it had had no childhood in it. Such things are the mother tongue of our imagination, the language that is laden with all the subtle inextricable associations the fleeting hours of our childhood left behind them."

John Cowper Powys tells in his own *Autobiography* of how a child's imagination has the "ecstasy of the unbounded", how it can find "the infinitely great in the materially small". For Morrison, "it's always now". His songs recapture just this sense of "dreaming in God".

George Ivan Morrison was born in East Belfast on 31 August 1945, an only child born to working class parents. His father George was an electrician working in the nearby docks on the river Lagan, his mother Violet worked in a mill. Both were in their mid twenties, and had married on Christmas Day 1941 at St Donard's, a local Church of Ireland establishment just down the road. Van was born a Virgo, the astral sign of creativity and restraint. The surname Morrison suggests Scottish ancestry, and a 1970 *Rolling Stone* article even describes his father as a "Scottish dockworker married to an Irish wife". In the vexed and violent history of John Bull's other island, many Scots had been encouraged to emigrate westwards, and set up a bulwark of good anti-Papist stock against the natives.

Van was born in the house where his mother had grown up, 125 Hyndford Street, a small two bedroom terraced house. A short walk away is the tree-lined Cyprus Avenue, along which he would wander, entranced. Although later transformed by the power of Van's imagination, the working class suburb of Bloomfield is largely indistinguishable from urban sprawl anywhere. The fields in the low-lying coastal plain surrounding the Castlereagh Hills have long disappeared under a jumble of housing estates, factories and shops.

The young Van was, as Rod Demick told John Collis, "a little isolated, an only child. Never a great communicator, even when he was relaxed, talking to friends." The countryside is still within easy reach in Bloomfield, patches of fields and woodland invading the close packed suburbs. As another childhood friend revealed to Collis, "it seemed as if the countryside started right there. Just green fields." Seemingly on every corner, drab buildings are emblazoned with messages of evangelic faith. The rich cadences of the *Bible* continue to echo through Van's work.

This was solid evangelical territory, in a city that was soon to ignite into religious civil war. Both Catholics and Protestants, though, were actively welcomed – and employed on the teaching staff – at Orangefield School For Boys. It was here, in 1956, that Van began his secondary education, having first attended Elm Grove primary on the Beersbridge Road, just round the corner from home. As he told *Rolling Stone* in 1972, "I wasn't even aware of religious prejudice until one day a couple of kids I'd never seen before came up to me and started swinging. They were going around punching out Catholics or Protestants, I forget. They stopped when we said we weren't whoever they thought we were. The whole thing was unreal." For all the twists and turns of his spiritual pilgrimage, intolerance towards other faiths, or unbelievers, is notably absent from Van's songs, or interviews. He has never shown, as did Dylan in the late 1970s, the arrogance of a religious zealot.

In his treasure trove of a biography, Steve Turner records Van's happy and conventional childhood, "swimming in the nearby Beechie River, digging holes in the garden and roaming over building sites", while himself remaining a loner, watching events from a distance. A teacher describes him as furtive, like a March hare. Many people thought he was, in the words of George Jones, "totally cracked". A neighbour remembers locking herself out of her house one day. "A man I was talking to saw Van and asked him if he'd climb over my garden wall and go through the back door to let me in. He just shook his head and walked away." The young Morrison was the kind of child you would always find indoors, his head deep in a book. Up in his bedroom, he made his first attempts at writing poetry, and sang to – or at – his pet dog, Maxie.

Van grew up during a time of austerity, in the aftermath of the Second World War. Queues formed patiently for "Utility" goods, and food and clothing was rationed well into the 1950s. Work was centred on Belfast's labyrinthine waterfront, its massive shipyards demanding a small army of boiler makers, joiners, tinsmiths, electricians, and engineers. In the early 1950s, just as Van was beginning primary school, George went over to stay with relatives in Detroit, searching for a steady job over there, and working on the railroad. As Van told Ritchie Yorke, "He went to check things out. Later he was supposed to bring the rest of the family over but it didn't work out. He did send me some American clothes, but the other kids were jealous of them." For all that, for Van the United States became a mythical land, flowing with milk and honey, and wonderful music. He moved there in his imagination.

George Morrison was known at work as introverted and quiet. His one abiding passion was his record collection, one of the largest in the whole of Ulster, and this sense of musical all-inclusiveness was passed down to his son. Van later told Paul Jones that "my father had records from the big band era. I forget exactly – maybe Woody Herman or something. He was one of those collectors." Van's mother Violet, small and vivacious, a mill worker who loved putting on a show at parties, was herself a good amateur singer – "everything from Al Jolson to 'Ave Maria'", as Van proudly recalled.

This was his real schooling. During term time, he told Yorke, "When we had music classes, we'd sit and blow recorders. If that was a musical education, then I just wasn't impressed. But at home I just lapped it up. I love classical music too. It all started way back when I was two-and-a-half years old. Ringo, my father's friend, would bring over some Hank Williams records and sit on the stairs and listen to 'Kawaliga'. My grandfather would keep an eye on me while my mother and father were at the movies and I would make him play records over and over again. All night long, on an old His Master's Voice record player with a big horn. He dug it too." Country music was a particular favourite with the young prodigy, who would noisily demand "Big Bill Campbell at the Grand Ole Opry, 'Texarkana Baby' by Eddie Arnold and Tex Morton, the yodelling cowboy, singing 'Big Rock Candy Mountain' and 'My Sweetheart's In Love With A Swiss Mountaineer'. What a record!"

Running parallel to these discoveries, and drawn in almost subconsciously from his mother, was a love of Irish traditional music. Performers like Cork's Na Fili and the McPeaks family from Antrim, were later to become regular attractions in the Belfast folkclubs. More immediately – and, for the time, eccentrically – Van developed a taste for the blues. This was music rooted deep in black experience, and brought over from Africa on slave ships, as brutally appropriated as its first singers, but Ireland knew all about forced repatriation, and human beings being treated like animals. The Scottish author and musician Jim Wilkie – and later Van – argued that the blues also owed much to the Gaels who colonised the southern states during the late eighteenth century. Those passing by the Morrison household might overhear a Mahalia Jackson spiritual, a Louis Jordan "jump blues", the blaring be-bop of Charlie Parker or the different complexities of Jelly Roll Morton, Billie Holiday and Duke Ellington.

A particular favourite was Leadbelly. In 1978, Van told Jonathon Cott, "He was my guru. Somebody once sent me a huge poster of Leadbelly beaming down with a twelve string guitar. I framed it and put it on the wall, and I've had it on the wall everywhere I've been. One day I was looking at it and thinking, I've got to get rid of this, it's doing me in. So

I took it down and was about to throw it out. At that moment I was fiddling around with the radio, and I tuned in to this station and 'Rock Island Line' by Leadbelly came on. So I just turned around, man, and very quickly put the picture back on the wall." He elaborated for Mick Brown on a 1986 promo album: "Between Leadbelly and the Carter Family, that's how I got into singing."

In Belfast, many of these recordings could be purchased from a cycle shop in the city centre, which carried racks of rare blues seventy-eights among the bicycle clips and reflectors. Its owner, Dougie Knight, compared the blues to the sonata form, for the benefit of the young Van: "The artist sets up a theme and then decorates it." Knight's customers included members of the city's Jazz Club which met every Tuesday in a room at the Old Seaman's Maritime Hotel. Here they would discuss such scholarly esoterica as "small band Ellingtonia".

Much to their own surprise, these eccentrics were the far flung ripples of a musical wave. Soon these working enthusiasts would be rolling out of bed at five am to catch a half-hour blues programme on the American Forces network. The likes of Memphis Slim, Jesse Fuller and Champion Jack Dupree now considered it worthwhile to include Belfast on their European itineraries. It was a white, trad trombonist, Chris Barber, who personally underwrote UK dates for the likes of Little Walter, Sonny Boy Williamson, Howlin' Wolf, Muddy Waters, Roosevelt Sykes and multi-instrumentalists Sonny Terry and Brownie McGhee, who settled in England as a result.

It was Barber's Jazz Band, too, who introduced in 1951 The Washboard Wonders: Beryl Bryden on washboard and Barber himself on double bass accompanying guitarist and banjoist Lonnie Donegan's blues tinged North American folk songs. This 'skiffle' interlude was to emerge as the highlight of the act – so much so that Leadbelly's 'Rock Island Line' was lifted from the Barber outfit's *New Orleans Joys* LP as a single. It sounds tame now; it was a nuclear explosion at the time. Its closest relation in terms of primeval rowdiness was 'rockabilly', a strand of rock 'n' roll summarised by one critic as "the blues with acne". Donegan became the uncrowned "King of Skiffle" in 1957, and the impact of this homemade and essentially amateur music had all kind of strange and fruitful outgrowths, long after every tea-chest bass and washboard had ended up on a bonfire, and the thimbles were back in mother's sewing box. The Beatles, for one, came out of skiffle's rough and ready, anyone can do it, manner. Like punk, without the electricity.

As Morrison told Steve Turner, "What I connected with was that I had been hearing Leadbelly before that, so when Donegan came along, I thought everybody knew about it." From Dougie Knight's tuition, Van instinctively understood the trick of the thing, to use the same formula as everyone else, but then subtly tweak it, and develop an individual sound by allowing one's own personality to come through. Just like punk, or any art form, really, from a symphony to an epic poem.

A instrument dubbed a "zobo" – you blew through it – was the principal deviation from the rules in Morrison's first skiffle group, The Sputniks, started when he was eleven with friends from school. "The skiffle thing was starting to happen. I formed a skiffle group." Van was already proficient on a secondhand guitar bought for him by his father. Like Joni Mitchell, a continent away, learning ukelele from a Pete Seeger manual, Van would endlessly practise. The chosen form of torture, for him and the neighbours, was *The Carter Family Style*, a guitar tutor written by Alan Lomax, the folklorist who had first recorded Leadbelly. Learn from the masters, and you can't go far wrong.

Music was already more than a hobby. Talking to Chris Welch of *Melody Maker*, he is emphatic on this point. "I think I did have delusions. At one time I thought I wasn't going to live very long. The thing that saved me was my interest in music. I wanted to know more chords, to sing better, to play more horn, to do arrangements, more music!"

A parallel musical education saw Van graduating from playing the recorder to taking private lessons on the saxophone. He was also learning how to pick out a tune on the piano, and was soon to stumble upon how to bend "blue" notes on the harmonica, on which he was to later prove a master. In The Sputniks, Van served mostly as singer and guitarist, a natural focal point as the group stretched out its limited repertoire at wedding receptions, youth clubs, church fetes, parties and every talent contest going. There they would compete against comedy impressionists, knife throwers and Shirley Temple wannabes. An exercise in humility. When The Sputniks fell apart, most members were undismayed. Even to youthful eyes, skiffle was seen as a vocational blind alley, a folly to be cast aside as the world of work beckoned. Except, that is, for their lead singer.

He was told of another skiffle group, composed of students at the Belfast College of Technology, who had gained most of their reputation by playing on the back of a truck, on Greenville Street. Their name for each new engagement was picked at random from a pack of playing cards, just like *Alice In Wonderland*. The Deuces, Aces, Jokers or whatever fate had titled them that night, were a couple of years older on average than Van, at an age when such gaps matter. Singing drummer Roy Kane and guitarists George Jones and Billy McAllen told Van, half jokingly, to go away and learn the saxophone. It took Van three weeks, and almost cost the goodwill of his neighbours. Steve Turner prints the reaction of one: "I remember it vividly. Many's the time I shouted at him out of the window." This was not yet the big time: equipment had to be carried on and off buses, if the gig was beyond walking distance.

Two further influences had yet to impinge on the young Morrison. In 1956 a prematurely ageing Bill Haley And His Comets covered a song from the "race" charts, 'Rock Around The Clock'. Post-war conformity cracked like an addled egg, a nuclear fission between black and white musics, previously each ghettoised. All it needed was a young champion and there, suddenly, was Elvis, with his seedy flash garb, "common" good looks, lopsided smirk and lavishly whirled glacier of brilliantine from quiff to ducktail. And, or course, a voice that could move mountains.

Here too, as if beamed down from Venus, was Louisiana fireball Jerry Lee Lewis, banging the ivories like a man possessed, a man indeed who had exchanged the Lord for the Devil, and was going straight to hell. British audiences were treated to package tours involving the sleazy majesty of Gene Vincent, the gospel testifying of Little Richard, and Chuck Berry, sly as a fox and turning dumb lyrics into art. The first rock poet. Most important of all in cultural terms was Buddy Holly, not just for the typhoon of sound he stirred up – the loudest thing anyone had yet heard – but his importance as the first white rocker to write his own songs. The results may have been a little saccharine to Van's taste, but the point was made.

As was the sudden appearance of home grown rockers, the grin happy Tommy Steele and Cliff Richard (whose initial menace must never be discounted), leaping up the British charts while failing to impress anyone back in America. It would take The Beatles to do that.

Meanwhile, Tommy Steele's first hit, the now laughable 'Rock With The Cavemen', had been overtaken in 1956's autumn Top Twenty by 'Bloodnok's Rock 'N' Roll' by intentional humorists, The Goons. This was the high summer of the Light Programme's *Goon Show*, featuring Spike Milligan, Peter Sellers, Harry Secombe and Michael Bentine. A movie for the ears, Milligan's bizarre scripts were chock full of incongruous analogies, off-hand cruelty and stream-of-consciousness connections; *Monty Python's Flying Circus* in embryo. Van Morrison rarely missed The Goons on Sunday mornings, and would repeat them word for word in the school playground.

It was at Orangefield that he came into his own, both as leader of The Sputniks, and as a budding wordsmith. Like the young John Lennon, also a Goons aficionado, Van would compose fragments of verse and prose in private notebooks, for his own delight. His inner moods, carefully shielded off – as they still are – from outsiders, lurched between melancholy and rhapsodies of mysterious exaltation. "A child-like vision leaping into view." Van would be walking along the street, then suddenly transported out of his time and space into another reality. Such inner journeys were common to poets like Blake, Wordsworth – with his intimations of immortality – and WB Yeats. Thom Gunn records in *The Occasion of Poetry* hitchhiking in France and suddenly experiencing "a revelation of physical and spiritual freedom...like the elimination of some enormous but undefined problem". Suddenly he had the energy "for almost everything". Colin Wilson, one of Van's favourite authors, has also written about a similar sense of timelessness. JB Priestley's review of Wilson's *The Outsider* argued that such dream states were not confined to the aristocratic (by birth or intellect), or the avant-garde: "Stockbrokers may have strange dreams, that butchers cutting off chops may be touched by intimations of immortality, that the grocer, even as he hesitates over the sugar, may yet see the world in a grain of sand." Priestley himself was a man of strange visions, obsessed with time running out of joint, however drably he tried to paint himself as a bluff Yorkshire squire.

Meanwhile, Violet Morrison had seen a different kind of light. She became a Jehovah's Witness, a religion, parallel to Christianity rather than part of it, which preaches strongly about the end times, and the imminence of Armageddon. A world view, though not a faith, that Bob

Dylan has taken to recently in his live concerts, to terrifying effect (though the last sad wheezings of his vocal cords add to the pathos). Van would join his mother at services at the local Kingdom Hall. A later song on the subject was one of his most uplifting, and the extravagant rejoicings and lamentations of the ceremony must have affected his later music, even if transformed from Jehovah to the flesh. Not the least attraction of the religion was its essential democracy, in which the congregation led the way. No priest or pastor here, to urge his flock to communal hatred, or fixed intolerance.

Even a film as innocuous as Bill Haley's *Don't Knock The Rock* was banned throughout Ireland, and local rock 'n' rollers were finding it hard to keep going in a climate of official disapproval. Barred from the staider youth clubs and most adult functions were a new breed of charismatic front men, like Belfast's Johnny Johnston, leader of The Midnighters, and Brian Rossi, the stage name of one Brendan Rosbotham, a Celtic Jerry Lee, snarling on stage like an animal, and pounding his keyboard with any part of his anatomy that came to hand. He was a man out of time.

The first wave of rock 'n' roll had broken on the shores of outrage, scandal and parental disapproval. Dark days were now come indeed, with a new breed of US pop stars: interchangeable, doe eyed, bashful and insipidly good looking, they all seemed to be called Bobby. The British rockers who did survive these cotton wool years, Johnny Kidd And The Pirates and Screaming Lord Sutch, kept their gig sheets full because of their blood-and-thunder stage acts, rather than frequent chart action. That said, Kidd's 'Shaking All Over', which Morrison has since reprised many times on stage, was perhaps the finest native grown rock song of its time.

A different kind of musical heritage comprised Irish staples like the weepy 'Rose Of Tralee', the sentimental 'Danny Boy', or the lilting 'Star Of The County Down' – watch this space! – songs embraced wholesale by the six hundred professional showbands operational in Ireland by the late 1950s. They bore names that reflected a would-be Stateside sophistication – The Miami Showband or The Dixies – or togetherness – The Royal Showband, The Clubtime, The Swingtime Aces. Modesty was not at a premium. The unspoken but inflexible rule was that each showband should never contain less than eight musicians, heavy on the brass, and should come costumed in braided stage suits and neat haircuts. Women knew their place in this set-up, looking patiently pretty and sitting demurely on high stools whilst awaiting their turns to display synchronised dance steps, add vocal harmonies or even be allowed to sing lead occasionally, a breath of fresh air in a sphere dominated by male bonding.

"Featured popular vocalists" were brought forward to either specialise in areas thought unsuitable for the usual singer or simply to let him knock back a swift half-pint of Guinness. A tradition which Brian Kennedy continues in the current Van Morrison live set-up. The showband scene bred its own bravura vocalists such as Dermot O'Brien of The Clubmen, or Tom Keely of The Abilene Showband, given prominence on domestic record labels like Envoy, Release and Emerald. A record contract was a far-fetched afterthought, although The Royals and The Miamis were signed, respectively, to EMI and Pye. The results were regularly aired on the Light Programme, which led to occasional tours of England, generally during Lent for southern showbands. A career highlight would be a St Patrick's Night appearance in the Medway Town's Shamrock Club. The Dixies reached a summit of sorts as special guests on ITV's *Charlie Drake Show* with a "hilarious" arrangement of Buddy Holly's 'Rave On'. It was from such low expectations that Van would have to break through with Them. His solitary struggle rewrote the rule book as he went, preparing the way for the likes of Thin Lizzy, The Boomtown Rats and U2, all of whom aspired to something more than the odd play on the Jimmy Young prog.

Yet the showband formula has endured. As late as 1981 Coast To Coast came complete with brass section, monogrammed blazers and gyrating cowgirls intact. They even scored a big UK hit, reviving the Royal Showband's 'Do The Hucklebuck', an Irish chart-topper almost twenty years earlier. Following the days of rock 'n' roll, showbands had polarised into traditional and modernists, just like jazz. The Fontana Showband went as far as renaming itself The Impact, but even so their teenage guitarist, one Rory Gallagher, coerced the bass guitarist and drummer into forming a splinter group that disconnected from the main band altogether. When the trio failed to make the impact Gallagher had hoped for, the young maestro climbed back onto the bandwagon.

"Showbands have destroyed some of the country's finest musicians," snarled Thin Lizzy's Phil Lynott in 1972, "and the guys themselves know it. They actually apologise for being in showbands. Even Eric Bell [Thin Lizzy's guitarist] will tell you it almost drove him crazy playing for two years in The Dreams. The bread made him join." "You'll get a really great jazz saxophonist having to play 'The Twist' by Chubby Checker," agreed Rory Gallagher, "and a drummer who really wants to be in a ceilidh band or someone like me who just wants to play Chuck Berry – but you'll do it for a laugh at a certain point. I knew from day one that I was only passing through."

Van's final months at school were spent with a variety of local bands, a moving feast drawn from the same small pool of local talent. Best remembered locally were Deanie Sands and The Javelins, essentially the previous group with extra guitars, led by a polio victim called Evelyn Boucher, who sang with callipers on her legs. Van took turns to sing. He left Orangefield in July 1960, without qualifications or any real direction in life. One of his teachers told Steve Turner that "he slipped through school without making much impression. He believed in nobody but himself." A crucial asset for his future career as a writer and musician. "If he'd listened to me, he would never have written a line."

By now Van was registered with the Musicians Union, and his MU card meant that, if not already spoken for of an evening, he could be reached by any showband suddenly a man short. It was no surprise for Van to be contacted late Saturday afternoon to deputise at a dinner-and-dance in Coleraine or a coming-of-age celebration over the border in Sligo. He was receiving actual money for playing – but he did not play anything like often enough for it to stave off the chill of workaday reality. For a provincial talent to make it in pop, it was still necessary, as it had been for palais vocalists like Frankie Vaughan or Ireland's own Ruby Murray, to tramp a well-beaten path to London. Thus was the career trajectory of Ross McManus, father to Elvis Costello, who took a rather different route in his own career. It was to prove Van's salvation as well, but not yet.

Dreams of musical glory, kept alive by the occasional evening gig, illuminated Morrison's daytime occupation – arranged through a neighbour in Hyndford Street – as an apprentice fitter at Musgrave & Co, a local engineering firm. Within a few weeks, he was gone. Tommy

Hannah had been a colleague, and told Steve Turner that, from the start, "you could see that his heart was elsewhere. He didn't want to be there and the foreman didn't really want him to be there either." Van had only gone on his mother's orders, and he had little in common with his fellow workers, who could rarely get a word out of him.

After a short spell in a "meat-cleaning factory", Van swapped blue for white overalls, and went into partnership with his friend Sammy Woodburn on a window cleaning round. As he joked in a later song, it always remained a career opportunity, if music failed to pay. Nevertheless, it was a serious business, not just messing about. Van told Sean O'Hagan in *Select* that "when I started touring my cousin was doing it for a while. I wanted to keep it going, but he had something else to do. I actually bought a window cleaning business – I was president of a window cleaning business and I had people working for me." Talking to Steve Turner, Roy Kane remembered Woodburn as "a Ted with a big drape coat. He had naturally curly hair and a wild turn in his eye. Wee Van always used to do the downstairs windows because he couldn't climb up the ladders."

It also freed him to choose his own hours, in case the MU should demand his presence at some outlying palais. Van kept his musical options open with The Javelins, now without Deanie Sands, who made do with harmonica and electric guitar in lieu of a brass section. The addition of Wesley Black on piano precipitated their growth by 1961 into a fully fledged showband, a crack four-piece horn section now in place, featuring Morrison on tenor sax. Their metamorphosis was complete when they took a new name, indicating their own high sense of their own musical abilities.

The Monarchs had taken up their throne. Bow-tied and white-socked, they aped the Americans in more boisterous fashion than most. In monochrome publicity shots, the impact of their bespoke shocking pink jackets (yellow for Jimmy Law, their new singer) was somewhat lost, but the sharp corporate persona immediately impressed. Van would never look so tidy on stage again, but he knew that this was the way forward. As he told *Now Dig This*, "We became a showband because in Ireland you had to have more bodies to work. Groups weren't really happening. You had to have a horn section. You couldn't work properly if you didn't."

Rehearsals took place in an old furniture van, and the band would sometimes double up with The Federals – who featured Van's window cleaning partner Geordie on sax – as The Half Cuts, playing wild rock 'n' roll. The Monarchs became a fixture at Thomson's Restaurant in Belfast, with Morrison's madcap contribution a particular highspot. Showstoppers like his rare singing spot on Neil Sedaka's 'I Go Ape' came complete with knee-drops, grovelling, scissor kicks, dancing on the tables – and Van's general tumbling about during saxophone breaks. His lack of inches came in useful for a demonstration of the Double-Decker, a short-lived British dance fad, in which Van, sax wailing, was piggy-backed around the stage on Jimmy Law's shoulders. He was the focus of the group: as Tommy Hannah told it, "He was such a quiet fellow, and yet when he heard the music he came alive." During a song called 'Daddy Cool' he would hurl off his shirt, and deliberately split his trousers, all while rolling around the stage. Johnny Rogan even records a version of 'Yakety Yak' in which Van would dress up as a caveman.

Morrison briefly left The Monarchs, and put in stints with The Great Eight and Harry Bird's Olympics, though when they came to call him for a gig once, his mother told them that he could not oblige, as he was up in his room writing poetry. Soon, though, he was a Monarch once more.

An approach from a Glaswegian singer called George Hethrington helped the group to sort out who exactly was serious about music as a proper career. Hethrington and six of The Monarchs, including Van, amalgamated as Georgie And The International Monarchs, as grandiose as it was wordy. These global superstars toured Scotland in an old van, headlining over a diversity of local turns, playing their own set, and then backing rock 'n' roll singer Don Charles, whose act climaxed with his current – and only – Top Fifty entry, 'Walk With Me My Angel'. Taking his advice, the group relocated to London.

Such was showbusiness: unsure whether you would be sleeping in a cheap B&B, or the back of the van that night, wedged in next to the amplifiers, driving back from an evening gig. It was life closer to the streets than Hollywood, shampooing your hair in public conveniences, eating in greasy spoon cafes, sleeping when and where you could. As Van later recalled, "We'd hang out in the park and sleep there because we just didn't have the money for a hotel." Once they parked by mistake in the House of Lords' car park.

Just when The Monarchs, reduced to a diet of drinking chocolate, were about to give up in despair, they met their guardian angel Don Charles again. He put them up in his flat, cleaned them up, and gave them an introduction to his agent, Ruby Bard, who also represented The Temperance Seven and Georgie Fame, making ends meet on the US air base circuit. His and Van's path would cross with due regularity over the next thirty years, to their mutual benefit. Hethrington and The Monarchs found a regular niche in Irish clubs like Birmingham's Hope-And-Shamrock. It is odd to think of the latter-day poet and mystic playing rock and roll toilets, but such is the apprenticeship that even the great must undergo. Even as blessed a creature as Sting once played string bass in a student jazz band.

Persistence and hard work in this life provide their own luck, and The Monarchs suddenly found themselves invited to play a season in southern Germany. Their name change had proved prophetic, and they were the first English speaking band to be booked straight into nightclubs, rather than an endless stream of GI bases. Georgie And The International Monarchs played two months in Heidelberg's Odeon Keller, then moved on to the Storyville Clubs in Frankfurt and Cologne. Ritchie Yorke quotes from Van's private journals, whose breathless style and ability to sum up rapid experience in snapshots of language indicates a writer in the making.

> Heidelberg. Tram lines. The Odeon Keller, lots of good beer. My one and only movie scene. The Bahnhof. Mark Twain Village. The hotel brawl. Bratwurst. American cigarettes. Soldiers. And the music fills the room as I'm writing Miles Davis music. Big Ricky. Cognac. My surprise birthday party. Seven sets a night. Seven nights a week. Matinees Saturday and Sunday. The eagle flies on Friday. An apprenticeship they call it, paying dues. That's what it's called…Right Pete Right Paul now. Waiting for the Volkswagen to come.

Note the quickfire references, fast cut like a movie. Morrison had already learnt well from Beat novelists like Jack Kerouac. The film images refer to a German movie called *Glide*, in which he made a fleeting appearance. As to the lifestyle he so vividly pictures, even national service would have been an easy option. One noted Birmingham agent considered sending British groups over to German clubs as being "rather like training a thousand metre sprinter by making him run five-thousand metre courses". It turned boys into men.

Supplies of Preludin and Captigun tablets, amphetamine based appetite suppressants, outlawed in Britain, were stocked in most all-night establishments. "To keep going, I popped a couple of pills," confessed Ace Kefford of The Vikings, "but we were more into getting legless on German beer." Georgie And The Monarchs likewise drank their pay; some members more than others. The Scottish contingent's keen consumption of steins of lager became so serious that subsequent dismissals and replacements were to transform The Monarchs – with a new "Georgie" – into an all-Irish concern by the time the German season finished.

The need to augment their standard club repertoire gave bands based in Germany a marvellous opportunity to experiment on stage. "We played everything," affirmed Ace Kefford. "Rock 'n' roll, blues, making things up, with three of us sharing lead vocals, just to fill up the time." Van was to turn this into a lifetime's habit: as he said recently at a show in Bournemouth, "I'm not going to play anything tonight that most of you know." His face alight with concentration, his vocal spots with the Monarchs embraced the rock 'n' roll end of blues and country, with Little Richard, Gene Vincent, Fats Domino, and James Brown – whose records had been available in Britain via EMI since 1960 – particular favourites.

Talking to Johnny Rogan, fellow Monarch George Jones indicates the importance to Van's future career of this experience. "That was where Van became the basis of what he is today. For the first time in his life he had met American coloured GIs who dug soul, blues and all the music that he was weaned on. Van drifted away every day to get near coloured guys who talked the same language as him. He suddenly became a big influence on The Monarchs. We started playing all this soul music in the clubs of Germany and we really began to like it." The roots of Caledonian soul, no less.

Individual highlights included Elvis's 'Hound Dog', prefaced by a verse of 'Que Sera Sera' – a trick he repeated on the Pacific High radio show in 1971, Screamin' Jay Hawkins' 'I Put A Spell On You' and the countrified 'I Can't Stop Loving You', a recent Number One single by Ray Charles. Van was especially strong on Ray Charles – little knowing that more than thirty years later he would share Wembley Stadium with him. It was a rare evening in Storyville if Van did not perform a prolonged 'What'd I Say', the call-and-response chant that Charles had first improvised in 1959 at a Pittsburgh dance. Like his later showstopper, 'Gloria', the song could last a full hour, with Van bringing the emotional temperature up and down at will. For dramatic effect, he would signal all bar the drummer to abandon playing, then appeal to the audience to clap along in time, until the horns and guitars surged back in. An old trick, but one that still works.

A more personal testament was 'One Two Brown Eyes', Morrison's first composition to reach a public stage. As he told Ritchie Yorke, "I mainly wrote boy/girl things and some blues songs." George Jones elaborated for Johnny Rogan. "Harry Mack was the scapegoat of the group...but he did recognise that Van had writing ability. We used to play a cover of 'Daddy Cool' which Van would start off, and from the centre solo until the end he would totally ad-lib. He'd change the song *every* night – making up all these different verses." None of these early experiments in songwriting were even in the frame when Ron Kovacs, a bald Dracula clone, and grey eminence of the German division of the CBS record company, invited a thrilled Monarchs to make a one shot single in a Cologne studio. They were paid about fifty pounds each for the privilege. Van reckoned later that "it was a really bad song, but we gave it a dynamite instrumental track". For the A-side, Kovacs insisted on 'Boo-Zooh', a non-song that needed an explanatory 'Hully Gully' after its title on the record label, indicating a mutant form of the Twist. It could have been worse, just. Other dance crazes of the time included the Fly, the Shimmy-Shimmy, the Gorilla Walk and the Slop!

The picture sleeve features a large George, superimposed on the rest of The Monarchs. Morrison appears stage left and his face neatly cut in half, wearing a white straw hat that would look slightly better on a donkey. The music itself is largely a novelty number without any real novelty. The Monarchs, too, were not self-conscious artists, as Van was himself to be, but he reminisced to Ritchie Yorke about these long lost days with genuine affection: "It was a completely different scene then.

Things weren't so personal. We had a kind of showband where egos weren't involved and people weren't getting uptight over small things. We all swapped instruments and had a good time. But in no way was it my scene up front. I was riding by the side."

Back home, the beat boom was pushing such showbands aside, like a runaway train scattering all in its path. It was time for Van Morrison to find his own direction.

'Boo-Zooh' took Georgie And The Monarchs into the German Top Ten during 1963's cool, wet summer, but it was an unrepeatable and freak occurrence. By the time The Monarchs finished in Frankfurt in November 1963, every other request was for 'Twist And Shout' or 'She Loves You'. Likewise, a Belfast teenager could now scan the pages of *City Week*, and select an evening out from multitudinous jive hives like the Cavern Club in Lisburn Road, lent authenticity by its dim lighting and arched ceilings, just like its Liverpool namesake.

Every town was now expected to have a "sound" all its own. Thus 'Blarney Beat' was purveyed by shaggy monsters The Chosen Few and The Green Beats, who later backed Dusty Springfield. North of the border there were new hip names like The Interns, The Mad Lads and The Gamblers; teenagers with shiny guitars and stars in their eyes. Many started their careers begging elderly promoters for intermission spots among the showbands. If lucky, they would take the stage between nine o'clock and just after the pubs closed, when the grown-ups and the showband would return, to bring the evening to a close in a squarely 'professional' manner. Both fancied that the Beatle inspired rubbish to which their children had just been cavorting would soon fade away, just like "serious" rock musicians and their followers when punk later raised its acned head.

However, there were plenty of older musicians who found post-1962 British Beat exciting, rather than a threat. On his return from Germany, Van Morrison joined The Manhattan Showband for a string of one nighters in England during the spring of 1964. During a visit to Newcastle's Club A Go Go, Van and the Manhattans' guitarist Herbie Armstrong first encountered The Alan Price Combo. With his jacket discarded, and shirt tails hanging out, their pint size singer Eric Burdon's orange peel complexion was bathed in sweat as he drove the band through a savage 'Smokestack Lightning', Bo Diddley's 'Pretty

Thing' and other Chicago blues standards. A ritualistic obsession had led Burdon to scrawl the word "BLUES" in his own blood across the cover of an exercise book in which he had gathered lyrics from import forty-fives. He had a voice to match. The agony and ecstasy of their frenzied recitals had earned his group the nickname of "Animals" which they were about to adopt officially – possibly at the suggestion of Graham Bond.

They were not alone in their championing of music which Van had thought previously was confined to his father's record collection. It was as if the sounds of his childhood – at the time found laughable and deeply eccentric by friends and relations – were now taking over the world. Chris Barber's Jazz Band was probably the first white act to cover Muddy Waters' 'I Got My Mojo Working', the British R&B crusade's anthem. A close second was '(Get Your Kicks On) Route 66'. Other contenders were Ma Rainey's 'See See Rider', 'Hoochie Coochie Man', and John Lee Hooker's 'Boom Boom'. Two Barber sidemen, Alexis Korner and Cyril Davis, had furthered the cause of R&B, irrespective of personal popularity or financial gain. Indeed, Davis was to die young, and Korner respected but far from rich (except in spirit, and the testimony of those he had encouraged). The first meeting in 1957 of their Blues And Barrelhouse Club in London's Soho drew an audience of three. More heartening were attendance figures five years later at the G Club in Ealing, patronised by zealots from Middlesex and beyond. Among young enthusiasts who took their first tentative steps on stage here with the house band, Korner's Blues Incorporated, were Paul Jones, Long John Baldry and a nervous London School of Economics undergraduate named Mike Jagger.

The idea of making a living from R&B still seemed a romantic folly, when The Rolling Stones' hit the Top Thirty in 1963 with Chuck Berry's 'Come On'. In the G Club's watching throng were subsequent Kinks, Yardbirds and Pretty Things, all destined soon to appear on ITV's *Ready Steady Go* and BBC TV's *Top Of The Pops*. The Downliners Sect, a band doomed to cult status, were fronted by the gifted Don Craine. On stage, he sported a deerstalker hat – as distinctive a gimmick as Johnny Kidd's eyepatch or Manfred Mann's beatnik beard. The Sect also boasted an R&B harmonica virtuoso in Ray Sone, and a typical Sect concert could swerve daringly from Bo Diddley to rural blues, throwing in the dredged-up skiffle of 'Wreck Of The Old 97', slick ditties like 'I Want My

Baby Back', and country and western novelties like 'May The Bird Of Paradise Fly Up Your Nose'.

The Sect were on stage at Ken Colyer's Studio 51, just off Covent Garden, when Van Morrison and Herbie Armstrong found themselves with a night off prior to a St Patrick's Night engagement in Camden Town. They decided to sample London's oldest jazz club. Of all the English R&B outfits he had seen thus far, Morrison was most taken with The Sect. Still buzzing from their energy and wildness, he wandered into the March night, lost in dreams of a yet unimagined future. He turned round to Armstrong and shouted, "That's it, that's the sort of group I want to have!" The experience followed through to Van playing Armstrong a new song he had just written, called 'Could You, Would You'. Morrison himself recalled the experience, as if in morse code. "Went to this 51 Club. There was this group called The Downliners Sect, you know. I thought this is great. I have to do something like this in Belfast. So that was the whole idea behind it. A sort of Club 51 situation."

Another set of impassioned pioneers were The Pretty Things, whose guitarist Dick Taylor had been the original bassist with the Stones. On stage, it seemed as if everything – music and equipment – could fall to bits at any given moment. Their drummer Viv Prince was a lunatic of the first order, and hugely influential on the teenage Keith Moon. Among other devotees at their shambolic gigs in the seamier watering holes of London were the young Malcolm McLaren, future punk Methuselah Charlie Harper, David Bowie – who under his given name of David Jones led his own band The King Bees through a matching set list – and an awestruck Van Morrison. When he returned home, he told George Jones that "we had to grow our hair long like The Rolling Stones, The Yardbirds, all the London bands".

The Pretty Things' stage act was more open-ended than most; culminating in a continuous performance underpinned by Bo Diddley's trademark "shave-and-a-haircut-six-pence" shuffle rhythm, with Phil May rising from quiet intimacy to full blooded scream. Likewise, the "most blueswailing" Yardbirds – who had taken over The Rolling Stones' residency – were developing lengthy extemporisations, or "rave-ups" – similar to those led by Van Morrison during 'What'd I Say' with The Monarchs. Psychedelia merely added (different) drugs to these free-form excursions, and changed the world.

Meanwhile, back in Ulster and – musically – the dark ages, Van brought this new kind of aggression back to an uncomprehending audience, giving voice to something deep within his own dark soul. John Collis recounts an extraordinary story told by Harry Bird, leader of The Regents Showband, with whom Morrison briefly played saxophone. The occasion was a young farmers' dance in Randalstown, a five hour marathon during which Van relieved the two main singers with an impromptu version of Elvis's 'Blue Suede Shoes'. As he started singing, the audience stood mesmerised. "I edged forward to look – his face had gone purple! His eyes were stuck out like organ stops. He was freaking out, going crazy, and the crowd watched in amazement, wondering if he was going to have a stroke. We couldn't let him sing any more – he was scaring the people." One is reminded of the film *Back To The Future* where at a school hop Michael J Fox goes into a Hendrix routine, playing the guitar behind his back, drowned in feedback, playing like a dervish. The crowd watch open mouthed, struck between horror and embarrassment. Music, literally, before its time. Van would have to create the right environment for such mayhem, and blaze a path for a whole legion of mad front men – Joe Cocker, Roger Chapman. Arthur Brown – who would similarly learn how to speak in strange tongues.

Back in the real world, Brian Rossi had installed himself at Belfast's Plaza (run by Mecca ballrooms) as lunchtime disc jockey, and drummer of the eleven piece Golden Eagles. Their gimmick was to bring on two girl hoofers to front the group and exhibit the latest dance sensations from the States. Pan's People in waiting. More to the point, they were the biggest group in Belfast, in every sense. When he heard of a vacancy for a guitarist, Herbie Armstrong phoned Rossi from a public call box, only to learn that the Eagles were also looking for a featured singer to double on saxophone and harmonica. Van, also crammed into the phone box, immediately put himself forward. Armstrong and Morrison – now with noticeably longer hair – passed a brief audition, and that same night began work for a princely eleven pounds a week, with free matching stage suits, white with gold thread. No wonder that Van has eschewed any kind of uniform on stage, ever since.

Having played two Chuck Berry numbers at the audition, Van was given his own R&B spot where the wildest applause was reserved for two Ray Charles' compositions: 'What'd I Say' and 'Sticks And Stones'. Then it was back to ballads, and Rossi's smooth patter. Van must sometimes have wondered if this was the closest he would ever get to playing the music of his choice, and yet still earn a living wage. The usual weekly stipend for a semi-professional member of a beat group was a beggarly thirty shillings (one pound fifty), okay as a hobby, but impossible as a life style. Thus it was that Herbie Armstrong stayed put in The Golden Eagles after Van responded to an intriguing advertisement in the *Belfast Evening Telegraph* for musicians to launch an R&B club. Taking London's lead, an increasing number of such clubs were forming in the provinces: Swansea's R&B Cellar, Bluesville in a Sheffield pub, the Downbeat in Newcastle docklands (where The Alan Price Combo held court). A national circuit was slowly and painfully coming into being. Only one other enthusiast responded to the advert, which turned out to have been placed by three blues enthusiasts, Jerry McCurvey, Jerry McKenna and Jimmy Conlon, subsequently known to everyone as the "three Js". Van was sufficiently inspired to seek out suitable premises, in an unlicensed two hundred capacity hall within the Maritime Hotel.

At such short notice, Van could not book the musicians whom he wanted most to play with, presumably Herbie Armstrong and bassist Tito Tinsley, both from The Golden Eagles. So "I got another lot of people and we went into this club as Them". These other people were a rough R&B combo, already extant, with whom Van had just fallen in with, and to whom he would eventually prove to be the cuckoo in the nest. Like Topsy, in terms of musical creativity, he just grew and grew. The Gamblers had been formed in 1962 by bassist Alan Henderson, drummer Ronnie Millings, and guitarist Billy Harrison, who took up the story for Trevor Hodgett in the fanzine *Wavelength*. The group gigged "round scout halls and legion halls and wee functions". Harrison was the only one brave enough to sing, and their repertoire was largely rock 'n' roll: early Presley, Little Willie John's 'Fever', 'The Hippy Hippy Shake'. Prior to Morrison joining, they had just acquired the services of schoolboy Eric Wrickson on organ.

Van himself was brought in as a saxophonist, and brought with him the R&B component: Muddy Waters, Howlin' Wolf, Blind Lemon Jefferson. Harrison had not even known that Van could sing, but "he wanted to do a few songs. In those days there were no egos about anything. If you had the balls to sing, get up there and do it." They began sharing vocal duties, half and half, with Van blowing into saxophone or harmonica between the verses. "Then Van more and more was doing the numbers. It allowed me to concentrate more on the guitar. There was no conscious decision about it."

The band rehearsed in an attic room above Dougie Knight's bicycle cum record shop. A representative from Philips came to hear them, but reckoned them the "biggest load of rubbish" he had ever listened to. Perhaps it was the blues material which Morrison was bringing into their set list, though – when recently interviewed by Trevor Hodgett – Eric Wrickson emphasises that The Gamblers were Billy Harrison's group, not Van's. "His band had been backing Bridie Gallagher, who was the Irish equivalent of Max Bygraves. At the same time The Manhattan Showband had come together to play in the Orchid, with Morrison on sax. They actually did an R&B set as a showband. We were speaking to Van afterwards, and Van said, 'Well, I like the rhythm and blues sets, but the rest I can do without,' and Billy said, 'We have a rhythm and blues band. Why don't you come along?' Within a week, he was a permanent fixture."

By 1964, The Gamblers were running out of places to play when Van proposed that his new band take the stage on opening night of the prosaically named Rhythm And Blues Club. Their own name was a greater cause of anxiety. A band also called The Gamblers had just replaced The Tornados as backing group to the fragile rocker Billy Fury. Then Eric Wrickson remembered *Them!*, a 1954 horror movie about an army of giant ants roaming California, hungering for human prey. An air of menace and mystery was needed, and the new name – no defining "the", no humour, no quarter given or received, outlaw chic personified – exactly fitted the bill.

As Harrison told *Wavelength*, "Eric Wrickson came up with the name when we were sitting in the rehearsal rooms, and we decided to let the hair grow, which was El Freako for Belfast, and not wear uniforms. This was our difference. We were a group – but individuals at the same time." As was Van, who had once suggested the idea of a group who would play in longjohns and grandad vests. If Them did not go quite that far, the days of mohair suits were over for ever.

CHAPTER TWO

The Story Of Them

On Tuesday 14 April 1964, a message seemingly in code appeared in the classified pages of the *Belfast Evening Echo*. It was the kind of conundrum beloved of Sherlock Holmes, placed by some dastardly criminal mastermind. "Who Are? What Are? THEM." Like some deranged paper chase, each evening brought a further twist of the knife. On Wednesday, "When? And Where? Will you see THEM?" On Thursday, "Rhythm and Blues and THEM. When?" These three questions were finally answered – as in an Arthurian quest – on Friday evening, shortly before the gig itself.

Rhythm & Blues Club
Tonight – 8.30 pm Introducing "Them"
Ireland's Specialists In Rhythm & Blues
Maritime Hotel College Square North

If this was the only advance publicity, then undoubtedly it helped ensure a poor attendance at this mysterioso happening. The Maritime's lack of a drinks licence might also have played its part. Those who did attend, however, spread the message through word of mouth, and the two hundred capacity venue was nearly full for the next gig. A week later, and people were queuing down the street from six pm to get in. Billy Harrison lapsed into religious imagery when describing audience response. "The Maritime Hotel became a place that people made pilgrimages to. It became the fount of blues learning in Ireland."

The process was two way. As Van later put it, the band were "feeding off the crowd". Then giving back, tenfold. Harrison described to Trevor

Hodgett, "We were nutters on stage. There was no routine. You get this circle built and everybody has a good night. You didn't really want to stop. It was an unbelievable period." Spontaneity fed directly into Van Morrison's own method of writing and performing. "He was always great at ad libbing. He could just conjure words. My recollection is that Van didn't write songs – he wrote ideas and then the song came as he was performing. He never had a song written down – maybe words here and there on cigarette packets – but you'd start to diddle about between numbers with some riff and he'd put something on top of it and gradually it would evolve. Everything was refined on the road. He was so good at ad libbing that all he needed were his ideas and he would blend them around." The same process as "toasting" in reggae, or rap. Indeed, a technique that goes right back to the earliest poetry, recited by travelling bards. On a good night, Van could – and still can – elevate the results into a lifetime's experience.

As ever, Morrison remained an enigma. Promoter Eddie Kennedy told Johnny Rogan, "He would be singing and he'd lay down on his back and play the sax. And even when the club was choc-a-bloc with four hundred people you could hear a pin drop when he played that sax – and then he'd go berserk." Emotionally, though, the singer remained the calm at the middle of a hurricane. "He was such a peculiar guy. He was so cool you couldn't believe it. Morrison was a man of very few words. Even off stage, the sum total of a Van conversation was 'Hi, man'."

Club Rado, as it became known, for no apparent reason, was noted for its lack of the customary violence that marred – or supplemented – pop evenings elsewhere. Them's fierce commitment to R&B, and the mystique and fire of the group drew a new kind of audience. Belfast undergraduates – largely male – were growing bored with jazz, and the beatnik image it was now saddled with. Here was a different kind of underground music, aggressively uncommercial, and full of menace to those outside the cult. Club Rado was a place to pose as a would-be Mick Jagger, while also the subject of attention of town girls in fishnet, suede and leather, jabbering incessantly until Them sauntered onto the boards. The band were already a focal point, particularly on those occasions when, as Van noticed, "the audience and the musicians would be as one". A kind of committed gaiety transpired with onlookers assuming the dual roles of rhythm section and accompanying choir, joining in with Van on 'What'd I Say' in the manner of pentecostal worshippers, anointed with the holy spirit. All this in a teetotal zone.

This kind of unspoken symmetry between musicians and audience in which both seemed to inhabit a private world, as ultimate insiders, has fuelled all the most startling developments in British rock: the Cavern, UFO, the Roxy, even the fleeting nightclubs which hosted the New Romantics. As Van said later, it was "like a whole number. This was before the Fillmore or anything like that. But it was the same kind of vibe happening, and this was in Belfast." It arises from an audience's idea of itself as something special, which the greatest TV music shows – *Ready Steady Go*, *The Tube* – have barely approached, and the worst – *Top Of The Pops*, *The White Room* – have so obviously faked. It is like the fierce partisanship and live buzz of the home supporters whose team is on a roll, something also barely glimpsed on the telly. The kind of charisma which the early Them had in spades, an unbottled, sweaty intensity.

The group plunged far deeper into R&B than The Monarchs in Germany had ever dared. Grown up, black man's music, sung and played with total commitment. Their standard set included T-Bone Walker's 'Stormy Monday', 'Help Me' by Sonny Boy Williamson, Jimmy Reed's 'Baby What You Want Me To Do', and pages from the Muddy Waters and Chuck Berry songbooks. A gentler influence was Sam Cooke, while their fifteen minute version of Bobby Bland's 'Turn On Your Love Light' surfaced as a signature tune of sorts. Eric Wrickson remembers that it would start "as practically a dirge" then work itself up into a frenzy. Van might be "one of the boys, uncomplicated" off stage, but he had an "incredible live act of tearing off his clothes, falling on his back and singing very well at the same time". The set list was oddly similar to The Grateful Dead when they were still called The Warlocks, and playing biker bars. As with Van, the Dead would continue to interpret these songs right up into the nineties, half as nostalgia, half as something new, and rich, and strange.

As Morrison stated, Them lived and died on stage at the Maritime Hotel: the records and tours were the light cast by a dying star. The pinnacle of their act was one of the first of his songs which their lead singer dared debut on stage. 'Gloria' was a refinement of an earlier composition, it centred on a three chord monologue, and depending on the singer's mood, would often last up to twenty minutes. A friend lucky enough to witness it remembers that some nights things would get extremely smutty, with Van carefully describing item by item what garments Gloria was removing in the singer's room, and precisely what she was doing to him to make him feel "all right". He also confirms the hypnotic nature of proceedings, with the sardine packed audience hanging on Van's every word.

This vein of musical aggression carried forward. In 1975, Allan Jones could sense a later rock revolution in progress when he reported back to *Melody Maker* on an early gig by rough R&B band The 101ers. Their lead singer was one Joe Strummer, soon to form The Clash. Their gig at the Charlie Pigdog club sounds like Club Rado revisited, though in a nastier universe, and one talked up by Jones to draw publicity. "The 101ers screamed their way through a twenty minute interpretation of 'Gloria', which sounded like the perfect soundtrack for the last apocalyptic days of the Third Reich."

Largely through the advent of the bootleg CD, there has been a miraculous resurrection of early live performances, long since thought lost, by bands whose real life was on stage. Cream in America, setting out the agenda for the guitar hero, Little Feat slipping and a sliding their mutant boogie, Television's final tour, their twin guitars in endless dialogue; all have been reprised on silver disc. Other key moments of rock history remain tantalisingly unrecorded, or exist only as odd fragments: John Mayall with a young Clapton who could seem to make time stop (listen to the live take of 'Stormy Monday') Sandy Denny's Fairport before the crash, Mighty Baby's live alchemy.

Them were such, a violent chemistry that could be never recreated in any studio, feeding as they did off themselves and the energies of their audience, but by the very nature of the technology of the time, only the most rudimentary of recordings survive. Even these are not commercially available, although anyone who has made the mistake of buying, say The Kinks' *Live At The Kelvin Hall*, or the Royal Albert Hall side of The Rolling Stones' *Gimme Shelter* will know what they are probably not missing. Doubly ironic, how many of Bob Dylan's early concerts have come down to us (unofficially) in near perfect state?

That said, Johnny Rivers specialised, when self-exiled in France, in long R&B workouts which entranced the demi-monde of the South, whipping them into states of frenzy. The recorded results that survive are about as wild as a night out with Little Jimmy Osmond, or a dinner date with Karen Carpenter. Perhaps it is best to leave Them live at the Maritime as a legend, and thus all the more precious for those lucky enough to have been there.

Club Rado was a collective exercise, so that whatever the local rivalries that Them induced, other bands would merge with them into a community rather like the mid sixties' San Francisco. The Misfits' drummer would often deputise for Ronnie Millings; or Van duet on stage with Keith McDowell of The Mad Lads – and later borrow his idea of singing Dylan's 'It's All Over Now Baby Blue' – or for showmen of the calibre of Johnny Johnston or Tony Ford to vault on stage for a couple of numbers. Van had yet to learn their mastery of stagecraft, but his voice was everything it would ever be. Seemingly old beyond his years, Van could slip comfortably from suppressed lust through lazy insinuation to intimate anguish, sometimes mingling ecstasy and gloom in the same line. His voice was the opposite of the kind of vocal purity that many English singers coming from the choirboy tradition affected, the finest exemplar being Colin Blunstone of The Zombies. Van was more like Ian Paisley – a near neighbour, in fact – shouting rather than purring, making a sales feature of his slurred diction and stentorian vehemence as he strained his two middle octaves through a muffled public address system.

Just like Mick Jagger, in fact, without his aggravating mock Cockney pose. The Rolling Stones had coincidentally played Belfast a month after the opening of Them's club. Their show ended in a riot after twelve minutes, but the fact that the Stones had already already managed three Top Thirty appearances, alongside chart appearances by Manfred Mann and The Animals was immensely heartening to the likes of Them. Heartening, but deeply frustrating. Van's band functioned beyond the territorial waters in which the London based record companies were prepared to fish for new talent. On the plus side, Them were undisputed masters of their own terrain, certain of a full workload from around eighty clubs within easy reach. As bands were used to playing two twenty minute sets per booking, it was quite common to cram in three separate engagements over the course of one weekend evening. Eric Wrickson totted up a night's work for *Wavelength*. Them played "the Dance Studio in Donegall Street – half an hour there – then nipped round and done half an hour at the Plaza, and then shot across and done half an hour in the Fiesta, and then an hour in the Maritime".

The financial aspect of this was startling. Wrickson again: "Big money in those days would have been twenty-five pounds – but you'd have gathered up your three twenty-five quids before you actually went to the Maritime. Also we were on the door in the Maritime. It was sold out at seven o'clock at night with two hundred and fifty people paying in ten shilling notes. We reached the stage of playing seven nights a week, four times a night."

Them were also starting to push the envelope, extending their sets almost into infinity. This at a time when a rumour that Georgie Fame had demanded to be allowed two full hours at Romano's Ballroom prompted questions to the Musicians Union. Them grabbed all the work going. During a month underscored with run-of-the-mill dates like the Spanish Rooms in the Falls Road and Sammy Houston's Jazz Club, there would be side trips into ballrooms like Derry's Embassy, with its heavy drape stage curtains. They would regularly drive over the border to Dublin and as far south as Waterford.

Such pilgrimages were not without their dangers. Like lambs to the slaughter, the city boys would arrive in a country town where the 1950s still held sway, their "girly" long hair a particularly red rag to those for whom even quiffed Elvis was not yet a symbol of masculinity. Within a minute of the first number, a crewcut roughneck, bold with Guinness, might have to be restrained from charging on stage to strike a blow for decent entertainment for decent folk. Others in the audience confined themselves to howls of derision, sporadic barracking and outbreaks of slow handclapping. All reprised a few years later when The Pink Floyd regularly had coins hurled at them in suburban Meccas – a world not yet ready for Syd Barrett – and with added savagery when the disintegrating Sex Pistols worked their way westward on their one and only tour of the US. No rock singer has been assassinated on stage by an irate audience – yet – although Marty Balin was clubbed to the ground by Hells Angels at Altamont, and Frank Zappa hurled into the orchestra pit at London's Rainbow (one reason why that venue should be bought back from the religious group who own it, and reopened in triumph, in my view). Another and finer religious experience came to those who attended Van's performance at that same venue in 1973, but we digress wildly.

Back in Belfast, and in the nature of such things, other groups were copying Them's repertoire – even 'Gloria' – and their off hand appearance. Like all local bands who had reached market penetration in their own area, Them could either stand still and be overtaken by newer heroes or else move on, and eventually leave their home town. Even The Beatles had quit Liverpool as soon as decently possible. Immortalising yourself on tape was the first step – though there were then few bona fide studios outside London other than customised sheds, garages and living rooms. With unconscious symbolism, the earliest extant recording of Them was a version of 'Turn On Your Love Light', taped by a fan studying electronics at Queen's University who had access to an Aladdin's cave of tape recorders, editing blocks and jack-to-jack leads.

A copy reached the ears of Mervyn Solomon, a local businessman who also happened to be the brother of Phil Solomon, a London impresario who represented The Dubliners, the schlock-rock of The Bachelors and an assortment of ceilidh bands. Mervyn arrived at the Maritime during the tour-de-force of 'Turn On Your Love Light'. Short skirted girls with urchin faces and pale lipstick ringed the stage front as if hypnotised by the tiny lead singer, who would also blow wild typhoons of saxophone and harmonica. Morrison's gift of a kind of mysterious inner calm, grace under fire, convinced Solomon that the group was worth his brother's attention. His decision had Dick Rowe scurrying across the Irish sea to see Them for himself.

As Head of Artists and Repertoire – A&R man to the biz – for Decca records, Rowe had made the dreadful error of turning down The Beatles on the evidence of an admittedly awful demo tape of showbiz tunes and tired instrumentals. Even since, he had searched feverishly for the next big thing, signing up The Rolling Stones, The Nashville Teens and The Moody Blues. Now he heard that Decca's great rival EMI were paying court to The Wheels, Belfast's first Beat supergroup, led by Brian Rossi, and with Herbie Armstrong and bassist Rod Demick from

The Telstars. Years before the growth of independent labels like Electra or Island, any band worth its salt needed to sign for a major label, or else it was exile to the likes of Top Rank, and chart oblivion.

Rowe had to act fast. Them were promising enough to be summoned over to Decca's recording studios in West Hampstead. For those still too young to legally sign away their rights, Rowe had to secure their parents' signature for a standard two year contract, with an option to renew if there was cause for hope. The Wricksons refused, so Eric was out – and later joined Wheels – replaced on organ by Patrick McAuley.

Given this boost to his career, McAuley was disconcerted to find session organist Arthur Greenslade on standby. That was not all. Of all Beat group players, the drummer was most likely to be replaced in the studio by an anonymous pro, paid by the hour. Even the first Beatles session. for 'Love Me Do', made use of Andy White, who in a later, hairier incarnation replaced the irreplaceable Bill Bruford in Yes (result: musical decline, financial well being). Beat groups playing live tended to accelerate and slow down as the spirit took them. A studio drummer was the first step on the path to click tracks, and computer generated sound, neatly cutting out the heart and soul of rock music, so essentially a live phenomenon. In this and succeeding sessions, Bobby Graham came in on drums, as did Ulster expatriate Phil Coulter on keyboards – a name that will reverberate throughout the whole Van Morrison story – and guitar prodigy "Little" Jimmy Page – a nickname to distinguish him from fellow session guitarist "Big" Jim Sullivan. Once grown up, Page would take the opposite course, using his studio expertise to form the (defiantly) greatest live rock band of the early seventies, Led Zeppelin, for whom even the issue of hit singles seemed to be a prostitution of their talent, and ambition.

Coulter was a rising songwriter. His composition 'Puppet On A String' was to bring the barefoot and sultry Sandy Shaw success in the Eurovision Song Contest. Strangely prophetic, as Shaw's whole career, even her punning name, was the creation of men, from Chris Andrews' songwriting, to Coulter's own double take, to a later career revival under the tutelage of Morrissey. Meanwhile, Coulter was put in charge of the day-to-day organisation of Them, rather like the similar role played by Norman Rossington in *A Hard Day's Night*, but without the comedy. The spirit of Them continued to glow in the studio, if fitfully. Harrison was to play the famous lead riff on 'Baby Please Don't Go', with Page supplying the "solid 'chunk' in the background", while as lead vocalist, Van Morrison was impossible to replace. As Mervyn Solomon told Johnny Rogan, his talent shone out, literally a star. "Van was one of the greatest artists that I have ever dealt with. I felt that Van should have been taken away and made a soloist. I felt we needed a modern jazz group behind him with flutes." An extraordinary premonition of *Astral Weeks*.

Morrison was much like the young Dylan, who would use the studio as a place to compose, and try out new ideas. "He was always coming up with snippets of lyrics and melodies." This was not easy, pre *Sergeant Pepper*, when groups were still expected to finish recording within an allotted three hours, or an evening session with a jobsworth locking up well before midnight. Not the least of Jimi Hendrix's revolutionary acts a few years down the line was to build his own recording studios, Electric Ladyland, where he could jam whenever he damn well liked. Van's ambition lay in a different direction to the rest of the band, of whom other members have recorded a near terror of Harrison's own brand of determination. Solomon names no names, but neatly indicates the divide between looking after one's career and vision. "At that point the group would do anything. They were determined to get on. Van always knew what he wanted and he sulked if the others didn't do it the way he liked. But he wasn't a prima donna – not at that point."

Talking to Ritchie Yorke, Van regards Them by now as "out of context". He seems to bear them no particular regard: "If I hadn't been with Them, I just would have been in another band...it was no big deal for me." As if to confirm this, Dick Rowe chose a cover of Slim Harpo's 'Don't Start Crying Now' as Them's first A-side on 4 September 1964, thus ignoring the songwriting skills of their lead singer, and for a second time in his life throwing away the crown jewels.

It sold well back in Ulster, but did not trouble the British Top Fifty. Van's first recorded vocal begins without accompaniment, and has the buzz and rasp of a wasp. The song itself is ultimately disposable, and the listener's interest does not perk up again until the very end, with some intricate guitar work, Byrds-like country rock, before its time.

Another Slim Harpo song, 'Got Love If You Want It', was rewritten with mod-speak lyrics to become 'I'm The Face' by The High Numbers, soon to rename themselves The Who. Here was a game of which Presley, The Beatles, The Police and Simply Red were to prove masters, pretty white boys who could take black music, whether a blues song by Arthur Crudup, Tamla girl groups, reggae or soul, and make it palatable to a mass audience. The only difference with the British R&B scene was that some of the white boys were far from pretty.

Trad jazz trumpeter Kenny Ball – already washed up by this new wave – regarded the craze for R&B as just "rock 'n' roll with a mouth organ". Fine, if the mouth organ was played by the likes of Van, or Paul Jones, maestros both. He had a point, though. Identikit groups with names like The Howling Wolves, The Boll Weevils or The King Bees – with a pre-name change David Bowie still acting his first role – were suddenly fighting for a piece of the action.

In retrospect, the most important aspect of Them for Morrison was the band's moving full-time to London. Echoes of his residence there would echo through later songs, and he was to move back to Holland Park, after years spent in America. Meanwhile, he and Them were on the treadmill of one nighters, often truly hellish, especially when England's only motorway terminated in Birmingham. After days of inactivity, a telephone call would ensure that within the hour the boys would be shoulder-to-shoulder in a draughty transit van, driving, driving, driving to strange towns, strange venues, strange beds. Meanwhile, their first single crackled from the crowded wavelengths of the new pirate stations.

Billed as vendors of "Raving R&B" (as opposed to the flashier "Maximum R&B" of The Who), Them's most important gigs were back in the capital, strutting their stuff in supercool new clubs like the Pontiac in Putney or Alexis Korner's short lived Beat City. That night, Van was unshowy to the point of inertia until the exasperated order came from Phil Solomon to move himself. Van's reaction, spiteful but effective, was to buck and shimmy, a composite of every rock 'n' roller he'd ever admired; flickering across the stage like a firefly when not required to commandeer the microphone. Guitarist Dave Mason of The Hellions, then house band at Soho's Whisky-A-Go-Go (and later a member of both Traffic and Fleetwood Mac) was particularly struck by

Morrison's stage antics. "Man, he was crazy. He would jump up and down, and leap on top of the speaker cabinets." Another convert to Them's cause was a youthful Rod Stewart, pre fame and coxcomb hairstyle, who accepted Van's invitation to come over to Belfast to play the Maritime.

Stewart's own roots in folk music, learned from busking around Europe even if they were well obscured by the 'Do You Think I'm Sexy' years, must have rubbed off on his new friend Van, particularly his love for the tender side of Dylan. Indeed, Stewart's first three solo albums seemed to presage a career as long and distinguished as Van's own, but something went wrong when Rod made his own transatlantic crossing, selling out sensitivity for self-promotion. From coxcomb to cock rocker. Financially *he* should worry, but there is a place in people's hearts that the likes of Rod or Phil Collins or Prince or Madonna vacate because of their very superstardom. A place that the likes of Van Morrison or Richard Thompson or Neil Young call home. For proof, simply check the quality and commitment of their fanzines!

Meanwhile, the band slogged on. A support slot to Screaming Lord Sutch dragged from Morrison the memorable comment: "I wasn't born in Swindon, but I'm dying here." Them immediately rose above the common herd with their second single, 'Baby Please Don't Go', written by Big Joe Williams, a Mississippi bluesman of the 1920s. Decca determined to release Them's arrangement, now justly regarded as definitive, as a single before anyone else. A fairground, cockleshell organ provides sweetness, but the song is driven by seesaw electric bass, and the riff doubled by Van's harmonica. His vocal line is desperate, pleading, this tale of county jails and hard labour slurred out to a cocky beat. The backing goes quiet while Van's singing becomes playful, staccato, pleading, forlorn in turns, with a side quote from The Animals' 'I'm Crying'. Throughout, Van's voice owes much to Burdon and Jagger, but there is already a sense of him being his own man.

The new single appeared in the shops early in November 1964 with a severely edited version of Van's party piece 'Gloria' on the B-side. The Wheels, with Herbie Armstrong, released the same song as an A-side, without success. 'Baby Please Don't Go' entered the *New Musical Express* charts at Number Twenty-Three after the group mimed it – with Van neglecting to "blow" his harmonica – on a Yuletide edition of

ITV's epoch making *Ready Steady Go*, headlined by The Rolling Stones. It later supplanted Manfred Mann's '54321' as the programme's theme tune. After a seven week climb, the single hit the Top Ten.

Old friend and rival Georgie Fame was currently at Number One with 'Yeah Yeah', written by "jazz sage" Jon Hendricks, whose song 'Centrepiece' would also later feature in Van's repertoire. Meanwhile, he was at last gaining exposure to a whole new audience. I remember watching a young Them on *Top Of The Pops* and, even though The Animals were my favourite group, I had a feeling that there was something beyond the pale about this bunch of hairy thugs. With Phil May, say, there was a kind of youthful charm beneath the snarl. Even Bill Wyman's moronic image, all vertical bass and bored gum chewing, seemed a bit pasteboard. Van looked the real thing, the sort of lout you would avoid staring at in the street, and walk rapidly away from – but not actually running, so as to alert him.

There was something cro-magnon in his smilelessness, the band's lack of musical embellishment (no Brian Jones here, adding all kinds of tonal contrasts), and the fierceness of his delivery. This was not a game, and these were not grinning kids. Indeed, this seemed not far removed from the primitive thump that Chess releases like *Rhythm And Blues All Stars* – released on the Marble Arch label in Britain – were bringing onto the mass market where once they had been the preserve of young fanatics like Keith Richard or Keith Relf. While the Stones were still grammar school boys acting tough – and neatly dressed at that – a metaphorical darkness seemed to gather around Them, at least in my adolescent imagination, although the rest of the group fused together into a street gang behind their charismatic leader. Yet I rushed out and bought the single or, more accurately, waited until I could get an ex-jukebox copy, with its centre knocked out.

One thing about Van Morrison on the box. Whether you liked him or not, you could not take your eyes off him. He exuded the same "who are *you* looking at?" air of confrontation as Trevor Burton of The Move, or Pete Townshend. A star was born.

"Everybody was fairly innocent then, a bit of a cottage industry," smiles Dick Taylor today. "We thought we'd last maybe two or three years. We never felt that we were in the entertainment industry as such." Yet, despite themselves, The Things, Them and all the fresh harvest of R&B hitmakers were becoming celebrities.

'Baby Please Don't Go' had propelled Them into stardom, though live appearances still revolved around the same circuit. They zigzagged from the Bird Cage in Plymouth to the Agincourt in Camberley to Southport Floral Hall to Basingstoke Technical College to the Rock Garden Pavilion in Llandrindod Wells to Margate's Dreamland to the Palace Ballroom on the Isle of Man. Often they would have to drop everything to fit in *Saturday Club* or a trip to the deconsecrated church in Manchester where *Top Of The Pops* was shot.

With Phil Coulter acting as chaperone, there was a matching round of interviews, in-person appearances, photo calls and shopping excursions for new stage gear. The group had embraced ties and uniform orange shirts during the Millings-McAuley interregnum, though they still managed somehow to look scruffy. They also were becoming a cause celebre, even without a publicist like Andrew Loog Oldham or BP Fallon acting on their behalf and planting stories in the press. The outrage that Them provoked was natural, not manufactured.

A BBC schools' programme denounced the "moronic" nature of 'Gloria' – modern art, now we look back – complete with an accompanying clip of the band in action. What greater incentive could there be to the bored schoolchildren being lectured to rush out from the school gates and buy the single! There was an underlying humour to the group, its most obvious manifestation the cartoon of a Andy Capp type figure lazily reclining on their drum kit, but it got lost somewhere amid the Ulster accents and patois. Their personalities, at least as publicly perceived, would not sell water in the Sahara.

'Here Comes The Night', their oasis so to speak, was the creation of thirty-six-year-old Bert Berns. In January 1965, Bert had jetted across the Atlantic. A canny New Yorker, his studies at the Julliard School Of Music had been the working apprenticeship for his subsequent career as record plugger, score transcriber and session pianist. Hard and thankless work , but it brought him the long wished for job of arranger and producer around the studios of Tin Pan Alley in London and the Brill Building in New York. He was among the first of a new breed of music hustler, of whom Guy Stevens and Joe Boyd were the most glorious later exemplars, masterminding British psychedelia for scant reward.

Berns – who was to save Morrison's career at a later, crucial stage – proved himself as a fine composer too, writing songs of the quality of 'Twist And Shout', 'Under The Boardwalk', 'Cry To Me', and 'Everybody Needs Somebody To Love'. Recorded initially by black US artists, such material was soon pounced upon, like juicy mice, by the hip cats of the British R&B establishment. Berns' other great talent was for turning a studio session into something more, a place to make music. As Billy Harrison told *Wavelength*, "I remember him coming out of the console: he walked over to the drum kit, grabbed a stick and started beating on a cymbal and saying, 'Let's get this thing cooking,' and created an atmosphere. Suddenly everybody went, 'Yeah. We're not sitting here tied to these seats, we're allowed to express ourselves.' Berns just created a whole freedom of atmosphere within the studio. Hellova producer. The guy was magic." Van put it more negatively. "Except for Bert Berns, I felt that those people who said they were producing Them didn't have a clue."

Even before Berns joined Decca, 'Here Comes The Night' had been suggested as Them's next single. The perfidious Decca had hedged its bets by rushing out a version by Glasgow's Lulu And The Luvvers, which spent a week at Number Fifty before disappearing forever. Them's superior version was issued in March 1965, boosted by slots on *Thank Your Lucky Stars* and *Ready Steady Go*, and crashed straight in at Number Six, its rise to number one blocked only by The Beatles' 'Ticket To Ride'.

Alan Clayson describes the single as a "latin slanted ballad of lustful envy", which is just about right. A drum rattle – like a call to arms – then Them enter on the chorus, stately with full organ and steady stick work. Each succeeding verse – sung by Van in an almost frisky way to a shuffle beat – reveals more about his betrayal. The chorus, by contrast, is sung with a kind of luxurious aching, with a super relaxed guitar break somehow screwing the tension even tighter. Suddenly the passing of each night is unbearable, Van imagining exactly what she is doing with her new lover. An ignoble song, darkly voyeuristic, but I defy any reader to deny that it is a situation unknown in their own lives. Matters end with a passion choked Van repeating "long and lonely night" over and over, until faded out, his first essay in pure sound. A song which exudes tragic inevitability, with Van taking on two completely different vocal parts, as if on an endless loop, over and over and over again...

Them made a guest appearance at the *NME* Pollwinners Concert at Wembley Empire Pool, on 11 April 1965, on a bill that also featured two future musical partners, Georgie Fame and Tom Jones. The bill marked the high water mark of Britbeat: The Beatles, Rolling Stones, Kinks, Animals, Searchers etc. It also featured Freddie And The Dreamers and Cilla Black, but then nothing in life is perfect. The *NME*'s Derek Johnson remarked prophetically that "the band's lead singer generates more genuine soul than any of his British contemporaries".

Them were at the peak of their career, even if they continued to display a dumb insolence towards the media and fans. Meetings with the band were fragmented and pocked with swearing and unfunny quips, anticipating the more self-conscious "bad attitude" of The Sex Pistols and Siouxsie Sue on the Bill Grundy show. Interviews were delivered in a thick brogue, almost incomprehensible to hardened journalists more used to harmless tricksters like the Fab Four. A trick repeated by Bob Marley And The Wailers who could retreat into Jamaican patios at will. Phil Solomon had imposed a uniform on Them of matching slim-jim ties and stylish suits. This backfired, when the resulting photo shots resembled a grown up version of William and The Outlaws from Richmal Crompton's children's books, ties ripped asunder, (metaphorically) muddy knees, scowls on their unwashed faces fit to curdle the finest cream. Them did capitulate to one photo session in swimming trunks at an outdoor pool in Ruislip, but the effect was more a borstal outing than youth club high jinks.

The *New Musical Express* for 23 April 1965 includes Them in its "Lifelines" section. The band had temporarily settled to a line-up of Billy Harrison on guitar, Alan Henderson on bass, Pat McAuley now on drums, and his brother John on organ. Common to all is a "casual" taste in clothes and a "self taught" musical education. Oddities crop up, like the band's biggest disappointment being the failure of their first single, and their first important public appearance being *Thank Your Lucky Stars*. No mention of the Maritime Hotel. Van, five foot six with blue eyes and fair hair, gives his biggest influence as a "feeling for the blues". His biggest thrill as "talking 'blues' to John Lee Hooker". His favourite colour is green. Tomato juice is his drink of choice. Ray Charles, Steve McQueen and Roland Kirk all receive namechecks. He likes fresh air and swimming. One detail gives the game away: the final two questions separate out personal and professional ambitions, but Van's answer is resolutely the same to both, "to make it in the pop business". Which he certainly did.

Defeated in his attempts to clean up Them's image, Solomon decided to use it as a calling card. A largely unsmiling band – Van has a kind of self satisfied smirk, dressed in unmatched leisure wear and tieless – they are described on the back cover of their eponymous LP, released in June 1965, as "The 'Angry' Young THEM". Apparently the invention of publicist Les Perrin – master of the famous "two phones" technique – before he abandoned ship, this angle was a throwback to the kitchen sink school of *Billy Liar*, *Lucky Jim* and John Osborne's *Look Back In Anger*. As the sleeve notes put it, "These five young rebels are outrageously true to themselves. Defiant! Angry! Sad! They are honest to the point of insult. When asked to produce a track that they considered as 'a pretty song', their answer was simply 'No! This is our music, you either like it or you don't'."

After such a ringing endorsement of anarchy and dissonance – which sounds more like a taster for The Velvet Underground in their "Sister Ray" period – the actual music was a little disappointing. The most vital presence was that of Morrison. "So alive and vibrant are the pure, basic thoughts that he writes, that it seems incredible that one man can have so much talent. His phrasing is so wonderful that in his hands even the most banal lyrics take on a new depth and meaning…and become touched with genius." A good career summary, though these abilities flash briefly, if tellingly. Particularly in its original vinyl incarnation, with the snap, crackle and pop of that medium as compared to the smooth inanities of CD's digital perfection, this remains a fine example of its genre, rough and ready British R&B, with a wild vein of Celtic poetry running through it.

The album opens with three songs by Van, which is at the very least a vote of confidence in his songwriting. 'Mystic Eyes' "expresses the sheer exuberance with which these boys got together. This number was intended simply as a non-vocal track – but on the session Van

Morrison began to sing a few phrases towards the end – and suddenly the song came alive." Van discounts this story in a later interview: "The lyrics were just words from another song I was writing at the time. We put it on tape the second time round." Strange, because it certainly doesn't sound that way. The closest thing to a Them rave up on disc, harmonica driven and almost a Bo Diddley beat, when something quite extraordinary happens. Here is Morrison's first essay into hypnotic song-poetry. It is as if Morrison was impelled into these strange and chilling words, and he starts quietly, as if talking to himself. "One Sunday morning, we went walking down by the old graveyard" – the next words are unclear, possibly jump cut in the studio, or deliberately slurred – "and looked into his mystic eyes". "His" eyes, not "your". This is a love song to God, or the universe, or a carved headstone, not to a woman. A Decca press release of the time reveals that the song was written after seeing children playing in a graveyard. "The bright lights in the children's eyes...the cloudy light in the eyes of the dead." Morrison repeats the title phrase ad infinitum as organ, drums, maracas and bass swell together into a near epiphany.

Fantastic stuff, and on a small scale what Morrison would do ever after, drawing the listener (and his musicians) into a private world of symbols and portents. A world all the more terrifying from being accessed from the everyday, like Alice climbing through a mirror into Wonderland, or Narnia lurking at the back of a wardrobe. The twist in Morrison's songs is that, once in, there is often no way back.

'If You And I Could Be As Two' is "the boys' favourite track", a slow, swinging rocker with spoken introduction and middle section. Sunday again, with autumn leaves on the ground, and a girl in a blue dress. "The storm was over, the ship sailed through." Morrison's words are closer to prose than poetry – a walk in darkness – delivered with an aggressively Irish accent, compared to the American tinge of Van's singing voice. This *is* a love song, the same theme as – coincidentally – The Spice Girls' Number One ('2 Become 1') as I write these words, but with bitter regret rather than coy invitation.

'Little Girl' is the first recorded example of Van's obsession with childhood innocence – "ten years old" – and a kind of mutant take on 'Good Morning, Little Schoolgirl'. There is a sense here of Van as a passive observer, noting everything but unable to act, or even move.

Far more frightening than voyeurism, that's for sure. Van repeats "in my soul" over and over, as if in terminal agony. He is one of the few singers who can convincingly convey both meanings at once.

The sleeve notes prophetically describe 'Gloria' as "without doubt an R&B standard of the future". It now sounds more punk than R&B. With stern military drums and a perky beat, bass driving like a whip, Van sounds out of control from the start. Hoarse, slurring his words like a feral cat, he spells out his girl's name like a magic spell. There is no guitar break, just the riff louder (four times), a flourish on the organ, the backing grows quieter and Van sounds breathless, lascivious as he tells of his lover's approach. Masterly drumming, which speaks volumes. There is a subliminal pause between "comes to my room" and "makes me feel okay", a glitch in the narrative, which suggests that they are doing something other than the *Times* crossword. At the end, the drums speed into an orgasmic beat.

'You Just Can't Win' boasts lots of natural echo and hiss, and references to Van's new life in London: "take a tube to Camden Town", and "you're in Park Lane now". He has already learned how to make his lyrics concise and to the point, with nothing to spare.

Another pointer to the future follows. "John Lee Hooker, hailed as one of the greatest R&B singers in the world, wrote 'Don't Look Back'. Perhaps it isn't so extraordinary that this soulful ballad sounds uncannily like a Van Morrison composition. Obviously, they have a great deal in common." Prophetic words, as Hooker 'n' Van were almost a double act by the early nineties. The Blues Brothers, or perhaps more accurately Father And Son.

With 'I Like It Like That', "Van again comes up with a superb rendering of his own composition". Except that it sounds more like subdued Animals than Them, and the song is deeply dull. Frisky lead guitar, but songwriting by numbers. Morrison's vocals at the end take on a nightmarish Captain Beefheart/Edgar Broughton quality, though.

Them's version of 'Route 66' begins with jazzy piano and a Jaggeresque vocal, but the backing swings far more strongly than the Stones' version. A song of hope and excitement, especially for Morrison with his father's stories about life in the USA, and Van's voice takes on a Stateside tinge. A fine twangy guitar break, and Morrison comes back even bouncier, sounding wistful on the line about California. In five years, he would be living there.

An original pressing of *Them* in the Geoff Wall archive displays no name at all on the front cover except the Decca logo, shades of the deliberate anonymity of The Rolling Stones' stunning debut. If you don't know who the band are, you shouldn't ask. Its members are all dressed casually, without a tie in sight. Van is central, perched on the ornate arm of an antique settee, right leg raised, black leather boots, light blue cord trousers, and matching blue sweater, with long curly hair, covering his ears. His expression is unreadable, full of subdued humour rather than menace. His Irish mouth and eyes are slightly smiling.

Them's first album cruised smoothly to the top of Ireland's charts, and the group were welcomed home as conquering heroes. The cover shot includes Peter Bardens, who had by now replaced John McAuley on organ. As he had already ghosted keyboard parts for Them in the studio, this was not too drastic a departure. Bardens was a more than competent keyboard player who went on to the heavily psychedelic Village with Bruce Thomas – later of The Attractions. Their single 'Man In The Moon' is one of the finest of the era, and on the Head label. Enough said. Bardens then made two spooky and underrated solo albums, and formed Camel, a kind of second division Caravan. He continues to flit in and out of the Van Morrison saga, that everyday story of musical folk.

McAuley's departure was the first of many, and Them's family tree would be almost beyond the pen of Pete Frame. Steve Turner identifies at least eight line-ups in his book, and even this is not definitive. Peter Bardens did come with "added value". Van would haunt his organist's north London flat – shared with Mick Fleetwood, with whom Bardens had played in Peter B's Looners with a young and drug free Peter Green. Here the three musicians would consume a rich diet of what was fast becoming known as "soul" music, though no one had yet attached the word Caledonian to it.

As well as singles by James Brown, The Supremes, The Righteous Brothers, Nina Simone and Wilson Pickett – saturation plugged into the Top Fifty by pirate radio – these soul brothers were soon in close communion with such as The Drifters, Fats Domino, Chris Kenner and Bobby Bland – from whose *Two Steps From The Blues* album, a 1962 collision of gospel and R&B, Van plucked 'Turn On Your Love Light'. Similarly erudite gems were infiltrating the repertoires of former R&B units in Britain now looking and sounding dangerously like pop groups. It is an era fondly remembered – and then given a bitter twist – on Elvis Costello's *Get Happy* album, of which even mint copies come with their own coffee stain. Party music of the finest stamp.

All kinds of British recording acts were trying soul on for size. 'I Can't Stand It' and 'Every Little Bit Hurts' had been thrust out as consecutive Spencer Davis Group A-sides. Cilla Black – of all people – squeaked her way through The Righteous Brothers' Phil Spector epic 'You've Lost That Lovin' Feelin'' – about as accurate a copy as a Taiwanese Cartier watch. Them's on stage concessions to soul were legion. 'I'll Go Crazy', 'You've Lost That Lovin' Feelin'', 'In The Midnight Hour', 'Dancing In The Street' – plus 'Turn On Your Love Light', Chris Kenner's 'Something You Got', James Brown's 'Out Of Sight', Fats Domino's 'Hello Josephine' and Screaming Jay Hawkins' 'I Put A Spell On You'. All were recorded in consideration for the group's forthcoming second LP, *Them Again*, along with a radically new influence,

Them laid down a cover of 'It's All Over Now Baby Blue', Bob Dylan's farewell to the folk scene and his own adolescence. The Animals had already taken the traditional blues 'House Of The Rising Sun' from his first album, and (literally) electrified it. Dylan returned the compliment by hiring a rock section for one side of *Bringing It All Back Home*, though he had recorded with a band as early as the sessions for *Freewheelin'*, producing the crunchy 'Mixed Up Confusion'. The Animals gave him the confidence to do this in public, though the reactions at the Newport Folk Festival, and in Europe 1966, were as if he had spat on the grave of Woody Guthrie. The messiah, turned Judas.

No wonder Alan Price is proudly on show in *Don't Look Back*. The Byrds took their ground breaking version of 'Mr Tambourine Man' from Dylan's rough demo with Happy Traum – which is why half the lyrics are missing from their hit single – offered to and refused by The Pretty Things. In Dylan's own view, though it might of course have been a put on, Manfred Mann were his most effective interpreters. Towards the end of *Don't Look Back*, ie when he is not pointedly ignoring Joan

Baez, or openly laughing at his clone Donovan, Dylan gazes longingly at electric guitars in a shop window in Denmark Street. A year later, on tour with The Hawks, a Band in the making, he rewrote the language of rock music. Dylan's lyrical stance was now that anything was possible, no subject was too arcane or strange or mysterious for a pop song, and Van Morrison was to follow enthusiastically in his wake.

For the moment though, 'One More Time', Them's first A-side to be written by Morrison, flopped badly. Bert Berns had returned to New York to busy himself with Bang, his new record company. In his absence, Tommy Scott – who ran a production company with Phil Solomon – came in as Them's main studio overseer. He also supervised a girl singer/songwriter called Twinkle (though presumably not by her parents), all of whose Decca flip-sides were written by Scott. As a resentful Twinkle explained, "I just had to put up with it." Scott was to benefit from an almost Twinkle-like monopoly on Them B-sides, writing the flipside of 'One More Time' under the pen name of "Gillon". Neither is the greatest song ever recorded.

Them were on a downward slope. In August, Billy Harrison began asking too many awkward questions about where all the money was going. The group were "walking, talking, eating, sleeping, playing, working music all the bloody time", their only indulgence watching cartoon films at the local fleapit before gigs. As he told *Wavelength*, he "went for the jugular and created a big row. The band was in agreement with me that things weren't right, but when I broached the subject I was left standing on my own. The union rep with no members!" Harrison decided to jump before he was pushed. After occasional gigs with The Pretty Things, he joined the GPO in London, and now works as a marine electrician back in Ulster. Much like Van's dad.

Van was now renting a flat in Notting Hill, scene of race riots ten years earlier, events given a high gloss in the movie *Absolute Beginners*. He shared his life with his girlfriend, an older woman called Dee, who some feared was a management plant, put in to protect their main investment. By all accounts she was half minder, half surrogate mother, and would "put his scarf on for him and give him money for his bottle of wine and his cigarettes". Whatever the truth in that, she left a deep mark on Van's lyrics – some say her early death was the inspiration for 'TB Sheets' – as did his new neighbourhood, the simmering cauldron from which London psychedelia would be spawned. A time and place since mythologised in fiction by Michael Moorcock, a long term resident. The birthplace of his anti-hero Jerry Cornelius.

By August, Pat McAuley and Bardens had also left Them, and two new members, guitarist Joe Boni and drummer Terry Noone, appeared in publicity photographs, but never recorded. Meanwhile, Van and bassist Alan Henderson had returned to audition a new Them, spending some time back at the Maritime rehearsing. New to the fold were guitarist Jim Armstrong from The Melotones, sixteen-year-old John Wilson, drummer with The Misfits (and, later, Taste), and The Broadways' Ray Elliot, with his Manfred Mann beard and Don Craine deerstalker. Elliot was picked for his ability to play "jazz chords" on organ, doubling on saxophone, flute and vibraphone. *Astral Weeks* in embryo.

John Wilson remembered that "the others used to make fun of me, 'cos I was so young and I was influenced by buying clothes in Carnaby Street and all this sort of stuff. They used to say, 'Don't worry, Junior, you might meet a pop star tonight'." He remembers a band whose taste for drink took much away from their live performances. Talking to *Wavelength*, he also remembered what seems to be a consensus view on the subject of this book. "But there was a definite charisma when Van performed. Van always had something about him. Whether you liked it or not, you could never take away from the fact that he was different from all other human beings, and here he is today, still being different."

Wilson also remembers the young Morrison as being "always creative, but no one ever nurtured him in those days. He was just a commodity, like a tin of beans." The new band played a forty minute set at the Top Hat club in Belfast that September. The local magazine *City Week* described the change of direction from straight down the line R&B, and which Van was to pursue ever after. "There was an emphasis on soul jazz that would have raised an eyebrow if played by any other local group. The sight of Van Morrison and new boy Ray Elliot chase-chorusing their way through a two tenor version of 'The Train And The River' would even have stimulated a Royal Showband fan who had arrived a night early."

It was a direction that did not satisfy everyone, and the power was even turned off at one gig because it was not the expected heavy R&B, but something "light and jazzy". No such limp wristed nonsense on Them's fifth single, '(It Won't Hurt) Half As Much', dredged up from a Berns session, and no chart action either. When it failed in Britain, its flipside 'I'm Gonna Dress In Black' became the A-side in the States, just as had 'Gloria', which climbed to Number Seventy-One in the US Hot Hundred.

Like Britpop thirty years later, British Beat – learned largely from American models – was passed back across the Atlantic to reinvigorate a moribund music scene. The Byrds took off from The Searchers' fusion of Merseybeat and contemporary folk, while The Count Five's hit 'Psychotic Reaction' was an unspoken homage to The Yardbirds. Similarly, The Shadows Of Knight made 'Gloria' a Stateside hit, shorn of its organ both literally and metaphorically. For the sake of decency, the line about Gloria coming into the singer's room was also cut. Decca now pulled an uncharacteristically bold stroke by reissuing 'Mystic Eyes', as a single. It rose to Number Thirty-Three on the *Billboard* chart, helped on its way by the release of a promotional film of a stoic Them – with new drummer David Harvey – miming one early autumn morning on London's Embankment as commuters looked on, askance. It was to be the beginning of Them's greatest adventure.

In a profile for *City Week* that November, Van namechecks Bobby Bland, Sam Cooke, Otis Redding, Booker T and Stevie Winwood. His likes are "girls, walking in the country, swimming, keeping busy, fans, Paris, poetry". His solitary ambition is to "make it...". For which it was necessary to make his own Atlantic crossing.

Decca rush-released Them's second and last album in January 1966. The cover of *Them Again* exuded truculence, and the band's usual unsmiling demeanour – with both Morrison and Elliot smoking cigarettes right down to the stub. Van is smart but casual in jacket, pullover and open shirt, surly looking, bull headed: he has had a major hair cut since the last LP sleeve. The band's new line-up looks anonymous, with Alan Henderson sporting a college scarf, and Jim Armstrong's glasses a dead ringer for Peter Asher out of Peter And Gordon. The album itself, described later by Van as a "mish mash" and "not really any good" is a sixteen track rag-bag of loose ideas. Even more than the first album, that indefinable sense of a band making music together, for itself and for others, has evaporated. This is music, played largely by sessionmen and without any sense of its intended audience. There is none of the continuity and flow of the early Stones albums, or the first Manfred Mann LP. That said, the album is never less than a good example of British R&B. It takes care of business.

The anonymous sleeve note draws attention to the changes taking place under the surface, praising "Them's efforts to break away from the popular image of long haired maracas shaking pop groups. On this album Them have introduced vibes, sax and flute. They are not content to stand still musically and are moving towards a 'sound' very close to the jazz idiom. This is an album to enjoy! To dance to! But it is also an album for connoisseurs."

As to Van Morrison himself, the sleeve note is open about his famed difficulty, though perceptive as to its reasons. "He sometimes throws his advisors into a frenzy of hair tearing despair...moody, unpredictable, perverse, often downright wilful – but always creative. On sessions, when asked to alter the phrasing of a number or increase the tempo, he will say with quiet rebellion, 'No, I always sing this way...the way I feel.' And he is invariably right."

As to the piece of plastic enclosed, it is "a stormy, tempest driven album, an album for those looking for an 'experience'. And in every phrase, every note, a supremely great album." In their dreams. Tom Scott and Phil Coulter's 'I Can Give You Anything' was composed "one stormy midnight. This is an aggressive, stomping number, written with Van's raw, savage voice in mind." Greil Marcus describes Van's singing here as "an attempt to communicate all he knows and all he feels, never letting down, never throwing away a line", but not yet finding the "freedom for which he was searching".

Some memorable moments loom out of the darkness. 'Turn On Your Love Light' opens with churchy organ, and Van at his most seductive and pleading, howling like a wild animal over the closing chorus. He engages in some vocal ventriloquism: Eric Burdon in Tommy Scott's 'Call My Name' with its close links to 'Don't Let Me Be Misunderstood' and Stax brass, a tranquillised Fats Domino on 'Hello Josephine'. 'Something You Got' is his own tribute to one of his favourite songwriters, Chris Kenner. The last person he sounds like on

'It's All Over Now Baby Blue' is Bob Dylan, though. A bass riff, delicate syncopated guitar, subdued drums, and Van at his most relaxed and regretful. His accent is a strange mix of Irish and American, but the overall tone is a sad sweetness, light years from Dylan's huskiness. The song fades out on Van, embroidering the original melody line, as if lost in his own thoughts. A mark for the future, and a note of regret for past glories, the original Them perhaps.

Writing later in *Rolling Stone*, Greil Marcus composes a symphony of words to describe this track, an early example of how Van can both inspire and be inspired by his musicians. "The band composes itself out of a very hard, dominant bass, working over crucial notes instead of patterns; an acoustic guitar; organ; drums; and electric vibes, as a high pitched, painful lead instrument. Each note stands out as a special creation – 'the centuries of emotion that go into a musician's choice from one note to the next' is a phrase that describes the depth of this recording. Played very fast, Van's voice virtually fighting for control over the band, 'Baby Blue' emerges as music that is both dramatic and terrifying." Marcus can only compare Buffalo Springfield's 'Out Of My Mind' – in which another shy genius, Neil Young, gives a terrifying account of paranoia and incipient madness – as music for "the loneliness of a dark night". Music that I would only play with the lights full on, speaking personally.

Of Van's original compositions, 'Could You Would You' is 'Here Comes The Night' part two, though it has thunderous drums and a pleading, passionate tone all its own. 'My Lonely Sad Eyes' is like Jagger at his slowest, with Van's new technique of eliding a whole sentence as if it is one word. The regretful atmosphere, and allusions to "some sunny windswept afternoon" prefigure later, greater songs. There is a lovely sense of a dying fall about the tune. 'Bad Or Good' is rendered "in shouting gospel style", with a touch of Mac Rebennack, and meaningless words. A second cousin to The Animals' 'Bring It On Home', complete with raucous chorus.

Far more interesting is Morrison's song 'Hey Girl', which opens with gentle flute and piano, and lopes along like a pony and trap on a country lane. The whole thing is a dry run for 'Cypress Avenue', addressed to a young girl, "so young I don't know what to do". He holds her hand in the "morning fog" – shades of 'Into The Mystic' – and they watch boats in the bay, then climb to look down on "the city down below". Here in embryo is the mysterious atmosphere of *Astral Weeks*, a Belfast of the mind, and a troubling sexuality. Van declares that "little girl I want to walk your dog", a euphemism in Rufus Thomas's famous song for sex. The song ends in mid air, with Van watching her baby sister. The song is very reminiscent of Doll By Doll's 'Hey Sweetheart', the same intense feeling of overflowing joy. The way that Van stretches out the word "sailing" to at least twice its usual length and the break in his voice as he sings "little child" is worth the LP's price of admission alone.

As the sleeve notes put it, 'Hey Girl' was "written and sung by Van as a poignant, wistful love song, but it is infinitely more than that. Those with an awareness of the complex frustrations, brought about by overcrowded cities and the neglected humanities of a neon society, will see in this composition a deep, underlying protest of a boy caught up in an indifferent world." The final song, side two track eight, sounds at first like a straightforward rave up. However, 'Bring 'Em On In' is again far more than that. "Van mentions districts and place names of London. Queensway in particular is very like New York's Greenwich Village. One could almost say that Van really 'goes to town on this track'." Although Van and Them are Irish lads from Belfast, and share a love for the "ould country" they are now based in London. "Where," says Van, "it all happens." Van is driving his Jaguar car – surely wishful thinking at the time – then suddenly he is walking down Queensway, where an old friend invites him in, whether for sex or drugs or a copy of coffee is unclear. Another jump cut, and he is stepping off the boat from Ireland, walking slowly to the car park and his beloved Jaguar "out of my mind". A song in code.

'Bring 'Em On In' maps out a whole future career. Just as well, for in Britain at least, Them was a band in rapid decline. A new single, Tommy Scott's 'Call My Name', might have better suited Herman's Hermits. To add insult to injury EMI issued a version of the same song by Belfast rivals The Wheels. No one any longer knew quite what Them was or stood for – apart from Morrison's brooding presence.

This led to outright piracy, with a counterfeit Them doing the rounds, and often failing even to turn up to venues daft enough to book them. Solomon's response was worthy of a gangster movie. He issued a public threat to the agency concerned. "Our Them have lost worldwide bookings because of confusion caused by this other group. I intend to cause similar confusion by booking our duplicate Fortunes and Pinkerton's Colours – I've registered the names. I shall only give way when I have compensation from Terry King's agency for all the work we have lost." Matters were resolved speedily.

Another bunch of imposters began gigging as Them in the USA, where *Them Again* had charted. If nothing else, this indicated market demand, and a US tour was set up. Meanwhile, there were a few commitments to clear up. Chris Murray gave *Wavelength* his account of possibly the last gig Them played in England. It was at at Ashton-Under-Lyne, at the local Mecca palais. A moody Morrison, drinking orange juice prior to the gig, reluctantly signs a press cutting pre gig, having first used it to sop up some stale beer. Nice. When the group hits the stage to demands for their hit singles, they face boos and cat calls as they launch into a series of unknown blues numbers. As the evening progresses, and the crowd thins, Van comes "into his own, belting out the blues in a bellicose manner".

In May 1966, Them touched down at Kennedy airport for a press reception, quite lacking The Beatles' ready wit in such circumstances (a species of on-air truculence which Van has adhered to ever since). Then straight to California for some radio interviews, and on to a football stadium in Arizona for their first concert on American soil. These modern bands just don't know how mollycoddled they are! Van virtually gulped down the microphone as he strained against a public address system built for sports commentators.

The highlight of the equally hectic two months that followed was a three week residency in June 1966, two sets a night, at the three hundred capacity Whiskey-A-Go-Go on Sunset Boulevard, LA. The instrument-by-instrument build-up to the first verse of 'Baby Please Don't Go' enabled Them to be introduced each in turn, with Morrison coming in last on surging harmonica. Here, given once more the luxury of a residency, and a semi regular audience with whom they could build up rapport, the band reinvented itself, resurrecting the spirit of Club Rado. Surviving photos of the time see a sinister combo – Henderson in shades, Armstrong dressed all in white, flanking Van in the centre, all mod hair cut and bum-freezer jacket. They crowd onto a tiny stage, no bigger than a pub alcove. Only Ray Elliott, in striped blazer and Sherlock Holmes hat, can raise the ghost of a smile. The small crowd, standing within touching distance, soon shed their California cool, and stormed the stage during an especially bravura 'Boom Boom' or when Van simmered things down to the spoken middle section in 'Gloria'. Just as he did at the Maritime Hotel, he would then elaborate and stretch out his monologue, piling the tension tight as a drumskin. As he had duetted with Belfast chums like Johnny Johnston or Keith McDowell, now he shared the microphone with the leather trousered singer of unknown support act, The Doors, as yet unsigned to any record label.

In *Riders On The Storm*, John Densmore recalls that on the final night of Them's residency "we all played 'Gloria' together. Two keyboards, two guitars, two drummers, Alan – the lovable but always into the 'drink' bass player – and two Morrisons." The resulting performance lasted twenty minutes. Tapes from the Matrix in March 1967 capture The Doors still playing their own take on 'Gloria', alongside R&B standards like 'I'm A King Bee'.

Back on opening night, the Whiskey was "buzzing with anticipation. The VIP booths at the back were full." This even affected Densmore's own performance that night, with him speeding up on drums on their opening song, 'Break On Through'. Robby Krieger had to nod his head up and down in the right tempo, to calm him down. During the intermission, it was everyone for themselves in the struggle to find a seat. "Them brashly took the stage. They slammed through several songs one right after another, making them indistinguishable. Van was drunk and very uptight and violent with the mike stand, crashing it down on the stage. When he dropped his lower jaw and tongue and let out one of those yells of rage, something Irish in me made my skin crawl with goose bumps. Ancient angst."

John Rogan records Morrison threatening the audience with his mike stand, and thrusting it into the speakers with a hail of feedback resulting. On one night, he stood on a swaying amp, and waved his arms like wings, urging himself to fly. Densmore is bemused why "a guy with so much talent had to drink to get up on stage". Given Jim Morrison's later problems with alcohol abuse, this is both sad and prophetic. Looking back, he recalls not Them's performance, but "their drunken, brawling foreign charisma. Jim thought they were great." The two Morrisons, Jim and Van, would howl in harmony, call and response, on a rambling and epic 'In The Midnight Hour'. Touring with Ike and Tina Turner had taught Mick Jagger all kinds of new stage moves. In just the same way, Jim Morrison learned quickly from his near namesake's stagecraft, his apparent recklessness, his air of subdued menace, the way he would improvise poetry to a rock beat, even his habit of crouching down by the bass drum during instrumental breaks. The Doors' mainman was to make such antics more self conscious, more of an act. He also learned bad habits. As Armstrong pointed out, "At that stage, Jim Morrison was a typical Californian grass head, whereas we were from a drink background, and somewhat loath to take any of the other. So we started Jim on the drink really." He had his own journey to make into the unconscious, a more sinister and dangerous path than the one Van was to take, and one that saw Jim in a poet's grave in Paris within five years.

Ironically, Jim was not present when Densmore was given the chance of a lifetime, to witness early versions of what was to become *Astral Weeks*. Like Patti Smith after him, Jim Morrison was obsessed with the fusion of poetry with rock music. Before his early death, Jim published three booklets of verse, quite separate from his rock lyrics, and would devote part of The Doors' set to his epic spoken piece 'Celebration Of The Lizard'. Van was going in the same direction, at the speed of light.

Densmore accompanied him to a party after the Whiskey opening. It's two in the morning, and everyone is talking and drinking except Van. "He sat on the couch, moody and glowering, and didn't say a word. All of a sudden he grabbed a guitar and started singing songs about reincarnation, being in 'another time and place'." The song is 'Astral Weeks'. "This was sheer poetry merging with rock 'n' roll. I wished Jim had been there. The apartment fell silent and all eyes were riveted on Van. Hearing him sing about 'walking in gardens all wet with rain' I found my eyes welling up. It was as if he couldn't communicate on a small talk party level, so he just burst into his songs. We were mesmerised. It didn't seem appropriate to shower Van with compliments, because his music came from such a deep place. So when he finished there was silence for a minute or so. A sacred silence.

Then everyone went back to talking and partying." A priceless moment of rock history, and if Densmore's memory is accurate, then part of *Astral Weeks* predates the demise of Them, let alone the Bang sessions.

Even if Jim had missed such manna from heaven, the bond between him and Van endured. Densmore recalls walking along Santa Monica Boulevard a few months later when Van Morrison drove by. "He rolled down the window and said he was back in town and asked how Jim was doing. I know Jim admired and cared for Van." By now, Van had moved permanently to the States, as a solo artist.

Meanwhile, other pioneers of psychedelia were learning the strange places that rock music could go, by supporting Them at the Whiskey. The tension and yearning of Van's music ensemble certainly left its mark on the misnamed Love – still in their garage phase, with Arthur Lee coming on as a black, more fragile Mick Jagger. Lee was another rocker whose songs were turning strange, and a man who would achieve his own unique lyricism, tinged with darkness, on 1967's *Forever Changes*. Also appearing at the Whiskey was Captain Beefheart And His Magic Band, whose own peculiar take on the blues even outdid Van's. Howlin' Wolf on LSD, from Neptune. Another support act was The Association, purveyors of stoned harmonies, whose influence crossed back to England. Mod group The Action played their songs as part of their rich transformation into Mighty Baby, the English Grateful Dead. These few months set rock music's parameters for the next twenty years, perhaps forever, and it is fascinating that the last ditch stand of Them was among such company.

Popular music was like a great coloured beach ball, in the air and up for grabs. Multifarious chemicals, a mood of youthful optimism, and developments like the stereo LP and improved PAs, all fuelled the revolution. Van was there, his Belfast truculence cracking like a carapace at the dawn of the Summer of Love. Them crossed from LA to San Francisco to headline at Fillmore Auditorium. A multi-coloured audience sat cross-legged and silent on the floor amid flickering strobes and ectoplasmic light projections, stimulating chemically induced glimpses of the eternal. All part of the psychedelic experience, the kind of "blowing your mind" which Van Morrison later so objected to, and which his own music helped people travel through, and survive. Like any other common-or-garden genius, Van's mind was already quite strange enough, without the assistance of hallucinogenics.

The Fillmore's promoter, Bill Graham, bustled about, similarly drug free, clipboard in hand, enforcing his own order amongst the apparent chaos. Graham's own background was in avant-garde theatre, and later that night he introduced Morrison backstage to a young actress who in true hippie style had reinvented herself as "Janet Planet". A woman of independence before her time, Janet was combining a career with bringing up her son Peter, as a single mother. Whatever transpired between Van and Janet, their very names a half-rhyme, she was present for the remainder of Them's American gigs.

Dazed by the kind of music they were encountering first hand in California, Van and the other members of Them were facing a future both uncertain and unresolved. Van found that "as far as ideas and stuff were concerned, America was the place for me...people understood, for probably the first time, what I was talking about". By now, they were certainly no longer a singles band – if they ever had been – and only performed the loathed 'Call My Name' if it was specifically requested. Such an occurrence was extremely rare, and the song failed to trouble the Hot Hundred.

The vultures were gathering. Roy Carr of *NME* described Them as "the archetypal, morose British R&B club band: an ill matched bunch of imageless transport-caff cowboys with clapped out equipment who achieved some degree of immortality and notoriety in spite of their sullen selves". Meanwhile, the band were roughing out an early version of 'Ballerina', a song of awesome beauty inspired by Janet, and premiering it in concert in Hawaii. Tensions were rising to a head, though. There were disputes over money, and one night in San Luis, Van began stalking Ray Elliot with a heavy microphone stand, with serious intent at bodily harm. Elliot and David Harvey had, for all practical purposes, already left the band, choosing to stay in America and take their chances in the brave, confused new world of underground rock. As the tour wound down, Them scattered like petals before the wind.

Van and Alan Henderson gravitated back to Belfast, and played two final concerts, in Derry and Dublin, with drummer Sammy Stitt. During their absence, in June 1966, Decca had released 'Richard Cory' – a bitter song about a factory owner, one of whose worker's even envies his suicide – from their final recording sessions as a single. Written by Paul Simon, the performance is close to folk-rock, and sounds uncomfortable and unconvinced. Decca even cancelled a rival version by new signing The Animals to give Them's version precedence. With the group away in America, and unable or unwilling to promote it, the single failed to chart, and followed 'I Can Only Give You Everything', lifted from *Them Again* as a US only single, into merciful oblivion. Not quite, in the case of the latter, as The Troggs thought highly enough of this rousing thrash to insert it on 1967's *Trogglodynamite*, and were still encoring with it twenty years later.

Them hardly existed as a working unit anymore. "Sometimes the band was just whoever turned up," Morrison later admitted. Jim Armstrong's place was taken briefly by Eric Bell, once of The Shades Of Blue and later to form Thin Lizzy. The increasingly uncommitted Henderson drummed up a shifting nucleus of new members in hangouts like Crymbles where Belfast rockers congregated to borrow equipment, compare notes, betray confidences and boast about imminent record deals.

Economic necessity now obliged Them to trade as a four piece with Morrison on guitar and saxophone as well as vocals. The set included 'Gloria' and 'Turn On Your Love Light', in loose arrangements bordering on jazzy pop, a post R&B style also adopted by the likes of Georgie Fame, The Artwoods and The Mark Leeman Four. In Hull The Rats, with Mick Ronson on guitar – another future Van collaborator – released as A-sides Mose Allison's 'Parchman Farm' and Cannonball Adderley's 'Sack O' Woe'. It was a style to which Morrison would return in the nineties. For the moment, and in the light of what was already seeping over from California, thanks to programmes like John Peel's *Perfumed Garden* on Radio London, such musical stylings already sounded tired and out of date.

So it was that "Van Morrison And Them Again" made their concert debut in July 1966 at Square One, a new Belfast venue. Van was dressed in a blue cloak and flower power suit from San Francisco, a fashion messiah. Likewise musically, as he tore up the set list and launched into a blues improvisation. His hired musicians grew increasingly apprehensive as Morrison tried out new and unrehearsed songs, and free-form associations, a musical high wire act without a net. Fine if the whole band had grown together, but even Captain Beefheart needed to have carefully drilled his musicians first. Bell told Steve Turner that Van was like a jazz musician, "inventing the lyrics as he sang, taking the volume right up and then bringing it right back down". The gig was more a shambles than a revelation, and Van seemed to have ceased to care what either his band or his audience thought of him. Free expression merged with a lack of any inner censor, even in between songs, and the torrent of swearwords at Carrickfergus Town Hall provoked a near riot among Teddy Boys who thought such language should be confined to the pub, not a place of entertainment. A hail of copper pennies engulfed the band, before the lacerated musicians evacuated the stage. The incident was serious enough to make the news on regional television, complete with an interview with an unrepentant lead singer.

Most bizarre of all was a song taped during the 'Richard Cory' session. 'Mighty Like A Rose' – *not* the later Elvis Costello composition – is a turn-of-the-century parlour poem set to music. Had the song been released as a single, it would have affiliated Them with the kind of olde tyme whimsy then prevalent in the Top Twenty.

Morrison was like a drowning man, clutching at straws. He even considered joining The Wheels, now reduced to Rod Demick and Herbie Armstrong. Turner records that Morrison met Armstrong outside a fish and chip shop in the Creggah Road, and expressed interest, but that "he had a phone call to make to Bert Berns in America". He also made a talent spotting expedition back to Club Rado where Taste, Rory Gallagher's new group – with John Wilson on drums – were resident prior to a two year stint in Germany.

On the advice of Phil Coulter, Van had bought a reel-to-reel tape recorder on which to lay down demos of the kind of impressionistic song-poems he had played to John Densmore, and later tried out so disastrously on stage with the pick up band formerly known as Them. Demos of new songs like 'Brown Skinned Girl' and 'TB Sheets' were sent out more in hope than anticipation. They have yet to be caught in any bootlegger's net, more's the pity.

As if to emphasise his growing isolation, Alan Henderson had a new version of Them back on the road, with Kenny McDowell from The

Mad Lads on lead vocals. They were to release four albums of descending worth, of which the first, *Now And Them*, lies unjustly forgotten (though Zap did contrive a vinyl reissue). It is a transitional work, half R&B, half West Coast jamming. This latter style is best heard on the fine, Eastern influenced 'Square Room', close to similar lengthy excursions by the similarly underrated US band Kaleidoscope. For all that, the band is like *Hamlet* without the prince, and the sleeve notes by Carol Deck of the obscure rock magazine *FLIP* have an underlying tone of desperation. "These are Them now and now is Them. They've been through some changes, bad times and good times and learned from all of it. I think it's going to happen for Them now. I think you'll like Them."

The world didn't, particularly. The out of tune 'I Happen To Love You' doesn't help, and the peace and love atmospherics – even the cover is a weak pastiche of Milton Glaser – come a cropper with the band descriptions. Alan Henderson is "a bit rough", while Ray "doesn't trust people" and drummer Dave Harvey "doesn't stand out in a crowd" and is "slow, at everything".

The most interesting song is 'Walking In The Queen's Garden', partly written by Morrison, but credited only to Them, and thus a reverse of the usual practice. The words are sung in an annoyingly sotto voce brogue, but enough emerges to intrigue, with waterfalls, silver spoons, "purple haze" and all. Now where did we hear that last phrase before? The much repeated "Now you've got the point, I'm going to another joint" functions as a kiss off from Morrison to his old band. Even the surrealistic opening, "the duke is such a drag, with his yellow flag" could well have been the artistic resolution of some dressing room squabble. Or not. Tommy Scott told Johnny Rogan that Van "came up to me in Los Angeles and said, 'I've written this thing, do you think it's too disrespectful?' I don't think he ever recorded it." It certainly joins a very short list of songs about Prince Phillip. 1971's dire *In Reality* spelt Them's demise, though there was a brief reformation in 1979, the aural part of which has recently emerged on a German CD.

A splinter group, The Belfast Gypsies, featured the McAuley brothers. Their solitary LP was recorded by Kim Fowley in Sweden, its cover boasting the name Them Belfast Gypsies, to confuse unwary punters. It finally gained a British release in 1978, with typically meticulous sleeve notes from Brian Hogg, whose *Bam Balam* fanzine kept the names of such as Them alive during the glam rock years. The album reprises a jaunty, faster 'It's All Over Now Baby Blue' – with seemingly an extra emphasis given to the line about "forget your debts, they will not follow you" – and the strange single 'Gloria's Dream'. This is a weird take on the original, slightly slower and more distant. It is a foggy night, and the party is getting hot, and Gloria's still happy to go upstairs, and everybody's going round and round and round, as if drugged. There's a touch of the atmosphere of Gavyn Bryars 'The Sinking Of The Titanic', music refracted from beneath the waves.

Jackie later joined Fairport's first singer Judy Dyble in a short lived harmony duo called Trader Horne (named after John Peel's aunt, or granny, or some such whimsical relation). Their solitary, beautiful album is now highly collectable, as is McAuley's own first solo effort, recorded with prominent jazz musicians like Henry Lowther. Jackie went on to become Lonnie Donegan's guitarist and arranger, and to form the band Poor Mouth, its name taken from a Flann O'Brien novel. Two of Van Morrison's own influences, as it happens. Talking to *Wavelength*, he remembered his time with Them, stuck on the ballroom circuit. "People used to ask Van, 'Do you know any Cliff Richard numbers?' and he just wouldn't answer them. Just give them a look."

Them received their finest obituary in a posthumous single, issued by Phil Solomon's new Major-Minor label in September 1967. Morrison remembers times "when friends were friends/and company was right", laughing, drinking, making "the scene" at the Spanish room on the Falls Road. He looks back to Club Rado too:

> *"Now, just about this time with the help of the three Js*
> *Started playin' at the Maritime*
> *That's Jerry, Jerry and Jimmy*
> *And you know they were always fine*
> *They helped us run the Maritime*
> *And don't forget Kit*
> *Hitting people on the head and knockin' them out.*

> *That little one sings and that big one plays the guitar with a thimble on his finger runs it up and down the strings*
> *The bass player don't shave much*

73

I think they're all a little bit touched
But the people came
And that is how we made our name."

Good times, even if they had also been "wild, sweaty, crude, ugly and mad". Interviewed in 1973 by Roy Carr, Van was already making a rapprochement with his past. "For a very long time I didn't realise just how good some of the records I made with Them were. The minute you start denying something you did, I think you're in real trouble."

Response to Van Morrison's demo tapes suggested that the true spirit of Them still resided in his dumpy frame. Decca showed interest, and arranged for four solo tracks to be recorded back at their West Hampstead studios. Had he re-signed with Decca, though, Morrison would have had to play the record company game, something he had already made it quite clear he was not prepared to do. Cabaret appearances and an unthreatening persona were not on his chosen path.

A more tempting offer came out of the blue from Bert Berns at Bang Records in New York, the phone call that Van had to return just as he was being offered musical oblivion with The Wheels. This was a major crossroads in his life. It was still not too late for him to resume his apprenticeship at Musgrave and Co. He would be ribbed by workmates at first for having had ideas above his station, but then he could perform weekend gigs with The Wheels, or as a support act whenever a big name came to Belfast.

The alternative was a step into darkness, a once and for all attempt at a solo career. America was the land of opportunity, the source of Morrison's rich musical heritage, a place of endless possibilities. Berns was an old friend and ally. Janet Planet was patiently awaiting Morrison's return as well, and was unlikely to move from California to Belfast. There was really no contest. Van took a one way flight to New York.

CHAPTER THREE

Lost In A Fugitive's Dream

Morrison had broken from his first manager, Phil Solomon, but remained in fear of him. Even the urbane Phil Coulter was "emotionally intimidated" in his presence. Solomon was unaware of this himself, telling Johnny Rogan that "I take exception to the word 'intimidated'. That was a figment of Morrison's imagination. All I did was instruct an American solicitor to take action. He certainly wasn't the Mafia." But why mention the Mafia in the first place: Morrison hadn't.

As to Van, in the end he had not been worth managing, "although we poured a lot of money into him". He becomes a little emotional at this point. "The man is as thick skinned as a crocodile. Morrison will do these things to suit Morrison because he's not a professional. He never was and never will be. That's the tragedy of Morrison. He was a genius who never reached fulfilment. I think his career has come to a complete halt. He sells records to a few people who love his work."

In his book, published in 1984, Rogan argues that had he remained with Solomon, Morrison would now be one of the most commercially successful rock acts in the world, "with vast album sales and several hit singles", though artistically spent. A solo Bachelors, a male Lulu.In fact, Morrison's popularity has continued to grow ever since; he has staying power precisely because of his restlessness, always one step ahead of his fans. Much the same as Joni Mitchell or Neil Young, who have had similarly long and successful careers. As Bill Flanagan once wrote, "Van didn't feel he fitted in the world in which he found himself", so he started to build one of his own.

Phil Coulter was one friend who realised the desperation of Van's position. "He didn't do a lot of gigs. He was on a downer. It was question of taking Van out of East Belfast, where he wasn't the most bankable of artists." One night, just before taking the plane, Van spent an evening drinking with Dougie Knight, and listening to blues albums. "At one stage he decided he was going to swim across the Lagan", but was persuaded against it. Days later, he heaved his guitar and suitcase from the glass domed terminal at Kennedy Airport, and took a taxi to Bert Berns' apartment in Manhattan. In early 1967 Berns had left Atlantic, to form his own independent record company, divided into the pop label Bang, which scored a number one with The McCoys' 'Hang On Sloopy', and Shout for black soul music. Finance came from the Ertegun brothers and Jerry Wexler, so Atlantic were still exercising some control on their former employee. He in turn financed two days at A&R studios on Times Square – Van paid his own air fare, and recalls only one all day session, from four in the afternoon until midnight – in which to produce eight finished songs, enough for four singles. No one had mentioned the possibility of releasing a whole album.

Morrison later remembered the deal as not "really that spectacular money wise. But I really respected Bert as a producer." He was "somebody I wanted to work with". As he told Ritchie Yorke, "I'd wanted to go to California, but I ended up in New York. I didn't know where New York was at and I had to find out. I just kept California in mind until I could do it. A lot of interesting things happened on the East Coast." Bert Berns was "a businessman too, like a very heavy business cat. He was into a business thing." Quite how was finally revealed in the song 'Big Time Operators', which suggests an organisation more akin to the Mafia, "vicious and mean", who bugged Van's apartment, tried to have him deported, and threatened to arrange a drugs bust if he didn't toe the company line. The same people who named his first album *Blowin' Your Mind*.

Morrison turned up with a tape of original songs, recorded on acoustic guitar with (literally) a tambourine man in the background. Berns liked the bareness of the sound, but when Van arrived in the studio on 28 March he found three guitarists, including Eric Gale, a bassist and drummer waiting for him: "It was like a big production number and I felt that a lot of it was unnecessary." The first day centred on the song 'Brown Eyed Girl', changed from its original title 'Brown Skinned Girl' so as not to offend any racial sensibilities. Twenty-two takes later, with backing harmonies by The Sweet Inspirations, a final version was in the can, and the ensemble went on to record 'Ro Ro Rosey' and 'Goodbye Girl' and a song that was the very opposite of a commercial single, the nearly ten harrowing minutes of 'TB Sheets'. A highly personal song, and performance, after which one of those present remembers Morrison as being "just torn apart. He was sitting on the floor in a heap, like a wrung out dishcloth, completely spent emotionally."

The following day, four more songs were laid down, 'Who Drove The Red Sports Car', 'Midnight Special', 'Spanish Rose' and 'He Ain't Give You None'. Van's frustrations with the session musos becomes increasingly marked, so that on studio chat before the last named song, his resolute Irish tones can be heard declaring that "I think it should be freer, you know. We should have a free thing going, you know." He clicks his tongue to suggest the rhythm in his own head. "At the minute we have a choke thing going." He expanded his frustration in a 1970 interview with *Rolling Stone*. "Bert wanted me to write a song that would be a hit, but I just didn't feel that kind of song. Maybe it was his kind of song, but it wasn't my kind of song." This difference of approach, art versus commerce, fed through into the recording process. "I'd write a song and bring it into the group and we'd sit there and bash it around, and that's all it was. They weren't playing the *song*, all they were thinking about was putting *drums* on it, or putting an electric guitar on it, but it was my song and I had to watch it go down." Van flew back to Belfast, and his parents' home, where he began to put together just this kind of song, the embryonic *Astral Weeks*. "I think it just changed to coming from a deeper unconscious level. It was more to do with getting in touch with the unconscious."

The impetus that was to lead eventually to the release of such crazily uncommercial material, and to Morrison's whole solo career, was a three minute, three second song about young love. 'Brown Eyed Girl' crept slowly into the charts, coming to rest high in the national Top Twenty, alongside 'Light My Fire' by old friends The Doors and The Fifth Dimension's 'Up Up And Away'. The single had more in common with the latter, a good time anthem, perfect sunshine pop for the Summer of Love. As he told New York's *Go* magazine on a telephone line from Belfast in August 1967, "Now there is no limit to what I can do. I plan to use the type of instrumentation I like and be completely free. This is only the beginning for me. Writing and singing are just as important to me, and I'll always be an artist. I'm not planning to fall into the background. My material is my own and whatever I do now will be completely solo."

Within weeks, Berns had summoned his protege back to New York, and booked him into a hotel on Broadway – within safe view and bugging range of Berns' office – where he was soon joined by Janet Planet and her son. Berns put together a pick up band of Charlie Brown on guitar, bassist Eric Oxendine and Bob Grenier on drums. They played a blur of small clubs and media appearances, even performing on the lower deck of a steamer pottering along the Hudson river, during a celebratory party. Van's greatest contempt was reserved for TV appearances where he was required to mime to the hit single, the ultimate indignity for a musician who thrived on the twists and turns of live performance. Conversely, such strategies freed him to spend time in Greenwich Village – where everyone from Dylan to Joni Mitchell to Jimi Hendrix had first come to public attention, and to frequent the musicians' bars and coffee houses around Eighth Street, the Village's main thoroughfare, without too many people pestering him for his autograph.

While Morrison was away, playing a string of East Coast one nighters, Bang released an arbitrary follow up single – 'Ro Ro Rosey' – and, in October and without bothering to inform their creator, threw together an LP, *Blowin' Your Mind*, from the session tapes. Van only found out when a friend mentioned on the phone that he had just bought a copy, and the force of his reaction can only be guessed at. Some tracks were little more than jumbled arrangements coalesced by a guide vocal. Nevertheless, the album reached Number One Hundred And Eighty-Two in the US, and gave Morrison added credibility with the West Coast underground. From 20-22 October, Van played the Avalon Ballroom, the cradle of free-form rock.

The cover of *Blowin' Your Mind* is a pastiche of the psychedelic posters in which the Avalon specialised, except that the brown curlicues fail to resolve themselves into words: the whole point of the original trick, language that only those in the know can decipher. Greil Marcus described it as a "monstrously offensive, super psychedelic far out out-of-sight exploding" design. Van's face is inset, circled in blue light, but pugnacious and short haired, with a withering stare. Peace and love are further distanced by Bang's logo, straight out of a smoking gun. The cover shot is by Rodriguez of Los Angeles, the antithesis of San Francisco.

Bert Berns' sleeve notes fail to convince as a mood statement of the times. Half catch at trendy laid back language – "a multi-coloured window through which one views at times himself and his counterself...erratic and painful...whose music expresses the now! the real now!! the right now of his own road, his ancient highway" – and half actually make good sense. Berns locates Van's Celtic crossroads, the competing influences of the blues and his homeland:

> Born and raised in Ireland of mother and music and radios of stained wood and torn cloth speakers that touched upon him with few but precious fragments of South and Soul. The Belfast boy of typical destiny who counted thousands of picket fences, decayed; leading him to Conservatory and the brass future of sound and distance. His books; his cathedral. Land of Eire and Leadbelly.

Berns grasps the fact that Morrison is a genuine poet among a sea of fakes and stoned wordsmiths. "No clouded lyrics promising jungles of purple birds", but instead "an infinite yearning, a hope to express the shape and smell of sheets embracing life and death". He is also spot on about Morrison's ability to focus in on tiny details, as all true poets do, to "still hold tight to the real of dust of bottles and heartbreak", while well aware of his client's independence. Even when surrounded by "men of coin and dialect", like Berns himself, "Van blows and Van sings and Van screams and Van listens and Van says 'up them all' and becomes Van and now he can live with himself".

The album's most hostile critic was Greil Marcus, who found it "painfully boring, made up of three sweet minutes of 'Brown Eyed Girl' and thirty-two minutes of the sprawling, sensation dulling 'TB Sheets', a track that stood out from the rest if only in its embrace of the grotesque. The other cuts simply merged into one endless, uninspired blues run...faceless chunks of time." It was like a half hour of Elvin Bishop's 'Drunk Again' – evidently not a frequent visitor to Greil's turntable – "only much much worse". Morrison had been freed of all restrictions – song, melody, verse, chorus – but far too early. Talking with Marcus, Van seems to concur, explaining that "I've got a tape in Belfast with all my songs on that record, done the way they're supposed to be done. It's good and simple, doesn't come on heavy. 'TB Sheets' isn't heavy. It's just quiet."

The 1991 *Bang Masters* gathered up out-takes and studio chat, which puts the original album in a wider frame. It opens, as these things always do, with the single. 'Brown Eyed Girl' is a song of joy, Van's voice first wistful then laughing. There is a strong soul shuffle, bass led, with Steve Cropper-like guitar and an organ somewhere in the background, sweetening the sound. The alternate take is less driven, with the guitar riff as yet unfocused, Van's acoustic strumming more upfront, and his voice more nostalgic, less upbeat. After all, this is a song about looking back. Morrison is now "all on my own" when he meets an old girlfriend, "overcome" thinking back to their young love. The lyrics are pure Wordsworth, emotion recollected in tranquillity, with the affair set among images of misty morning fog, a rainbow's wall, a waterfall. Love al fresco, "in the green grass behind the stadium", finding Nature where he could. The fact that all this is in his mind – "they put out publicity to the fact that it was written specifically about somebody I knew, but it wasn't" – makes it all the more perfect an experience. Paradise regained, in Belfast.

From this straight into a soundscape of urban lust, jealousy and sexual disgust. 'He Ain't Give You None' is also directed to a "little girl", with a slow hustle of a beat, spidery lead guitar – at one point he urges "let's go, Eric", Gale not Clapton. There is something of the loose intensity of the early Velvets here, and the sense of forbidden fruit: "You can leave now if you don't like what is happening." References to London seep through, with warnings to stay away from Notting Hill Gate – "I lived there for a while, but I moved out" – and old John flogging his daily meat on Curzon Street. Much like the "meat rack tavern" in Buckley's *Greetings From LA*, best not to enquire too closely. A song of absolute lust, with a laughing Van remembering "when we were down in the alley" with something close to a leer. His sexual boast of outdoing her "daddy" – either husband or pimp – and the very term for sex's sweet motion, "jelly roll", seem light years distant from the Summer of Love. The delighted contempt of the singer, the song's graveyard pace, the stately organ and stinging guitar: all compare to *Highway 61* period Dylan. The alternative take four on *Blowin' Your Mind* is a far less joyful affair, more threatening. There is a druggy ambience, with veiled references to getting up and getting down. The "grass" mentioned is for rolling up, not in.

Any listener drawn in by the lightness of the hit single must be reeling by now, and it's too late to stop now, we are straight into 'TB Sheets'. In the previous song Van confided to the listener that he got "messed up" in Notting Hill, and here is a Dickensian tale of death and decay in a big city. Organ and drums go free form, then a stately groove, fitting Van's voice like a garrotte, led by nagging lead guitar. Van's harmonica hurts the ear, then he's in like a terrier, lecturing his girlfriend, "Julie" about it not being natural her staying awake at night, dying.

John Collis pins this all to the death of Dee, Van's lover and landlady from those days (another candidate being the singer's cousin, called Gloria of all things, who died young). He compares the song's rich luxuriance of detail – the smell of germ drenched bedding, a glint of sunlight that pains the eye – to Keats, whose fevered poetry was itself fuelled by consumption. This is an equal achievement to the slithery dread of the earlier poet's 'Lamia', a young man's song of death, with Van half entranced and half appalled, recreating the whole desperate situation in the studio, acting out both parts. Things start with a fragmented argument, with the girl's raging jealousy. "Your little starstruck innuendoes. Inadequate season. Foreign bodies." Someone once questioned if Dylan was better than Keats, as if this was some kind of contest. Well, here we have a scene straight out of *Dante's Inferno*, witnessing a torture. Check out Van's desperate snuffling after breath, the pleading for water, the urgent need to escape, the panic in his voice on "gotta go". The only alleviation of pain – apart from his guilty laughter – is to turn on the radio, and let its tunes infuse the "cool room". In later songs the shaft of sunlight would prove to be a blessing, a sign of divine grace, but not here.

The utter desolation of 'TB Sheets' could be seen as a living hell from which Van's whole later career has been a search for escape into meaning. Rather like the film *Shadowlands*, dealing with CS Lewis's coming to terms with pain. It is a song which he has very rarely performed live, as if that is any kind of surprise.

Side two of *Blowin' Your Mind* is a more relaxed, low key affair. 'Spanish Rose' screws Van's voice up to breaking point, with a 'La Bamba' beat. Piffle. 'Goodbye Baby (Baby Goodbye)' is sung tougher than its writers, Bert Berns and Wes Farrell, would have intended. As to Van's own 'Ro Ro Rosey', it sounds like it took longer to sing than it did to write. "She's just sixteen and she's not yet grown", a delve into the writer's unconscious. Van's voice seems to fragment at the end, into Joycean shards of language.

'Who Drove The Red Sports Car' is something else again. "A piece of my life, if that means anything." Jazzy piano and sharp drums, while Van articulates a dream, deeply private yet universal, with layers of sensual recall. "Who did your homework, and read your *Bible?*" This half spoken reminiscence, patterned as a string of questions, suddenly steps up a gear, with Van caught out in the rain. "I had nothing on but a shirt, and a pair of pants. I was getting wet. Saturated." In what can only be called a religious moment, his voice swells into epiphany, as two women – Maggie and Jane – invite him up into the warm and dry, as if into paradise. The way that Van emphasises the "t" in wet, Woody Allen like, and his closing laughter and throwaway "don't mind if I do" are priceless. There is really no song here, just a riff and a stream of memories, but from this Morrison creates a thing of hope and beauty, the other side of the coin to 'TB Sheets', heaven after hell. As he tells the musicians, "That's a bag. Now you gotta turn it upside down, put it in a rack, fold it, press it, call it a record." This record closes with 'Midnight Special', a roar of delight with female chorus.

As Van later told Mick Brown, "It wasn't really an album, it was four singles. They put them together to put the album out. The blind leading the blind." He told another journalist that "I don't think that album really had anything to do with where I was at". For all that, he returned to the same studio to cut eight more tracks that November. Berns said he could "do whatever you want to do" but when the sessions came around, "there was about a ten piece rhythm section and out of that, five people we didn't need. The engineer just didn't seem to care about the sessions at all. And I didn't have my chance at 'my shot' as Bert put it."

The results had none of the drive or conciseness of the first Bang session, but finished tracks did include early, inferior versions of 'Beside You' and 'Madame George', some of which appeared on 1970's ludicrously titled *The Best Of Van Morrison*. As the singer explained, "It should have been called 'The Worst Of…'. When I started I was told I would be able to do my own thing, but then it got sabotaged. I actually redid some of the songs on *Astral Weeks* just to show how they really should be done." Which alone made the exercise worthwhile. Released in late 1970, *The Best Of Van Morrison* features a ludicrous sleeve to match, with Van's face the size of a pimple, which then expands all around him, like a cheap graphic from *Doctor Who*. The back cover photo is far more appealing, but as it is the same one used on the front of *Astral Weeks* – the success of which had prompted this vault scraping exercise – that is hardly surprising.

Of the new tracks, 'It's All Right' sounds like a private message, while 'Send Your Mind' is plain odd, with lots of false endings. There is an eastern edge to 'The Smile You Smile', the guitar winds back on itself like a sitar, while Van talks to trees and sunshine, and feels his girlfriend's lips against his. Stoned rather than twee. 'The Back Room' is the real story of rock 'n' roll, dressing room frolics with Van at his most Jagger-like. Wine, and "something to turn you on".

The same material was reshaken and recycled in 1974's *TB Sheets*, boasting one of Morrison's best covers, a painting of the artist sitting in an armchair in a symphony of brown, as heavenly light streams through the window. Here at last are the two early sketches for *Astral Weeks*, an album which became what it was "because everything was stripped away". 'Beside You' here is, conversely, far rawer than the finished version. The ending is far more explicit, "go ahead and do it one more time baby", and the tune not quite in place. 'Madame George' lacks the sad sweetening of strings, and is set instead against a studio party. As Bill Henderson comments, "You have two opposed views of the same scene. On *Astral Weeks*, 'Madame George' takes place inside Van's head, looking at the revellers. The Bang version is outside looking in." He also points out the extra lines in the first verse, which make the transvestite theme all the clearer, whatever Morrison's later denials. "And then your self control lets go, suddenly you're up against the bathroom door...you're in the front room touching him." The song starts with Van saying "put your fur boots on", and ends with taking a train "up from Dublin to Sandy Row", leaving it all behind.

A third song – which first surfaced on *The Best Of Van Morrison* – is cut from the same cloth. 'Joe Harper Saturday Morning' has much the same tune as 'St Dominic's Preview', and sounds like a missing link from *Astral Weeks*: "I'm not what so many people see." A strange account of a request for money, set in a garden, in the rain of course, with an "old queen", and ending at a bus shelter. "The shine of glory all around did not disguise what we did." A coded tale, about a young man selling his body for small change.

(The real Joe Harper started the blues nights at the Maritime and was a noted loner.)

The *Bang Masters* CD gathers up more loose ends, with a previously unreleased 'I Love You (The Smile You Smile), an acoustic demo of a song about a dream girl with whirlpool eyes, who can take him to paradise. Sony have also recently issued a gold CD of the original album, with five alternate takes, and slightly improved sound. Bill Henderson's exemplary sleeve notes to the *Bang Masters* catch the scattershot creativity of these recordings, a seed bed of later invention. "He was busting with ideas, with talent, with a special vision. Every artist works to balance skill and intuition, but in young Van Morrison's case it was more than a balancing act – he was juggling hand grenades."

Any future plans were forever abandoned after Berns' fatal heart attack in December of the same year. Van was genuinely shocked. "Bert was really a nice guy. It was really weird when he died. Like one day he was in the office, and then the next day he was dead."

The curse of 'TB Sheets', perhaps? At this time, *The Beat* published an extraordinary personal interview with the singer. "Sometimes I think I may just be an underground thing. I can't mix, you see, that's my problem. You have to be able to mix if you want to be in show business." Playing with Them had become "a trial, a sort of endurance test like the Indians used to make people walk while they hit them with sticks. It was no longer people making music and grooving together. It became a whole conscious business trip. It became sick." As of now, Morrison wanted just "to do my own thing and groove with it. I want to turn people on."

Wavelength have also transcribed a Dutch radio interview from 1967, which at first I thought was a misattribution, from Scott Walker's days studying plainsong at Quarr Abbey on the Isle of Wight. The phrasing, though, could only be Van. He describes going into a monastery for a brief spell, so upset had he become with the pop scene – "it's so false, it's not real" – and the direction his life was then taking. "I didn't actually want to be a monk. They said they would let me stay there for as long as I intended to stay. To think, read and philosophise, this type of thing. They said if I wanted to come back any time I could come back." In terms of his music, and its new inner, lyrical assurance, Morrison never left.

CHAPTER FOUR

And The Healing Has Begun

It was time for another kind of retreat. Van, Janet and her son Peter moved two hundred miles north of New York to an apartment on Green Street, part of the bohemian district of Cambridge, Massachusetts, and situated between Harvard University and the Massachusetts Institute of Technology. He often performed in clubs in nearby Boston, like the Tea Party and the Slade Hill Cafe, where he was backed by local band The Montgomerys. Boston had produced The Remains, among the best bands of the time, who had recorded 'Don't Look Back' from Them's first LP as a single. It also spawned the Bosstown sound, a marketing hype that died in the water. Boston's current kings of R&B were The Hallucinations – The J Geils Band, in embryo – and The Colwell-Winfields Blues Band.

After a quiet wedding, Janet devoted herself to furthering Van's career, while her husband played local club dates and college functions. Anybody hoping for rock 'n' roll showmanship was disappointed. He would strum away quietly, providing background atmospherics, and seemingly lost in a world of his own. Van would take his time between numbers, tuning-up, sipping beer, and mumbling directives to accompanists, and the occasional verbal sideswipe at the more rowdy of his audience. He was in danger of being consigned once more to musical oblivion. 'Ro Ro Rosey' and further singles from the Bang dossier had died a death outside the Hot Hundred. There was further humiliation when Van joined The Hallucinations on 'Gloria'. Jon Landau remembers how "frustrated and out of control, he stood on the stage shouting meaningless phrases and incoherent syllables like some crazed demon". Peter Wolf came to his aid, shouting, "Don't you know who this is? This man wrote the song."

Morrison formed an electric band, including Berkeley School of Music graduate Tom Kielbania on bass and Charles Marriano on sax, but this did not suit his new, stream of consciousness songs. Kielbania moved to double bass, the other musicians departed, and a twenty-two-year-old flautist, John Payne – a Harvard philosophy student who doubled on soprano saxophone joined. Like Kielbania, a musician closer to jazz than rock, he was recruited by the bassist, and came along to a gig at the Catacombs in Boston. "I listened through the first set and then Van asked me to join for the second. As soon as I stood there and started playing with him I could feel what he was trying to do. It was only when he played 'Brown Eyed Girl' that I realised who he was." Morrison asked him to join his band. "I said, Sure. I dropped out fast from Harvard, and went down to New York where he was planning to make a new album."

Hardly a power trio in the mould of Cream or Jimi Hendrix, though John Mayall had similarly dispensed with drums and electric guitars. Now a three piece, Traffic also relied heavily on Chris Woods' flute and saxophone, and Winwood's heartfelt vocals floated over a blend of folk and funk. Conversely, Marc Bolan was abandoning his elfin bongo led bleatings – always deeply suspect in my eyes – for electric rock. Van's new blend of acoustic jazz and poetry was an acquired taste, and one not yet appreciated by the world at large. "Only afterwards did people realise what we were doing. People may recognise it now, but then they didn't have a clue. We used to play clubs and people like Jimi Hendrix would come up and sit right in front and listen all night. It seemed the musicians dug it but the general public didn't know what we were into."

Andy Wickham, an expatriate Englishman who had also talent-spotted Joni Mitchell, certainly did see the potential, and immediately recommended Morrison to the label's vice-president Joe Smith. Van entered into a management deal with Inherit Productions, a New York firm who had recently seen Miriam Makeba make the Top Twenty with 'Pata Pata' in 1967. They brokered the deal with Warner Brothers, who were updating their image with new signings like The Grateful Dead, and Morrison was offered a two album deal.

There was one small problem. Morrison still owed material to Bang Records. In a move at once churlish and highly amusing, Van handed over master tapes of thirty bursts of worthless nonsense, most less than a minute long. Titles included 'Freaky If You Got This Far', 'You Say France And I'll Whistle', 'Dum-Dum George', 'Ring Worm', 'Walk And Talk' and variations on Berns' most successful song, 'Twist And Shout' ('Twist And Shake', 'Shake And Roll', 'Stomp And Scream'). Songs like 'Dum-Dum George' make far more sense if, as a theatre security guard told Ben Cruikshank, George is a nickname for Bert Berns (as a pun on ancient comedian George Burns).

The joke was back on Van when these same tracks were finally released, in Britain under the title *Payin' Your Dues*. Geoff Wall's review pointed out that "none of these solo acoustic sketches can be said to provide an insight into the development of Morrison as an artist". Had Bang done the indecent thing, and released them, it would have been as extreme a way to lose an audience as Lou Reed's *Metal Machine Music*, and that was deliberate. Van's musical talent occasionally surfaces, despite himself. 'Goodbye George' has some of the slow majesty of 'Madame George', more so in fact than the earlier version taped for Bang. Virtually unlistenable, the "songs" are full of deliberate nonsense – like the poems of Edward Lear, but without their underlying pathos or humour. 'Blow In Your Nose' parodies his first Bang album. "We're putting an album together and releasing it next week. It's got a psychedelic jacket, its groovy." Of course, the man who would have been most horrified by the viciousness of such as 'Dum-Dum George' – which ends with a snort – or the moronic retread of 'La Bamba' as 'La Mambo', is already dead. Thinking of the effect this tape must have had on the newly widowed Mrs Berns rather freezes the smile on one's face.

As she told Steve Turner, Morrison turned over a master tape "that he must have spent a few minutes making. It consisted of bursts of nonsense music that weren't even really songs. There was something about ringworms and then he sang something about 'I gotta go and cut this stupid song for this stupid lady'. I had two small babies, one born three weeks before Bert's death, and I just wanted to get on with my life. So I just let it go." In a vaguely similar situation, Neil Young was later sued by his record company, Geffen, for making "Neil Young records unrepresentative of Neil Young".

The first album for WB was produced by Inherit managing director Lewis Merenstein. *Sgt Pepper's Lonely Hearts Club Band* had established an album as a work of art in its own right, from its cover art to the flow of the music. *Astral Weeks* fulfils this criterion beautifully, with its two sides separately labelled "In The Beginning" and "Afterwards". The album remains curiously undated, free of segues, production tricks and psychedelic trickery. Outlines between rock and jazz dissolved when Van was on stage, so Merenstein's business partner Bob Schwaid chose the finest musicians available in New York. Tom Kielbania and John Payne were also on hand in case – as with Them – session men could not recreate what Van's own band managed on stage intuitively. Kielbania had the indignity of having to show Richard Davis the bass lines he had already worked out for these songs.

On guitar was Jay Berliner, who had worked with Mingus, a long time Morrison hero, and did not actually get to hear the album for another ten years. At the time, it was just another gig. "In those days I was so busy that I had no idea what I was playing on. I wasn't booked until nine pm, and so didn't play on 'Cyprus Avenue' and 'Madame George'. What stood out in my mind was the fact that he allowed us to stretch out. We were used to playing to charts, but Van just played us the songs on his guitar and then told us to go ahead and play exactly what we felt." Van told Ritchie Yorke that "those type of guys play what you're gonna do before you do it, that's how good they are". Elsewhere, though, he complained that "I was kind of restricted because it wasn't understood what I wanted". John Payne echoes Berliner's description of the sessions that resulted. "Ironically the image that you have when you listen now is of these guys who are all together, and they realise that they are creating a monumental work of art, but the fact is that this was just another session. The only guy who really looked as though he were getting into it was Jay Berliner. I'm not saying that they were all just sitting there, thinking another day, another dollar, but I couldn't say for sure that they weren't."

Providing percussion were Connie Kay of the Modern Jazz Quartet and Warren Smith, doubling on vibraphone.If there was a lead instrument, it was the slithery string bass of Richard Davis, who had worked with that arbiter of talent, Miles Davis. John Payne came in on flute and sax, after the sessioneer booked proved to be unsympathetic. All that was needed to complete the magic mixture was harpsichord and strings, dubbed on a week after the event by Larry Fallon, with Van again in close attendance.

A four hour session was booked for 25 September, seven pm till midnight, at Century Sound, a studio in New York's theatre district owned (coincidentally) by Brooks Arthur, the engineer on 'Brown Eyed Girl'. 'Cyprus Avenue', 'Madame George', 'Beside You' and 'Astral Weeks' were all recorded that evening. Van refused to give his musicians any clue about the music he was hearing in his own head. Payne told Steve Turner that "he seemed spaced out, he appeared as if he was in a lot of personal pain". There were no rehearsals, simply a brief run through and then straight into the music. "These guys just jammed together", as Turner gleaned from Tom Kielbania, reduced to a spectator during this extraordinary evening. "They went right through those songs and then cut all the solos out. If they hadn't done that every track would have been the whole side of an album." A little exaggerated, perhaps.

Payne kept up the pressure to join in, and succeeded when Merenstein said, "Well, everybody's feeling good so why don't we do one more song." Thus it was that he played on the one and only take of 'Astral Weeks', the first time he had ever heard the song. "I was the flute player from then on." Steve Turner records Morrison's working methods, much the same as Dylan in the studio, explaining nothing, hoping that alchemy will strike. "Van never discussed the song. He never talked about anything. The ending sounds rehearsed but it was the one and only take. I can remember Larry Fallon walking out and saying, we don't have a chord chart for this. But it was the only take and they named the album after it." Only somebody schooled in live performance would dare take such creative risks, or pull them off so spectacularly.

After a morning booking, the very worst time of the day for improvising musicians, and at which the playing was so lacklustre that the session was abandoned, the reassembled cast caught fire again at dusk on 15 October. As Richard Davis told *Rolling Stone*, "There's a certain feel about a seven-to-ten-o'clock session. You've just come back from a dinner break, some guys have had a drink or two, it's this dusky part of the day, and everybody's relaxed. I remember that the ambience of that time of day was all through everything we played." They produced finished versions of 'Sweet Thing', 'Ballerina', 'The Way Young Lovers Do' and 'Slim Slo Slider'. All kinds of rumours have since surfaced about forty-five minute songs, radically variant track listings, and the original idea of releasing a double album. The most radical cut since confirmed was about ten minutes taken from 'Slim Slo Slider', between the end of the lyrics and the final saxophone flourish. Van improvised wordlessly over a duet between Davis and Payne, his sax soaring as if it were crossed with a flute, sounding "as if it's coming from across a lake".

Astral Weeks had a sound all of its own, though the later work of Nick Drake perhaps inhabits the same world, that of drifting melancholia. In the studio at least, Morrison was very much in charge of proceedings, however uncommunicative. As Bob Schwaid told *Mojo*, "At the time I thought it was an avant-garde marriage of jazz and rock." It was at just this interface that Al Kooper – first in The Electric Flag, and then Blood, Sweat And Tears – and the (then) agit-prop group Chicago were working. *Astral Weeks*, of course, was something else again. "Really it was a combination of Van's approach to what he thought to be jazz with folk, blues, gospel and rock levels. At the time none of us thought that it fitted into any category." As a result, nothing was found suitable for single release.

Elvis Costello recently described *Astral Weeks* as "still the most adventurous record made in the rock medium, and there hasn't really been a record with that amount of daring made since". The album was released in November 1968, and only available on import in Britain until its release here in September of the following year. *Melody Maker* described it as "one of the strongest albums of the year. Van pits his small harsh voice against an interesting backing combination." The anonymous reviewer picks out 'Madame George', "which builds an overwhelming atmosphere of despair and decadence verges on genius." This was not the common view. The *NME* likened Van to a poor man's Jose Feliciano. "The gravel voiced Irishman has come a long way since he fronted Them. The songs themselves aren't particularly distinguished apart from the title track, and suffer from being stuck in one groove throughout." *Beat Instrumental* shrugged off the album as "rather Dylanesque", with 'Cyprus Avenue' just about passing muster, though "the remainder is lacking in originality, and there is a great deal of monotony about it".

As Morrison told Mick Brown, "I didn't really want to be in the rock 'n' roll scene, so I thought I'd have to do an album that was just singing, and songs that were about something. So I did get out of the rock 'n' roll scene to some extent. Then the critics started saying that it was a rock album! It's obvious to anyone with two ears there's no rock 'n' roll on that album at all. The whole point was not to make a rock album." As so often, it was fellow musicians who first picked up on its splendours. In Hollywood, the current king of hip, Johnny Rivers, regularly performed 'Slim Slo Slider', while David Bowie slipped 'Madame George' into his 1969 stage repertoire. Perhaps it inspired the notorious dress cover for *The Man Who Sold The World*.

On Joel Brodsky's cover photograph, Van is circled in black and looks down and inside himself, eyes closed and mouth in a slight smile. He is framed by trees, which outside the circle are tinted green, surrounded in turn by a black border. Sinister and dreamy all at once, just like the music. On the back cover, a long haired, clean shaven Van glowers in a patterned shirt, his eyes narrowed to two slits, like a killer.

Printed underneath is the ultimate rarity, a Morrison poem which does not also function as a lyric, though it does refer to various songs on the album. Written in free verse, and drifting out from the centre of the page, it uses repetition and internal rhymes to power it forward. A poem of place, its action is based around Van's adopted home in Cambridge, and breathes acceptance, settled love and happiness. The only false note is Van's self comparison with a sheep, even if it does chime in with "sleep" in the next line!

> *I saw you coming from the Cape, way from Hyannis Port all the*
> *way,*
> *When I got back it was like a dream come true.*
> *I saw you coming from Cambridgeport with my poetry and jazz*
> *Knew you had the blues, saw you coming from across the river,*
> *Told you on the banks of the river, carried you across,*
> *Loved you there and then, and now like a sheep,*
> *I close my eyes and sleep for love comes flowing streams of*
> *consciousness*
> *Soft like snow, to and fro,*
> *Let us go there together, darlin', way from the river to here and*
> *now*
> *And carry it with a smile, bumper to bumper*
> *Stepping lightly, just like a ballerina.*

This has the same combination of the personal and the transcendental as the eight songs it accompanies. As Van later commented, it was "probably the most spiritually lyrical album I've done". In a sweet little touch, Morrison's name is signed in childish script underneath.

I have no wish to disturb the underlying enigma of *Astral Weeks*, a large part of its continuing appeal, but Van himself opened up spectacularly about the album to Ritchie Yorke in his long out of print 1975 study, *Into The Music*. "*Astral Weeks* was a whole concept from beginning to end. It was all thought out up front. Originally it was supposed to be an opera. By opera, I mean multiple visual sketches. When I had written the songs, there was talk of a film. So it was a visually orientated concept." As to rumours of a forty-five minute track, "the truth is that I had a song at the time which was about forty-five minutes long, but it wasn't recorded for the album. I don't think I could ever do it again. I made a rough tape recording with just myself and another guitar player."

There were only two tracks which did not make the album. "One was about Jesse James and the other about trains. They were both just basic blues numbers. That's why they didn't fit in with the album." As to the meaning of what *did* make the final cut, "it's all in your head".

Of all the albums issued in the name of rock music, *Astral Weeks* inhabits a sphere of mystery and intrigue matched only by a select company indeed. *The Velvet Underground* – containing the black hole of 'Murder Mystery' – The Beach Boys' semi-abandoned *Smile* project, The Rolling Stones' *Let It Bleed*, perhaps *Scott 4*, certainly Dylan's work between the bike crash and *Nashville Skyline*, and The Beatles from *Revolver* to the "white" album. It is no coincidence that all these records date from the late 1960s, with the hippie dream potent but dying, and a sense of apocalypse – fuelled by drugs and paranoia – vibrating in the air. This music, otherwise so various, combines surface attraction, with a deep inner dread. All the albums mentioned involve elements of death and decay, set against a utopian desire for love and freedom. The best of Pete Townshend's work, *Tommy*, *Lifehouse* and *Quadrophenia*, put this struggle into a fictional form: in a different way Ray Davies spent endless concept albums teasing out these same jarring opposites, as did The Pretty Things in *SF Sorrow* and even Mark Wirtz in his *Teenage Opera*.

The same duality, buoyant and despairing all at once, touched lesser known but equally potent albums at a time when that medium was still fresh, and open to development. In Britain, the Bonzo Dog's *Keynsham* was a deeply serious work underneath the jokes, a picture of society as an open prison. In Kevin Ayers' *Joy Of A Toy*, childhood turns sinister. Blossom Toes' *If Only For A Moment* abandons acid whimsy for Brian Godding's thoughts on violence and political inertia. Fairport's *Unhalfbricking* deals with a series of violent deaths, autopsies and drownings, all oddly prefiguring the motorway crash which killed their drummer, while Procol Harum's *Home* is an (unacknowledged) suite about mortality. Both Van der Graaf Generator's *The Least We Can Do Is Wave To Each Other* and Bachdenkel's *Lemmings* are concept albums when that term was not a pitiable conceit, and both deal with how to survive a coming armageddon. *Astral Weeks* functions on one of its many levels as a survival kit for those strange times.

Even future mainstays of the worst kind of mid seventies pretentiousness were touched by the spirit of the age. Jon Anderson's fragile and moving 'Survival', on the first Yes album, and the debut LP by Supertramp present an extremely adult response to loss, homesickness and ennui. As *Astral Weeks* indicates so strongly, there is the sense of another, better reality tantalisingly just out of reach, a dream on which to base the drabbest of days. Of course, the widespread use of soft drugs at the time gave chemical access both to the vision, and the come down. Even Morrison, famously careful and puritanical in this area, afterwards admitted that his use of marijuana – though never LSD – helped him to voyage into the mystic.

American examples from the same era would include early albums by Neil Young, David Accles and Leonard Cohen, the first Mad River LP, The Youngbloods' *Elephant Mountain* and Nico's *Marble Index*. All are symphonies of darkness. This feeling of a descent into the void, first opened out in Lennon's extraordinary 'Tomorrow Never Knows', motivates many rock movies of the time, from *Easy Rider* to *Performance*. It is cunningly structured into *Gimme Shelter,* the story of Altamont. *Woodstock,* replayed as a Greek tragedy, although even in the jangly brightness of the Stones' *Rock 'N' Roll Circus*, Brian Jones looks like the spectre at the feast. Murray Lerner's movie of the third Isle of Wight Festival, *Message To Love* recasts the actual facts into metaphor, a line-up of the soon to die, ending in rain, a slow motion retreat into entropy.

Even among those who survived those times, there is a continuing interest in musicians who either died young or shuffled off into silence, leaving musical empires as their legacy – Syd Barrett, Nick Drake, Peter Green and Brian Wilson (almost), Hendrix, Jim Morrison. This is in part morbid, but also a genuine recognition of brief spirits who flowered gloriously, in a way impossible to sustain. The story, in psychic terms, of a whole generation.

Michael Moorcock's Jerry Cornelius books – located in Notting Hill, at much the same time that Van resided there – celebrate the same dying fall, as do the novels of Thomas Pynchon and, less overtly, the more terrifying fictions of Ruth Rendell. The critical theories of Lacan or Derrida or Barthes, which now dominate cultural studies, are also a product of those times, seeking to deconstruct the world into an infinite series of signs and power play, which forever abolished meaning.

More positively, the work of Iain Sinclair – perhaps the most important English novelist since Dickens – is a multi-layered treatment of hope deferred. Various late sixties survivors scurry through end times, trying to recreate a lost harmony through occult ceremonies, and magical rebirths. It is no coincidence that Sinclair's first film project, in mid sixties Dublin, was a series of street scenes to which were later added as a soundtrack the music of Van Morrison and Them.

The sixties, and its cultural products, live out Milton's poem *Paradise Lost*, Eden glimpsed and then snatched away. This could also be seen as the pattern of any human life, as could *Astral Weeks* itself, (re)birth to death. Many of the greatest artistic statements since codify the same sense of a forced retreat into the heart of darkness: *Apocalypse Now*, Bowie's *Station To Station*, Pere Ubu's *The Modern Dance*. There is even vicarious pleasure in such amputations, the way the normal fabric of everyday life is gradually torn and ripped apart in *Twin Peaks*. Nihilism has since become the spirit of the age, celebrated in everything from punk rock to Thatcherism, the novels of JG Ballard and Martin Amis, or even Damien Hurst's dead cows, sliced. To celebrate, of course, is not always to endorse. The purest musical soundtrack to all this was Joy Division's *Unknown Pleasures*. It ends with a song that says everything in its title, 'New Dawn Fades'.

The greatest music since the late sixties – from Gram Parsons to Bruce Springsteen, REM to the Smiths, U2 to Paul Weller – has tried to find a method of consolation, attempting to penetrate such emptiness, then transform it into something else completely. Just like New Order, in fact. It is this quest on which Morrison himself has been engaged, from *Moondance* to the present day.

Meanwhile we have *Astral Weeks*. For an album which means so much, I refuse to supply any kind of smart-alec interpretation which could harm the perception of this extraordinary work, either the reader's or my own. Fortunately we have Morrison's own comments, courtesy of Ritchie Yorke, to light the way. For all that, *Astral Weeks* remains as impenetrable and coldly majestic as the Sphinx.

Morrison described the title song as being "like transforming energy, or going from one source to another with it being born again like a rebirth. I remember reading about you having to die to be born. It's one of those songs where you can see the light at the end of the tunnel and that's basically what the songs says."

'Astral Weeks' was itself reborn five years later as the title song of the Canadian film *Slipstream*. It tells the same sad story as I have just outlined. "It's about a disc jockey who is straight and anti-commercial and his boss wants him to get an image. He won't conform so they destroy him. And I think that 'Astral Weeks' is in context with the film."

The song opens with a shiver, gentle guitar over a shuffle beat, then Van's voice suddenly fully mature and tender, open to all possibilities. He addresses both his unnamed lover and the listener – here as one – aiming directly at the place that Dylan sang about in 'Going Going Gone', where words cannot carry. The collective unconscious is suddenly found in a waste land where "the ditch in the back roads stops".

All is uncertain, this spiritual rebirth a question still, not a statement, and Van equates his move to a new world – both America and that of love – with a sense of being lost, "ain't nothing but a stranger in this world". He sees his own childhood reflected in his adopted son, and drifts away at the end of this endlessly circular song into dreams of heaven, repeated over and over, as his voice takes on a tone of wistfulness and surrender.

'Beside You' is "the kind of song that you'd sing to a kid or somebody that you love. It's basically a long song, just a song about being spiritually beside somebody." Sung in a kind of hushed exhilaration, an interior monologue with the drifting logic of a dream, Van recreates those strange visions of his own youth, seemingly outside of time and space, and transfers them to Janet's son. He drags out the final "child" seemingly forever.

'Sweet Thing' is "another romantic song. It contemplates gardens and things like that…wet with rain. It's a romantic love ballad not about anybody in particular but about a feeling." An extension of the line in the opening song about "lay me down in silence", and Van here locates the lost child within himself. His singing is totally ego-less and unemphatic, bored almost, like a cat purring. "Gardens all wet with rain" become a personal touchstone ever after, and one can supply all kinds of explication – water as a healing force, the baptism of love, the "champagne" of his lover's eyes – without quite touching their meaning.

'Cyprus Avenue' is about "a street in Belfast, a place where there's a lot of wealth. It wasn't far from where I was brought up and it was a very different scene. To me it was a very mystical place. It was a whole avenue lined with trees and I found it a place where I could think. Instead of walking down a road and being hassled by forty million people, you could walk down Cyprus Avenue and there was nobody there. It wasn't a thoroughfare. It was quiet and I used to think about things there."

That said, this is a song about being trapped, "conquered in a car seat", and reduced to tortured silence, just like in 'TB Sheets'. The need for innocence in the earlier song is now equated to going crazy, though the vision which then unfolds is out of time, and sexless. His dream lady in her antique carriage is only fourteen years old. Van's singing is totally possessed, moving from choked desire to exultation to hushed wonder.

Whoever decided to programme these songs, and divide them into two sections, the songs on side two of the original LP release are tougher, more assured and resilient. It is as if after these four songs of rebirth, Morrison can now enter fully into the adult world. Songs of experience, which inevitably follow songs of innocence. Even the backing music – however it was attained – is more upbeat, less lost in its own reverence.

"On the second side, 'Young Lovers Do' is just basically a song about young love. And he laughs mysteriously." Again the world is "wet with rain", but here is a sexuality missing from what has gone before. There is a Sinatra strut to Van's voice, a blues knowingness with Stax brass, and a string section which swirls where previously it drifted. The song is about growing up, an adolescent first kiss, and still conveys the same sweet mystery as 'Astral Weeks' but more upfront.

As to 'Madame George', "the original title was Madame Joy but the way I wrote it down was 'Madame George'. Don't ask me why I do this because I just don't know. The song is just a stream-of-consciousness thing. I didn't even think about what I was writing. The song is basically about a spiritual feeling. It may have something to do with my great aunt whose name was Joy. Apparently she was clairvoyant. Aunt Joy lived around the area I mentioned in connection with Cyprus Avenue." Morrison's (then) fiancee suspects the song might also refer to Van's father George, though he simply shrugs at the suggestion.

Ritchie Yorke fills in here. "Key mood words such as eye, goodbye, why, love are repeated over and over, inside a softly swelling and tumbling melody, until they assume instrument tone and proportion. It is soothing and scintillating all at once. Like standing, face to the wind, in a blowing snowstorm. Opposing sensitivities in stereo: hot and cold, hard and soft, brutal and gentle, love and hate."

"Child-like visions" turn sinister here, meeting a sexuality grown luxuriant and decadent. Van's tone is chilling, strangely confidential, gliding words together into serpentine coils. Whatever he subsequently said, he definitely sings about "playing dominoes in drag", *not* "is a drag", and the ambience is close to that of The Velvet Underground's 'Sister Ray', a more overt tale of transvestites and fellatio and a police raid. Whereas that song is a bleeding mass of feedback and confusion, this is stately, with richly textured strings that drift into perhaps the most beautiful coda in the whole of rock music. Van's voice softens into an all-inclusive love, taking on the whole world. A song of leavetaking, slowly fading as Van boards his train.

"'Ballerina' is the one track that I really don't know much about. I had a romantic image in my head about the San Francisco outlook. I was in SF one time in 1966 and I was attracted to the city. It was the first time I'd been there and I was sitting in this hotel and all these things were going through my head and I had a flash about an actress in an opera house appearing in a ballet and I think that's where the song came from. The song may possibly be about a hooker, but other than that, it's just poetry." And also of course about Janet Planet, an actress whom he met in SF that year, but he is going to hardly talk about this with his new fiancee at his side.

If anyone ever argues that Morrison cannot sing – an unlikely scenario anyway – then simply play them this. All human emotion is crystallised here, and subtly vocalised: desire, joy, hope, world weariness, consolation, awe and anticipation. The "angel child" here is also a fully mature woman. What sounds like a penny whistle comes in just at the end, almost subliminally. Van's Celtic phase starts here.

'Slim Slo Slider' takes as its subject "a person who is caught up in a big city like London or maybe is on dope, I'm not sure". If the twin poles of the rest of the album are Belfast and America, here is a third and unwelcome intrusion. The craziness of 'Cyprus Avenue' has come home, so that the streets of Notting Hill become "some sandy beach", in the junkie's eyes. In a horrible twist, the boy of the opening song transforms from son to illicit lover. We are back in the world of 'TB Sheets', and a twelve bar blues, and Van's chuckle is truly nasty. After all those rebirths, here is a song about winter, "white as snow", and death – about which Van sings almost joyfully – ending in dissonance, with a shrill saxophone almost neighing like the horse in the opening lines. One straight from the Apocalypse.

Astral Weeks is an album that startles and consoles the listener on each new playing, reaching deep into universal emotions and memories as only great art can. It has the strange bitter-sweet atmosphere of Shakespeare's last plays, with their mysterious transformations, the dead coming back to life. Morrison himself seems unsure of how he came to create such music. "A lot of these songs are not really personal and that's why I have to try to interpret them. A lot of them are just speculations on a given theme."

He later described such work as a "stream of consciousness", though it is a radically different technique to that of his fellow countryman James Joyce. In *Ulysses*, Joyce used the technique to show the fragmented inner life of his characters, with all kinds of base desires and thoughts. Morrison is closer to the more impressionistic style of Virginia Woolf, with her flows of feeling, and painterly abstractions. Van puts it more simply. These are songs not of fact but imagination.

"I wasn't into any romantic interludes when I recorded *Astral Weeks*, but when I wrote the songs I probably was. I'm definitely a romantic but I'm also a realist." Where Morrison does correspond with Joyce is this double vision, the love and compassion that both can bring to their portraits of others, Leopold Bloom or Madame George, seeing their tawdriness and defeats, but also the heroism with which they survive, and live out their lives. As Lester Bangs wrote about 'Madame George', "it's about a *person*, like all the best songs, all the greatest literature". This also explains the album's continuing power. It is about keeping going, "you breathe in, you breathe out", about life's perils and life's delights. Whatever the lyric sheet says, Van sings "to be born again, to be bored again" in the first chorus of 'Astral Weeks', and neither precludes the other.

Brian Hogg identified the strength of *Astral Weeks* to reside not in individual songs but "its cumulative air of passion and mystery. Even the excellence of the best of Them had not prepared us for this shock of brilliance. The album has since gained a legendary reputation, usually appearing near the top of any poll of the greatest moments in rock. Its detractors are few indeed, one being Van Morrison – "the arrangements are too samey" – while others have unfortunately been those given the job of writing his biography. Ritchie Yorke talks without hesitation about Van's musical genius, but Johnny Rogan sees only "the origins of a very questionable phenomenon...the premise that he is no mere rock musician but something akin to a mystical poet". The album's lyrics reveal "comparatively little of real substance" and on the printed page 'Madame George' is "a bloody awful poem but an intriguing piece of automatic writing". Even Collis compares the opening to 'Astral Weeks' with the kind of pretentious tripe so accurately parodied by The Bonzo Dog Band.

It is the same old problem of confusing words on a page with words as performed by a great singer – who also wrote them in the first place

– using the timbre of his voice and the backing musicians to introduce all kinds of ambiguities and meaning. The lyric sheet is a discourse that can only come to life when performed, and never subject to exactly the same interpretation twice.

As to Van himself, "when *Astral Weeks* came out, I was starving, literally. That's where that was at. I didn't really get recognition for that album until later. The critical acclaim was really good. A lot of people I knew liked the album and I knew they weren't just putting me on. And anyway inside I knew that it was good."

The music on *Astral Weeks* has that same life or death quality, and for anyone trying to discuss Morrison's work without taking that into account is disgraceful. The most moving account of its power was written by the late Lester Bangs, a rock critic not known for the generosity of his views, or any pronounced liking for the common ruck of singer-songwriters. Indeed, Bangs loathed would-be poets in rock with a manic intensity that Hunter Thompson reserved for politicians and the drugs squad. In this album, though, he found a man "in terrible pain" and yet the album was like a beacon of light, "a redemptive element in the blackness, ultimate compassion, and a swathe of pure beauty and mystical awe that cut right through the heart of the work". And the listener.

Bangs echoes my own view of the times from which the album emerged, "when a lot of things that a lot of people cared about passionately were beginning to disintegrate, and when the self-destructive undertow that accompanied the great sixties party had an awful lot of ankles firmly in its maw and was pulling straight down".

Bangs centres on Morrison's ability to turn words into an incantation, "most of all in 'Madame George' where he sings the word 'dry' and then 'your eye' twenty times in a twirling melodic arc so beautiful it steals your breath". Van is obsessed with "how much musical or verbal information he can compress into a small space and, almost conversely, how far he can spread one note, word, sound or picture". Here is an album about "people stunned by life, completely overwhelmed, stalled in their skins, granted one moment of vision and a whole lifetime with which to deal with it". Let's get personal here. In my case, it was watching the teenage Richard Thompson playing Les Paul arabesques in a small club, tongue tied and angelic, transporting the audience to another world, something I could neither explain nor forget. What's yours?

For Bangs, *Astral Weeks* represents a "great search, fuelled by the belief that through these musical and mental processes illumination is attainable. Or may at least be glimpsed." Morrison "never came this close to looking life square in the face again", but he has somehow excavated the insides of his own skull. As the very title suggests, it is as if Van is looking down on his inert body from above, from the "astral" plane, and indeed he has often spoken since of just this kind of out of body experience, and how as a child he could enter it, almost at will. None of his later work makes sense without being rooted back in this album, though nowhere is he ever again quite so emotionally abandoned. "Dry your eyes"...

Most other musicians, if granted the miracle of *Astral Weeks* would have continued to plumb its sound and atmosphere until, by the law of diminishing returns, their careers withered away. Such has been the history of James Taylor since *Sweet Baby James*, an album which also maps out a path for survival, and whose warmth still amazes when one comes to it fresh. Another alternative would be to withdraw from life – either literally or as a recording artist – and one dreads to think of what kind of mythology which would by now have grown around *Astral Weeks* had that been the case.

Van was made of sterner stuff: his odyssey as a creative artist had hardly yet begun. "There's a lot in between 'Gloria', 'Brown Eyed Girl' and 'Astral Weeks'. There's a lot of different things that I do and you can't get them all on one album. There's really nothing to talk about when you discuss it, because it's just the difference between art and show business." As he told the *New Musical Express*, "It's just what I wanted to do at that particular time, so I did it. There's a lot of stuff that I've never recorded that's totally far out. But I make albums primarily to sell them, and if I get too far out a lot of people can't relate to it." Enough related to Johnny Rivers' cover version of 'Slim Slo Slider' to make it a US hit, and Van's own work was an early staple of the burgeoning FM radio stations Stateside, whose improved sound quality, in stereo, and policy of more music and less disc jockey chatter was attracting a whole new campus audience.

Meanwhile, Morrison played support to Moby Grape, once cataclysmic but now squeezed dry by record company hype, and pedestrian jazz rockers Rhinoceros. Less of a mismatch was a gig with

Tim Hardin, another "Slim Slo Slider", whose muse floated on pools of melancholy. Unlike Van or Tim Buckley, Hardin reined in his songs to conventional structures, thus ensuring many cover versions by the likes of Bobby Darin. His introspective style was soon labelled as "self rock", and like self love it quickly atrophied.

Morrison refused to be thus pigeonholed, and battled on in venues where confrontation was almost assured. During a return to the Whiskey-A-Go-Go, he was described by the Los Angeles correspondent of *Disc* as "simply awful...loose, rambling songs that all sounded alike. They went on forever, and Van's nasal voice did nothing to vary the pace or inflection. We left after a solid hour of this torture."

A far more positive response came from Greil Marcus, the sharpest pair of ears in America, who attended a gig at the Avalon Ballroom in San Francisco, and reported back for *Rolling Stone*. Morrison was on acoustic guitar, backed up by acoustic bass and a hornman doubling on sax and flute, "a brilliant set in which he sang all of *Astral Weeks* as well as three songs from his previous record". Van was now performing 'Who Drove The Red Sports Car' and – more surprisingly – 'He Ain't Give You None' – with the same "soft, seductive rhythms, and it made them seem as if they were new songs".

The newly married John Payne had recently left, unhappy with life on the road, to be replaced by the British-born Graham Blackburn, who persuaded Van and Janet to move in February 1969 to Woodstock, in the Catskill Mountains. Here other rock icons were rejoicing in the simple life. Jimi Hendrix was rehearsing his next project, while Bob Dylan had retreated to a farmhouse in Bearsville, lying low. The Hawks, now renamed The Band, had a communal home nearby in the village of West Saugerties, and here developed *Music From Big Pink*, a new blend of electric folklore. The Morrisons rented a house high up on Ohayo Mountain, not quite a mansion on a hill, but getting there. Among their nearest neighbours was Clarence, a sculptor who had constructed his home from reclaimed scrap. It was just that kind of place.

Friends reported on Van's new domestic harmony, with Janet "as a very happy-go-lucky girl, optimistic about everything". John Payne told Steve Turner "she was very sweet. She worshipped him artistically. She was totally devoted to Van and his career and to believing in him."

Turner reprints a set of contact sheets by Woodstock photographer Elliott Landy that confirms this, the two cuddling in matching woolly sweaters, and sitting in a forest glade together, like elves. In Woodstock, the singer experienced a creative rush, producing pages of scribbled lyrics and notation peculiar to himself. He was moving away from the looseness of *Astral Weeks* and back to recognisable patterns, verse and chorus, with little or no vocal extemporisation. Turner reports on frequent trips back to New York to tape one song, 'Moondance'. As Blackburn revealed, "Van like to be spontaneous in the studio, but it's a spontaneity that he has to wait a long time to achieve. He would try and get himself in the mood and get a groove going. We'd be pulling our hair out, and then we'd have to do it all over again."

This musical perfectionism was matched by a withdrawal from live performance, although *Rolling Stone* reported how the Newport Folk Festival was "retightened" in July 1969 by "the bitter romanticism of the short and stocky man". A photograph of the event shows him backstage, chewing his nails, and glaring like a dangerous animal. Van was also beginning to display a purist's rejection of the music "industry" that has persisted ever since. As he told the *Melody Maker*'s Richard Williams (a principled, donnish rock critic who himself later jumped tracks to become a sports journalist) in 1973, "See I definitely don't fit into what's happening in the showbiz scene. Most people in that scene think it's weird that I'm not coming in and telling everyone how great my records are and what my new suit's like. Everyone else is doing it – hyping their records, hyping themselves. I really don't care what those people think, I'm concerned with getting to my audience."

Frustrated by the lack of action, Blackburn eventually left, as did Tom Kielbania to get married. Van wanted to get away anyway from the loose, semi acoustic jamming of *Astral Weeks*, and to form a band, a Band even, in which he would be both focal point and leader. It was the same process that Dylan had undergone in 1965, but by now what had been taboo, for "folk" singers at least, was almost mandatory. For Van, more importantly, it was a matter of gaining total creative control. As he told Mick Brown, "*Astral Weeks* was a breakthrough for me creatively, but then again I didn't have any particular rapport with those musicians. They were session jazz musicians who worked in another area. I couldn't say 'you're my band' sort of thing – 'do this'. Because I didn't have the sort of rapport it takes. But when I found those people I could use live and on the album that was a more ideal situation, and it worked".

Morrison re-established contact with The Colwell-Winfields Blues Band, who had also moved to Woodstock, and were in the process of breaking up. Van's new electric band included their bassist John Klingberg, Jack Schroer on alto and soprano sax and Colin Tillton doubling on tenor sax and flute. Schroer had already played session with Boz Scaggs, a refugee from The Steve Miller Band when their music was still mysterious. Scagg's career provides an interesting contrast with Morrison's. A sweet voiced soul crooner, he left behind hippie daze for hip acceptance, becoming the American counterpart to Robert Palmer, though nowhere near as pretty. Scaggs started with the tough 'Loan Me A Dime' – with masterly slide guitar by Duane Allman – but his work petered out into mellow mush. Van's work remained too pungent and individual ever to meet such a fate.

Another session player, Jeff Labes, came in on keyboards, alongside drummer Garry Malabar and Guy Masson on congas and percussion. The same double-whammy in the music's engine room as on *Astral Weeks*. In the studio, Van was joined by a trio of backing singers, Emily Houston, Judy Clay and Jackie Verdell, part of the general sweetening of the sound. Already present and correct on lead guitar was Jack Platania, head hunted locally in summer 1969 by Van's English road manager, and himself a former Bang records artiste.

Platania's interview with *Into The Music* is the best insight we yet have into this time, a creative seedbed for Van. He had first met Morrison through Bert Berns' wife, and was later persuaded to audition for his new band. "I went up to his place up in the mountains. Usually all his places are up in mountains, mountain tops, all his houses for some reason. They always have that vantage point, they all look like Inverness or something." The first Van Morrison band also featured the drummer from The Fugs. "We did a lot of live gigs and Van was in his transitional period. Financially he wasn't that well off at this point. We played all sorts of gigs. After a while the group disbanded, he got rid of everybody except me and him. We did several gigs, just as a duo. We played the Newport Festival and such. Then after a while he started forming another group."

In the studio, and planning his next album, Van's manager Lewis Merenstein had brought back many of the musicians from *Astral Weeks*. Richard Davis was hanging around, but never used. Platania: "Van sort of manipulated the situation and got me to play, got rid of all them all. For some reason he didn't want those musicians. They brought me into the studio, Mastertone, on Forty-Second Street, and that's where the album began. A lot of it was live." When recording proper began at A&R studios, Van "really took the helm". He "spent a lot of time mixing". Platania remembers "some magic, some fun times". The most important out-take, a song called 'Caledonia Soul Music', was to prove prophetic. "I played slide on that track with an empty beer bottle that I picked up off the floor of the studio. That was never included on the album, it was a long piece." Van wrote out the basic chords, and off they went.

Moondance was released at the dawning of the 1970s. It was consciously presented as music for a new era, as richly human and positive as the best work of The Band, and had the same tightness of purpose. No extraneous guitar breaks, or vocal arabesques. An album which dealt with joy, not inner pain. If the greatest albums of the late sixties had been about surrendering self control, this was the polar opposite, ten lessons in how to run your life happily. Fittingly, Lewis Merenstein was again in overall charge, but this time Van joined him behind the mixing desk, and took a producer's credit. 'Come Running' had grown in the studio from an unpromising acoustic demo with no hookline into a hypnotic cry of pleasure. Released as a single, it cracked the US Top Forty, as did *Moondance* in the album charts.

The front cover has five extreme close up shots of a bearded Morrison, whose dark eyes avoid the camera and look pensive, lost in a world of their own. His mouth is turned down in soulful contemplation. On the back cover, a clean shaven and unsmiling Van confronts the viewer direct, his expression unreadable. Much the same is true of the music inside, which is curiously impersonal and guarded. It is general rather than specific, following Apollo not Dionysus, crafted rather than being wildly inspired.

With its emphasis on romance and Celtic mystery, it is strangely reminiscent of the verse of Robert Graves. In his book, *The White*

Goddess, a grammar of poetic myth, Graves identified the figure of the muse, both real woman and a shadow of the earth mother, who inspires great poetry (that written by men, at least!). It is a role that Janet performs here. As Steve Turner notes, Van "appeared to idolise Janet, and saw her not merely as a lover but as a saviour". When he sang that her loving made him righteous, "he was consciously using the language of religious redemption".

Ritchie Yorke again provides rare insights from their composer into the genesis of individual songs. "'And It Stoned Me' is about a real experience. It's just about being stoned off nature. Remembering how it was when you were a kid and just got stoned from nature and you didn't need anything else." Coincidentally, Van had abandoned his use of even soft drugs by this point, regarding them as slowing down his work rate. This song celebrates a natural alternative.

Water, as so often in the *Bible*, is a sign of God's blessing. Moses strikes the rock, and a fountain gushes, John the Baptist immerses Christ's head, and Jesus himself turns water into wine. It also represents spiritual grace – the sweet streams of the Psalms or the Song of Solomon – and, in pagan terms, death. Charon guards the River Styx.

The song flows along smoothly, with Van's voice pure liquid, relaxed and ecstatic all at once. Horns eddy, even the acoustic guitar break and piano tinklings are like ripples on a stream. As to the lyrics, their setting is resolutely rural: a county fair, a mountain stream. These childhood visions come into view, and prefigure both sexual satisfaction – "jelly roll" – and spiritual grace.

The song evokes a dream state, one of those out of body experiences from his childhood, whose (literally) other-worldly calm Van evokes in the best of his music. As he told Steve Turner, "I was about twelve years old. We used to go to a place called Ballystockert to fish." They stopped in the village, and asked an old man "with dark weather-beaten skin" in an old stone house for water. "He gave us some which he said he'd got from the stream. We drank some and everything seemed to stop for me. Time stood still. For five minutes everything was really quiet, and I was in this 'other dimension'. That's what the song is about."

In 'Moondance', this romance is translated into an adult setting, perfect music for and about fucking. His lady's blush is not that of embarrassment. "With 'Moondance' I wrote the melody first. I played the melody on a soprano sax and I knew I had a song so I wrote lyrics to go with the melody. That's the way I wrote that one. I don't really have any words to particularly describe the song, sophisticated is probably the word I'm looking for. For me, 'Moondance' is a sophisticated song. Frank Sinatra wouldn't be out of place singing that."

A largely acoustic outing, though anchored by electric bass, with piano, guitar, saxophone and flute all played soft and embroidering Morrison's voice, tender, exuberant and seductive by turns. This is a rock musician singing jazz, not a jazz singer, though the music itself has a jazz swing, triplets rather than four square on the beat. Van's song does indeed sound like a saxophone, and he even imitates one towards the end. The first of many songs of autumn, with which a Virgo like Van would feel immediately attuned.

"'Crazy Love' is about basically what it says it's about." The song opens directly with Van's voice, close to the mike, suffused with joy, almost shocking in its intimacy, and beautifully underpinned by his female chorus. Here the girl in 'Moondance' combines with the blessing of the opening track, "I'm running to her like a river's song", and Van has written a secular hymn. There is something both touching about the line "she's got a fine sense of humour when I'm feelin' lowdown", reflecting what outsiders observed in the relationship, and one feels somehow that trouble could be brewing later. After all, a muse needs comfort as well.

Just that kind of mutuality runs through 'Caravan', with Van offering himself as a healer, getting down "to what is really wrong". The gypsy life and the radio are both images of harmony, images that bless. Van is "getting back into the romanticism bit with gypsies and all that. I'm really fascinated by gypsies. I love them." The song is also based on a real memory, as is so much of *Moondance*. Up in Woodstock, the nearest house was far down the road, but he could hear music playing. "I could hear the radio like it was in the same room. I don't know how to explain it. There was some story about an underground passage under the house I was living in, rumours from kids and stuff and I was beginning to think it was true. How can you hear someone's radio from a mile away, as if it was playing in your own house? So I *had* to put that into the song. It was a must." The music has that same buzz, a confident strut, with Band-like piano, and Van in full throttle. His interplay with Platania's softly picked guitar touches the soul.

Anyone who fails to feel a shiver down their spine during the next song must be at least six feet under. Bass thrums like a boat in motion, and the song comes back to water as a means of magical transformation. The only other song this majestic about setting sail is Procol Harum's 'A Salty Dog', but the words have more in common with Alfred, Lord Tennyson – no less – in his poems of leavetaking. There is the same sense of crossing over, both to another land and into death, as in his 'Crossing The Bar' Of course, the song also deals with the mystical union of good sex, and the visionary stillness of 'And It Stoned Me'. It is a song which works on about five levels at once, and Van's own comments reflect this multiplicity of meaning. (A deconstructive critic could fuel a whole wasted career on unpicking the variants that follow. A slippery text, as the saying goes.)

"'Into the Mystic' is another one like 'Madame Joy' and 'Brown Skinned Girl". Originally I wrote it as 'Into The Misty'. But later I thought that it had something of an ethereal feeling to it so I called it 'Into The Mystic'. That song is kind of funny because when it came time to send the lyrics into WB Music, I couldn't figure out what to send them. Because really the song has two sets of lyrics. For example, there's 'I was born before the wind' and 'I was borne before the wind', and also 'Also younger than the son, Ere the bonny boat was one' and 'All so younger than the son, Ere the bonny boat was won'." To make things even more confusing, the lyric sheet prints "sun" here, not "son". "It had all these different meanings and they were all in there: whatever one you want is in the song. I guess the song is just about being part of the universe".

This from a man who punningly titled a later song 'Here Comes The Knight'. Betsy Bowden's book *Performed Literature* deals with just such dichotomies, showing how Bob Dylan can at times sing two words at once. One of the joys of live music is that all kinds of meanings can be entered into by the singer, as compared to the finality of a printed text. Even such texts are themselves only a final compromise, and literary detectives have long established how poets like Tennyson, Yeats, WH Auden and Robert Graves have often retrospectively changed their poems in succeeding editions. The same process, really, as when Van reinterprets one of his earlier songs in concert, though in that case often the words remain the same, while everything else – the pace, meaning, music and atmosphere – changes. But then of course Morrison is *not* a great poet, or so Johnny Rogan keeps on telling us.

'Into The Mystic' echoes the previous song, "I want to rock your gypsy soul", but it cuts deeper, with Van's voice rising from a gentle hum – moody as a fog horn – to an extraordinary point when he sounds as if he is drinking air. Stax horns bubble in the background, with Platania's electric guitar beautifully understated, embroidering the vocal line. At the very end, almost subliminally (it does not appear on the lyric sheet) Van sings "too late to stop now", suggesting that the song also describes an act of love.

It is a phrase that will become a key point of later live concerts. Meanwhile, back at *Moondance*, Brian Hogg feels that its second side is an anti-climax, it "treads water" to adopt the mastering image. The truth is a little more complicated, although Van himself describes 'Come Running' as "a very light type of song. It's not too heavy. It's just a happy-go-lucky song. There are no messages or anything like that."

Well, not quite. The imagery is just like that at the end of 'Madame George', a train passing, wind and rain – here as in Dylan's 'Percy's Song', or Thomas Hardy's poem 'During Wind And Rain', an image of implacable nature against which human life and death play out their little games. Van and his lover "dream that it will never end" while knowing that of course it will. Even the injunction to "put away all your walking shoes" has a temporary sound to it.

Meanwhile, the song is very close in its sentiments to Dylan's roughly contemporary 'I'll Be Your Baby Tonight', with the same mixture of tenderness and lust. Van's voice duets with a tinkling piano, and chunky brass on the chorus, like a smoother and better produced 'Brown Eyed Girl'. The ensemble come together for "you gotta rainbow if you run to me", just like an encore. What woman could possibly resist?

A drum shot, and 'These Dreams Of You', jaunty on the surface, but an odd mixture of accusation and affirmation. I presume that the uncredited harmonica player is Van himself. The lyrics are "the result of a dream I had about Ray Charles being shot down. That started off the whole song. The line 'you paid your dues in Canada', I don't really know where that comes from. I just have a romantic image of going to Canada and that's about it. The song is basically about dreams." Nightmares more like, with Van's lover telling lies, walking out, ignoring his cries, throwing him out, and slapping him on the face; odd behaviour for an angel. Van's voice sounds almost strangled on the final chorus.

"'Brand New Day' expressed a lot of hope. I was in Boston and having a hard job getting myself up spiritually. I couldn't relate to anything I heard on the radio. Then one day this song came on the FM station and it had this particular feeling and this particular groove and it was totally fresh. It seemed to me like things were making sense. The drums were playing really laid back and I didn't know who the hell the artist was. It turned out to be The Band." Van was sitting outside his house, on a grassy bank. "I looked up at the sky and the sun started to shine and all of a sudden the song just came through my head. I started to write it down, right from 'When all the dark clouds roll away'. I'd turned on the radio and I just thought that something was happening. The song was either 'The Weight' or 'I Shall Be Released'."

The resulting track is hymn-like in its sense of quiet devotion, much like 'I Shall Be Released' of which this is virtually a rerun, written by Dylan with whom Van later sang it in *The Last Waltz*, or Fairport's 'Now Be Thankful'. A song of freedom but the lines about old betrayals – sung with a kind of bitter luxuriance – bite deep, like a former sinner confessing his past. Van's voice is odd throughout, straining for meaning as the music plods beneath him, with Platania sounding like Steve Cropper played too slow.

"'Everyone' is just a song of hope, that's what that is." It's only a wild guess, but the line about "pipes and drum" suggest a darker inner meaning, the marching bands of Ulster. 1969 was the year in which Belfast broke out into civil war, with British troops brought over almost as an army of occupation to keep order. The community had split into mutual no-go areas, and this seems to indicate Van's wish to "walk again down the lane" is not merely the desire to rekindle childhood. Whether this meaning was intended or is accidental, there is a psalm-like cadence to the words here, and we are back with the opening song, "by the winding stream". The music is happy enough, like the most cheerful parts of *Astral Weeks,* on speed.

"'Glad Tidings' is about a period of time in which I was living in New York. A friend of mine wrote me a letter from London and he'd written on the envelope 'Glad Tidings from London'. So I wrote 'Glad Tidings from New York', and that's where I got the idea." An odd song which makes no sense, literally. Van certainly sounds happy enough, slurring his vocals over a bouncy beat, but the words are an odd mix of the surreal – fairy tales coming to life – and the impenetrable.

Seamus Heaney once wrote a poem called 'Whatever You Say Say Nothing', and there is the same kind of caution here, an injunction not "to read between the lines" – exactly what you do when reading poetry, of course, so rather a redundant warning. 'Glad Tidings' seems to be reprising some of the problems Van experienced with Bang; businessmen talking in numbers, people who interrupt "when you're in trances", strangers who "make demands". Even the opening and closing line, "and they'll lay you down low and easy", could be either about murder or an act of love. Brian Hogg describes "those close, almost claustrophobic horn riffs, wrapped in a freer, more open style", and there is certainly a dark undercurrent here, as in so many of the songs. Even 'Into The Mystic' could be a metaphor for dying. Dancing beneath the moon is dangerous, a recipe for madness or stirring up the dark.

The original American issue of *Moondance* boasts a gatefold sleeve, with a photograph of Van and Janet squatting in the woods, bent over some kind of occult symbol, woven into cloth. Jon Landau considered the album's only flaw that of perfection. "Things fell into place so perfectly I wished there was more room to breathe." For all that, "Morrison has a great voice, and on *Moondance* he found a home for it".

As Van told Richard Williams a couple of years later, "I'd like to have got the same musicians again and recorded the album live. That would have been a killer. That is the kind of band I dig. Two horns and a rhythm section – they're the kind of bands I like best. But the musicians weren't the sort of guys who work live gigs, they only work in the studio."

Strange then that virtually the same line-up appeared at the Fillmore West on 26 April 1970, and laid down a storming set. Van plays rhythm guitar and saxophone, and the band is as on the album, though with a different drummer, and minus the three backing singers. The *Moonlight Serenade* bootleg CD, on the Italian Teddy Bear label (!), illicitly proves Van right about the strength of this band live. While lacking the honey smoothness of the album – from which everything is played, apart from 'Brand New Day' – there is a snap and crackle to their playing missing from the studio set. And Morrison live on stage is like a fish back in water, revelling in the grace and danger of real time, taking risks and interacting with both band and audience.

"The incredible Mr Van Morrison", a downbeat voice announces, a couple of bars of staccato piano, and we're straight into 'Moondance', jazzier and slightly faster than on the record. The song stretches out with Van's voice shadowed by tinkling keyboards, and a half spoken "set my heart on fire". 'Glad Tidings' is somehow more committed a reading than on the original vinyl, the twin saxophones punchier. 'Crazy Love' Van says three times, presumably to the band, and he sings by turns pleading and proud, to a churchy organ. Every twist and turn of his vocal is right in focus, including a growled "makes me righteous" which hits some primeval part of the listener's soul. Straight into a cheerful 'Come Running', where every instrument – piano, horns, guitar, Van's wife – are percussive: the organ break is like Brian Auger, then everything slows down and Van seems to be singing in a dream, "do you remember, you came walking down, when the sun came shining through the trees, and you said" – pause for repeated, stabbing "do you?"s – "and I said you I want to give you, gotta give you, wanna give you, gotta give you, the rainbow in my, in my, in my, in my soul". Startling.

'The Way Young Lovers Do' is more passionate, more abandoned than the *Astral Weeks* original, with wilder breaks. An incredibly speedy 'Everyone', with keyboards imitating a spinet and jaunty flute, gives way to 'Brown Eyed Girl' in which the band suddenly sound ill at ease, out of phase with Van's loud thrummed acoustic guitar. It lacks the bounce of the original, which they seem hardly to know. Maybe Morrison suddenly sprung it on them. Van counts one, two, three, four, and we're back in safer territory, a Band-like good time groove to 'And It Stoned Me' – the Robbie Robertson style lead break, mathematically perfect, is set against chorded piano, just like the Woodstock backwoodsmen – which segues into 'These Dreams Of You', with wild saxophone. As Van sings "Ray Charles was shot down", Jeff Labes runs his hand down the keyboard, Jerry Lee Lewis style. The whole band suddenly stops during Van's growled "hush-a-bye", and for that brief moment it is just as if your own heart has ceased beating. In 'Caravan', he vows to get down on his "hands and knees" to see what's really wrong. The band slows and quietens down, almost to silence, before Van brings them up again.

Without any fanfare, he opens sotto voce on 'Cyprus Avenue', his band subdued, as he stutters painfully on "tongue gets t t t, every time I try to, yeah my insides shake, yeah" then suddenly everything comes into focus, the music speeds up and the organist imitates Garth Hudson. Van sings "I'm extremely wasted" as if the words are a death bed confession. Brass comes in, Van repeats "nobody" like a prayer, then "you were standing there" at least six times, the band noodle, "in all your revelation" six times, "in all your" ten times, like a sexual climax, then the whole phrase, then "wait for me to come" over and over again with urgency rising in his voice. A dreadful pause, then he roars "it's too late to stop now" as the music swells behind him. He breaks off to introduce the band, seemingly still in a trance, then "you were standing there in all your revelation", over and over again, "wait for me to come" even more urgent and sexual than before, shortening to just the first word as he gets further worked up. Another sickening pause, then Van asks his band for a "big G" chord, and back to the climax.

Twelve minutes of musical mayhem, after which 'Into The Mystic' sounds drained, until Van starts moaning on the "fog horn blows" line. He performs the same trick of repetition on "want to rock your soul", leaving words behind. A concert to rank with the greatest by anyone, and which gives the lie to Van being uncertain and ill at ease on stage, though of course this is a sound recording only. Video evidence of a live 'Cyprus Avenue' from the Fillmore East in October 1970 shows a visually uncertain figure, dumpy and uncharismatic at first, who seems to grow as the song gets going. Lester Bangs captured his stagecraft in words in his review of this same concert, describing a shamanic invocation, almost as if Morrison is taken over by a higher power.

> He drives the song, the band and himself to a finish. With consummate dynamics that allow him to snap from indescribably eccentric throwaway phrasing to sheer passion in the very next breath he brings the music surging up through crescendo after crescendo, stopping and starting and stopping and starting the song again and again, imposing long maniacal silences like giant question marks between the stops and starts and ruling the room through sheer tension, building to a surge of 'It's too late to stop

now!', and just when you think it's all going to surge over the top, he cuts it off stone cold dead, the hollow of a murdered explosion, throws the microphone down and stalks off the stage. It is truly one of the most perverse things I have ever seen a performer do in my life. And, of course, it's sensational: our guts are knotted up, we're crazed and clawing for more, but we damn well know we've seen and felt something.

Back on 5 April, Van had played the Fillmore East, in New York, though still at the bottom of the bill, bizarre as that might now seem, just like Bob Marley And The Wailers playing small clubs and pubs on their first British tour, and proud to be asked! Harry Weiner was there, and writing in *Wavelength* remembers "a constant din of chatter". Many of the audience had never even heard of him. "What finally caught my attention was the sight of this short gentleman, who through the marijuana haze looked akin to a billygoat, singing with a power and intensity the likes I had never bared ears to. He never smiled. Through the classic stops and starts, Van repetitively walked from one perimeter of the stage to the next, stopped, sang a lyric somewhat like 'I walked on over here' continuing this motion and refrain several times, sometimes with his back to the audience, as the band followed his groove empathetically and emphatically, even as the audience continued to buzz."

At the other end of the musical spectrum, a tape has emerged of acoustic demos laid down between 1969 and 1971. 'Ballerina' is fragile, naked sounding, "child you were headed for a fall". Pure stream of consciousness, emphasised by the solo voice and guitar, "I'm mumbling and I can't remember the last thing that was running through my head". Three songs from *Moondance* are jumbled together with three more from the next album, and five previously unknown. 'These Dreams Of You' is sad, driven along by a tambourine, 'And It Stoned Me' even slower and sadder, Van sounding close to tears, with Janet harmonising. 'Come Running' has a different tune, more Dylanesque, with the words in a different order.

Of the songs new to me, 'Bit By Bit' is a gentle, slow song about surviving, and happiness. It sounds as if Van is sleepwalking, mentally. 'Hey Where Are You?' is back in *Astral Weeks* territory, but without the desperation, with string bass and lightly blown flute (like Harold McNair's work with Donovan). The drifting lyric describes a stoned day. Sample lines: "As the raindrops came down on Sally's head, she cuddled up in her coat of red, and said." There is an altercation at a bus station, with a "grey man". It all sounds like a very bad Van Morrison impersonation. 'Lorna' is a love song to Janet, perhaps, "see you laugh in a photograph, that's all I wanted to do, see your swishing walk and talk your baby talk, that's all I wanted to do". It inhabits the innocence of 'Cyprus Avenue', like Dante and Beatrice, a song also of lost, platonic love from his early teens. "Carry your books to school, that's all I wanted to do", sung with tenderness and longing. Like many such demos, it has the strange quality of making Morrison sound as if he is in the same room as the listener.

'I Need Your Kind Of Loving' seems again to date back to the acoustic trio, and shows just why Van disbanded them, despite their musical competence. He drifts, lost in a world of his own, and without the careful setting of *Astral Weeks* it can sound aimless rather than free. 'Rock 'N' Roll Band' is a song about lost time and faded hopes, "we flagged the highway drivers down, on a ride to nowhere". A "soul time", dancing to a "rock 'n' roll band with three guitars and drums and a saxophone". A lovely song, which deserved release.

Meanwhile, *Moondance* was attracting a rising tide of critical acclaim. An advert titled "Glad Tidings from Van Morrison" describes him as "Irish, ginger and poker faced…a howler and a growler". *Rolling Stone* brought in two of their biggest guns, for a joint review, in March 1970. Greil Marcus and Lester Bangs agreed that here was an album of "musical invention and lyrical confidence". Van's music is unique because "what one hears is not style, but personality". He seems to achieve "some ancient familiarity" with his musicians. An imagination, "visionary in the strongest sense of the word", joins with "verbal magic as inventive and literate as Dylan's". As to the album in hand, it displays a "stately brilliance". "It's a good thing that he doesn't have much stage presence, otherwise it'd be too much to take."

Early subscribers to *Zigzag*, me included, read John Tobler enthusing that "I cannot tell you how extra-terrestrially brilliant it all is". Even the *New Musical Express* thought the album was "near to being a brilliant piece of work". The presiding wise old man of the SF scene,

Ralph J Gleason, identified for readers of the *San Francisco Chronicle* the main source of Morrison's inspiration, a timeless continuum of folk poetry. "He wails as the jazz musicians speak of wailing, as the gypsies, as the Gaels and the old folks in every culture speak of it. He gets a quality of intensity in that wail which really hooks your mind, carries you along with his voice as it rises and falls in long, soaring lines."

John Collis sneered at this comment in his biography, commenting that "it is a long time since the old folk in my culture sat around wailing" but that is a pity, not a counter-argument. Morrison taps into an oral tradition which can still be heard in pubs in the wilder parts of Scotland and Ireland, as the drink flows and the choruses start. An unself-conscious, pre-literate kind of sound rarely heard in public now, except perhaps at football matches and in the more evangelical kind of church, or after a car crash (or in the privacy of those busy making love or dying), a frightening and feral thing indeed, but deeply healing to those who utter it. Singers like Dick Gaughan or Christine Collister or June Tabor of Salif Keita also possess it, none of them exactly easy listening. It can also be located in field recordings of myth or ritual. Just go to Padstow on hobby horse day, and listen to the endless chant as it goes from pub from pub. To Johnny Rogan's particular disgust, Gleason's review ends as follows: "He sounds like a young Irishman haunted by dreams, a poet, one of the children of the rainbow, living in the morning of the world." There is more truth in this one line, though, than in the whole of Rogan's book.

In a 1996 *Mojo* readers' poll, *Moondance* came in at Number Forty, and the common rock fan spoke. People like you or me. Oliver Dudek saw the album as helping to "coin Morrison's reputation as rock's mystical poet", while M Warley of Maidstone considered that there was "more spiritual depth and mystical lyricism" here than "in all the West Coast psychedelic music of the sixties, or the angst ridden outpourings of the singer-songwriters of the seventies. A *Rolling Stone* Top Hundred albums listing placed the album at Fifty-Nine. It "just may be the most romantic rock 'n' roll album ever recorded. Van Morrison's voice, as sensual as warm honey, coats each song with an irresistibly seductive power."

In July 1970, the same magazine printed an interview with Van conducted by Happy Traum. One of the secrets behind the happiness so evident on *Moondance* is revealed: Janet had recently given birth to

Van's daughter, Shannon. He describes the process of composing songs: sometimes it is hard, and something inside *forces* him to write, "sometimes it just flows out, but I can't be forced to write by someone else. I can't be forced to do anything." Does he find it painful to sing his songs. "Oh no! I dig singing them. It's not painful at all! If it were painful, I wouldn't do it. I don't want to inflict myself with pain. Christ, no. All this stuff about you got to suffer to produce good music, is just bullshit. Because you don't produce good music when you're like that. You gotta be happy."

Van namechecks Leadbelly again as his main influence, then goes into a digression that could have come straight from *The X Files*. "I don't think he's really dead. A lot of people's bodies die, but I don't think they die with them. I think a lot of them are still hanging around somewhere in the air. It can't be that weak because these people are so strong...they can't die, they just leave something behind. I just don't believe that those people will ever die." Surely this is the very point of any tradition, whether music, poetry or playing tiddlywinks, that the wisdom of the dead feeds through to the living. *Moondance* attempted the same kind of spontaneity as the blues masters. "We did a rhythm track and then the vocal, or sometimes the vocal and the rhythm track and then added the horns. But mostly it was live." As to *Astral Weeks*, it was originally a rock opera, with a definitive story line. 'Madame George' is not a drag queen, "if you see it as a male, or female or whatever, it's your trip. I see it as...a Swiss cheese sandwich. Something like that." Which explains precisely nothing.

Songs from *Moondance* were widely covered by other performers. Johnny Rivers' *Slim Slo Slider* album also included 'Into The Mystic'. 'Moondance' was recorded by Irene Reid, 'Brand New Day' by Dorothy Morrison, from The Edwin Hawkins Singers, and Esther Phillips, fresh from the Monterey Jazz Festival. Phillips also performed 'Crazy Love'. Warners had no qualms about renewing Van's contract, expecting him to release two albums per year, with matching singles. Equally welcome was an offer from a New York publisher to bring out a book of Morrison's poetry and prose along the lines of Bob Dylan's free association novel *Tarantula*, or Van's near namesake Jim Morrison, Lou Reed and Marc Bolan, all by now published poets.

Rock music had lost its visionary gleam. By the end of 1970, Hendrix was dead and Jim Morrison rapidly heading the same way. The Beatles had disbanded, and the Stones were in disarray after Altamont. The great psychedelic bands were largely decayed, or feeling their way towards a prolonged life by empty showmanship – Jethro Tull – or through grandiose concepts. File under "progressive rock".

It was a time to retrace one's steps, and Dylan was at an artistic nadir, with *Self Portrait* and the false dawn of *New Morning*. Fairport had taken a Band route with *Full House*, as had (more surprisingly) The Grateful Dead, retreating into the myths and legends of their respective nations. Quietude was all the rage, with James Taylor and Jackson Browne – fine and sensitive songwriters both – typifying this move, no longer taking on the world, but taking one's own psychic temperature instead. Don Maclean's hit single 'American Pie' was symptomatic: rock music had become its own history.

There were several ways out for the most sparkling performers of the hippie daze, particularly for those cursed by fate to sing the words they wrote. You could internalise such melancholy, the death of hope, so deeply that those who did it properly – Tim Hardin, Tom Rapp, Nick Drake or, in a different sphere, Syd Barrett – never really came back. Secondly, one could simply cease to perform or record. David Accles retreated to England before a brief return with *American Gothic*. Roy Harper threatened, as ever, to retire, but fortuitously never actually got round to it. Thirdly, you could bland out, so that, say, Keith Christmas shed the mystery and keening passion of his early work, Ralph McTell lost focus, and – in a different world altogether – Frank Zappa exchanged political satire for soft porn.

The most fruitful solution was to branch out into your own chosen musical world, and then simply keep going. Sandy Denny's solo career saw her embracing jazz and MOR, while Kevin Ayers tried whimsy, and Al Stewart history. Michael Hurley followed a particularly individual furrow, into stoned weirdness. The most symbolic change was Daevid Allen, who had been present in Paris 1968, and evolved a whole pixie mythology to both express and disguise his thought systems. Peter Hammill picked away at the scabs of his own consciousness, while Peter Gabriel used Genesis as a vehicle for his own brand of polite surrealism. Tim Buckley abandoned renaissance folk for the furthest reaches of the avant-garde, and on *Starsailor* he howled like a banshee, against choirs of fallen angels. This was the archetypal post-hippie soundscape, made home by the post-Syd Floyd, and taken to its logical ends by German bands like Can and Popol Vuh: a vast, rhythmic and mythical inner world in which to roam, as if forever. Unable to earn a living from such music, Buckley drove a New York cab for a while, then returned with the (outwardly) more palatable white funk of *Greetings From LA*, and a tight Philadelphia rhythm section.

Van has never been as musically extreme as the likes of Buckley. He would be more closely allied with his occasional musical colleague Robin Williamson, who focused down from the multi-cultural paint box of The Incredible String Band to an intense exploration of Celtic roots. The risks taken have been in terms of song structure, not musical shapes. The one period during which Van was experimenting with a series of new musics – with help from The Crusaders and Mick Ronson, and including a bizarre move into comic monologues – was from 1974 until 1977, his lost years. Perhaps the defining point of his career came now, with that all important third album.

Morrison contemplated ignoring the white soul launch pad built by *Moondance*, by turning to an a cappella LP in the "street corner" fashion that had been as prevalent as gang warfare in the black and Italian ghettos of US cities. It was a direction similar to that assayed by Laura Nyro, in *Gonna Take A Miracle*, with Labelle. Nyro is in some ways the female equivalent of Van: her early work was similarly self-referential and emotionally fragile, while retaining a commercial edge, and shot through with the influence of black music. Both give their best in live performance, either on stage or in the studio, both have produced songs whose central mystery remains potent and unexplained. Van's idea was dropped, though a veiled indication of what might have been is detectable in the title of his third WB album, *Van Morrison, His Band And The Street Choir* (originally to be called *Virgo's Fool*).

It was a key decision. Ever since, his music has alternated between the twin poles of *Astral Weeks* and *Moondance*, drifting impressionism and tight, compact, tuneful songs, while never straying beyond them. Van has developed his sources, making excursions into Irish folk, down the line R&B and big band jazz, and extended his invocation of the heroic dead. Leadbelly in *Astral Weeks*, William Blake and the eternals, Jackie Wilson, John Donne, Rimbaud and Alan Watts later. The rest of his career has deepened and extended these early concerns: an Irish childhood, the healing power of the countryside, a search for spiritual consolation. Meanwhile, he was treading water.

Morrison spilled the whole story to Ritchie Yorke. "I really don't think that album is saying much. That album is like a kick in the head, or something. 'Street Choir' was to be an a cappella group, so that I could cut a lot of songs with just maybe one guitar. But it didn't turn out; it all got weird. Somewhere along the line, I lost control of that album. Somebody else got control of it and got the cover and all that shit while I was out on the West Coast. I'd rather not think about that album because it doesn't mean much in terms of where I was at. Someone was on my back to get something cranked out, even though they knew it was wrong. A couple of songs on it were hit singles but the album didn't sell well and I'm glad."

It is the usual story. By the time a new musician has a hit album, he or she has usually done their best work, and their music is settling into a recognisable – and marketable – style. More of the same for a few years, the public begin to notice, and commercial decline sets in. The truly great know implicitly how to keep going in their own chosen path, changing as they see fit, being creatively selfish, and knowing that their public will eventually latch on. David Bowie, say, as compared to Dire Straits. Making a career out of restlessness.

On its American release in October 1970, *His Band And Street Choir* was initially as well received as *Moondance* – more so in its sampler single, 'Domino', which topped 'Brown Eyed Girl' as a Top Ten single. Album sales imposed a law of diminishing returns on forty-fives issued after its release – which is why 'Blue Money' sneaked to Number Twenty-Three, and 'Call Me Up In Dreamland' faltered just outside the Hot Hundred. On the front cover, Van's face – full beard and long, wavy hair, lips slightly downturned, shirt buttoned to the collar but no tie – is superimposed on another shot, standing glum in a patterned kaftan, his eyes like slits. On the back of the CD booklet (and US gatefold sleeve) he and his band sit on the grass, Van's Irish eyes are smiling for a change, as he wraps his right arm around one of his fellow musicians, proffering something, water from a mountain stream perhaps, in a paper cup. Van appears in his prime. The rest look like Woodstock veterans, grown slightly old and seedy.

As to the music, Van is again listed as producer, with new drummer Dahaud Elias Shaar acting as his assistant. The album design is down simply to Janet, who also provides sleeve notes. Van plays guitar, harmonica and tenor sax, and Schroer, Platania, Klingberg survive from *Moondance*. Keith Johnson comes in on trumpet and organ, and Alan Hand on keyboards, but the ensemble lacks the tightness and direction of before. Professional, not inspirational. The "Street Choir" of singers comprises Ellen Schroer, Martha Velez, Janet Planet, David Shaw, Andy Robinson and Larry Goldsmith. Velez is a particular and pleasant surprise: after a solo album of electric blues, with Clapton on lead guitar, she later recorded one of the earliest albums of white reggae. *Moondance's* trio of female soul singers – Emily Houston, Judy Clay and Jackie Verdell – return on one track, 'If I Ever Needed Someone'.

Janet Planet's sleeve effusion sounds a little desperate. Note the word "must". "This is the album that you must sing with, dance to, you must find a place for the songs somewhere in your life. They belong to you now, dear listener, especially for you. Let your body go." As to Van, she seems to be trying to convince herself that he is a changed man. "There is so much light here, and incredibly I have seen Van open those parts of his secret self – his essential core of aloneness I had always feared could never be broken into – and say...yes, come in here. Know me." They say that love is blind, but Janet is surely alone at marvelling at the cover photographs, seeing "the good feeling that radiates from him now".

She does make one extraordinary claim. This music is far away from – and musically inferior to, some would add – "the former reality of a confession of the nature of 'TB Sheets'. All that really did happen to Van, make no mistake. Only there wasn't anyone else there with him. To lay that bare once and for all – he was sickening alone, afraid and ranting to be neither."

If this is true – and Van's wife is more likely to know than any journalist – then many mysteries are explained: Morrison's evangelical belief in music as a healing force, his notorious grumpiness, his restless energy, his haunted look, the way in which he can set the everyday against the timeless. One could interpret Joni Mitchell's whole career, say, as a reaction to her near-paralysis by polio, leaving her with an inner fragility, matched by a hunger for new experience and entertainment that at times seems almost greedy.

It is a strange fact how many writers have been dangerously ill during childhood or early adolescence, giving them the time and solitude in which to enter their own imagination. Alan Garner once made an extraordinary radio broadcast in which he remembers thinking so hard that he noticed a flickering; the interplay of night and day as they passed. Morrison's own childhood trances take on much the same intensity. His ability to look down on his own sleeping body is akin to many recorded by those hovering between death and life. On the other hand, it seems doubtful that such a major event in Van's life would not have been recorded in print, either by himself or his friends and relations.

The photographs in the CD booklet suggest that Van's band is part of some communal lifestyle, Grateful Dead style. The songs are now credited to the vaguely sick-making "Van-Jan Music". Girlfriends and babies appear in one shot, with Van's stepson Peter on a bike, and Shannon cradled in the arms of a mini-skirted Janet. The album has much the same downhome quality, and a matching brainlessness. It is vaguely reminiscent of Dylan's *Nashville Skyline*, but then how do you find a musical expression of contentment without sounding smug? Pain is always more fun, for the listener at least.

There is an interesting demo of 'Domino', with Van and his producer deciding to drop the flute part as too complex. The words make far more sense, emphasising the original theme of seduction, with memories of a girl with long blonde hair and the lights down low. They also change the song's pitch. As Van says, "That's a better key for me, it gives me the chance to wail more." The recorded version is a punchy affair, with words that mean little, though threatening the whole feelgood thrust of the album. "It's time for a change." Van is declaring notice, early. The music is something else again, toughly joyful, with an early Van hymn of praise to the radio, on which this song finds its true home.

After this encomium to Fats Domino, 'Crazy Face' namechecks Jesse James. This could well be one of the missing songs from *Astral Weeks*, a long slow sadness, and then an extraordinary sustained note (on baritone sax?). Van repeats the same strange words, which could be Tombstone or Ulster, perhaps even a young Van playing at cowboys. 'Give Me A Kiss' has the innocence of the early Beatles, set to a rolling beat. Good time music, with Van scatting happily. Some studio chat, with Van telling his band not to worry, then 'I've Been Working', a hypnotic strut, live in the studio. Van sounds like a hip preacher, testifying to love, "set my soul on fire".

'Call Me Up In Dreamland' is about life on the road, with "radio" as a verb, and laughing sax. 'I'll Be Your Lover Too' is gorgeous, a slow acoustic wallow with Van's voice drenched in tender emotion, and memories of Derry. Morrison proudly asks "how's that?" at the end. 'Blue Money' seems to be about a top shelf magazine model, maybe this is how Janet paid the rent during their wilderness years. The music sounds like Georgie Fame And The Blue Flames, boozy horns and a nonsensical chorus. 'Virgo Clowns' – Van and maybe Janet – has a lullaby feel, with the singer offering support to the woman who can in turn "take away all my misery and gloom". Van and Platania duet on acoustic guitars, one in each speaker, with a sliding sax playing bass lines. Slightly maniacal, stoned laughter follows, like a Cheech and Chong movie. The demo version is slower and more melancholy, and cuts deeper.

'Gypsy Queen' is closest to the original concept, with Van singing falsetto, almost like a woman, and a rich vocal chorus. The lyrics are almost Van by numbers – dancing, rain, moonlight, cars in motion – as are those to the throwaway blues 'Sweet Jannie', about young love. "I've been in love with you baby/ever since you were in Sunday School." The demo of 'If I Ever Needed Someone' is sweet and mournful, with Van wringing real need out of the simple words. The poetry is in the performance, the singer's slight delays, the way he breathes. The band version is slightly jauntier, more public, with Van's vocals less anguished and a sweet soul chorus taking the strain. 'Street Choir' starts appropriately with churchy organ, and a gospel choir. Heavenly trumpets, anyone? The lyrics are perversely bitter, 'Positively Fourth Street' sung in sorrow rather than anger. Van proves conclusively that he is a sweeter harmonica player than Dylan, though. There is a sad, slow majesty to this performance, which hints at better things to come.

John Platania considered, though, that "it's still a great album. Whether he will say it or not, he was more concerned with getting singles out. I don't know how much of it was pressure, but I think he had designs on getting air play. They were very hook orientated songs.

I think he digressed from that later." Eighteen hours of additional material was left on the shelf.

The reviewers, as usual, were waking up to a new talent, slightly too late. For Jon Landau, here was "a free album, another beautiful phase in the continuing development of one of the few originals left in rock. The song he is singing keeps getting better and better." For Royston Eldridge in *Sounds*, soul music is "an expression of emotion, an outlet of feeling and a music that belongs to Van Morrison as much as it does to Otis Redding". Richard Williams asked the readers of *Melody Maker* "Has Van Morrison eased up?" and found the singer "too relaxed, too happy", lacking his customary terseness. For *Friends*, Morrison remained "one of the few white performers to make use of black music in a creative rather than derivative way". Brian Hogg later found the album "ultimately a lesser work, a rushed and sometimes shallow collection", while for Van himself, "I really don't think that album is anything much. There really isn't anything I'm saying there."

Talking to Michael Walsh, John Platania gives new insights into Van's career at this time. "We worked a lot. He was out on the road quite a bit more than he would ever have really wanted to." Van was forced to "hustle" for money, just to survive. "He wanted to work with me, with my group. He wasn't in the greatest financial situation". Schwaid and Merenstein, the architects of *Astral Weeks*, "ripped him off quite a bit", and the guitarist thinks that is why they were cut out of the production of *Moondance*. "He wanted to get rid of them, because they were ripping him off." Van's salvation was a lady called Mary Martin, who "straightened his affairs out and really got him secured in the Warner Brothers stable. She was really important in financial terms and in a guiding managerial role at that part of his career. She fixed up his publishing, and that's when the money really came in."

Offers of work flooded in, too. "Then we did *Street Choir*, in between Woodstock and New York. 'I've Been Working', all that stuff, that comes from being stressed out from driving up and down New York State thruway to Woodstock. We were on the road quite a bit, doing tours of California and the Midwest, more than he really wanted to, but he had to work to keep the band together, it was a big band. Then Janet got him to leave Woodstock and move to California and we were still working, and that's when *Tupelo Honey* came in."

CHAPTER FIVE

Caledonia Soul Music

Morrison gave an interview to *Sounds* in December 1970, half promising a live album, recorded on two track, and the release on vinyl of the complete *Astral Weeks*, an "opera" lasting a couple of hours, with other singers taking some of the strain. The very idea of a rock opera has now been tainted beyond compare by the likes of Andrew Lloyd Webber, but it has long occupied the minds of some of the genre's true originals.

SF Sorrow, the original version of *Tommy*, The Kinks' *Arthur*, Peter Hammill's *Fall Of The House Of Usher*, with a libretto by Chris "Judge" Smith: none made Mozart feel nervous, but all had their own sense of fate, and a wayward majesty. In the folk firmament, that sad genius Peter Bellamy's ballad opera *The Transports* has been performed by others since his suicide, and worked well. Another visionary dead before his time, Randy California, wrote two compacted epics, the science fiction extravaganza *Future Games* and the terrifying political fable, *Potatoland*: both will grow posthumously.

Out in weird city, Frank Zappa structured even The Mothers' early albums as complex libretti, and later works like *Joe's Garage* were carefully plotted, if turgid. Ambitious epics by the likes of Kaleidoscope (the UK variety) and Julian's Treatment, have a small but vociferous pocket of admirers. Roger McGuinn's solo concerts often had as their centrepiece his explanation of – and songs from – the never completed *Gene Tripp* project, and artists as diverse as Captain Sensible and David Bowie have made recent attempts at the form. All of these attempts are strongest on atmosphere and individual songs, weakest on plot development and overall structure. It is no coincidence that perhaps the two most mercurial talents ever embraced by rock, Captain Beefheart and Vivian Stanshall – both seduced from the fine arts – have created a world of their own devising: Beefheart's *Trout Mast Replica*, Viv's *Sir Henry At Rawlinson End*.

Morrison matches each in creativity, but his is a narrower, more focused genius, more genuinely egocentric. Van Vliet and Stanshall are in retreat from themselves, rushing headlong into their art. The idea of tracks from *Astral Weeks* parcelled out to individual voices is a hard one to swallow. The protagonist of each song seems to be a different side of Van himself. That said, the slimmest chance of this project ever being realised is mouth watering.

Stranger things have emerged from the vaults. Mind you, in the case of, say, Arthur Brown's one way trip to hell *Strangelands*, one wishes they could be locked back in a vault, and the key thrown into the deepest ocean.

Back in the realms of the possible, Van also talks about working with The Modern Jazz Quartet, and producing an album by Lorraine Ellison – "she's terrific". As to his current stage set, outside of his own compositions "I do some Hank Williams songs, and some Ray Charles stuff, some instrumentals, like Horace Silver – sounds weird, doesn't it. Hank Williams and Horace Silver."

His Band And The Street Choir was the last album to be issued during the Morrisons' residence in Woodstock, newly made famous by a rock festival held some miles down the road. At first the place had been like Haight Ashbury in the woods. Artie Traum remembers how "you'd see Joplin, Hendrix, Morrison in the street, playing the clubs. The combination of old school Republican farmers and drug crazed hippies certainly produced an interesting atmosphere."

The Morrisons' landlord wanted to move back into his property, but there were more pressing reasons for their move West. As Van told Richard Williams, "Woodstock was getting to be such a heavy number. When I first went, people were moving there to get away from the scene. Then Woodstock itself started being the scene. They made a movie called *Woodstock* and it wasn't even in Woodstock, it was sixty miles away. Everybody and his uncle started showing up at the bus station, and that was the complete opposite of what it was supposed to be." John Platania told Steve Turner: "He didn't want to leave but Janet wanted to move out West. He was manipulated into going." Janet's family still lived in California.

Before he left, in early 1971, he played a series of "farewell gigs" at New York's Fillmore East. These were supposedly in preparation for a European tour, with planned concerts at London's Festival Hall and in Scandinavia, Germany and Holland, a BBC "In Concert", and filming back in Belfast. All not to be.

Geoffrey Cannon – one of the most precise of rock critics – provides a verbal sketch of the proceedings, as if in shorthand. Van "shags on in shades and a sheepskin jacket. Sings like he's not there. Moves mike backwards and forwards like disconnecting a plug." For the next song, he stands rigidly in wait, sideways on to the audience. "Later wanders backstage, hands on hips, head down, looking like he's trying to decide something. He's small and jerky. His delivery is slurred. Slightly bending over the mike, raising his right hand up, then pulling it down, like a lavatory chain."

In a dramatic moment, half way through 'Into The Mystic', he removes his shades, consumed with tension, fists clenched. "He seems desperate to keep hold of his own body." Cannon senses a dialectic of distrust between Van and his audience, especially when he sings 'Danny Boy' (a song almost beyond credibility due to a million sentimental readings), with more apparent seriousness than anything he has written himself, "coming on like an opera baritone". It is as if he is taking the rise out of his listeners, a dangerous strategy. The microphone cracks, like a pistol shot, and we're into 'Cyprus Avenue'.

On the line about getting tongue tied, "he gets totally contorted, frowning into the mike. Then silent. Then snorts. He seems unable to find a way out." "Here I am" (repeated three times). "I'm caught!" and he throws his left arm across his face, kicking his right foot to knee height. A desperate little move, Cannon notes. "I'm extremely wasted, and I'm pouring spaghetti bolognese over you." The audience dissolve into embarrassment, laughter, contempt. Van shouts: "This is the real thing, Jimi," and even that master of stoned stagecraft could not cap what comes next: we are in the realms of Syd Barrett or Twink in full mania.

"Stop me from loving you, baby" (mumbled).

"And you was standing there" (twice).

Organ plays quietly. Van scratches his hair.

"And you were standing there."

Twiddles his mike. Stands sideways on. Then launches into abuse.

"Someone here's talking. We came here tonight to work. Someone here is talking, so we can't work. That means, if you talk, it's coming back on you. You wanna shut up and watch us work or what?" Pause, as the audience register the shock of having the spotlight turned on them, so to speak. Then Van again: "The lights are a fucking drag. Can we turn the lights off." Someone near Cannon angrily shouts, "Turn off the amps." Van cackles at this. "Okay, you pay for them, so you can have them back on."

A pause, then, "We could stop any time. It doesn't matter. We could just stop." He starts the song again, running around the stage like a headless chicken, then trips over a lead. Morrison replaces his shades, and plucks a nit out of his mouth. Audience shouts of "this could go on forever!". Van "flings his head from side to side like a maniac". His shades fly off, with his head still bent. He grips the microphone with rigid arms. "It doesn't matter what you do to me…because it's too late to stop now." End of concert and, almost, Van's career.

A girl afterwards says, "Wow, he has such balls to give such a terrible performance," but the next night he creates just the same mayhem, after an early show electric with promise and anticipation. Cannon points out how Van's triumphs and disasters flow from the same root. "His nature compels him to create his songs, new, each time he's on stage. The song has no separate existence from his will to make it live one more time. To sing his songs 'accurately' or 'competently' would be an act of contempt."

As a result, Van turned down frequent invitations to appear at the gargantuan open air rock festivals of the time. His one such experience, at Randall's Island was a disaster. The audience seemed more intent on chucking paper planes at each other, and finding himself ignored, Van and his band sat down petulant and cross legged on the stage, until they were finally taken notice of.

John Platania, in turn, noticed Van's confidence on stage ebbing away. "There were many times when he literally had to be coaxed on stage. His motto was 'The show does not have to go on'. He would create the choice of whether he would go on stage or not." In just the same way, Joni Mitchell once calculated that she had cancelled as many concerts as she had actually played. Stage nerves are as much to do with audience expectation as the musician's own self belief. As Morrison later explained, "I've never been comfortable working live. I'm still not. I was never able to adjust to it because when I started and you played dances, you would finish a couple of songs and just walk through the audience. No stuff about being a star."

Robbie Robertson also knew all about stage fright, and even wrote a song about it. He and Morrison co-wrote a song for the 1971 album *Cahoots*, on which Van made a guest appearance, trading vocals with Richard Manuel. Ritchie Yorke comes up with a theory that the title 'Four Per Cent Pantomime' is an arcane reference to whiskey, the difference in alcohol content between Johnny Walker Red and Johnny Black. As the song is about gambling at cards, this seems a little far-fetched, though a bottle of hooch does get smashed – as do the singers – for no apparent reason. Van and Richard shout vocal lines at each other like long lost soul brothers, while Garth Hudson chords expansively, a defrocked church organist.

Robbie Robertson watched amazed as the two singers – both masters of their own melancholy – inhabited a plateau of pure inspiration. "They were acting this whole thing out. For a second, it became soundless – all hands and veins and necks. It was almost like the music was carrying itself." Mary Martin had introduced Dylan to The Hawks in the first place, and noted how "for Van, Richard was the real soul of The Band". A generally held opinion, and when Manuel died – as with Pigpen of The Grateful Dead – a light went out that the parent band was unable to ever fully replace. By that time, The Band were a spent force anyhow, with Robbie Robertson long gone.

Van is affectionately referred to by Manuel as "The Belfast Cowboy", a name that stuck. There is a subtext to the song, about the rigours of life on the road. "Mr booking agent please have mercy, don't book the gigs so far apart." Enough was enough, and Van cancelled his European tour, pleading that he was unable to put together an adequate band. Mary Martin put out a press release, claiming "it's only because he is so much of a perfectionist, that's the only reason".

Even if – as Platania claims – she had rescued his career, Van decided that Ms Martin was next for the chop. "I feel I'm not the type of artist who can have a manager. That puts the music business through quite a few changes. It means that they have to deal with somebody who's not a puppet, who doesn't function like a clockwork robot." This seems a little unfair to such a creative a force as Mary, whose arrangement of a blind date between Dylan and a Canadian bar band changed rock music for good. It is more truly a reflection of the same artistic restlessness which sees Van constantly sacking and hiring backing musicians, and ensuring that no two successive albums are the same.

One thinks of Tony Hancock, another grumpy, dumpy genius, whose paranoia that he was not the main attraction led to him dispensing of the services of his co-stars first, then his writers Galton and Simpson, and finally himself. Morrison has a more unshakeable sense of self belief, and the need to remain in full creative control, as he told John Grissim Jr, of *Rolling Stone* in 1972.

"It's ridiculous. If I'm gonna work with somebody, they're going to be working for me and not the other way around. The word 'product' keeps coming up. And if I'm the product, then these people are supposed to be an extension of how I operate. And if they're not, they're operating against me. It's part of an older generation set-up. I want to do it the way of right here and now. I don't want to live by anyone's old philosophies."

Van's move to the West Coast was part of this brave new world. "There's a lot of good energy building here. People smile more than they did back East. They seem happier. The vibes here are very similar to the ones in Belfast when I was first working bands there. A lot more musicians here are playing together and doing things for sheer enjoyment rather than for the bucks." In April 1971, the family moved to San Raphael, a rural settlement to the north of Marin County. Their home, high on a hilltop, comprised an acre or so of oak, redwood and wild iris. Here he could create Caledonia soul, and even the name of the district, Inverness, was a reminder of Van's Hibernian roots. The lifestyle here was almost a parody of such Joni Mitchell albums as *Ladies Of The Canyon*, but a fellow adopted Californian was even closer emotionally. Jesse Colin Young had been a tough New York folkie, but mellowed out with his band The Youngbloods, a charismatic, bluesy combo with a jazz drummer and a guitarist who doubled on electric piano and answered only to the name Banana. They had moved West, too. Young's first solo album, *Together*, released on the band's own Raccoon label, is the most moving of all evocations of this feted – and fated – lifestyle for Young sang songs about living on a ridgetop, and grey, misty days which still can touch the heart. Morrison's next album was to radiate the same kind of rich fulfilment, and Young was later to half-jokingly complain that whenever he formed a new band, Morrison would steal its members.

Van was now fully domesticated. Janet spoke to *New Spotlight*, though whether she is describing Paradiso or the Inferno is a little unclear. "He doesn't like a lot of people around. Really he is a recluse. He is quiet. We never go anywhere. We don't go to parties. We never go out. We have an incredibly quiet life and going on the road is the only excitement we have." One thinks immediately of the line from 'Old, Old Woodstock', "my woman's waiting by the kitchen door". Or the heavily ironic joke, why does a woman need legs? To walk from the kitchen to the bedroom. And eventually out of her man's life! As John Platania later told Steve Turner, "Janet wanted to get into acting but Van wanted a traditional woman at home and I know that bothered her. She was young and just wanted to step out on her own. She controlled a lot of his musical direction. She had a big, big influence on him. She sang backing vocals for him, helped him choose material, offered business advice. She was a strong person. People used to offer her modelling assignments and acting roles, but Van flatly refused to allow her to do these things. The lack of socialising drove her crazy."

When he did get out, Van particularly enjoyed the work of a local band, who had likewise migrated from the East. Asleep At The Wheel brought western swing, the "hillbilly jazz" popular during World War Two, up to date: they were later to notch up a 1974 chart entry with a revival of Louis Jordan's 'Choo Choo Ch'Boogie', also covered by their British counterpart Chilli Willi, led by the wondrous Martin Stone. Another country rock band living locally were Clover – who later spent time in England, and backed Elvis Costello on his first album – and Lamb. A musical kleptomaniac, Morrison was to hire Lamb's keyboard player and Clover's steel guitarist to play on his albums.

Idyllic as it may now seem, Van himself regarded this period as "intense". He was contracted to produce two albums a year, with chart singles an expected extra. Since moving from Woodstock he had been forced to recruit a new band. "It was a very tough period," he told David "Kid" Jensen in 1990. "I didn't want to change my band, but I found myself in a position with studio time, and I had to ring up and get somebody in. That was the predicament I was in." Sometimes, he even allowed these musicians to come back to his place.

Johnny Rogan describes pianist Mark Jordan and guitarists Doug Messenger playing into the early hours. "Van took them into new territory, ad libbing both lyrics and melody in a way that they had never previously seen."

To capture such fleeting wonders, Van invested in a sixteen track home studio so that he could tape whatever he chose, with whoever it pleased him to invite over, and with no time constraints. Like Pete Townshend with The Who, he could plan a forthcoming album in detail, before the full band came in. Plans to record Jackie DeShannon proceeded no further than one co-composed single, 'Sweet Sixteen' – and rumours of a romantic involvement, brusquely denied by Morrison. No such gossip attached itself to Van's musical collaboration with John Lee Hooker, though it continues to this day, longer than most marriages of the time, including Van's own. Hooker had long been an influence on bands like England's Groundhogs, and his songs were now being covered by the likes of Sam The Sham, The Doors and The J Geils Band. All this helped set up a collaboration with Hooker's "favourite white blues singer", Van Morrison, who sang and chopped out guitar licks during two days of loose sessions from which were salvaged lengthy versions of 'Goin' Down', 'TB Sheets', and 'Never Get Out Of These Blues Alive', the title song of the resulting album. He also appeared on Hooker's next LP, 1973's *Born In Mississippi*.

Morrison gave his home studio the grand title "Caledonia Productions Incorporated", in deference to his own ancestry on his father's side, and as a taster for his Caledonia Soul Orchestra. That old curiosity shop of rock knowledge, Alan Clayson, reveals that Woody Herman's 'Caledonia (What Makes Your Big Head So Hard)' was a turntable fixture in San Raphael around this time. Morrison was obtaining control, as he had long desired, over every link of the chain of the recording process, from studio to pressing plant to market place. In 1974, Caledonia Productions published a seventy-four page book of

Morrison's thoughts on the music industry, and life in general, which was intended to do away with the need for journalistic intrusions. As its title suggested, the aim was to be as "true" as possible, "the music, of course, is its own statement".

After the Fillmore East debacle, even here Van was now calling the shots, and playing at the kind of small, intimate venue where his music really shone, and inspiration could flow, unfettered. In September 1971, a relaxed, jokey Morrison appeared in front of about two hundred fans at Pacific High Studios. He and his band just tore the place apart.

First up is a relaxed 'Into The Mystic', which rolls along like a lazy wheel. 'I've Been Working' is led by jazzy piano, and a fat electric guitar, out of Chicago blues. Van's vocals and the shadowing horns are at times hard to decipher from each other. "And you send me," Van whispers, as if to himself. 'Friday's Child' is a song about leaving home, with a stately keyboard riff, like Chris Stainton from Joe Cocker's Grease Band, and the realisation suddenly dawns that this is a grown up version of what Cocker's Mad Dogs And Englishmen were attempting, plus poetry. The way Van sings about "rainbows at your feet" is peerless. The singalong "it's too late to stop now" is borrowed from 'Cyprus Avenue', but here it's just a chorus.

Of all things, Van now resurrects an old favourite from his days in Germany. He opens with a semi serious 'Que Sera Sera', but Doris Day soon gives way to Elvis Presley, and a version of 'Hound Dog' which replaces the King's sexual tension with a joyful strut. The rhythm guitar riffs, Keith Richard style. From that to 'Ballerina', of all things, "twenty two stories long". The album version's urgency yields here to a fulfilled, almost lazy rendition. "I'm mumbling, and I can't remember the last thing that went through my head." Two songs from the forthcoming *Tupelo Honey* follow, the title track sung as if in a trance – Van adopts a Caribbean accent on the final verse, Ray Davies style – and 'Wild Night', a single "which comes out next week". The band wakes up, and Van dances through the reckless melody, laughter in his voice.

"I'd like to slow the tempo down, and do a rendition of somebody else's tune." 'Just Like A Woman' really should be commercially available, with Van singing with infinite tenderness, making the song his own, and daring to ad lib Dylan. He omits words, repeats them, and adds "is this queer in here" – bringing out the sexual ambiguity of the song – and "I was weird and you were weird too". *Tupelo Honey's* 'Moonshine Whiskey' is joyful, then slows into a dream sequence. "I wanna put on my hot pants", indeed. Van promenades down funky Broadway, then gets in the water and watches fish swim, and the "bubbles come up", making bubble sounds to match. Well weird.

In 'A Hard Road, Dead Or Alive', Van plays the Belfast cowboy for all he is worth. "The new sheriff sent me a letter", and what sounds like a trombone leers suggestively. Van makes up the words as he goes along. 'You're My Woman' is another *Tupelo Honey* taster, a hymn of survival. 'These Dreams Of You' is bouncy, 'Domino' a shout of joy: "I just wanna hear some rhythm and blues music. R&B. On the radio." Shouts of "get it on", and this extraordinary river of music flows on, into 'Call Me Up In Dreamland'. "Why don't we take it at the top and start all over again", and for a blissful moment you think he is going to do just that. The *Inner Mystic* bootleg mistitles the next song 'Blue Monday', but Van has not pre-empted New Order, and we have another *His Band And Street Choir* track live and cheerful. 'Bring It On Home To Me' cuts out Eric Burdon's menace, and adds "I can do the boogaloo" to a sleepy run through. The final song, 'Buona Sera, Senorita' opens with a musical quote from the '1812 Overture', and is pure music hall, almost The Bonzo Dog Band. "Kiss me goodnight", and you feel that the audience would, if they could.

There are no stage nerves in evidence here, but only a few weeks later, Van was due to play at Winterland, one of San Francisco's biggest venues. Two days before the gig, he announced his retirement from live gigs, and when finally pressured to appear, he ignored the audience throughout, and refused an encore, until Taj Mahal talked him into it backstage. The solution was virtually at his back door. One night at the Lion's Share club, a few miles drive from his home, Van sat in with Ramblin' Jack Elliott, whose untutored phrasing had left its mark on the young Bob Dylan. The older Dylan laughed out loud when he found out that this "authentic" cowboy was also of Jewish extraction. The evening worked so well that Van began to make unannounced appearances there – thus relieving the pressure. He performed iconoclastic covers of songs like 'Everybody's Talkin'' – the theme song of *Midnight Cowboy* – and 'Misty', Johnny Mathis's supper-club warhorse. One night, Van performed a solo, acoustic set, joking with the audience – "I hope you can see the comedy in all this" – and experimented with scat singing, a technique from his show band days. He was then joined on stage by John Lee Hooker, for some intense blues, and a pick up band of Rick Danko from The Band, and Dylan's confidante Bobby Neuwirth. They ended with 'Ballerina', in which Van exerted his whole being, eyes closed, lost in the music.

Stephen Pillster told Steve Turner that spontaneity was the name of the game. "He would call up his band early in the afternoon to see if they fancied having a blow that night. I would then call the club owner, who would just cut one of his acts for that night, and let the headliner open for Van. We could pretty much go in at two hours' notice." With his confidence flowing back, a coast to coast tour was set up for early 1972, as Van had a new album to promote.

For *Tupelo Honey*, Morrison selected backing musicians with the assistance of Ted Templeman, the Warner Brothers house producer recently assigned to him, though Van considered that "he dumped on me later on". Templeman was also to produce the simple minded Doobie Brothers and the snaky, slip 'n' slide rhythms of Little Feat. Once drummer with soft rockers Harper's Bizarre, Templeman had already worked with Captain Beefheart, so he was well used to musical mavericks, though he later claimed, "I'd never work with Van Morrison again as long as I live, even if he offered me two million dollars in cash. I aged ten years producing three of his albums."

Largely written in Woodstock, before the move, *Tupelo Honey* was released in November 1971, and reached *Billboard*'s Top Thirty, and 'Wild Night' – the first of many singles taken from the album – peaked at Twenty-Eight. Van told the *NME* that "some of the songs I put out as singles were much better live. Maybe they were like five minutes live. Well on a single it'd be something like three minutes. So that's a compromise. It's just all this red tape that the record companies give you about three minute singles."

Another example of Van's constant quest for inspiration over packaging, and his determination to keep things live. This fed into his views on his latest record. "I wasn't very happy with that album, it wasn't really fresh. It was a whole bunch of songs that had been hanging around for a while. I never really listened to it much. I've got

a bad taste in my mouth for both *Street Choir* and *Tupelo Honey*."
Those who actually bought it begged to differ.

The album art reflects Van's original intention: "I was really trying to
make a country and western album." On the front cover, Van in
sleeveless T-shirt, hippie length hair, and patterned loon pants leads
Janet along through a leafy glade. Sunshine pours through the trees,
just like honey. The atmosphere is deeply Pre-Raphaelite, with Van
playing an Arthurian knight and Janet riding a white stallion. She has
Guinnevere's fey beauty and her waist length tresses catch the
sunlight. On the back cover, a sepia shot which could come from a
different century, Van is dressed like a Mississippi gambler, in bow tie
and suit. Janet, in a floor length, floral dress, caresses his knee. Van is
almost smiling, as is the horse, which looks straight at camera. By Van's
left hand is what appears to be a stuffed cat, but in another photo it
gazes up at Morrison with matching awe.

The artwork "reads" as an image of married love – there are no
children or strangers present to intrude on this mutual self absorption
– and of pioneers, colonising the prairie. There is that same sweet
gravity as in David Accles' stirring 'Montana Song'. This is undercut by
the way Janet looks subservient – being led, standing while Van sits
above her. Here is an Eden which one somehow knows is bound not
to last. (The art director is one Ed Thrasher, a name seemingly straight
from punk rock, which evolved to rid the world of albums precisely like
Tupelo Honey.) Morrison seems to recognise this in comments which
others have seen as churlish, but I would regard as simply realistic.
"The picture was taken at a stable and I didn't live there. We just went
there and took the photo and split. A lot of people seem to think that
album covers are your life or something."

Not necessarily, but the best ones do reflect the kind of music they
package, and the sounds here – published by Caledonia Soul Music –
are full of the dreaminess and romance of the cover art. Recorded at
Wally Heider's studio in San Francisco, as was much of The
Youngbloods' work, it exudes warmth and a Band-like serenity. The
musicians chosen include some names from Van's past – Jack Schroer,
percussionists Connie Kay and Gary Mallaber – and the nucleus of The
Caledonia Soul Orchestra. Bill Church is on bass, Mark Jordan on
keyboards, Luis Gasca on trumpet, and Boots Houston and Bruce

Royston both play flute. Janet Planet joins in on backing vocals. Two temporary additions are guitarist Ronnie Montrose, who is more noted for heavy rock, and the steel guitar of Clover's John McFee. The band lock into a mellow groove, masking the fervid creativity of the studio sessions. Templeman captures Van in full flow: "Van's ability as a musician, arranger and producer is the scariest thing I've seen. When he's got something, he wants to pull it down right away with no overdubbing. He works fast and demands the same of everyone else. I've had to change engineers who couldn't keep up with it."

The music on *Tupelo Honey* melds into one seamless whole, so that a track by track analysis seems inappropriate. As *Melody Maker* opined, "There are those albums which one enjoys so much that one doesn't want to review them, but just play continuously". Steve Peacock in *Sounds* gets things just about right; the music is "colourful without being garish, exciting without being frantic, full of well being and joy without being complacent". A few stray observations. The centrepiece is 'You're My Woman', a long cry of need. The title track has a little boy lost feel, and peerless singing. Deep soul, with Van breathing deep at the end. 'I Wanna Roo You' is in private code, and waltz time. Its subtitle 'Scottish Derivative' indicates another attempt by Van to rediscover his Caledonian roots, with country fiddle and a farmhouse feel. 'When That Evening Sun Goes Down' is emotionally a dead ringer for Dylan's 'I'll Be Your Baby Tonight', another song of married contentment. Van chuckles at the end. He later admitted that he had written 'Moonshine Whiskey' "for Janis Joplin or something", though it is not autobiographical in the same way as Leonard Cohen's 'Chelsea Hotel Number Two'. That kind of empty sexuality, "giving me head on an unmade bed", is the very obverse of *Tupelo Honey*. A far closer comparison would be Richard and Linda Thompson's *Pour Down Like Silver*, sensual rather than sexy, songs of love and need, half directed to God. Indeed, there is something of the new convert – to domesticity, not the altar – in songs like 'Starting A New Life'. "She's an angel"!

The reviewers were highly positive. In *Rolling Stone*, Jon Landau found a deep well of inspiration: "Every repeated play reveals its deeper level of meaning. Van consistently and consciously develops the theme of 'starting a new life' through the growth of his own strength and confidence." Just as with his live concerts, he was developing the form, "making increased use of the album as the unit of communication as opposed to merely the song. Everything is perfectly integrated." For *Time Out*, the album was "a summit", for *Zigzag's* John Tobler, "If all music was as good as this, there would be no need for anybody to make any more".

The most penetrating insight came from rock mastermind Charlie Gillett, writing in *Cream*. "Many of his songs take about a year to get across to me, but the point is that I keep playing them until they do. Meanwhile I hum the tunes, sway my shoulders to the rhythm, and marvel at the way the songs each draw me into their very different moods. He is really way out on his own, oblivious of what others are doing, forgetful of his own past, concerned only to say, today, he's glad to be alive."

For Richard Williams of *Melody Maker*, although *Tupelo Honey* does not represent a return to the anguish of *Astral Weeks* or the sensual tautness of *Moondance*, "it consolidates *Street Choir's* sense of happiness and makes something worthwhile out of it".

The greater the public demand to see Van play live, the less confident he became in his own abilities. He would quit the stage immediately if distracted by feedback, a dead microphone, audience interruptions or anything else not in the pre-written script. Van was taking enough risks with his music already, without further uncertainties. He was at his greatest on stage when he seemed to forget his audience completely, lost in a Belfast dream. Again, the trend towards playing in huge sports stadiums, with fans squatting on the floor, was not to Morrison's taste. He began to refuse encores, and to talk seriously about abandoning the whole pointless charade.

A poor quality tape of his gig at the Aquarius Theatre, Boston on 19 May 1972 captures Van pre-Caledonia Soul Orchestra, a man in transition. The music is heavy on the brass, with the opening number, 'I've Been Workin'' highlighted by Van's harmonica solo, which degenerates to rough barks and whoops, like a rabid dog. Next in is a rough and ready version of 'Astral Weeks' with electric bass and loosely picked lead guitar, seemingly intro-ing forever. Van's singing seems to echo itself, when he provides his own backing chorus, and the whole thing sounds aimless and forced. After a perfunctory 'Caravan', he breaks into laughter, and the atmosphere noticeably relaxes. Next he scats through the good time 'I Will Be There'. Whoops from the audience, and two "oh boys" from Van.

'Moondance' has Van a dead ringer for Jim Morrison at times, talking his way through. Virtuoso piano. The voice sounds Islamic, summoning the faithful to prayer. "Suck my soul", then he outdoes Robert Plant, sending his voice here, there and everywhere. There is a subtle undercurrent of swing throughout, and his cover of 'Misty' emphasises this. On the other hand, 'Tupelo Honey' sounds like a lament here, with Van sculpting arabesques of melody out of the air. This is communication between artist and audience, literally, beyond words, and they reply in turn, with wordless cries of pleasure.

Much retuning then, almost as a reward, Van grants a rare preview of 'Listen To The Lion' from the forthcoming album. It starts in a kind of holy quiet, then picks up like a steam train, Van bouncing lyrics off his female backing chorus, and slowing the song back down into silence. Huge applause. 'He Ain't Give You None' seems an unusual choice, maybe an affront to those shouting for better known material, but it draws some applause from those in the know. It has been bled of its original spite, and is now almost a celebration, with plenty of gutbucket saxophone. The audience clap enthusiastically through 'Wild Night', in 'Domino' the band falls silent, and Van plays off them alone. 'Cyprus Avenue' closes proceedings, a gentle meditation until he talks about being "assassinated". Despite that sudden shock, this is a more inward version than at the Fillmore, with Van caressing the final words like a charm. Ugly feedback, which Van ignores, and the backing chorus sings "revelation" over and over again, as Van growls beneath. During the stop and start chorus, Van answers a solitary heckler with "if you don't like the show you can always leave". Someone else shouts out "shut the fuck up", whether to Van or the heckler is unclear, and the air is suddenly edged with menace, as Van screams out his climax.

A review in the Boston *Globe* described the evening as "a near perfect pop music concert", while Van himself enthused about "the energy, man. I'm not down yet." Five sell out concerts in six days.

Van further revealed himself in two interviews published that summer. John Grissim Jr's *Rolling Stone* piece begins with a description of the fated Winterland gig of the previous year, which saw

Van breaking up his band and Street Choir. "I felt I wasn't getting across. Really the only thing that's important is that I play music for people to hear." He also confirms his underlying sense of humour, emphasised by a photo at the top of the same page of him sitting with a coffee mug balanced on his head. "Part of the way I look is not to be taken seriously. It's kind of like I'm a straight man. All I need is a partner and I could go into business. That's what I am, the perfect straight man. A lot of people haven't figured it out yet."

He admits to not knowing exactly what some of his songs mean: "There are times when I'm mystified." He agrees with Grissim that there is a strong visionary element to his work. "It's strange, because I don't see myself as a mystical type person. But then every now and then these weird experiences happen. Like I'll be lying down on my bed with my eyes closed and all of a sudden I get the feeling that I'm floating near the ceiling looking down. I couldn't say whether that's supposed to be astral projection, but it's pretty freaky when it happens."

In July, fellow Irishman Shay Healy interviewed him for *Record Mirror*, having watched him play live. "The tightness of the band was amazing and with tiny movements of his fingers behind his back, Morrison guided them through." Van himself sings "fantastic riffs with a control that was astonishing". All the more surprising, then, when Janet tells Healy that "he doesn't like performing because he doesn't like the idea of all those people looking at him. Really he is a recluse." As befits such, Healy literally pursues Morrison as he makes for Boston public library. "I'm a Phoenician, man. You probably are too. I'm really into this sort of stuff now, finding out about the past and things." A dimension he would explore far more, in his own future. Van is re-entering the past musically, too. "I love old Louis Prima numbers. I like Tony Bennett. In fact I like all good singers and that's why I like some of the showbands, because they have good chanters."

These new obsessions, tribal mysteries and the exploration of the human voice, were twin rivers, feeding into the triumphant album *St Dominic's Preview*, which climbed straight into the US Top Twenty on the back of the sudden rediscovery of his live power. Released in July 1972, it became Van's highest charting album so far. Its original title was to be *Green*. In an unconscious irony, St Dominic was the saint who instituted the Spanish Inquisition, for after the sweet harmonies of *Tupelo Honey*, there is a sense of loss and pain in the best of these songs.

On the front cover, Van sits alone with his guitar, and with his eyes raised to heaven, a symphony of blue, fronting two huge ornate doors, studded with Celtic designs and presumably those of St Dominic's Church. There is a rip in his jeans, and his boots are scuffed. He is clean shaven and with a gypsy scarf around his neck, like a down at heel troubadour. On the back cover he is again solitary, lost in his music.

The music is again co-produced by Ted Templeman. New faces this time around include saxophonist Jules Broussard, who had previously played with Boz Scaggs, Bernie Krause on Moog synthesiser, and pianist Mark Naftalin, a refugee from the Paul Butterfield and Mike Bloomfield blues bands. Once a Beau Brummel – SF's answer to The Beatles – guitarist Ron Elliott released a solo album of his own, 1969's *Candlestick Maker*. Back on drums is Connie Kay, from *Astral Weeks*. Indeed, the album sounds like an amalgam of all the better parts of Van's earlier career.

'Jackie Wilson Said' was apparently inspired by a line from 'Reet Petite'. Van begins a cappella, then a tight arrangement hits in. There is an element of bad luck to this song. Presumably written to Janet, she soon stopped smiling at Van and left him, while Wilson suffered a heart attack on stage in 1975, and was never again able to walk or talk, let alone sing. 'Gypsy' starts bouncy, but gets melancholic and itchy feet, all at the same time. The very opposite of the songs of domesticity on the previous album. In these two songs, Dexy's Midnight Runners' whole career lies, waiting to be born.

'I Will Be There' is a simple twelve bar blues, jaunted up with odd chordings and honky tonk piano. Van evokes the spirit of Ray Charles, and again plots restlessness, this time in the service of the loved one. It is a heavily realistic quest, though, with Van grabbing Coca-cola, his toothbrush and his underwear. From that it is a bold move to segue into the eleven minute 'Listen To The Lion'. Van plays Hamlet.

We are back in *Astral Weeks* territory, a bass led shuffle and Van lost in his own poetic universe, but here his voice takes wilder risks: growling, a near death rattle, feral grunts and roars. Talking in tongues. A male chorus replaces the string section of the earlier album: the song itself is a personal odyssey, beginning in love. The rhythm picks up, like a sailing ship, and Van traces the Viking route from Denmark to Caledonia, and then on to America – the Golden Gate and New York City – "looking for a brand new start". The forgotten narrative of his race, sailing the seas before recorded history, making a journey without maps. Van himself later described the song as "a stream of consciousness work". The real journey takes place within, searching for one's roots and the spirit of unquenched creativity of William Blake's "Tyger". This is no children's game. When Van sings "I shall search my very soul", you know that he means every word. Ritchie Yorke wrote about the "miraculous energy funnelled through its ideal medium, dropping down on your head like a windfall of autumn leaves. At times it reaches such ecstatic heights that you feel like it's almost going to tear your head right off."

No respite, we're straight into 'St Dominic's Preview'. Lovely complex chords, a reference to cleaning windows, and a song about Ulster. Van himself is back "in San Francisco, trying to make this whole thing blend". As he told John Grissim, "I'd been working on this song about the scene going down in Belfast. And I wasn't sure what I was writing but the central image seemed to be this church called St Dominic's where people were gathering to pray or hear a mass for peace in Northern Ireland." A few weeks later he was playing a gig in Reno, Nevada. During dinner, he picked up a newspaper, "and there in front of me was an announcement about a mass for peace in Belfast to be said the next day at St Dominic's Church in San Francisco. Totally blew me out. Like I'd never even heard of a St Dominic Church."

This is like the writer Iain Sinclair's visiting a Hawksmoor church in London's East End, and recognising it exactly from a dream he had a few days before, the germ which became the full blown disease of *Lud Heat*. As befits the Belfast situation, the song is in code, "orange" boxes and "flags and emblems", people determined "not to feel anyone else's pain". The refusal of "commitments" might well lay behind Alan Parker's film, which does exactly that, using R&B to escape urban violence. In this strange melting pot of a song, the most Dylanesque Van ever gets, we get references to Edith Piaf, Yeats and Hank Williams. It ends at a record company reception, with Van unable to get his sense of foreboding over to his fellow rock stars, "flying too high" to notice.

Talking to Shay Healy, Van pointed out, "I'm definitely Irish. I don't think I want to go back to Belfast. I don't miss it with all that prejudice around. We're all the same and I think it's terrible what's happening. But I think I'd like to get a house in Ireland. I'd like to spend a few months there every year." 'Redwood Tree' is a song of reconciliation, which seems to graft Van's Belfast childhood onto California, where redwoods actually grow. "Keep us from all harm", an invocation to the spirit of the ancient wood.

The album ends with another ten minute epic, 'Almost Independence Day', with Van trading acoustic guitar licks with Ron Elliott, and Bernie Krause's Moog synthesiser, like a foghorn in the Bay. Krause had earlier worked on The Byrds' 'Space Odyssey'. As Van told Ritchie Yorke, "It wasn't my concept to write a sequel to 'Madame George'. I like the song though. It was just contemplating organ and the Moog. Everything was recorded live except that one high part on the synthesiser. I asked Bernie Krause to do this thing of China Town and then come in with the high part because I was thinking of dragons and fireworks. It reminded me of that. It was a stream of consciousness trip again." Danny Holloway of *NME* thought that it sounds "as though it was made up in the studio", a drifting seascape, a dream of freedom.

For Brian Hogg, this is a "mesmerising, meandering song". Other reviewers discern the same ethereal qualities here. For Stephen Holden in *Rolling Stone*, "the deeply compelling quality of Morrison's trips is embodied in their very evanescence; in the fact that the forces he conjures are beyond precise articulation and may only be suggested." For *Sounds*, Van himself has "almost become a myth" for British audiences. The music here is "smooth as hot chocolate and yet taut as an elastic band stretched to snapping point". For Dave Marsh of *Creem*, "Morrison has a way of making spiritual statements that would sound either false or trite from almost anyone else. He has always dealt with a certain kind of spiritual regeneration, a type of self discovery."

As Van himself told Ritchie Yorke, "The album was kind of rushed because of studio time and things like that. But I thought it was a good shot, that album. There were a lot of good songs on it. *St Dominic's Preview* was more into where I'm at, more into what I was doing." The album is credited to Caledonia Productions, and the music – as on the previous album – copyrighted to Caledonia Soul Music. The unreleased track of the same name, lasting a good twenty minutes, consists of Van endlessly intoning those same words, and bringing in the instrumentalists behind him, by barking a gruff "mandolin" or "get down". Interesting, but too relaxed to rise much above background music. Caledonia itself comprises the wilder parts of Scotland, an area never conquered by the Romans, who therefore expunged even its name from their maps, and built Hadrian's Wall to face it out. Morrison discovered a "certain quality of soul" when he first toured Scotland with The Monarchs. More directly, the modal scales of bagpipe music are part of the swirling majesty of his own musical signature.

Danny Holloway of *NME* went over to interview Van in San Rafael, in the late summer. "Driving to his house, the small dirt roads present hair pin turns without ample warning. Past the front gate, there's a long up-hill walk along the driveway, until the perched mountain home becomes visible. The house is completely secluded, and surrounded on all sides by redwoods." In the interview itself, Van proves just as isolated and impossible to penetrate.

He only seems to come to life when discussing his favourite music, The Band, Mose Allison, Gil Evans. "I don't like screaming guitars and stuff like that." Van was now hosting a regular music show, for no fee, at KTIM, San Rafael. In an interview with *Spotlight*, he explained: "I play records that normally wouldn't get played and the whole thing is pretty laid back and spontaneous. I suppose it's one of the only underground stations in the true and original meaning of the word. It's nice to play records that I dig and turn other people on to them." Much as he was to do with his covers of other people's songs.

Meanwhile, Van's home sixteen track Caledonia Studios was up and running. Once he even rented it out to friends. "I let people use it one time but it got all weird, about twenty cars in the driveway and people lying all over the ground stoned and stuff. So I didn't do that again." Van had by now appointed as manager Steve Pillster, who had previously overseen Dan Hicks And His Hot Licks, a good time music band formed by the drummer of The Charlatans, the original psychedelic pioneers.

More dramatically, Janet had finally moved out with their daughter Shana, as Shannon was known, beginning proceedings for divorce and for financial recompense for her emotional support. The album provided the final catharsis. John Platania: "When we started recording Janet was still in the house, but she was definitely on her way out. She would make subtle complaints about the relationship but nothing specific. All that she would say was that he was difficult to live with. By the time the album was finished she had definitely left."

Van seemed to compensate by opening up in live performance. It was almost as if with his personal life in disarray, he could make the stage a second home. As he told Ritchie Yorke, "I am getting more into performing. It's incredible. When I played Carnegie Hall in the fall something just happened. All of a sudden I felt like 'you're back into performing' and it just happened like that. A lot of times in the past I've done gigs and it was rough to get through them. But now the combination seems to be right, and it's clicking a lot." He was about to embark on his own personal odyssey.

In Britain, Van was not forgotten. In the "world vocalist" section of the 1972 *NME* readers' poll, Van tied at Number Fifteen with David Bowie, Randy Newman and Paul McCartney, a startling achievement for a man who had not performed on these shores since 1968. Meanwhile, he continued to play occasional concerts on the West Coast, with a band now officially named The Caledonia Soul Orchestra. "It was a combination. I brought the piano player in. He actually moved there. Jeff Labes."

Rough tapes exist of two sets performed back at the Lion's Share, San Anselmo in February 1973. The general ambience is relaxed, with lots of tinkly electric piano. 'St Dominic's Preview' leads into a funtime 'Hey Good Lookin'' – plenty of sax – and the menacing blues 'I Just Wanna Make Love To You', slowed right down. A preview version of 'Hard Nose The Highway' follows.

The evening show is more relaxed still, opening with a cover of that classic under-achiever Harry Nilsson's 'Everybody's Talking', the theme song from the film *Midnight Cowboy*. A seedy tale of urban cowboys and a man who, literally, flogs his daily meat, before beating up a client and taking a dying Ratso down to Florida. 'I've Been Working' has mutated into Sonny Boy Williamson's 'Help Me', and boasts a risque last verse, "I feel like lying down, bring me my nightshirt, put on your morning gown". The majestic 'Wild Children' is another preview from the forthcoming album, and leads straight into 'Listen To The Lion', a song which the venue's name might well have inspired, and the real king-pin of the set. It stretches out to epic length tonight, rising and ebbing like the tide. Next up is 'Misty', then even more bizarre 'The White Cliffs Of Dover', the old World War Two nostalgic chestnut, more usually sung by Dame Vera Lynn in front of a squadron of cheering servicemen in full uniform. An example of Van's deadpan sense of humour – the song is performed with great seriousness – and perhaps also a touch of homesickness tucked in there somewhere. 'Little Jimmy' returns from *Astral Weeks*, Van's childhood ghost.

In April, Morrison returned to San Anselmo to make an appearance with Jackie DeShannon, and it was now that rumours began to circulate about further live appearances and a joint album, like Kris Kristofferson and Rita Coolidge. As Van told Cameron Crowe for *Rolling Stone*, "There was never a duet album planned. There was no team up. There was nothing. The whole thing was just the magazines talking. They write about something they don't know anything about, just to make money. That's how these magazines exist." For all that, DeShannon opened for Van's four night engagement in May 1973 at the LA's Troubadour, a small venue whose media profile loomed disproportionately large.

Playing here was the exact opposite of burying yourself away in, say, San Anselmo. Sharon Lawrence reports Van as sounding "like Eric Burdon in his heyday", and "as relaxed as he ever will be". This from a performer who could also be "full of pain and so nervous it hurt to watch". Peter Jay Philbin reports an opening set by DeShannon, using Van's band and singing 'Santa Fe', the track she co-wrote with Van. Even more important, the opening night saw Van's first ever live appearance with a string section, in addition to six musicians who – with Platania, Labes and Schroer all on board – had now evolved into perhaps Morrison's greatest ever concert band. Van himself conducted the group from his microphone stand, while continuing to perform "as if a thick sheet of glass" surrounded him.

The *It Ain't Why, It Just Is* bootleg captures the same residency. From the first note the music is bright as a button, a band whose time had come. 'I've Been Working' ends with the injunction "hold back too much" and blowsy brass. Then a gentle swinging, and a fragmented rhythm for, of all things, 'Young Lovers Do'. The string section sit on top like cream on a rich trifle, then go off into their own world. The effect is still startling as it surges out of the speakers, like a complex musical quilt, with everything balanced and answerable to Van's voice. A perky version of 'Purple Heather' follows. Van's voice is infinitely tender, and the string section is straight from heaven, and the whole thing brings tears to the eyes. That timeless alchemy of an unashamedly male voice backed by a string quartet – the sour and the sweet – Elvis Costello and The Brodsky Quartet, The High Llamas, Bob Dylan's version of 'Hard Rain' in Tokyo. The kind of music to be buried to!

A functional 'Come Running', to draw breath, then back to *Astral Weeks* for 'Sweet Thing'. At last here is a live band who can match those studio cats, so quickly discarded. This is neither rock nor jazz, and certainly not jazz-rock, but a new amalgam, which swings and drives along, all at once. The guitar solo is ego-less, part of a musical conversation, along with Van's voice, which is flexible and light as an eel. The song ends with a meal-a-deux, the lovers dining on each other.

'Blue Money' is another jolly interlude, with vaudeville chorus, much like the album version. 'Green' is from the next LP, and there is no irony intended here. Van's voice cries, the guitar weeps, and strings sigh. 'Wild Night' is like a musical jigsaw, each piece fitting perfectly. The performance ends with a nine minute 'Caravan', in which the musicians get the chance to improvise, and Van effortlessly heightens and lowers the tension, and introduces the band – special emphasis on Jeff Labes. Then 'Cyprus Avenue' a song by now just like the Dead's 'Dark Star', or Richard Thompson's 'Night Comes In', or the whole set list of King Crimson in the early seventies, different every time. Here it is melancholy and wistful, and Van gets particularly tongue tied, with added wood blocks. He breaks through on the word "railroad", you briefly wonder why, then he backtracks to the full verse. Spine tingling, as are the strings behind "six white horses and a carriage" while a piano ripples upwards. The song has never sounded so haunted, with the lady a close cousin of John Keats' 'La Belle Dame Sans Merci'. Love and death. Van mentions England with genuine longing. Singer, audience and band end dissolved in laughter, after a succession of false endings.

David Bowie exhumed Them's 'Here Comes The Night' on 1973's *Pin-Ups*, an album of his favourite songs from the British Beat boom. Everyone from Bryan Ferry to John Lennon was recycling musical history, matched with a new seriousness in the rock weeklies, stuffed full of refugees from *Schoolkid's Oz* and the underground press. Typically perverse, Van covered two songs on his next album, one an Irish traditional air, the other originally sung by a foot high, green felt frog (with a man's hand up it).

John Platania told *Into The Music* that *Hard Nose The Highway* was recorded at a studio at the back of his house, high on a hill. "It was a great album to work on. It was very loose, he usually gave everybody free rein to play. He never wanted screaming guitars. He had a sound, he had a vision." For one song, 'The Great Deception', Van was literally on his back, recording it as he lay flat on the studio floor, to ease the pain. "He was singing on his back because he couldn't stand. He improvised, it was done off the top of his head, completely, even lyrically. The guide vocals, sixty maybe seventy per cent, was stream of consciousness, right off the top of his head. I think he redid some later on."

As Van himself told Ritchie Yorke, *Hard Nose The Highway* is the first album over which he exercised complete control, in a way never known by fashion puppets like The Clash. I saw the "White Riot" tour and my heart turned to stone, even if my senses pulsed. Van can trigger both pleasure centres. "As a concept for the album, I was just trying to establish how hard it was to do just what I do. Plus there were some lighter things on the other side of it. One side has a kind of hard feeling while the other is soft. That's just about the concept of the album." It was originally conceived as a double LP.

To quote a headline in an Irish daily newspaper, "Van Morrison gives childhood a big boost". Released in July 1973, *Hard Nose The Highway* folds out to show a symbolic and cosmic painting, Magritte on LSD, just like Miles Davis albums of the time. It is determinedly multi-cultural. A young Van squats on his haunches. Behind him the moon rises over green fields. Cut-out cattle show the stars shining through. An old Chinaman in a straw hat grasps his staff and looks up sightlessly to heaven, seagulls fly above and a strange shrouded figure – death? plague? – stands in front of distant cliffs and a calm sea.

Behind Van is the modern world, jumbled and chaotic, with winos, drug addicts and hookers outside a bar, two ancient disembodied heads looking the other way, and what could be either a fence or prison bars. At the top left, leading into infinity, the white lines of a highway can be seen. What it all means is beyond comprehension.

The band is virtually the LA concert line-up – Jeff Labes, Jack Schroer, John Platania – with the full string section, and added horns. Gary Mallaber remains on drums, and David Hayes comes in on bass. Backing vocals are shared between Jackie DeShannon and The Oakland Symphony Chamber Chorus. The latter appear on the opening track, 'Snow In San Anselmo'. Van told Yorke that it is "a sketch on when it snowed in San Anselmo. It's about the images that were happening when it was snowing there for the first time in thirty years." This hardly captures Van's vulpine howl, the atonal backing voices – just like Keith Christmas's equally creepy 'The Forest And The Shore' – the picture of a world whose energy has dripped away. A shorter 'Desolation Row'.

'Warm Love', a US Top Forty hit, is "just a boy and girl song, walking on the beach. It's a young song." I can't really add to that, except to note that this is a musical love affair, with the girl bringing her guitar. Now who mentioned Jackie DeShannon? My own mental picture to this song is the scene in *Zabriskie Point*, where the sand dunes are full of naked couples making love, just before the whole thing explodes and The Pink Floyd rock out. *Melody Maker* called it a "smashing single", while John Tobler for *Zigzag* thought it "a second cousin to 'Crazy Love' and nearly as good". Van sings near falsetto, and the tune is fragile and darting as a butterfly in flight.

'Hard Nose The Highway' is an oblique look at his career. Over to Van. "There's three things happening. The first verse is an image of Frank Sinatra going in the studio and saying 'Let's Do It'. He makes an album then walks out and takes a vacation. It's an image of professionalism. The second image is of Marin County. If you take something into a shop to be fixed and they say come back in a week, and you come back in a week and they say, 'I dunno man, that won't be ready for two months.' There's that kind of attitude in Marin County." It also seems to be a covert reference to The Grateful Dead, at a creative peak but also dicing with excess. The famous dead keyboard player syndrome, three down already, and all three can now jam with Garcia.

"The second verse is kind of being weary with the scene. I just can't get into that cult thing. The third verse is about record companies, promoters and all the business people in music. The theme running through the whole thing is 'Seen some hard times' which I definitely have." Van continues on the road, and it is soon to take him back to Belfast, though not to perform.

'Wild Children' – "war children" in the opening verse – brings together counter-cultural figures from the 1950s, Rod Steiger, Marlon Brando, James Dean and Tennessee Williams. Van has the power to make them into myth. "I think that 'Wild Children' kind of stands out in particular. For all of the kids born around that time, there was a heavier trip to conform. For example, uniforms at school. There's definitely been a whole breakthrough. Growing up in another country and getting our releases through figures from America, like the American anti-heroes. They were somebody representing something." Phased electric guitar, almost progressive rock, but with an underlying swing rather than a dismal thump. And Van's voice in this exercise in nostalgia is smooth and flowing as the river he evokes. Now I wonder where Bruce Springsteen got that idea from?

The hard side of the album closes on what Ritchie Yorke describes as "one of the most stinging indictments from any observer, let alone a rock artist". Van injects a bitterness I can only compare to Viv Stanshall's lines about Marc Bolan, "slick as a lithograph", sung with the loathing of an Old Testament prophet. This is Bob Marley's 'Babylon', a few years early. Morrison wrote the song having received a letter from a self styled revolutionary, asking for a sizeable donation. "I met this revolutionary guy. He came on to me like he was interested in the scene. He may have been legitimate. But I just don't like people who write you a friendly letter and then half way through ask you for a large sum of money, after calling themselves revolutionaries. That's where the song started from." He told Steve Peacock of *Sounds*, "That song is for all the phonies. Hollywood is just another of the illusion trips. Fantasy trips that just fit into the deception. A lot of people in Hollywood are into their own scene, and believe their own publicity."

But never Van, except when he writes it himself. 'Green' by Joe Raposo from *Sesame Street*, was written to be sung by Kermit the Frog, who also takes a cameo role in Spirit's *Future Games* musical maze. It must be remembered that rock stars watch a lot of daytime TV: Nick Salamon from *Bevis Frond* even appeared on *Countdown*, and won.

Van was also a father, which gives permission to watch kids' programmes without embarrassment. He saw the song as a "statement that you don't have to be flamboyant". Of course there are two underlying puns, being green is better than being "blue", ie sad, and green has long been associated with the Irish. Van has often been photographed as if he were an emanation of the woods, on *Astral Weeks* and *A Sense Of Wonder*. Perhaps he is a leprechaun – that would explain so much. An early anthem for the ecology movement, along with 'Big Yellow Taxi'. *Records And Recording* said a tad unkindly of this track that "even the kindest critic would call it a heap of slush". The *Melody Maker* thought it was "not a bad track, just strange", while for John Tobler "Green is the unifying factor of the record".

Rather an odd observation, as the next song opens with the colour brown. 'Autumn Song' rambles on for ten minutes, new age music early, like a film in slow motion. Post-modern, even. The chorus quotes the chords to Hendrix's 'Wind Cries Mary'. Van describes it as "just an ode to autumn", though Keats can sleep easy in his bed. We have gone through the seasons, and we are back to "Christmas of the night" at the end. One song to go, the timeless 'Purple Heather', which quite lacks the bite of the live version, more like a lullaby. It is a reworking of the traditional song 'Wild Mountain Thyme' as sung by Dylan at the 1969 IOW Festival. "I really dig the way we did it: it worked out well I think." An old song from the repertoire of the McPeake family, and Van's first foray into folklore. The whole of side two is mood music, unthreatening, tranquil, and the kind of sounds you'd like behind you when you are reading a book. This one will do fine!

Geoff Barron of *Melody Maker* finds the album themed by its use of colour, a paint box in words. He is prescient in picking out the words "let your inspiration flow", the major theme in Van's later work. Nick Kent in *NME* describes Van as the "finest male soul performer around". He also outdistanced Dylan when "both moved on to their separate forays into the realms of laid-back pastoral positivism". For Brian Hogg, though, "Van over-reached himself, unable to see his limitations".

The real venom came from, of all people, Ritchie Yorke. The hugely respected Charlie Gillett had commented in *Let It Rock* that "although the music is often interesting, it doesn't have a convincing emotional basis. The prevailing mood is of clean country air. Despite the lack of lyric inspiration and of melodic focus, the record is attractive to listen to." Fair comment, I reckon, but Yorke gets out his Mary Whitehouse impersonation: "The real sadness is that a tree had to be chopped down to provide the paper on which that review was printed. I would be ashamed to wrap my fish and chips in it."

Van seemed to agree, though. He told Cameron Crowe of *Rolling Stone*, just before setting off for Europe, that the album was already "long gone and totally in my past". He is not a rock 'n' roll musician, and never was. "I've made rock 'n' roll records, but then I've made jazz records and country and western records. They always want to give you a label." His only concern was to keep going, creatively. My only present is the gig tomorrow night, and the gig after that. That album doesn't have anything to do with my life or the way I live. It's just a record of old songs. Yet I'm sitting here talking to you to promote the album...which is already old. This whole business is just a game."

The album was released in Britain on 20 July 1973, to coincide with Van Morrison's first tour here since Them. Anticipation was near breaking point, about the hero's return home. One British magazine even called him "the Marlon Brando of rock 'n' roll". A mysterious recluse.

By now, The Caledonia Soul Orchestra had settled down to a steady line-up of guitarist John Platania, Jeff Labes on keyboards, Jack Schroer on saxophone, Bill Atwood on trumpet, bass player David Hayes ("borrowed" from Jesse Colin Young) and drummer Dahaud Shaar. There was a string quintet of Nathan Rubin, Tim Kovatch, Tom Halpin, Nancy Ellis – visually the focal point, with waist-length blonde hair swaying in time as she bent over her cello – and Terry Adams, scored by Jeff Labes. Platania reckoned later that "I would say that tour represented the height of Van's confidence as a performer. Up until then it was often touch and go as to whether he'd go on stage." The orchestra were almost constantly on the road for a year, hard nosing the highway through America, Europe, and back to the States.

As Ritchie Yorke wrote, "Gone were the nerves, the neurotic attacks of stage fright, the nightly fit of post-gig depression", all symptoms of a man who cared too much about his audience, not too little. "Christ, he was actually enjoying himself out there." The audience reaction was ecstatic, from the most committed fan to hardened journalists. This was one of those tours that forever affected anyone lucky enough to be in the audience. Sharing the presence of genius.

Michael Watts took in a July 1973 concert at the New York Philharmonic. "Morrison is essentially a craftsman rather than a showman, avoiding even eye contact with his audience and allowing them the luxury of few spoken words. That he achieves such a ridiculous empathy with them is due less to any outward show of personality than to the power of his music, always building, cutting instantly from one song to another, until the emotions are milked and squeezed to a head. Perhaps all said and done, he's the ultimate showman."

Watts talks about the "rapture" of the audience, and a "well nigh poetic experience". The *NME*'s Roy Carr took in the first European gig, at the Carre Theatre in Amsterdam. He compared Van favourably with Presley in Vegas and James Brown at the Apollo, couching his description in religious terms. "I bore witness to what I can only describe as a most incredible non-performance. Damn it, the man hardly moved on stage. I have to own up, never have I been so enthralled by such a premeditated lack of visual entertainment." Van exits, kicking his legs up in the air, "the most triumphant exit since Mohammed Ali blitzed Sonny Liston".

At a record company reception, Van passed through the scrum unnoticed. "A lotta people wanna catch me on an off day. If they succeed – it goes along with the myth." He asks after The Pretty Things. "David Bowie's only doing what Phil May used to do. He's just wearing different clothes."

In late July, Van started his British tour in Birmingham, then two nights at the Rainbow, Bristol, Manchester and Newcastle, followed by two nights at Dublin. The 'A' circuit. Richard Williams was in poll position for *Melody Maker*, and evokes the evening beautifully, with a detail he reserves for sports reports, nowadays.

"Birmingham Town Hall, jammed solid, bursts into relieved applause as the small, slightly tubby figure slides between members of the rhythm section and places himself between the saxophonist and the string quarter." First up is 'Blue Money', then the new single, 'Warm Love'. Bill Atwood and Jack Schroer play a "piquant muted-trumpet/alto sax line" as Van imitates Smokey Robinson. Between songs, Van stands immobile, left hand on the mike, right hand half way down the mike stand, rocking to and fro. He rides the music, keeping up the tension.

A slappy backbeat from Dave Shaar introduces Bobby Bland's 'Ain't Nothing You Can Do', "given a solid bar blues treatment, with big trumpet led riffs". Labes' Hammond organ solo brings back memories of Georgie Fame at the Flamingo. The string quartet comes in on 'Into The Mystic'. As Van sings about the foghorn blowing, a baritone sax answers him with a "deep, booming blare". Jeff Labes' "rhapsodic blues piano" provides an intro to Ray Charles' 'I Believe To My Soul'. "The stop-time breaks, leaving space for Van's vocals, are incredibly precise and dramatic." Van stands at the back of the stage, hands on hips, while his trumpeter takes an exuberant solo.

'These Dreams Of You' features Schroer on raucous alto-sax. Williams thinks he looks too young to produce such a mature sound. "The ghosts of a hundred Harlem jump altoists rise and applaud – and the angelically pretty blonde cellist smiles wide." 'I Just Wanna Make Love To You' is "slow, oozy, menacing funk, and Platania steps out of his normal role as provider of One Thousand And One Unforgettable Fill-Ins to take a stinging solo". The audience roar along lustily. 'Sweet Thing' is "a fleet six/eight swinger, the strings building soaring climaxes with the aid of Shaar's quicksilver drums, while Van plays tricky rhythmic games against them". Platania plays feelings rather than just notes, and the song settles into a steady four beats to the bar. To close the first half, Van reprises an old Them song, 'Friday's Child', "properly reticent".

During the interval, Van's microphone is moved off the eight foot high stage and onto the strip in front of the audience, so that he can communicate more intimately with his audience (though most now cannot see him!). Another Them epic, 'Here Comes The Night'. The audience start to let go during 'I've Been Working', featuring a jagged alto solo "shot through with sunshine", and a screaming coda. 'Listen To The Lion' is "misty and floating", 'Green' – he slips in a thank you "with all the professionalism of the hardened cabaret performer" – and a strutting 'Gloria'. The audience is on its collective feet, bellowing the chorus.

There is that adrenaline rush of a good Morrison concert, "the hall is ablaze with joy". A gale force 'Domino', then 'Brown Eyed Girl', which now features a startling acceleration into the second verse. Van slows the tempo right down for Sam Cooke's 'Bring It On Home To Me', and goes into some strange movements, including back bends. His voice begins to crack on a finger snapping 'Moondance', but he has been singing for an hour and a half by now.

"As he goes into 'Caravan', the atmosphere feels as if it's wired direct to a nuclear power station." The strings make a surprise entrance, "with an ethereal four part invention of great purity and logic". "Turn it up", and Van is sliding across the stage, bending and kicking his legs. The ensemble return for 'Cyprus Avenue', no longer tortured, a joke almost during the "tongue tied" segment. But when Van cuts the band dead, and waits for silence to drop, Williams' nerves are still stretched taut. "He holds the audience like a puppet master, delaying until we're ready to snap," then unleashes the command "it's too late to stop now". "The band crashes, he spins on his heel, and stalks off. It was all you could ever have wanted."

Steve Peacock interviewed Van at London's Europa Hotel, for *Sounds*, and got him to open up a little. As to his songwriting, "sometimes it's a stream of consciousness and other times it's about a certain thing". The latter now predominates, with real stories like 'The Great Deception'. Van has regained his taste for live action, but – as with his songwriting – strictly on his own terms. "I'm not going to wear circus clothes and jump around, I may stand still all night, not even move my little finger, or I may dive off the stage. There's no set pattern. This band can't do a canned show. We have to get off." How often does this happen? "Almost every night. Almost home runs, you know." Van and two of his musicians also spoke to "whispering" Bob Harris for BBC2's *Old Grey Whistle Test*. Van talked about a forthcoming live album, and some movie scores he was involved with. His answers are opaque as usual, guarded, terse. We are not talking about the Cockney wit here of Phil Collins, or the intellectual rigour of Bowie, Eno, Sting. More like a wary politician, guarding every word. John Platania gives the game away, though. "Contrary to popular belief he is having a good time."

Platania also told John Tobler about another factor behind The Caledonia Soul Orchestra, Ed Fletcher. "He's a spiritual advisor. He sort of keeps our heads up. He's a very up person, a positive person. He's also MC for the tour." Along with Fletcher, support act Al Stewart – just then turning from bedsitter images to songs steeped in European history – and a sell out audience, Steve Peacock was there at the Rainbow, for a gig which *Q* was to include in its list of the one hundred greatest ever. There was "a kind of electric anticipation in the air, a building pitch of excitement as the set built, a kind of freewheeling fever of joyous relief". Music which went "straight to your heart like a cannonball".

The Rainbow gig was broadcast live on Radio One and on BBC2. Andrew Bailey of the *Evening Standard* described the performance as being "preceded by an air of expectancy as heavy as that before a performance by Olivier or Nureyev". At one point, Shana toddled onto the stage, like one of Blake's holy children, and Van seemed almost to catch fire as he sang. Unburdened by any instrument, he conducted his Orchestra with brusque nods and direct eye contact, counterpoising new songs with forays into his rich past, Them songs and R&B stand-bys of the kind that had got The Monarchs through rough evenings a decade before. He even indulged in high kicks worthy of The Tiller Girls, and the occasional grin.

And yet the Colston Hall gig the next night was marred by bad sound, a cold audience and an inert band. "If the Rainbow was an electric storm, Bristol was smog, with an occasional flash. The whole thing felt slightly desperate." With someone who takes risks on stage like Morrison, this is an occupational hazard, the difference between real ale and canned beer, live but dangerous and prey to atmospherics. It's the price you have to pay.

"I was doing what I was doing when The Rolling Stones were still at school," Van told Roy Carr in *NME*. The music business is still "draining the thing dry. The same people are still in charge. They're just a little updated." His success has brought artistic freedom, as seen at the Rainbow. "I guess I've been one of the lucky ones – in spite of everything. Really, it was kinda like winning the football pools." Carr reminisces how the young Morrison "exuded a mystique of authenticity and aggro on stage". He was like a drunken docker spoiling for a fight. Everyone ran for cover. "There was so much vocal pain in his heart and fire in his belly...all the the animal kick of Tarzan suffering from a hernia. But with control, man. With control." An authority at the mike which the years have merely deepened.

The double album *Them Featuring Van Morrison* was released in November to cash in on Van's new popularity. Mitch Howard, also writing for *NME*, notes how Van develops from attacking his songs to working his way into them, and employing "his characteristic circular chord changes".

The Troubles in Ulster had intensified since 1969. The presence of British troops – originally sent in as a temporary measure, to separate the warring factions – had merely enflamed the situation, and provided target practice. The place was becoming Britain's Vietnam, a running sore with no solution in sight other than ultimate withdrawal, and that option was politically unacceptable. Already run down urban landscapes were further disfigured by bombs and random killings, partisan graffiti and forced internment, armoured patrols and frequent body checks. Ethnic cleansing was in progress, with the army as an unwanted third party, attacked by both sides. Seamus Heaney, an Ulster Catholic involved in the civil liberties movement in the late 1960s, had written directly about these ancient tribal blood rites in his book-length poem *North* before himself escaping the massacre, moving south to Dublin. He was part of a new generation of Irish poets – from both religious communities – who dealt with the Troubles through history, myth and folklore.

Van Morrison rarely alluded directly, either in songs or interviews, to the civil war that had engulfed his birthplace. His music was an implicit defence of love and peace, the voice of Woodstock nation (no armed patrols or kneecappings there). Like James Joyce or Samuel Beckett, he had chosen exile, cunning and silence. Nevertheless, the psychic death of his native land darkly shadowed his work, and made evocations of a paradise glimpsed in childhood unbearably poignant.

Back in America, Morrison played two concerts at the aptly named Shrine Auditorium in Los Angeles, a venue associated with Ray Charles. He upped the quotient of blues covers, and dressed like a rocker in black leather. It was here that the "Marlon Brando of rock" tag was first attached to him.

On 20 October, Van and an unnamed girlfriend travelled to the Irish Republic for a short holiday. Arriving without publicity or fuss, they checked into the Sutton House Hotel, a converted mansion overlooking Dublin Bay. The cover photograph for *Veedon Fleece* was taken then and there, just as all eight of its songs were written during this brief period. Van spent some time filming in Belfast, revisiting the places of his childhood: Hyndford Street, Cyprus Avenue, Orangefield School. Back in the Republic, he hired a car, and took off into the depths of the countryside, visiting Cork, Killarney, and Arklow, even kissing the Blarney Stone. He told a reporter it was "good" to be back in Ireland. Van looked up old friends, watched a few showbands, and taped a two hour show for RTE's *Talk About Pop* in Dublin, performing solo on guitar.

The half hour actually broadcast – and since wiped – provoked an uproar. Even its producer claimed that the programme was "dreadful television and unforgivable rudeness on Morrison's part. It wasn't even clever." Morrison strummed his guitar to drown out interviewer Tony Johnston, and literally turned his back on him. Van had been granted full artistic freedom, only to produce a shambles. The musical scraps that have survived are still of interest, though. Van bashes out an early version of 'Mechanical Bliss' on the grand piano provided, then the tune turns into a magical version of 'Snow In San Anselmo'. Even better is the otherwise unreleased 'Drumshanbo Hustle', a funny but bitter tirade against the music industry. The town in question was where Morrison once played with a showband, and was ripped off. Music undertaken as a career is a form of prostitution:

> *They were trying to muscle in*
> *On the recording and publishing*
> *Oh you were puking up your guts*
> *When you read the contract you had signed.*

The song also seems to allude to the divorce from Janet, going through as Van toured Europe. Marriage is a different form of contract, and more easily broken.

> *I was talking to the judge just before we left the countryside*
> *Paper in his hand trying to find a way, going by the book*
> *Rip the pages out before we bring the final curtain down.*

Van also talked about being asked to appear in a film about Irish rock musicians. He had caused much upset when he had cancelled two shows at Dublin's Carlton Theatre, with only a few days' warning, though later explained that he had never known about the concerts in the first place. By way of recompense, in December *Sounds* announced that Van had agreed to play four concerts in Dublin that spring, as part of a week long musical festival, along with The Chieftains, Tim Hardin, jazzers Humphrey Lyttleton and Ronnie Scott, with Elmer Bernstein conducting the RTE Symphony Orchestra. All future career directions.

Van flew back home, and reassembled The Caledonia Soul Orchestra to record this new Irish material. Two other themed projects were in progress, a country and western album – with songs like 'Wild Side Of Life', 'Crying Time' and 'Banks Of The Ohio' laid down but never released – and a Christmas project. "We tried to do it last year, but we were under too much pressure. You have to start making a Christmas album on 1 January, if you want to get it out. We'll probably do a few original songs, and some of the old things like 'White Christmas' and that thing 'Chestnuts roasting on an open fire'. All that romantic stuff."

With a broken marriage behind him, Van was finding fresh inspiration in the landscape of his youth, as the beautiful and mysterious *Veedon Fleece* would signify. The years of self imposed exile were over. As years went on, Morrison was to pay increasing attention to his own Irish heartbeat.

It's Too Late To Stop Now, a double album drawn from concerts at the LA Troubadour, Santa Monica's Civic Auditorium and the Rainbow, was released in February 1974. The front cover: Van looks angelic, lit in blue, looking down as if in a trance; the first "o" of his surname has become a four pointed star, illuminating the stage. Behind him a shrouded figure plays violin. On the back, Van is picked out in red, a devil now, eyes closed, grasping the microphone, effortlessly powerful, a dead ringer for Captain Beefheart.

There are no overdubs: what you hear is exactly as it happened. The record also doubles as a "greatest hits" compilation, a series of live snapshots as to where Van now was in his career. He described the album as "basically a re-statement. It's just that a lot of these songs come off better live. They're different anyway, when done live. Basically it's interpretations of the songs: a lot of them are better than my original records. Songs do mature with age, I think." Because of the refusal to allow overdubs in the studio (the bane of so many "live" albums, the occasional dud note being all part of the roughness of on stage mayhem), 'Moondance' was omitted. It had a wrong guitar note. "Van has a sense of black and white about things like this," his business manager Stephen Pillster explained. "So it really was an absolutely honest live album, perhaps the first ever."

It is a wonderful distillation of a tour which Myles Palmer of the *Times* had described as demolishing "all barriers between the soul, blues, jazz and rock genres. The ensemble playing was simply the most sophisticated and unusual I have heard in a decade of continuous exposure to pop." For *Record Mirror*, Van was "*the* voice of rock 'n' roll". For Robin Denselow of the *Guardian* "it was a tense, thrilling and emotional night, for Morrison has become arguably the finest white blues singer in the world".

The album recreates a typical concert, picking out the plums, and parcelling them into four suites. The CD reissue is a double, full price job lot, so many of us stick with the vinyl version, which does seem to capture the rich fullness of the live sound, un digitalised.

Side one opens with Bobby Bland's 'Ain't Nothing You Can Do', Van in full shout and a brassy, leery sound with curt Chicago blues guitar. A song of despair and masochism, under its punchy surface. Its emotional and musical opposite, 'Warm Love' has Stax horns and Steve Cropper-like guitar, with Van's vocals staccato and effortlessly proud. Strings float ethereally behind 'Into The Mystic'. A piano tinkles like a fountain, joined in the crystalline mix by wah-wah guitar and harmony brass. Through headphones, you are centre seat, front row. The bass duets with Morrison's so flexible voice, "Just want to rock your jelly roll soul". The sacred and the profane, *Astral Weeks* and *Blowin' Your Mind*, all as one. Back to *Moondance* again for 'These Dreams Of You', driven by David Hayes on bass, over whom Van extemporises, a piano flutters like a butterfly, and saxophones go crazy. The mention of Ray Charles prompts a cover of one of his songs, 'I Believe To My Soul'. The strings come in again, a touch of heaven, the rhythm speeds up, slows, changes round, and Van emotes masterfully, between the peremptory strut of the brass riff and the swoon and swirl of the violins. Music so self confidant it could talk, and the sax break almost does. Massive applause follows, just to remind you that there is an audience present.

Side two opens with 'I've Been Working' off *His Band And Street Choir*, with the same glorious rush as Ian Dury And The Blockheads a few years on, those same hyperactive keyboards. Van sounds so happy, doing what he likes best. He is curt and almost threatening on Sonny Boy Williamson's 'Help Me', then relaxes into verbal improv, along with the odd soul grunt. 'Wild Children' was, according to its composer, "a killer, it's much better than the version on *Hard Nose The Highway*. When we recorded that song, we weren't really into it. I'd just written the tune. Ideally you should take a song on the road for a couple of months and live with it for a while." There is a greater sense of longing in Morrison's voice, with a rich textural backing. Platania sounds like Pete Banks from early Yes – when they were still trying to play music – there is the same gentle jazz swing and melodic intrigue. The song sounds weightier, more like a Hollywood epic, just as the arrangement takes on a widescreen sweep. The song seems not so much as to stop as to start again, like an endless circle. 'Domino' is full of itself, taken fast, rhythmic yet tuneful, with the percussive drive of a quick march. "Just want to hear some rhythm and blues music on the radio", and next up is just that, Willie Dixon's 'I Just Want To Make Love To You'. Van testifies like a preacher, pees on Jagger's cover version, and the edginess in his voice is doubled on electric slide guitar, its spookiness worthy of Ry Cooder himself. The string section is almost Moorish, like Led Zeppelin's 'Kashmir'. "Heart of stone," Van rasps, a desperate man.

Side three opens with another cover, Sam Cooke's 'Bring It On Home'. Morrison sounds fragile, then pleading, then anguished. He shouts out "Jack", as if seeking help, and Schroer takes over in the same vein, but wordless. Van thanks him, then adopts a West Indian accent, then wails. A psycho drama, with the pace of a funeral. Straight into 'St Dominic's Preview', with complex strings and Van singing his private words urgently. Hammond organ, like a slow Chinese burn. 'Listen To The Lion' ends in holy quiet. Bob Woffinden writes of "a beautiful cadence, which leaves the audience in a hushed state of perceptible awe". It has the impact of prayer, somehow even more intimate than the studio take. Van's voice takes on the quality of a man talking softly but very intently, so that you have to bend forward to catch each word. The singer and his musicians are in deep communion here, the aural equivalent of making love. Conversely, the barked demands for "water" are like the final request of a dying man.

The final side opens with a medley of Them's "greatest hits": 'Here Comes The Night' is heartfelt and sprightly, 'Gloria' punchy, with Van like a cat on a hot tin roof. 'Caravan' is much longer than the album version, but still without an ounce of spare fat. A beautiful string arrangement comes in at the end, measured, restrained, like a gavotte, as Van introduces the band. 'Cyprus Avenue' is the only possible finale, and starts with him almost throwing the words away. There is a lightness of touch to the backing, Jeff Labes' keyboards in particular, which is truly breathtaking. Hear instruments laugh, just like human beings, and then strings come in crying for the "rainbow ribbons in her hair" section, with a shimmering beauty that touches the soul. Van sings "in all your revelation" like a man granted a vision which robs him of coherent speech, repeating it over and over again, and then we are into the customary stop-start ending, with shouts and gasps from the audience and Van slurring his words lecherously. Mass applause.

The BBC Rainbow broadcast contained three songs not present on the final album: 'Brown Eyed Girl', 'Moonshine Whiskey' and 'Moondance', while RTE added two others, 'I Paid The Price' and 'Wild Night'. *It's Too Late To Stop Now* was originally intended as a three album set, an album of Grateful Dead proportions. Its American pressing comes in a sumptuous three piece sleeve, with extra colour photos of Van and his orchestra. A proper CD reissue would include the extra tracks from the Troubadour that were claimed by one bootlegger as official out-takes, and more shots from the well documented tour. Hell, I'd offer to do it myself. The BBC Rainbow broadcast could also be resurrected on video. After all, we are talking about one of the greatest rock 'n' roll concert tours, up with Dylan 66 and Marley 75 and early Springsteen, or U2's Zoo TV, or Primal Scream when they discovered Muscle Shoals, or REM when Stipe started shaving his head.

Even as it stood, the double album drew rave reviews. Steve Peacock of *Sounds* recalled an amazing night at the Rainbow, "halfway between an intimate club session and a spectacular soul revue". Van always injects a strong emotional charge, and the music here effortlessly transports the listener back to the concert hall. The album achieves "the drive and pace of an exceptional live show, with spontaneity tempered by thoughtful and subtle touches usually the result of careful work in the studio". In *Melody Maker*, Geoff Barron notes how Van has the magical ability to make time stand still. "The feedback across the footlights between artist and audience is almost tactile." Bob Woffinden wrote in *NME* that "his timing is immaculate and his rapport with an excited audience is the kind of thing that makes this album worth ten times what Warner Brothers are asking for it".

In February, the *NME* published Ritchie Yorke's interview with Van, who chose five desert island discs: *The Best Of Ray Charles*, an album of Renaissance vocal music, *Astral Weeks*, a record by Shakey Jake, and the as yet unheard *Veedon Fleece*. That same month, another European tour was announced, following hard on the release of *It's Too Late To Stop Now* on 18 March. Dates were announced for the Colston Hall, Bristol – on 21 March – and at the Sundown Edmonton, Manchester Free Trade Hall, Glasgow Apollo and Birmingham Town Hall. These were all major provincial venues, though the lack of a gig in central London seemed odd. Van and The Caledonia Soul Orchestra would then move on to Dublin, Paris, Munich, Brussels, Copenhagen and Amsterdam.Just as well that Van was starting to "dig travelling a lot – for its own same, rather than working". Pre-tour publicity named the whole she-bang the Van Morrison Show, mentioned "string and vocal sections", and announced that the CSO would open with their own instrumental section, as well as backing Morrison, who would himself first play a short solo acoustic set.

The Soul Orchestra had gone through some major changes. The *Veedon Fleece* sessions captured a band in transition, with guitarist John Platania already gone, replaced by Ralph Wash. (His name receives an "l" on *Veedon Fleece*). Bassist David Hayes and drummer Dahaud Shaar, remained for the new tour, but saxophonist Jack Schroer had been replaced by James Rothermel Jr (another escapee from the Jesse Colin Young band) and Jeff Labes succeeded on keyboards by James Trumbo. Trumpeter Bill Atwood was dropped, as was the string section. Van himself was now playing harmonica and saxophone. One of the greatest rock combos had not even lasted long enough to promote the live album which established its majesty. The new, stripped down combo was soon re-christened The Caledonia Soul Express.

John Platania told the *Van Morrison Newsletter* the sad news about the original *Band And Street choir* bassist John Klingberg. "He started to get really far out, as far as drink and everything. He died a few years ago. He died from too much drink. He was into drugs, so was Schroer." What had happened to "Brother" Jack. "He stopped playing and he couldn't keep up with things. As far as I know he is driving trucks, which is something he always loved. He is in the South West someplace driving a truck." Van later tried to reintegrate Schroer into a later line-up, but "Jack couldn't keep up and he was phased out".

The only evidence to what was going on musically lies in a rough tape of a Cambridge, Massachusetts gig from 14 March. Van revisits his old home, and many of his old songs, in a set list which sounds breathtaking. The first four songs alone comprise three lesser performed items from *Astral Weeks*, 'Ballerina', the title track and 'Madame George', intersected by 'The Streets Of Arklow' from the forthcoming album. When I die, I want to hear those same four songs, live with the original Caledonia Soul Orchestra, in its full pomp. It will almost be worth the trip! Back in this world, and in Cambridge, Mass, there is another new song, 'What's Up Crazy Pup', and a cover version of 'Caledonia', the two sides of the single, as well as retreads of the likes of 'Brown Eyed Girl', 'Moondance', 'Caravan' and 'Gloria'.

The problem is that after the icy perfection of the Rainbow concerts, this is musically amateur hour. The backing band sound thin and uncommitted – nothing short of a disgrace after the miracles of the year before. Wash's guitar runs are anonymous, Rothermel's flute and saxophone forced and out of tune, and Trumbo's keyboards dull. Even Van fails to rise to the occasion, and there is an awful sense of a band dragging itself along, going through the motions. Like a recently "downsized" firm, with those workers who survive struggling to fill in for absent colleagues. Perhaps Morrison's sickness soon after was psychosomatic, realising that whether through accident or design the heart had been ripped out of his enterprise, so recently the greatest live act in the world. There is an emptiness at the core, which one cannot solely blame on the poorness of the tape quality.

That said, Ritchie Yorke reports a "stupendous three encore performance" at the Capitol Theatre in Passaic, New Jersey on 17

March. Stephen Pillster talked about how "we had a certain momentum happening coming out of the States and everyone was really looking forward to those British dates. Then a day after we arrived, Van came down with the flu and a hundred and four degree fever, and we had no choice but to cancel out the first few dates." All those on the British mainland, for a start.

Such was the sense of disappointment that *NME* felt obliged to print Van's sick note on their front page. A Dr Hughes MCRS LRCP reports that he was called in to see Mr Morrison on 21 March, "when he had collapsed and retired to bed with a high fever. This man had a previous bout of fever when in Hawaii, three weeks earlier." The patient had returned to full activity before being fully recovered, and "in my opinion he will not be able to resume his occupation for several days". Is this Little Feat's 'Rock 'N' Roll Doctor'? David Hayes reckons "Van got a blood virus or something, it really hit him over the head".

Van certainly sounds feverish in an interview with Steve Peacock in *Sounds*: "I'm just a stand-up singer, and that's what it comes down to, and I'm also a poet and a musician." Does not his greatest artistry lie in writing, and stage work merely repetition? "If you're just a poet, but even then. Stage is much more creative. You can do both. If you just let it loosen up a bit it comes together a lot more."

Van had just about recovered when he played the small thousand seater Olympia Theatre in Dublin on 29 and 30 March, a Victorian masterpiece "all milky glass and swirling iron lattice work", more used to classical music than rock. Geoff Brown was there for *Melody Maker*, and noticed how many of the audience had hitched down from Belfast. Prominent in the front stalls was Christy Brown, author and subject of the film *My Left Foot*. Morrison clings onto the mike stand "as a stumbling man grasps a steadying arm". He opens with 'Astral Weeks' – what else? – but he is "singing in rapid-word-groups, each phrase followed by a painful swallow. He sings another phrase, head down, eyes stare from beneath raised eyebrows, furrowing his brow." He leaves the stage, while The Soul Express fill in with an instrumental 'Moondance'. Van returns with 'Ain't Nothing You Can Do', ironic in the circumstances, and somehow fights his way through an hour of music, including 'Into The Mystic' and 'Here Comes The Night'. Ed Fletcher comes on stage to apologise for Van's being ill, then back the man himself comes to encore with 'Come Runnin'' and 'Gloria'.

The second performance that night is far more relaxed. The Soul Express come on first, and play an instrumental set for about half an hour, tunes like 'Funky Hinkel', 'Orbital Transport', and McCoy Tyner's 'Song For The New World'. They have the same ambience as Tom Scott's LA Express, who backed Joni Mitchell's odyssey into jazz at much the same time. As an article in the *Van Morrison Newsletter* points out, The Soul Express are more of a pure jazz outfit than the Orchestra. Hayes appears to lead them from the back, and Wash's guitar solos are a constant delight. A short interval, then Van is on stage, in better voice and his phrasing more adventurous. He runs through 'Warm Love', 'Moondance' and 'Domino', then duets on alto with Rothermel for Fleecie Moore's 'Caldonia'.

Saturday's two performances are stronger still. On 'Moondance', Van "stops time, holds it suspended like a mesmeric silver ball held by thin string so that an hour has passed like a minute". On 'Help Me', Van's harmonica solo "boils to a belting crescendo and is then cut off as though an axe has fallen on it". 'Into The Mystic' again features Morrison and Rothermel duetting on saxophones, which purr "as though a hundred miles away and carried on a warm sea breeze". The band's smiles are blinding. The second set climaxes on a unique rendition of 'Listen To The Lion', but each performance of a largely duplicated set list is completely different. Here they are redefined in the "relaxing afterglow of an emotionally draining experience". The evening ends with a fracas – a bottle hurled by drunks in the balcony narrowly misses the road crew – and with Fletcher and Pillster taken off by the Gardia for questioning. Van himself had said nothing to the crowd except "thank you", leaving communication to the songs, "his voice searing to the point of pain, like volcanic lava pelting into your ears".

Questioned by Ritchie Yorke before going down with flu, Morrison reveals, "I'm just writing like a madman. I do so much I'm sort of caught." He is looking forward to two bookings at the Montreux Jazz Festival, one a jazz concert, the other a blues show, both scheduled to be recorded. He has also been invited to appear with the Denver Symphony Orchestra. He is also planning a book of poems and lyrics, and the release of *Veedon Fleece*, complete apart from a couple of remixes. Meanwhile, a less welcome release is *TB Sheets*, the title track of which seems oddly in keeping with Van's feverish performances in Dublin. Reviewing the album in *Melody Maker*, Michael Watts notes – almost with second sight – how Van's "poetic muse wings its way amongst the Gaelic mysteries, and lends his music a rare, unspecified eloquence quintessentially Irish". The keynote of his next official album.

Morrison flew on to Europe. During a return show at the Carre, Amsterdam, he stood centre stage with his acoustic guitar, Rothermel to his right on flute and Wash seated on a stool beside him, on acoustic guitar. 'Listen To The Lion', 'Almost Independence Day' and 'Astral Weeks' appeared in a set that included an outstanding 'It's All Over Now Baby Blue' and a surprise encore of 'My Lonely Sad Eyes'. While still in Holland, he recorded a new single, "a rhythm and blues thing called 'Caledonia'. 'Mixed Up Crazy Pup' is on the B-side." It was later claimed that Van wanted to see how quickly an artist could get out a single, and the band had emerged from the studio with mixed masters in six and a half hours. Enough time to record a whole album in the early 1960s.

The A-side was a cover version, with a slight change of title, of Louis Jordan's 'Caldonia (What Makes Your Big Head So Hard)', written by Fleecie Moore. Jeff Ward reviewed it for *Melody Maker*. "Great soul swing from one of the true great artists of our time. Heck of a lot of good feeling and good party humour packed into just a couple of minutes. A fine lift in the sax solo – is that the mastermind himself squirming over the bass lines. A slice of the real thing."

Van now returned to compress his cancelled British tour into two nights at the Hammersmith Odeon. Bob Woffinden of *NME* noted how the band looked "strangely insubstantial", but that they powered through a set that included 'Astral Weeks', a wonderful 'Madame George' – "three acoustic guitars and an insistent piccolo produced some beautiful gossamer sounds" – and Dylan's 'It's All Over Now Baby Blue'. "You get the impression that he probably folds his shirt up neatly before having sex. Where technical expertise and precision is something that he achieves with a stunning ease, unbridled zestfulness and passionate intensity are qualities that come unnaturally." Well, I wouldn't even *claim* to know! Watching the same concert, Martin Hayman of *Sounds* loved Morrison's guitar on 'Cyprus Avenue', "terse, flamenco like runs", while Michael Watts found "a conviction, expertise and authority not seen too often outside the best black roadshows".

Van sacked The Caledonia Soul Express as soon as the tour was over. 'There was nothing else to do within that particular context," he later explained. David Hayes told it his way to the *Van Morrison Newsletter*. "Van wanted to get out of Dodge for a while, so he split the band and went his way to explore new ideas. We said what the hell, let's play on." Platania talks of co-writing songs with Van like 'Family Affair' and 'There, There, Child', recorded but still gathering dust in the vaults. The new Caledonia Express recorded an album's worth of music, and were immediately offered a three album deal. In their naivety, they held out for more money, and the project foundered. As did the band. Van's Caledonian years were over for good.

CHAPTER SIX

Drifting

The next few years saw Van apparently lost and restless, recording all kinds of music only to refuse it commercial release, experimenting with different line-ups and largely disappearing from public view. His life seemed to be in some kind of turmoil, post divorce, and musically he turned his back on the creative pinnacle represented by The Caledonia Soul Orchestra, indulging himself in free flowing improvisation and songs which seemed to deliberately avoid the emotional depths and formal ambition of the, as yet, unreleased *Veedon Fleece*.

In June, he played the Lion's Share with his smallest band ever, the club's piano tuner John Allair on organ and drummer Steve Mitchell. It was "another chapter" he told the audience, and after a forty-five minute set by the duo – with Allair playing bass pedals with his feet, soloing with one hand and playing rhythm with the other – Van joined them for a set which included 'Rock Me Baby' and Lenny Welch's 'Since I Fell For You'.

Todd Tolces noted how, when Van played harmonica "he not only shook the harp, the mike, the stand and his entire body, but the stage vibrated beneath his feet while the ripples from altered air passageways floated through the PA over the bar and across the floor where dumbfounded fans listened in awe". Van announced that this line-up was to play Montreux, but it was not to be.

He was feeling the tug of homesickness. He told one reporter in May that he was "trying to get a soccer team together in the States, just for a lark". So this is why he was practising high kicks in concert, he was training for Wembley glory. "I had a short wave radio. There was just one place in the valley where you could get the BBC. I guess if you're brought up in Britain it's something you have to hear."

By the time he got to Montreux, at the end of June, Van had also ditched his manager Stephen Pillster and his band, arriving only with his girlfriend Carol Guida, described at the time as his "fiancee", and who had also shared his Irish trip. Ritchie Yorke gives a tantalising glimpse into the private scenes which had led to this impasse: "Few Van Morrison gigs are without their attendant backstage traumas, though his performance regularly wipes out the memory of whatever internecine strife has preceded it."

As to Pillster, "he just stopped doing what I wanted". The idea of a gig with the Denver Symphony had also dropped by the wayside. "It would just mean another rock singer had done something with a symphony orchestra. I've done the trip with strings already anyway. It's hard for me to do all that showbiz stuff." He had made a conscious decision, like Peter Gabriel in leaving Genesis: 'I was feeling part of the scenery. I had to get out from the machinery." He had "reached the point where I don't want to deal with those people. If it means I do less in my career, if I may fall short in some of my artistic spheres, then that's what'll happen."

Morrison played with a pick-up band at Montreux, a line-up slimmed down to the bone. Van himself handled acoustic guitar, alto sax and harmonica, with English bluesman Pete Wingfield – who had played with Blue Horizon signings Jellybread – on keyboards, black bassist Jerome Rimson from The Detroit Emeralds, and Dallas Taylor, once of CSNY and here with Bill Wyman, on drums. Taylor was soon replaced by English sessionman Peter Van Hooke.

Wingfield said that the band was put together almost by accident. He had originally been booked as part of a house band backing the likes of Muddy Waters and Buddy Guy, but they brought their own musicians, so at short notice he agreed to help out Montreux organiser Claude Knobs by backing Morrison. On the plane out to Switzerland, he met Rimson and Van Hooke, fellow members of The Olympic Runners, and eventually Rimson and Taylor joined Van as well. They found Morrison easy to work with, without huge musical charts for his backing musicians. "Basically he just either sings it or strums it on the guitar and just shouts out chord changes and we fill in the gaps. It was the easiest getting together of a set I've ever done."

At Montreux, the band operated somewhere between blues and jazz, lots of improvised instrumentals, and only 'Street Choir' previously released on vinyl. Only 'Bulbs' is featured from his latest recorded project, *Veedon Fleece*, and Van seems to have somehow cut loose from his history, drifting in search of land. The opening number, 'It's Not The Twilight Zone' has long, slow chords, and Van singing as if straight from his unconscious, and growling "honeycomb" or is it "heart of gold", over and over again. One of his spookiest performances, as befits a song which alludes to a fifties TV precursor to *The X Files*, a mutant version of Dylan's 'Leopardskin Pillbox Hat', if I hear the words right.

> *The carport took over, you left it ajar,*
> *You know I caught you before you went too far,*
> *But don't let it freak you when it gets to the bone,*
> *It's not the twilight zone*
> *It's just a party phone, honeycomb.*

'I Like It Like That' is a blues, with words that barely make sense, though "I don't want to be alone" certainly does. With electric piano predominant and its loose jazz vibe, this could be The Youngbloods with a deeper voiced singer, or played slightly too slow.

'T For Texas' is even more relaxed, a yet slower blues, and the story of Van's musical history. "I've been listening to this music ever since the age of three." He wants "a plain drink of water" – *Moondance* all over again – and an ice cream with a cherry on top. A song about "waiting for the summer rain", quintessential Van. Next up is 'Bulbs', Van on rhythm guitar and the bass like an electric *Astral Weeks*, probing, playing arabesques against Morrison's driven vocals. Then there is some tuning up, and into 'Buffy Flow', a saxophone instrumental in a minor key, paced like a slow lament and oddly touching.

'Heathrow Shuffle' is far more animated, another saxophone led instrumental, while 'Naked In The Jungle' is genuinely animated, with chorded, Chinese style piano and driving bass, and nonsense words. 'Street Choir' is a strange song to reprise, drums led and taken at a slow, stately pace, like a hymn. There is real sadness in Morrison's voice. After some al fresco piano – as if the band are waiting for inspiration – and an untitled harmonica instrumental, and before the final track, there is some booing, and a lady in the front row suggests that he go home and leave the blues to black people. Van responds in cold anger. "If you don't like it go fuck yourself, okay. There's a guy paying me to stand on this stage, and that's what I'm doing. If you don't like it, do you want to come up on stage and do it?" Wingfield busks on piano, like a silent movie. Van draws breath. "Do you want to come up here and do it? The only blues that you know are on your shoes." Does he mean sole music? As if in retaliation, Van goes into a frenetic take of the R&B standard 'Since I Fell For You'. The line "You, you, you, you...will never see the light" seems particularly apt, especially the way that he sings the word "you" like a knife stabbing.

Backstage, Ed Fletcher pointed out "they can't expect him to keep on singing 'Domino' for the rest of his life". Ritchie Yorke asked Van if he had made a conscious decision to drop his older repertoire. "I don't think anything is the be all and end all. I don't know what's happening. I'm just the same as everybody else. Sometimes it doesn't bother me in the least doing all that old stuff, and other times it does. It all depends on how it feels. I am definitely not a programmed performer. I can only perform when I feel like I want to perform and it's coming out of me." As to the charge of seeming not to bother about those who have come to see him, "I think I care too much about what the audience thinks". Afterwards, Van sat in the sunshine, reading Jean-Paul Sartre and Francis Schaeffer's *Escape From Reason*.

Heidelberg was the best German show: "We played for two and a half hours there." While in Europe, the quartet cut an album in one afternoon and two evenings – shades of *Astral Weeks* – all new material. Wingfield: "He'll suddenly say, 'Oh and I've got this other song' and reel off about nine verses. I can never quite tell when he's improvising and when he isn't because the words are always pretty individual, to say the least." Van himself reveals that on 16 July, he and the band had entered an Amsterdam studio, and recorded an album to be called *Naked In The Jungle/Mechanical Bliss*. It included an instrumental co-written with Wingfield. "I'm really happy with this one that we just cut. We just went in and did it the way it should be. Nobody messed about." The musical content is everything, "like blues and jazz, R&B". A whole album's worth of material, destined to be lost in the vaults.

Van later played rough tapes of some of this material on Tom Donahue's KSAN radio, claiming that they were ready for final mixing as his album after next, and that he now intended to take some time off for himself. He regales the laid back Donahue with two versions of 'Mechanical Bliss' and 'Not The Twilight Zone' sung falsetto in the key of C, which sounds like a masterpiece here, no problem, dragged out like a last man's dying breath, and then Van chuckles. The lyrics are barely audible but deal with reaping what you sow. 'Much Binding In The Marsh' is a cheerful sax instrumental which takes its name from a late fifties BBC radio comedy, and would make a good theme tune. Van tells Donahue that he gave up the saxophone to concentrate on his singing, but has been playing seriously for the last year. The sound is of fifties jazz, almost early John Coltrane, pre "sheets of sound". Naked In The Jungle' has an odd chorus about "freaking out". 'Foggy Mountain Top' is "back to the blues" and is much like Dylan's 'It Takes A Lot To Laugh, It Takes A Train To Cry', with references to going up on Highway One. It is the same song as that labelled 'T For Texas' at Montreux.

'Mechanical Bliss' itself was later issued as the B-side of 'Joyous Sound' in 1977, and is totally bizarre. Van sounds like Jesus, "they strike me for what I believe in", then takes on an English colonial voice, while the music plays the galloping major. Carruthers of the Foreign Office gains a mention, and there is a *Goons Show*, silly ass element, with funny rhymes though Van also croons like Caruso. The whole thing is like a Viv Stanshall spoof, without the quick humour. "Getting in and getting out." The lines about a "flick of the switch" and talking in a lisp suggest that this could be an ode to upper class buggery. On the other hand it could be a riposte to the heckler in Montreux. Things end with Rob Wyatt-like word salad, burbling in tongues. "Okay Chaps, step up a lip."

Four tracks "live in America" 1974 – 'Twilight Zone', 'Foggy Mountain Top', 'Heathrow Shuffle' and 'Naked In The Jungle' – are included on the *It Ain't Why It Just Is* bootleg CD, and sound suspiciously close to the Montreux versions.

Van claimed that he no longer recorded constantly because he just ended up with a studio full of tape. He also hinted that his version of 'Just Like A Woman' from Pacific High would be released sometime in the future on an album called *Highlights*, along with a live performance with John Lee Hooker. By the time of the Bremen gig on 10 July, Peter Van Hooke was firmly in the drum seat. Two songs survive from the "Musik Laden" show. Van, oddly Germanic in glasses and brown leather jacket, plays saxophone on 'Heathrow Shuffle' (looking wonderfully bad tempered), then sings 'Bulbs'. It is wonderful evidence of how he can inspire and drive on his musicians, without seeming even to notice them: the tension flying between the four intent figures is palpable. Music as serious as your life. For all that, in a highly comic moment, Van's microphone falls off its perch, and the camera switches to Wingfield, who improvises a falsetto vocal. Back to Van and a microphone back in its place. Pure Fawlty Towers. Then Van roars like a lion, the band burn behind him, and the meaningfully nonsensical words – "street lights all turn baby blue" – seem to explain the universe.

The same band played an open air concert at Knebworth on 20 July – only their third show together – entitled "the bucolic frolic". Early press releases had headlined Led Zeppelin, the new Mahavishnu Orchestra with Jean Luc Ponty, and "the full Van Morrison Show with The Caledonia Express". By the time of the concert, Led Zeppelin had dropped out and the billtoppers were The Allman Brothers, with The Doobies and Alex Harvey added to the bill. Opening before noon, when half the audience was yet to arrive – or come to consciousness – Tim Buckley made his last appearance in Britain, a sparkling set drawing largely on *Greetings From LA* and captured on the *Return Of The Starsailor* bootleg. *Sounds* discerned that "Buckley's aims seem similar to those of Van Morrison – creating a whole sound structure from a position somewhere between rock 'n' roll and jazz improvisation. Morry was going to have go some way to beat the impact Tim was getting." This must be the only time that Van has ever been nicknamed "Morry". It was not a name that has since stuck.

Chris Salewicz reported back for *NME*. Van looked "like a probationary teacher on his first day in the science department of an East End comprehensive. For most of his set he was largely uninspiring, though he managed times – notably on 'Into The Mystic' – when he succeeded to mentally scurf the listener's life and then lapse it into false calm again. Pete Wingfield's piano keys stuck time and time again and Morrison would appear an almost tragic figure as he struggled to reactivate the set, wiping his spectacles painfully and looking faintly ludicrous in his lace flied leather pants." He returned to encore on 'Brown Eyed Girl'.

For *Sounds*, though, Van "turned in the most engaging music of the afternoon. He looked as tense as usual to start off with but for once he loosened out very quickly, bringing 'Street Choir' right up to second number in the set, which had to be a significant gesture. 'Why did you let me down?' seemed to become a question which needed no answer, old history. At times as his set stretched out, it seemed that the Allmans were going to need to look to their boogie kings title, with Wingfield hammering away and Morrison rocking out." Another reviewer praised the light jazz style of the quartet, on songs like 'Since I Fell For You', and the audience was positive, many not bothering to stay for the headlining Allman Brothers.

Afterwards, Rob Mackie interviewed Van backstage, at the singer's own request. Many of his answers, however, are in his usual manner, much in the style of tax form replies, a quick agreement or disagreement. Van had himself chosen to cut down the size of his band, and to play more himself, but retain the old name. "Anyone who plays with me is The Caledonia Soul Orchestra." Is there anyone around who he likes listening to? Presumably Mackie is talking about fellow musicians here, so is particularly bemused by Van's reply of Isobel Barnett. Lady Isobel was a stalwart of panel games like *What's My Line*, and came to a tragic end after a shoplifting charge, when she was found dead in her bath. Fearsomely upper class, she seemed to be a fixture on early B/W TV, all pearl necklace and round vowels, coiffured hair and the face of an aristocratic chicken. Van is either being deadpan here, or is entering the "twilight zone" himself.

The answer comes from Pete Wingfield. "Van's crazy – but he's crazy in the nicest possible way. He'd probably say he was the only sane person around. He may seem solemn and unhappy on the outside but there's a bizarre sense of humour beneath. He likes British humour, The Goons and so on." He even got Pete to send over homemade cassettes of Tony Hancock.

Van led his new band, Hancock tapes et al, through a tour of the USA and Canada, low on support staff, but high on musical values. As Wingfield told *Beat Instrumental*, "taking a grand piano on tour is something that's hardly ever been done before, though I think Elton John might have done it. Although the hiring and freight charges worked out slightly more expensive than just hiring a different piano in each town, it was worth it to be playing an instrument I knew." Thus equipped,the band was ready for the high wire act that this twenty-five gig tour became, ready to improvise at a moment's notice. "Sometimes Van would suddenly decide he didn't want to play the set we'd worked out, and he'd launch into a number he'd just written and which we'd never heard, with Van calling out the chord changes to us between the lyrics." Bob Dylan had begun to employ the same trick, to keep himself and his band flexible, though often at the price of bemusing his audience. "There was very little formal arrangement. Van controlled everything with hand signals."

The thanks his band received for all this hard work was to be laid off by Morrison at the end of the tour, like discarded tissue paper. Wingfield remained respectful of his ex-employer, though, fully aware of his underlying vision. "For Van, the music is all – he has no stage act and no gimmicks. He exists in a vacuum – he knows nothing of the current scene. He listens to jazz and blues, never to rock."

On 29 August 1974, two days before his birthday, Morrison played the Orphanage in San Francisco, as part of a welcoming reception after his European tour. The gig was filmed, though never officially released. Director Craig Richins opens with shots of the Golden Gate Bridge and street scenes of San Francisco, and of fans queuing outside the venue. This is almost a travelogue of Van's West Coast years, and the announcer declares that two thirds of the original pressing of *Astral Weeks* sold in San Francisco. Fittingly, Van is accompanied by a young, local band. *Melody Maker* reported that "Sound Hole, the hard driving Marin County sextet with Mario Cippolina on bass, is Van Morrison's latest back-up band". He himself described them as "the hottest band in the Bay area". Van looks relaxed, in white pants and a maroon sequinned jacket, playing in front of the club's ornate, stained glass window, a rehearsal for his appearances on properly consecrated ground: St Mary's Stogumber and Glastonbury.

A good quality tape chronicles the concert, Van and his young band storming into 'Heathrow Shuffle', with massed saxophones, then a punchy 'Ain't Nothing You Can Do', like a fresh and fit Band and Street

Choir. No surprise, therefore, that 'Street Choir' is next, but the rendition is sultry and taken at an even slower pace than at Montreux. 'I Believe To My Soul' is boozy and brassy and relaxed. 'Snow In San Anselmo' is also taken without hurry, with Van seeming to imitate John Lee Hooker's gruff vocals, just as Joni Mitchell impersonates Furry Lewis in 'Furry Sings The Blues'. 'Moondance' sounds comatose, and Van's soundless grunts at the end could almost be him snoring. The tape begins to run slow at this point, so that 'Into The Mystic' is pleasant, but lacks mystery, and 'T For Texas' sounds bored. It is as if you can hear Van's creative batteries running down. The man needs a rest.

Interviewed backstage, he declared that playing small clubs had been good for him – "a club is nice, it's intimate, you can get down" – but that he was now finding how to transfer that kind of intimacy to larger arenas. Indeed, after this night, he decided to stop playing club dates. The manager of the Orphanage, Richard Hundgeon, claimed the exposure in places like the Lion's Share had damaged Morrison's box office appeal in California. It was almost as if he was beginning to be taken for granted.

Van continued to work with Sound Hole. They appeared together at the Great American Music Hall on 3 September when, after a thirty-five minute opening set by the band, Van joined them to perform songs like 'Ain't Nothing You Can Do', 'St Dominic's Preview' and 'I Like It Like That'. He continued to mine a jazz-blues seam, frequently blowing solos through his alto sax and mouth harp. It was at about this time that Lester Bangs saw Van on a late night network TV concert.

"Van and his band come out, strike a few shimmering chords and for about ten minutes he lingers over the words 'Way over yonder in the clear blue sky/Where flamingos fly.' No other lyrics. I don't think any instrumental solos. Just those words, repeated slowly again and again, distended, permutated, turned into scat, suspended in space and then scattered to the winds, muttered like a mantra until they turn into nonsense syllables, then back into the same soaring image as time seems to stop entirely. He stands there with eyes closed, singing, transported, while the band poises quivering over great open tuned deep blue gulfs of their own."

In November, he was due to tour Australia, and there was talk of some dates in Japan. To mark the year's end, Van appeared on 30

December at the Keystone club in Berkeley at a benefit for Tex Coleman. Coleman, a friend of both Van and John Lee Hooker, had burned his hand badly, and the gig was held to raise money for his medical expenses. Warm love in action. The evening began with a set by John Lee Hooker and ended with one by Elvin Bishop. Bishop was a veteran of Paul Butterfield's mould breaking Blues Band – ten minute raga rock solos, a multi-ethnic line-up, backing Dylan's bid for electric freedom at Newport in 1965.

In between, Van jammed an hour's worth of blues, backed by Bishop's regular quartet, working through numbers like 'Trouble In Mind', 'Swing It For Me', 'Baby Please Don't Go' 'Bring It On Home' and 'Help Me'. There were no rehearsals for the improvised set, as local hero Bishop played bottleneck, slide and swapped vocals with Van, who played harmonica and alto sax. Afterwards, Van admitted that he had expected the evening to be more relaxed. The Keystone was packed tight, and contrary to his wishes his name had been advertised in association with the gig.

It was not long after his European and East Coast tours, and he said of his new record *Veedon Fleece,* "The tour was fine but the LP was recorded quite a while ago and isn't what I'm doing now." Maybe not, but it remains his forgotten masterpiece, and it has failed to date a micro-second since its release.

With *Veedon Fleece* Van had come home in more senses than one. From henceforth, his records would obtain better chart placings in Britain than in the States, due partly to his decision to relocate his main home back across the Atlantic. Having written eight new songs in less than three weeks, he told Ritchie Yorke that "it is going to be more of what I'm into. It's going to be around *Astral Weeks* and *Moondance* but nothing like them."

Conversely, John Cale was a veteran of The Velvet Underground, and a man whose own music is full of pain, he would tell interviewers about his outbreaks of domestic violence, and scream on stage, sitting under a grand piano. Cale made the double edged comment that "Van Morrison's still pretty honest artistically. And that's pretty good considering that he doesn't have anything to be honest about anymore." It seems relevant to quote a man who once wrote that 'Fear Is A Man's Best Friend' when discussing an album which shivers with images of fear and dread, but which also contains visions of angels and country joy.

Veedon Fleece was released in late October, produced by Morrison and mainly recorded at the artist's own Caledonia Studio, and with musicians drawn from various editions of The Soul Orchestra. It is an album both literally and metaphorically tinged with green. On the front cover, Van sits in the grounds of a country house, whose turrets rear behind him. He has gained his mansion on the hill, if only as a guest. He sits on a green lawn that could only be in Ireland, dressed with amazing neatness in dark jacket, white shirt and tie. On either side lies a huge Irish wolfhound, dogs long associated in that nation with kings and poets. Tennyson, who travelled frequently in Ireland, brought a pet wolfhound back to England with him.

As to the new album, he explained that "I haven't a clue about what the title means. It's actually a person's name. I have a whole set of characters in my head that I'm trying to fit into things. *Veedon Fleece* is one of them and I just suddenly started singing it in one of these songs, it's like a stream of consciousness thing." If Veedon Fleece is a person, then he sounds like a character out of a John Cowper Powys novel, effortlessly strange and symbolic, a cosmic force almost. Powys would be an interesting influence, as his novels are enormous acts of nostalgia, mostly written in American exile, deeply tied into landscape and mysticism, and heavily Celtic. His novels are perhaps the ultimate example of the "stream of consciousness", huge narratives in which very little happens, apart from the quest for life's meaning, set in a universe in which even the tiniest stone is self aware, throbbing with life. This is also a rare glimpse into Van's own head, people with characters from his own subconscious – Veedon Fleece, Madame George, Linden Arden. One imagines a *Rawlinson End* type cavalcade of eccentric persons, all of them aspects of their creator.

Talking to Tom Donahue, Van enigmatically spelt out the title of the album V-E-E-D-O-N F-L-E-E-C-E – like a secret code – and said that "it means what it says". After listening to 'Bulbs', Donahue told Van "you always make great noises. The other things you do in songs beside the words. Listen to the man, he moans differently from the rest of them."

Musically, the album lacks the horn section of recent projects, with Jack Schroer adding saxophone where necessary, and a string section ready when required.

Van provided some invaluable clues to this complex work – for which I cannot even find a lyric sheet – in a conversation with Ritchie Yorke. The opening track, 'Fair Play' was, like all the tunes here, "written while I was in Ireland last October. I have a couple of friends over there and that is a phrase they use all the time. I was just travelling around Ireland and I wrote a song from what was running through my head. So that kind of spurred the idea and it just went from there. It was just a matter of thoughts I was taking in." There is an *Astral Weeks* feel, with acoustic bass and jazz drums, an open ended kind of soundscape, over which Van broods on his past and on what has befallen his native land. For Nick Kent, 'Fair Play' is "so damn hypnotic with its Debussy cocktail lounge piano".

The song reeks of Ireland, its architecture and great tragic heroes like Oscar Wilde, magicians of language. Through a matching linguistic skill, it recovers an Irish childhood, with sayings like the title of the song – a favourite saying of Van's friend Donall Corvin – and "tit for tat". Mixed in are memories of the Lone Ranger from Saturday Morning children's cinema, with his battle cry of "Geronimo". The Lone Ranger might have been subject to a spoof song by Quantum Jump, suggesting an unnatural relationship with his Indian side-kick Tonto, but his iconic significance as a masked man on a white horse, anonymously righting wrongs, remains. Hell, I was a member of his fan club at the age of eight, and still have the badge to prove it! Van's voice almost breaks towards the end, and he adopts a John Martyn-like stoned growl. This is not so much singing as putting pure emotion into the air, and watching it vibrate.

Perhaps the finest ever cover versions of Van's work are by Robyn Hitchcock, that collector of other people's eccentricities, as if he didn't have enough of his own to keep him going. Hitchcock centres in on the essential sadness and grace of this project. He performed 'Fair Play' at McCabes guitar shop in 1991, with a piano accompaniment for perversity's sake, and the record seems to stop on the word "dreaming", which Hitchcock repeats as if in a trance. He captures the eccentricity and risk taking of Van's singing – as few other musicians could – and by transposing it into his own upper class English demotic, shows how universal such vocal sounds are. The line about "arms and legs so black and blue" lends a sinister edge even here.

Hitchcock's version of 'Linden Arden Stole The Highlights' is similarly respectful, capturing that same swoop of words, like skating on an icy pond. Like all great copies, it takes us back to the original with added respect. The song is "about an image of an Irish-American living in San Francisco. It's really a hard man type of thing." For Brian Hogg, "Van's voice soars over a stark piano and string quartet, a song which in itself sounds more like a fragmented idea but achieves fullness by its being left that way, allowing its quality to remain unchanged." Again embroidered by Jeff Labes' piano, this is the story of an Irish expatriate, a good man who is pursued by an evil gang, and "cleaves their heads off". A man who takes the law into his own hands, just like the Lone Ranger, and there is a Wild West feel to all this, violence mythologised.

The line about living with a gun links into 'Who Was That Masked Man', "a song about what it's like when you absolutely cannot trust anybody. Not as in some paranoia but in reality. What it's like when there's nobody you can trust at all. The guy in the song is just stuck in a house with a gun and that's it period." It conflates the Lone Ranger, and the terrorist gunman of the previous song. Van's voice sounds tinged with mania, straining at its highest limit, and when he sings about "an evil in everyone" the song abruptly ends, having reached a point where it can no longer continue.

'Streets Of Arklow' "comes from when we took some time going around various places in Ireland. Arklow was one of them. So I wrote a song about what I was feeling when we were there checking it out." For Kent it shares the "doomy surrealist atmosphere" of Dylan's *John Wesley Harding* album, with the addition of "atmospheric Irish reed pipe". Van growls like a bear, and the beat picks up, but there is something ominous in the air still, even if "our souls were clean". Grass which doesn't grow: a sinister orchestra comes in as Van makes this point, like a storm stirring. The song makes a direct connection between Ireland – "God's green land" – and gypsies doomed to roam, their hearts full of fire.

'You Don't Pull No Punches, You Don't Push The River' "starts off as a love song then goes into a feeling, I suppose, like images of things.

Flashes of Ireland and other flashes of other kinds of people. I was also reading a couple of books at the time. The song has got a bit of Gestalt therapy in it too." For Nick Kent, "it's certainly crazy enough. Van starts off singing to some chick about 'soul satisfaction' but suddenly the arrangement breaks out with some mad flautist noodling away while Morrison carries on like a Belfast dervish. Complete lunacy, but it's great." On the other hand, *Melody Maker* considered it "almost completely lacking in the dynamics and tension which normally breathe life into such a tune".

The song opens with flutes and Van's evocation of a tomboy – the same mysterious girl as in *Astral Weeks*, half way to womanhood. Much the same image as in Led Zeppelin's much derided (though not by me) 'Stairway To Heaven', another wonderful piece of Celtic imagination, and about the passage from child to adult (and, some say, a girl's first period). Seamlessly, Van moves into a dream of the cathedrals of the West of Ireland, and a vision of William Blake and the Sisters of Mercy – much the same as in Leonard Cohen's song to his female muses, half human, half figures of myth. There is also a brief reference to Meher Baba, Pete Townshend's own guru, a man who literally became dumb for the last years of his life as a conscious path to enlightenment. In much the same way, Van's work since could also be seen as a journey into the silence. The grail quest has gone Celtic, a search for a highly personal and nonsensical symbol. Van's very voice seems to be on a quest, straining for each note, expressing in turn mystified hope, achieved joy and stern determination.

Johnny Rogan identifies the huge importance of this track in Morrison's artistic development. It represents "an experimental peak, a step beyond even his most ambitious work". Rogan picks up Van's reference to his recent use of Gestalt therapy, an attempt to complete the circle of emotional wholeness. It helps the patient become an active rather than a passive participant in his or her own life, taking full control, and would thus have confirmed Van's desire to take some time off from his musical career, in order to find himself. *Veedon Fleece* is very much part of that same process.

'Bulbs' is "definitely going to be the single. There's nothing to say about it." It is the most Californian song on offer here, and the perkiest, set to a guitar strum and electric bass. The song deals with "leaving for

America, with a suitcase in my hand", and suggests Van's excitement at his new life. The relevance of the title is beyond me, though Van is planted in the shadows, watching the streetlights, and their glow, which neatly contrasts two kinds of "bulbs". Like Linden Arden, his own father, and so many children of Eire, Van has been forced over the ocean to find work. I remember once standing with my Irish girlfriend on the western edge of Kerry, and her saying that the next land west was New York. It is strange to hear tales in such a remote community of relatives in Los Angeles or London, as if they were adjoining villages.

'Cul De Sac' is "just what it is. The title speaks for itself." For Steve Peacock in *Sounds*, the song is a "tour de force" which justifies the cost of the album alone. Morrison turns the usually slight and often flippant waltz time into "a churning barbed weapon signature which carries the song and the playing along in great rolling waves". The same title had been used a few years before for Polanski's odd film starring Donald Pleasance, a movie of entrapment and endings. There are also deliberate echoes of the creepy song 'Dark End Of The Street' – which Richard and Linda Thompson made into a psychodrama of attempting escape where there is no escape, as doomed as Romeo and Juliet – both in its tune and the sense of desperation, which Van's voice conveys here. He sounds like a beast caught in a trap, thrashing around.

Rogan talks of Gestalt therapy as being devoted to one's own wholeness, filling in emotional gaps by "owning" qualities in others that one would wish for oneself. 'I Wanna Comfort You' is "a song about just letting somebody put the weight on you. Like when things become too much for one person to handle, having someone to lean on. The end is like the reverse situation, of you leaning on them." Nick Kent thinks of prime Percy Sledge. For Peacock it rages like 'Cul De Sac', "in a smouldering, almost suppressed way". Morrison, meanwhile, sings "with unquestionable mastery. He takes terrible risks with timing, phrasing and even pitch, but he doesn't falter once." Van's voice is full as a flowing tide, yet half-choked with emotion.

'Come Here My Love' is "just a love song", in the style of Tim Hardin's 'Suite For Susan Moore'. Domestic and touching. 'Country Fair' is a prequel to Van's work with the likes of The Chieftains. In both subject and musical mood it evokes the West of Ireland, where time stops, and people still have time to poke their noses into everyone's business, and watch over those who need support. As my girlfriend pointed out, Ireland might (then) have still been a poor country, but it built cheap bungalows for its old people, rather than shoving them into care homes. For Van, his song is "just about things that you remember happening to you when you were a kid. You could say it's a bit like 'And It Stoned Me', it has the same kind of feeling anyway. It's the same kind of feeling, but it's not about fishing." For Nick Kent, the song is "like final tranquillity after the storm of metaphysical bantering heckled at us". For us mere mortals who actually buy Van's albums, it is like an acoustic shower of rain, comforting, healing, with flute as soft as the endless "damp" of the West.

My own greatest surprise at a Kerry country fair was the racks of American country and western tapes on offer. This is a society imbued by back transmission with American culture – and C&W itself derives largely from Irish folk music taken westwards – and this complex theme is central to *Veedon Fleece*, where one Irish Rover returns home, and finds America and Ireland subtly intermixed.

When I agreed to write *Celtic Crossroads*, my first thought was to hopefully turn a few people on to this album, above all others in Morrison's rich oeuvre. Since its release, it has functioned among many of my friends – alongside albums like *John Wesley Harding*, the best work of Kevin Ayers and Roy Harper, and the myriad offshoots of English folk-rock – as a touchstone of deep mysteries and some kind of inner healing after the excesses of the sixties. The same agenda as so many of the early psychedelic voyagers, however much they might since have gone out of fashion, and the likes of Johnny Rotten – whose work shows a total lack of consolation or self-knowledge – scrawl "I hate" on their Pink Floyd T-shirts. *Veedon Fleece* is subtler than anything ever dreamed up by Roger Waters, but it shares his need to explain and explore, and work out how the past can dominate the present. There is some common ground with that virtually overlooked statement of defeat, *The Final Cut*. It is a genuinely underground album which Morrison himself seemed to largely disown, and whose songs he has rarely covered live, as if they are either too difficult or too personal. It makes a perfect B-side of a C90 to back *Astral Weeks*, and seems to me that album's equal, though more mysterious still, more deeply in touch with Celtic roots. If *Astral Weeks* was a kind of precursor of Woodstock nation, positing some kind of lifestyle in love and peace, then *Veedon Fleece* provided sanctuary from the violent, amoral world since Altamont.

One reviewer described it as "a freer, more acoustically slanted work". Steve Peacock in *Sounds* found that "overall the album has the same kind of brooding, low profile intensity, but it is without the kind of desperate anger of *Astral Weeks*. An almost stately and very moving album". In *NME* Nick Kent reckons that half of Van's brilliance has stemmed form "his penchant for utterly inspired gibberish. Yup, Van's a smart yolwer all right, and now he's gone downright metaphysical." Geoff Barron of *Melody Maker* gets things as wrong as wrong can be, finding that side one "contains some of his least memorable shots at songwriting since *Tupelo Honey*, a similarly fated album". The album leaves its listener in a "relaxed stupor". Jim Miller took the same line for *Rolling Stone*. The album lacks focus and drive, and as a result sounds "self indulgent", while floundering in its own cliches. It is mood music for mature hippies (by which token, Van has invented New Age music, single handed). Morrison suffers from wobbly pitch, and "too often suggests a pinched vocal nerve drowning in porridge".

Miller may have tin ears, but he does discern what makes Morrison so enigmatic, and neatly encapsulates what I am trying to show throughout *Celtic Crossroads*. Although Van comes on like a flamboyant soul trouper, he "maintains an oddly detached, awkward stage presence. His vision is hermetic, his energy implosive: yet his vocation is public." These contradictions give his work great resonance, "his distinction lies in his fusion of a visceral intensity with an introspective lyric style". He is capable of "dismembering a song, using the fragments for audacious vocal flights".

Veedon Fleece was unmistakenly Irish in its inspiration and subject matter, forging a new kind of music from Van's shared Celtic past. As with all traditions, the solitary and private genius lying behind Morrison's work was part of a larger process. The Irish band Sweeney's Men – with Andy Irvine, Terry Woods and Johnny Moynihan – had already brought a rock sensibility to Celtic traditions, and thus proved deeply influential on Fairport Convention's own experiments in trad-rock, which fed back into a whole new generation of Irish bands.

Horslips – who had the heaviest drummer I ever heard live outside of Bev Bevan – recorded a concept album *The Tain*, welding contemporary rock to the ancient Ulster saga, *The Cattle Raid On Cooley*, and 1976's *The Book Of Invasions*, subtitled "A Celtic Symphony". The folksong 'My Lagan Love' appears, suitably transformed, in the "Fantasia" section of its second movement.

"Everything we did was the genuine article," keyboard player and flautist Jim Lockhart explained. "We wanted to take melodies that were inherently Irish or Celtic, and put them into a different form of music." Phil Lynott's Thin Lizzy, which shared many musical roots with Van, had already pulled off the same trick by rocking up the folk song 'Whiskey In The Jar' in 1973. One of their peripatetic guitarists, Gary Moore, had already jammed with whimsy and acid folk warriors Dr Strangely Strange. Although resolutely acoustic, Planxty were an Irish folk supergroup, first formed to back Christy Moore (no relation) who led a whole movement of players democratising their sources – Donal Lunny was particularly influential here – bringing local players to an international audience. Van's own future guitarist, Arty McGlyn, was part of this process, as was the worldwide success of the Gaelic speaking Clannad, who added synthesisers to the Irish folk tradition.

As if in response, Morrison was about to retreat back into the depths of his Celtic soul, entering a long, creative silence, from which it seemed for a time that he might never re-emerge. *Veedon Fleece* was exactly the kind of album to leave behind as a temporary suicide note. It continues to guard so many mysteries, and if there is a key to Morrison's locked soul, I feel it is somehow encoded here, written in his own musical version of ogun script. Van is the masked man, himself.

Meanwhile, Van was still drifting, trying to find a new direction for his life and his music. There were unconfirmed reports that he was looking to move to County Wicklow, attracted both by the Irish landscape and by the generous tax regime for creative artists. He was back at the Great American Music Hall on 24 and 25 March 1975, having told the *San Francisco Chronicle* that the shows would be experimental. "I'm getting into something different; out of old songs, more into an instrumental thing – freer type improvisation on horn." He was joined by pantomimist Joel McCord who was to appear both with the band and solo, and there was the possibility that Morrison and

McCord might also read some poetry. Other members of the band included Bernie Krause on synthesisers and David Hayes on bass. The audience would find Van "singing songs I've recorded, new songs I've just written and instrumentals. It's a different trip. I just don't want people to come expecting me to be singing 'Domino' or something."

In April, he returned to the Great American Music Hall to play another four sell out shows with a new quartet, presenting a much more "straight ahead rock" sound. David Hayes remained on bass, with Mark Jordan on keyboards – he had previously worked with Boz Scaggs – and former Stoneground guitarist John Blakeley. Tony Dey from the Ted Ashford group was on drums.

The ninety minute set on Sunday 21 April was again opened by McCord. Van played a number of his own songs – with new arrangements of 'Wild Night' and 'TB Sheets' – old R&B numbers like Rufus Thomas's 'Walking The Dog' and blues standards like 'Help Me'. The real surprise came at the end with an extended 'St Dominic's Preview' which included musical quotes from The Rolling Stones' 'You Can't Always Get What You Want' and Lou Reed's 'Walk On The Wild Side'. He returned to encore on 'Gloria'.

Melody Maker on 14 June 1975 carried a report by Todd Tolces of a one-off gig at the Keystone, Berkeley. Morrison appeared with the same musical team, which he "fronts with a regal conductorship". Bassist David Hayes was on loan from Terry And The Pirates – led by the shivery guitar of John Cippolina, once of Quicksilver Messenger Service. Guitarist John Blakely played the occasional lead break, but "kept most of his power in the rhythm structure", while "familiar Marin sessionist" Mark Jordan played keyboards. Van concentrated mainly on saxophone and only quit to let his punchy, soulful vocals clear the air around the hall.

The evening opened with 'Wild Night', at first slower and funkier than the record, then faster and ever fierier. "Van was off to a roaring start." He sang some slow blues and then some fast blues, and an instrumental close to Booker T's 'Green Onions'. 'Blue Money' was a crowd pleaser. The highlight of the evening was a cover of The Coasters' 'Under The Boardwalk', "executed in a dynamic and heartspoken way that only Morrison could've devised". Van shifted into high gear, and with his screaming sax wailing he erupted into an uproariously rocking 'Lovelight' – perhaps some of The Grateful Dead were in the audience – followed by 'Domino', the very kind of Top Forty material he had vowed to abandon. A delighted home crowd called him back for "a lengthy and absolute 'St Dominic's Preview'". A good place from which to step into the silence: for the next year or so, Van became invisible. His next public sighting was a brief and nervous appearance at The Band's farewell concert at SF's Winterland on 26 November 1976.

Nevertheless, a press release falsely announced that he would be headlining with southern boogie merchants Lynyrd Skynyrd at the Crystal Palace Garden Party in late August. Other, more complementary, acts would include the soft rock of James Taylor and Jesse Colin Young, provider of so many of Van's backing musicians. Did he take them back, like orphans, when Morrison came to discard them as spent forces?

Van had sacked all of his bands: now he seemed to sack himself. As a 1976 WB press release put it, sounding much like a musical suicide note, "as far as the past year was concerned, things simply came to a grinding halt. Everything just came to a standstill as far as being into the music. I simply stopped doing it for a while in order to get a new perspective. I wanted to change the way I was working. I wanted to open up new areas of creativity so I had to let go of everything for a while." This was not entirely altruistic: Van also talks about wanting "to get more of a solid business thing together". Talking to Robin Denselow of the *Guardian* in 1977, he realised that "I got to the point where music just wasn't doing it for me anymore. Something was telling me to knock it off a bit. I caught up with years of sleep." He still seemed to be reacting against the pressure of the 1973 world tour. "When you're committed to a series of concerts you lose all the spontaneity, it's not jazz anymore. The reason I first got into music and the reason I was then doing it were conflicting. It was such a paradox." One he needed mental space in which to resolve.

He was also approaching his thirtieth birthday, a time when anyone naturally needs to look back and reassess the direction of one's life. To mark this same event, in September 1975 Ritchie Yorke published Van's biography, though as Chris Austin predicted in *NME*, "Morrison is no Acid Casualty; he is likely to be around for at least another quarter

century, and even more likely to be producing better music all the time."
Austin also notes "an unpleasant tendency to backbite at his fellow
journalists", a career habit of Morrison biographers past and present.

Along with contemporaries like Dylan, Cohen, Neil Young and Joni
Mitchell, Van was entering uncharted territory, carving out a new kind
of career profile, as long term artists who happened to perform rock
music. Their predecessors had enjoyed a brief explosion of success,
then years of decline playing the revival circuit. Even Elvis was a deeply
nostalgic exercise now, mummified in Las Vegas.

Growing too old to be a conventional pop star, one could become
a drugged legend like Brian Wilson, a cult figure like Van Dyke Parks, or
fitfully active like John Lennon. Paul McCartney drove to the middle of
the road: Bob Dylan simply kept on the road, driving forever to
"another joint". Many switched tracks to work behind the scenes in the
record business, as managers, producers or musical hacks. Van's old
friend Phil Coulter had written hit songs for Dana – Eire's first
Eurovision Song Contest victor – and The Bay City Rollers. Van too
could have worked nine to five from home, submitting demos and
writing jingles in his portastudio. Mainstream pop royalties could be
ploughed back into pet projects, like Coulter's albums of orchestral
music, a largely private pleasure.

Instead, he followed a rigorous programme of self improvement, an
intellectual form of circuit training, making up for his lack of formal
education. He needed to locate his true inner self. As he told Steve
Turner, "People would be sitting and talking about Van Morrison and
I'd wonder who they were talking about. When I became famous it was
a complete drag and still is a complete drag. It's not relevant and what
people make out of it is completely unreal." He immersed himself in
classical music – Debussy became a particular favourite – and set
himself a reading programme of poetry, Celtic history and mythology,
and the supernatural, the mental seedbed from which so many later
songs were to grow.

He was particularly interested in exploring his childhood sense of
mystical rapture, being taken out of space and time, and looking for
"somewhere to put my experiences, to find out what they were". Thus
it was that he sought out "various other people who gave me
pointers. I wouldn't call them 'gurus'. I would call them 'spiritual

friends'. I don't believe in 'gurus'." The surnames of such people act as touchstones in his later work, much as landmarks and street names did before.

Van identified most immediately with the English visionary William Blake – whose devoted wife would remark, "I have very little of Mr Blake's company. He is always in Paradise." Indeed, the two have much in common, as anyone who reads Peter Ackroyd's recent biography will discern. Both were largely self educated and from a working class background, both saw visions, both believed in the potency of magic. Blake lived and died "in a glorious manner". "He was going to that country he had all his life wished to see and expressed himself happy, hoping; for Salvation through Jesus Christ – just before he died his countenance became fair. His eyes brighten'd and he burst out into singing of the things he saw in Heaven."

Morrison chose other poets who could provide a key to his visionary experience: the witty complexities of John Donne, or Wordsworth and Coleridge finding meaning in Nature and revealing these insights to the reader in "language really used by men". Hazlitt talks of "a chaunt in the recitation of both Wordsworth and Coleridge that acts as a spell upon the hearer, and disarms the judgement". Music was never far away from Van's mind. After all, Blake wrote songs, Donne "songs and sonnets" and Wordsworth and Coleridge made their breakthrough with *Lyrical Ballads*. As with Yeats and Joyce, TS Eliot and Kenneth Graham, Van was looking for writers who in their different ways could make language sing. It would be his particular genius to combine such high culture with the whole gamut of post-war popular music – blues, soul, rock, folk and jazz.

Morrison also explored his heritage as an Irishman, through the novels of JP Donleavy and Brian Moore's earthy vernacular prose about the Belfast of their shared childhood. He made a close study of the "Celtic twilight" of WB Yeats and dramatist Lady Isabella Gregory, a renaissance of national consciousness allied to the revival of Gaelic as a living language, and a new interest in ancient Irish legend and folklore. This in turn plunged Van into the vast literature surrounding Arthur, the once and future King. Further reading material ranged from Aristotle and Socrates to Gurdjieff's mystical design for living and Yogananda's *Autobiography Of A Yogi*.

As his 1976 press release put it, "I went through a lot of things within myself that I had to sort out". Van dived deep into the world of psychology, from Jung to Gestalt pioneers like Wolfgang Kohler, Fritz Perls and Max Wertheimer. He took out subscriptions to journals from the New Consciousness Movement and the New Age Society. He also underwent special relaxation exercises with a student of Ada Rolf, and Transactional analysis. "Most of these groups come to me. If there's something in it that I can utilise for making myself better equipped to deal with what I have to do. But that's it. It stops there. I never join any organisation." No guru, no method, no teacher.

Musically, Van was making a similar journey into himself. As he told the *NME*'s Roy Carr, "I think that it's part of the gig for musicians like myself to make people aware where certain things have their roots and that things don't just materialise from out of nowhere. It opens up musical cultures that they might not realise exist. If there's something in it that they can enjoy and even learn from, that's good enough." He renegotiated his deal with Warner Brothers: "overworked, overstretched, after *Veedon Fleece* I renegotiated the deal. It was a reaction to doing too much." His record company released a stop-gap single coupling 'Caledonia' and 'What's Up Crazy Pup', while dropping hints about a forthcoming 1940s swing LP with big band accompaniment.

Other projects which at least reached the talking stage included a proposed skiffle album with Bill Wyman, sessions with Joe Sample of The Crusaders, and a rock 'n' roll album to be produced by Al Kooper. There was even talk of Van joining musically with Phil May, then living in Paris, and at a loose end after The Pretty Things had become "like a body that had been fatally wounded but kept walking, not knowing how critical the wound was". There were other musical collaborations, with Carlos Santana, George Benson, and Brian Auger. Demos were recorded with Streetwalkers, featuring ex-Family lead singer Roger Chapman, a liaison thwarted by managerial and contractual disagreements. 'Flamingos Fly', was covered by Sammy Hagar, former vocalist with Montrose, for his debut solo LP, *Nine On A Scale Of Ten*. Tom Fogerty, having fled Creedence Clearwater Revival, later recorded two Morrison songs, 'You Move Me' and 'Real Real Gone' on his *Deal It Out* album.

Van was forced to issue a personal statement in early 1976, to the effect that "I've simply been trying out several experimental projects at various times and places. It's likely that a wide cross-section of these sessions will be released at a later date on a 'history of' sort of album." At least eight such tracks were recently scheduled on the *Philosopher's Stone* album.

Morrison was reportedly seen in the audience for Dr Feelgood, the Reading Festival and Eric Clapton. He played sessions for Bill Wyman's album *Stone Alone*. There is a strong Rolling Stones influence, with lots of slide guitar, crossed with Captain Beefheart on five tracks apparently recorded in 1975, which at a guess are from the R&B project. 'I'm Not Working For You', 'You Move Me' and 'When I Deliver' are brisk but ultimately unconvincing, more sweat than inspiration, like Chris Farlowe on a bad day. Van plays some gutsy harmonica, though. 'Sweet Release' is slower and more heartfelt, and self accusing: "I cut my nose to spite my face." On 'Joyous Sound', Van sounds like future collaborator Georgie Fame on a bouncy, almost reggae tinged song. It sounds like a template for Madness and the two tone explosion, a few years down the line.

Another stray tape emerged from this time, much in the vein of 'Joyous Sound'. The whole thing has an air of *Moondance* revisited, and remains eminently releasable. On 'I Shall Sing', Van sounds almost Jamaican, slurring simplistic words across a cheerful, big band backing. 'Laughing In The Wind' opens with a typhoon of brass, close to mid period Bonzos, with Van feeling lecherous in the springtime. "In a small cafe, just passing time away, I'm giving you the eye, no wonder to reason why." The precise, prominent guitar suggests that these tracks might be from the abandoned Joe Sample sessions. 'Street Theory' is a second cousin to 'Come Running', 'Foggy Mountain Top' (or 'T For Texas') is taken slower than before with good blues piano, and a harmonica break that almost talks. 'There, There Child' is live and has a New Orleans exuberance to the horn section. A wild guess here, but Van could be taking Shannon back to her mother "at your front door by the old oak tree", and paints a verbal picture of the starry night in this outburst of warm fellow feeling: "you ain't over the white cliffs of Dover". 'It Hurts To Want It Back' is back in the studio, and opens with steady rolling electric piano. Van sounds like Paul McCartney from

Van Morrison, into the music

Before and during: Van Morrison and Them appearing on *Where The Action Is*

Van and wife Janet Planet in Woodstock, from the photo shoot for *Moondance*

On a promotional cruise down the Hudson River in 1967, for Bang Records: l-r Jeff Barry, Bert Berns, Van and Janet

Van transported by his muse at the London Rainbow, 1973

A smoking Van, during one of his greatest concerts, backed by The Caledonia Soul Orchestra

Above: Van pictured with Neil Young and Joni Mitchell during Martin Scorsese's filming of *The Last Waltz*, 1976
Right: At the crossroads: the late 1970s saw Van focus on his Celtic heritage

Back in England, February 1979, after a
decade in America

With 1979's *Into The Music*, Van's career was
back on track

Van at the Capitol Theatre, May 1985

Van revisiting his roots at the 1994 Fleadh
Festival, still playing the instrument on which
his career began in the Belfast showbands

Blues brothers: Van with long term friend and colleague, John Lee Hooker

Jazz brothers: filmed at St George's Hall, Bristol in 1990, for Channel 4, with Mose Allison

With boyhood hero, Spike Milligan, who later inspired Van's instrumental 'Boffyflow And Spike'

Bob Dylan was an early influence on Van's musical development and their paths have crossed many times in the last twenty years, culminating in 1997's joint headlining tour

The elder statesman of rock 'n' roll

around *Let It Be*, percussive white soul. The final track, 'Feedback On Highway 101', has a pub rock sound to it, as does so much of this tape, newly energised, closer to entertainment than to art, working on the body rather than the brain.

In 'Street Theory', Van sings "its so hard to go back home", and by then he had abandoned plans to return to his homeland: "What am I going to do – move to Ireland and open a grocery store? I'm in the music business. I'm not gonna sit up on a hill somewhere writing songs that are gonna sell ten or twenty albums." Instead, he spent some time in London, regaining touch with the music industry. As he announced in the authorised source of a press release, "I am moving back to Britain for a while primarily because I want to get back to the roots, back where I started off". In life as in his music, "I'm getting back to basics – basic rock 'n' roll stuff. I like Britain as a place to live and it will be interesting to check it out again."

On his shopping trip he picked up a new manager, rock promoter Harvey Goldsmith, although as Goldsmith later told Johnny Rogan, "Everybody told me I was nuts! Every single person that had ever been involved with him, be it record company, publishing, promoting, agency or whatever, had a tremendous respect for him but everyone also said that he was the most difficult person in the world to deal with." Goldsmith always relished a challenge, and here was one of the best. In the spring of 1976, he booked Morrison into Virgin's Manor studios in rural Oxfordshire, the birthplace of *Tubular Bells* and all kinds of post-hippie jazz rock, in which Richard Branson found his first niche market to satisfy. It was the ideal place in which to get things together in the country, and coincidentally not that far from Traffic's Berkshire cottage, as the eagle flies.

Morrison, "at present living in Berkshire, following a nine year stay in America", was forming a new band, and the first project was to be an album, to be released later that year, and followed by British and American tours. His new manager, fresh from organising a tour by The Rolling Stones – forced like so many rock stars to live in tax exile – commented: "I must say how pleased I am that Van has chosen to return. It makes a nice change to see this reversal of the name drain in Britain's contemporary music scene." Goldsmith facilitated the stoned presence of Dr John, or Mac Rebennack, a longtime New Orleans session man, who could help Van pursue the rhythmic experiments of the demo tapes just discussed. As he told Rogan, after a long series of auditions "we ended up with Mac and Ray Parker and we put them all in the studio. After two days, Van decided that he wasn't satisfied with Ray Parker, who's got a jumpy, flamboyant style. Van tried all sorts of things. He had Chris Barber's jazz band down there doing some New Orleans stuff. It never got used, but it was fun. Van spent a lot of time at the Manor. He liked the place."

In his autobiography *Under A Hoodoo Moon*, Dr John recalls meeting Van, who mentioned his idea for an R&B album, and agreeing to be his producer. "I managed to hijack part of Stevie Wonder's rhythm section," Ollie Brown on drums, Reggie McBride on bass and Ray Parker Jr on guitar. "These guys were absolutely happening at the time; they'd just finished recording Stevie's *Songs In The Key Of Life*." Unfortunately, during a meal in Oxford, Parker – whose favourite guitar had been delayed coming through customs – broke the tension by laughing, which Van took as personal, and fired him on the spot. Dr John and the other two hung on with Van as "he may not have the best personality to deal with people, but the mystical quality of his voice could make you go through hell in dealing with him".

The sessions took on the quality of Whitehall farce. "I have memories of him auditioning a lot of guitar players – including many of the premier players in England, who had driven up from London to Oxford to make the gig. There were players all over the studio: I'd give one guy a downbeat, he'd hit one note, and Van would cut him off – "Next!". The whole Chris Barber Band came there to play on a tune, and they all got axed real fast, too. We never did find a steady player." Van and Dr John divided the task between themselves, and Marlo Henderson – another member of Wonder's band – overdubbed lead parts back in LA. Other problems intervened. "I had written some horn charts for the album and came to the studio ready to do the horns but Van had fired most of the horn section." And yet, as we have found with so many other fellow musicians, respect for Morrison's talent, and his mystic force, outweighs his personal quirks. "He's probably one of the few guys that I ever felt like punching out in the middle of a session, but I didn't do it – because I respected his singing so much. He's a very hard guy to deal with but his music is powerful. He's a mystical cat and

I got to respect that in him. I figure that the more talent there is in people, the bigger pain in the ass they usually are."

Most mysterious of all is a live-in-the-studio session which emerged on bootleg as *Amsterdam's Tapes*, and which John Collis dates as back in 1974. The Vara Studios tape is certainly later than that, as it features both Dr John on keyboards and voodoo vibes and guitarist Mick Ronson, once of David Bowie's Spiders From Mars and fresh from Dylan's "Rolling Thunder Review". There is a rhythm section of Leo Nocentelli on guitar, and organist Art Neville – one of the four Neville brothers from New Orleans. Jo Modeliste plays drums and George Porter bass. It could indeed post-date the Manor recordings, which surfaced officially as *A Period Of Transition*, but appear fresher and more spontaneous.

'I'll Go Crazy' is an uptempo duet with Dr John, with choogling guitar. 'Baby Please Don't Go' is a steady rolling update of the Them classic, again with lovely rhythm guitar from Mick Ronson. Next up is 'Wonderland' a piano instrumental, and a kind of precursor of acid jazz, which swings like a Scotsman's kilt on Hogmanay. The track listing of the tape in the Geoff Wall archives differs radically from that described by John Collis, which includes an update of 'Into The Mystic' and 'I Believe', though presumably not the syrupy mock-hymn recorded by The Bachelors. Here a horn-less 'Joyous Sound' follows, and then an early version of 'You've Gotta Make It Through The World' with swinging organ and audience applause.

Two cover versions come next, 'I Just Want To Make Love To You' – with tinkling piano and a screaming guitar – and Johnny Kidd's 'Shakin' All Over', a song much beloved of The Who as a crowd pleasing encore, and which ends here like a Led Zeppelin freak out. 'The Eternal Kansas City' is much like the version on *A Period Of Transition*, while 'Fever' is another re-tread, with backing like the early Brian Auger Trinity. After a rough and ready 'Foggy Mountain Top', the tape leaps to a Frank Zappa out-take of 'Dead Girls Of London', with Van on creepy lead vocals. In *NME*, Morrison said, "I think Zappa is a very intelligent human being. I think he's got a lot to say, about how it works, what you shouldn't let happen, and what he thinks *should* happen. I think it's really good that he's outspoken about that." Much like Van himself, the devastating honesty of an artist who always followed his own direction, whatever the financial or political consequences.

A review in *Sounds* back on 24 January 1976 considered the *Two Originals* re-release of *His Band And Street Choir* and *Tupelo Honey*, two lesser albums, but which improved with time, like fine champagne, "guaranteed to put a smile on your face and rhythm in your soul". Barbara Charone posits that Van had not become a superstar in the Elton John vein purely from choice, "because he didn't want to, shying away from the bright white lights and shiny black limousines".

Overdubs for the new album were completed back in LA. On Thanksgiving Day, 25 November 1976, Van joined other rock luminaries – including the equally reclusive Bob Dylan, Joni Mitchell, Neil Young, Eric Clapton and Dr John – playing for expenses only to mark The Band's farewell concert at San Francisco's Winterland Theatre. The results were filmed by Martin Scorsese as *The Last Waltz*, and also emerged on a triple album, and more recently as a bootleg CD, straight from the rough mix master.

The Band's lead guitarist and master of ceremonies Robbie Robertson wanted "a party with our friends, like a New Orleans funeral". Despite the jubilee atmosphere, Van was so crippled with nerves that this least clothes conscious of all rock stars – indeed, his down to earth appearance is a major part of his appeal – returned to his hotel to change his stage outfit, less than an hour before showtime. As he shivered in the wings, Van steeled himself to face a paying audience for the first time for well over a year.

The audience responded in kind, amazed that their local superstar was back on stage. A barrage of whistling, cheering and stamping greeted him, and rose to a crescendo as he tore into the folk song 'Tura Lura Lura (That's An Irish Lullaby)', "like a raunchy Ray Charles blues", in a duet with The Band's doomed pianist Richard Manuel. Morrison visibly relaxed and soloed on his own song 'Caravan', high kicking "cock proud" as he had done at the Rainbow back in 1973. The Band sound dead ringers for his band, circa *Moondance*. Adam Black of the *NME* reported that Van "strode forth, amply filling a sequinned cranberry leisure suit with a lace-up crotch". "It was one of the most magical performances I've ever seen him do," said Harvey Goldsmith. "He went out there and really stormed the place. All the artists like Clapton, Dylan and Joni were standing in a little area on the side, and everybody came out to watch him. To a person they all stood up and roared with the audience."

If the concert marked the death of The Band – and the communal lifestyle they represented – it also saw the re-emergence of Morrison on the world stage. He brought the event to life. "I didn't want the promotion but it was the right situation because of something karmic. It wasn't hyped, it was a pure situation." Van re-emerged to join the assembled cast for 'I Shall Be Released' – its composer Bob Dylan now centre stage, sharing a mike with Van and Robbie Robertson – but did not stick around for the scrappy instrumental work-out that followed.

Back in England, Goldsmith found Van a quiet house with a large garden in upmarket Kensington, which he flew over from the States to view, refused, and flew straight back. Eventually, his manager persuaded him to move into a rented house in the Los Angeles suburb of Brentwood, during the launch of *A Period Of Transition* in March 1977. His next permanent address would be back in England. Van's retreat from his public was at an end.

In an interview transcribed in the British fanzine *Nuggets*, Morrison described *A Period Of Transition* as "a specific project and it just came off the way I wanted it to come off". Co-producing the album with Mac Rebennack, he "kind of slowed me down which was really good for my head". By using the same horn section for every track, "that way it's a clean album". The LP reached Number Twenty-Three in the UK charts, and Forty-Three in America.

Van claimed that the album's title referred to the front cover, in which photographer Ken McGowan captures Van in an introspective state until finally he realises that this mood – as all others – is transitory, and the final shot captures a half smile. On the back cover, he is again pensive, washed out in monochrome, with his hair in a teddy boy quiff, which sums up the album's disconcerting shifts between the music of various decades. On *A Period Of Transition* Van is playing complicated games with time, and with the nature of his inspiration, not that many people realised this then. A zen album.

The closest album in spirit to this is Gene Clark's *No Other*, a hall of crazy, cracked mirrors; lyrically both show the post-hippie singer searching for love and inspiration through a desert of wasted hope.

Musically though, Clark's masterpiece soars and thrills: *A Period Of Transition* drags itself along like a three legged dog.

'You Gotta Make It Through The World' is in Van's words "a survival song". Like Clark's 'Life's Greatest Fool', human beings are condemned to exist in a world that hurts and kills, an obstacle course that no one survives. For Dr John, it has "a real spiritual sound", but Van sounds bored, after an initial groan and mumble before the backing kicks in, and the music fails to lift off, matching the doomy theme. There is a lack of joy here, even in the sax solo. Life's a bitch, and then you die.

'It Fills You Up' is an attempt by Van to express the inspirational spirit behind his music, taking him to "another realm…with kings and queens". The lyrics might say "you gotta do or die" but the vocals are disconnected and the music plods. "It fill you up to the brim, Jim" is not exactly inspired.

'The Eternal Kansas City' was inspired by a dream. During a stay in the Cotswolds Van came across a place called Birdland – I presume that this is the bird sanctuary at Bourton on the Water – and in a weird twist of logic and time transference cross-referenced this to the New York club forever associated with Charlie Parker. In a dream both images attached themselves to Kansas City, for no logical reason. In *Circus* magazine, Dr John describes this as "the song that Van got the whole album hooked up around. It was a real deep thing for him to focus on. It goes from a real ethereal voice sound to a jazz introduction and then into a kind of chunky R&B." So far, so good. The stage is set for an epic with the force and majesty of 'Listen To The Lion'. What we actually get is a shrill Las Vegas chorus, women foregrounded, men somewhere in the deep background, a (very) brief pastiche of Parker, then Van's brief lyrics, which mainly repeat the chorus.That's it, for a short and disappointing side one.

'Joyous Sound' is more like the real Van, as he starts to wail, and the lyrics describe themselves. Through music, the singer is in touch with heaven, the heaven of earthly love. A touch of a cappella at the end, "His Band and Street Choir" arrive at last. As to the next track, 'Flamingos Fly', "I've done three different versions in the studio. I've done it slow, a ballad version. I've done a mid-tempo version and I've done this version. This is the version I like best for release."

In speed terms, it's still not exactly The Ramones, but it drives along okay with Steve Cropper-type guitar. But where is Dr John in all this? The Vara studios tape presents his driving keyboards with far more depth and urgency. Van has squeezed the song dry of its poetry, and his voice nags rather than flies – just compare Clark's 'Silver Raven', in which the ex-Byrd soars high, following his muse. In comparison, Morrison's voice sounds like it has been injected with helium, straining for the high pitched stratosphere of David Surkamp.

'Heavy Connection' is "psychic stuff", and it does start with an authentic musical shiver, Van's voice playing off against the brass background, "from a whisper to a scream". Then he starts la-la-ing and all hope is gone. The lyrics are interestingly secret, Van in Amsterdam, receiving a "picture postcard" of the red light district. The central image – contact with one's lover as secret and necessary as that with one's dealer – is a drug metaphor, like Clark's 'From A Silver Phial', but quite lacking that song's desperation, and majesty. The ending takes off, with Van singing of love as a rainbow, and the backing musicians lose their cool anonymity.

'Cold Wind In August' is suddenly the real thing, a shiver of need between two lovers, and a bold fusion of fifties and sixties musical styles. Dr John, told Elliot Cohen that "there's a lot of nuances in his lead vocals. The song is a cross current from forties to seventies music. It's like where Ray Charles left off. It's a real tear-jerker that gets back to the basics of music." The paradox of the title is like a sudden chill of mortality, and Van's voice is driven. Jerry Jomonville's tenor sax at last shows a musician inspired, unleashing a long, slow scream. This California saga compares to WB Yeats' play *Purgatory*, the same events eternally recycled and unresolved, like an endless tape loop.

The final zen trick, however, is to create an album so well produced that all life and inspiration have been squeezed out of it, so that Van sounds as if he is singing inside a bell-jar. The backing musicians remain exactly that, in the background, anonymous, out of contact with Van's voice. Any one of the abandoned projects discussed above has more life and interest than this careful confection. The arrangements are described as "nut and skull": so where is the soul?

Reviewers failed to be impressed. Jude Carr in *Sounds* thinks the main problem is the anonymous backing, predictable songs, and Van's voice which "lacked true emotion, not enough feeling". For Nick Kent in *NME*, Van has attracted a phalanx of imitators: Bruce Springsteen, Graham Parker, Phil Lynott, Elvis Costello, Bob Seger. Indeed, Morrison has instigated a whole new strain of rocker – the small, ungainly, feisty loser with passion is his patent, first and foremost. The current album, though, furnishes "a slack, pale aural backdrop, signifying nothing". The album would better be called "a period in limbo". The *Melody Maker* finds the album dominated by trite choruses, unexciting, and the final impression – like the cover – oddly self conscious.

Van recognises that he does best to trust his own subconscious. As he told *Nuggets*, "I've written songs that I don't know what in the hell they mean. Like Kerouac" – the magazine prints "Cadillac" here, obviously not deciphering Van's Belfast drawl – "some of his prose stuff, how can you ask what it means, it means what it means. Either you dig it or you don't. That's what I like about rock 'n' roll, the concept."

CHAPTER SEVEN

Into The Mystic

The years of retreat were over. Van plunged back into the rock 'n' roll ferment and under Harvey Goldsmith's managerial guidance adopted a notably higher media profile. He recorded a "Midnight Special" for the American network NBC, broadcast in April. Harvey Kubernik reported back for *Melody Maker*: "Rehearsals started at one pm. Decked out in beige Levis and a blue shirt, Van looked quite the campus casual. The redhead was in a fiesta mood and very friendly during breaks in the action." Robbie Robertson, Levon Helm and Ringo Starr were rumoured to be appearing, but the the actual line-up of Van's band brought back two names from the past, John Platania and Jeff Labes, with Dr John on piano and Ollie Brown, the drummer from *A Period Of Transition*. Also on stage were bassist Anthony Johnson, three horn players including Tom Scott – who had led Joni Mitchell's flight into cocktail jazz – and two female back up singers. They demoed four songs from the new album, reprised later.

Morrison re-appeared shortly after eight pm, wearing the same burgundy suede outfit he sported at the last Band concert in Winterland. He launched immediately into a seven minute version of 'Moondance', with Carlos Santana and George Benson trading guitar riffs, and vocal harmonies by Etta James. Dr John took the baton for a couple of verses. Next up was a duet with Benson on Erroll Garner's 'Misty'. A surviving video shows wonderful interaction, almost like a couple making love, between Van's fluid vocals and Benson – a great guitarist, who played on equal terms with the likes of Miles Davis, before his descent into MOR vocals. It had started that afternoon as an unscheduled jam, now it was the highlight of the broadcast.

Morrison was like Lazarus, risen from the dead. "The show reaffirmed that Van is alive and well on stage, where he belongs. Reports of bottle casualty and a hard to get along with attitude were far from what I observed. A star is re-born." Added to which, the oracle – so long silent – now spoke. Cameron Crowe of *Rolling Stone* captured Van's first interview since 1973 (and from which the *Nuggets* transcript appears to be a straight steal). They met in Van's temporary home in the Los Angeles suburb of Brentwood, an urban neighbourhood "filled with a pleasant, folksy cacophony. Children are squealing as they play on their tricycles. A baseball game is going on down the street. The man next door is listening to a transistor radio and working on his car in the driveway." A setting of aggressive normality, like that satirised at the beginning of the film *Edward Scissorhands*.

Van is about to leave California, his home for the last six years, for good. His next base will be England. The poet is hiding under a suburban disguise, answering the door in a tweed jacket, and hopping into a rented Nova to a beach restaurant in Malibu, overlooking the ocean. "I never really fit into California. It's strange I stayed so long." Van looks peaky from staying indoors, and is set in his ways: "I get caught up listening to the same Ray Charles live album all the time." His own early albums are picking up sales again. "My trip at the moment is to integrate the records and the gigs. They just have to be taken separately together."

As to Patti Smith's updating of 'Gloria', "I could even dig that for what it was. It doesn't floor me like some things. But if something comes along like what Patti Smith is doing, I have a tendency *now* to accept it as what it is." He speaks with a rare directness about his years of drifting: "There comes a time when you have to let go of your ego. The ego is very useful for doing a lot of things, but it can also come back at you and blow your mind at times, and screw you up. I just had to let go on the whole thing, even the writing at some points. I didn't have anything specific to say."

The restaurant music system is playing, by complete coincidence, *Tupelo Honey*, but Van seems at long last to be coming to terms with such celebrity. "It doesn't matter if people are ripping me off, I just love it all, because it means that it was worthwhile...other people are getting things from it." This magnanimity was not to continue for long.

Van plunged back into the media flea circus, jumping through hoops of others' devising, including a press conference in Amsterdam. It is from this visit that the Vara studios tape most probably dates: three songs were captured on video. He also filmed an hour long performance in Hilversum, where he was joined on stage by Dr John, Mick Ronson, former Stackridge drummer Peter Van Hooke and bassist Mo Foster. Van Hooke was to become one of his longest lasting musical collaborators. According to John Altman, "He and Van were very close, they stayed in each other's houses." This mutual trust worked itself into their music. "Peter's contributions to Van's show...he gave a lot. He followed Van's dynamic shadings and often led Van into places *he* followed."

The same line-up played a showcase-cum-press reception in the exclusive confines of Maunkberry's – formerly the 55 Club – in Mayfair. *NME* raved, "and play he did, for a long time, with the one 'n' special Mac Rebennack tinkling the ivories so exquisitely a la Prof Longhair". Four of the songs that night surfaced for a wider audience on Granada TV's *So It Goes* in June. "Van seemed to be intent on dredging up his innards to express his Caledonian Soul Music, R&B standards like 'I Just Wanna Make Love To You', a new song called 'Venice', a harrowing little number entitled 'Twilight Zone'. "The whole firecracker ignited for the last number 'Kansas City' (his new single). Mick Ronson played guitar, held himself back well, Peter Van Hooke battered his skins with adequate abandon, Mo Foster was sturdy on bass, flaming red curls bobbing.

There was now a short interval, while the audience wolfed down free bangers and mash, then a musical jam, with Van – dressed in a silk shirt and white denim trousers – duetting with "a slightly sheepish" Roger Chapman. Crammed onto the tiny stage was a triple keyboard attack of Dr John, Julie Driscoll's musical partner Brian Auger, and Peter Bardens, a long lost colleague from Them. Graham Parker – the Donovan to Van's Dylan – skulked hopefully in the doorway but was not asked on stage. The ensemble, which also included Ray Russell and Alan Spenner, reprised an old Them favourite, 'Turn On Your Love Light', and the set list was Van's version of pub rock, a full flush of golden oldies. 'Help Me' went down well, and the final song, BB King's 'Rock Me Baby' featured black guitarist Bobby Tench, "looking radiant".

Roy Carr remembers the small audience packed together tighter than a Northern Line tube train during rush hour, as "Van wails passionately".

There was certainly a lot of punky aggression and truculence on show during an interview with Nicky Horne on Capital Radio, oddly similar to The Sex Pistols' on-air confrontation with Bill Grundy. The event was billed as Morrison's "first interview in years", but when Van and a chemically coshed Dr John arrived at the Capital studios, he greeted Horne's matey hello with "Who are *you*?". John Lydon, eat your heart out.

Horne told Johnny Rogan what happened next. "Morrison was obviously in a bad mood and you couldn't talk to Mac because he didn't know what planet he was on. He was standing there with a shillelagh in order to stand upright." Horne's first mistake: this is actually Rebennack's magic totem, from which he is never separated, rather like Gene Wilder's comfort blanket in *The Producers*, but with a voodoo charge. As to Van, "he didn't say a word. He was just looking very morose. He didn't talk to anyone." Not the best start to a good radio interview.

Once on air, Van rambled in a Dylanesque stream of consciousness manner, about meeting Dr John, then like an articulate punk – if that is not a contradiction in terms – he demythologised the whole process. "What I'm doing right now is I'm doing an interview for promotional purposes, no more no less than that. There's an album, so I'm available for talking." This is just like PIL labelling their album as *Album*, or Prag Vec including instructions on their first EP as to how others can make and release the same. Morrison is deconstructing his own media image, not that Nicky Horne either realises or thanks him for it. "There's no mystique around me. The only thing that's around me is this microphone...I can't see no *mystique* anywhere." Van bangs the wall at this point. Horne obviously feels like banging Van, in turn. "I started to lose my cool. He was blowing it. There were thousands of people who wanted to hear this man talk, who had listened to and loved his music."

Van, though, refuses any role other than that of following his muse. "I was born with a natural gift to play music and to write songs, and that's all I know. The rest of this stuff – I haven't got a clue what it's all about." A recording of 'Into The Mystic', of all things, plays the interview out. He leaves the studio without any further comment, and to the sound, metaphorically speaking, of Horne sobbing in the corner. "I have never done an interview that bad. I was really upset that a man I had admired for so long could blow it so totally. He really did destroy my feelings for him as a man." Van told Goldsmith afterwards that "I'm fed up with being a living legend. I want to be a star."

A similar interview with David "Kid" Jensen – a long time supporter – for Radio One is the subject of legend, and remains resolutely unbroadcast. A few hours after the Nicky Horne interview, Van climbed on stage at the Speakeasy, one of the spiritual shrines of sixties Britbeat, and spoke through his music. Van commanded the low platform of its stage, and did it all over again, this time with the help of Eric Burdon. Chas de Whalley was there for *Sounds*. "Ever looked Dr John the Night Tripper straight in the eyes? Ever stood *this* close to Van the Man so you can feel him breathe. You should have been down the Speakeasy the other Friday night. Playfully introduced as The Belfast Intruders, Van Morrison had a pretty neat little band behind him. And they were tight too."

The music started off as little more than a jam session. Often stopping for up to five minutes between songs, the menu was again pub rock, with old chestnuts like 'C C Rider', 'Baby What Do You Want Me To Do', 'What'd I Say' and 'I Just Want To Make Love To You' showing Van's Beat group roots. Requests for more sophisticated fare like 'Astral Weeks' or 'St Dominic's Preview' were studiously ignored, while "for a warm and romantic singer, Van made no attempt whatsoever to communicate with the crowd. Off mike, he faded into the wings, chain smoking the while. On mike he barked and bayed with his eyes tight shut, or else he stared wildly at a point above the audience's heads, stricken it seemed by a strange and dispassionate terror."

After a few trays of beer had circulated among the musicians, even Van began to loosen up, and new songs like 'You Gotta Make It Through The World' and 'It Fills You Up' bumped and bounced in all the right places. For Chas de Whalley, mired in punk, Morrison "was like a rock 'n' rollin' Sinatra but without the tuxedo". More to the point, Van's fellow Ulsterman Roger Armstrong of Chiswick Records grabbed Roy Carr of the *NME* by the shoulders and shouted over the music:

"This is more than just enjoyment for me, it's almost a religious experience."

Roy Carr later quizzed Morrison for a feature titled "Portrait Of The Artist As A Moody Bugger". Morrison finally reveals why he disbanded the original Caledonia Soul Orchestra, three years before. "That band was at its peak and I was beginning to realise that there was nothing else to do within that particular context. We'd been doing practically the same show for five years. The only difference was the addition of the string section. Instinctively, I knew when it was over." Van is dressed in a knitted pullover, and clasps a packet of Marlborough. "I wanna get as much fun and as much genuine satisfaction out of making music when I'm forty as I am now – or when I started out with Them – because that's what I do better than anything else." He admits to Carr that he has been too reclusive of late.

However, he is almost hermetic in his comments to Ian Birch of *Melody Maker*, so much so that the eventual article is titled "Morrison: A Silent Movie" when it appears. He takes to interviews like a duck to tarmac. "I hate interviews. I'm doing this for promotion purposes." He does let one bugbear slip, though. "People copying me are selling more records than I am." The cream of these interviews, a whole comedy routine in itself, is a dialogue with Vivien Goldman in *Sounds*. Even the title is a hoot: "I Mean, It's Good To See The Queen And The Duke Of Edinburgh Waving". Vivien – a noted reggae buff who herself put out a new wave single – is far from overawed to meet the great man, in a Kensington restaurant. Van covers his steak with sauce, and eats heartily, shocking the waiters by picking up strawberries with his fingers. There is a sense of prickliness, "the blue eyes behind the blue shades were challenging, daring you to show discomfort".

The results are set out in *Sounds* like a stage dialogue, all good knockabout stuff, with each getting as good as they give. The results are like a play by Harold Pinter. Menace lurks beneath the surface, and there are plenty of silences between the bouts of verbal fencing.

VG: "What brought you over here?"
VM: "BEA I think."
VG: "And what did you have to eat on the plane?"

VM: "Mystery food."

VG: "Like it could be anything, carved out of polystyrene. An ancient British art."

VM: "I don't know what it is, but it's terrible."

Van refuses to discuss his recent spiritual pilgrimage. "Can't tell you. It wouldn't be right for this paper. People who are interested in pop music would not be interested." Goldman suggests, in turn, that Van underestimates his audience. She drives him into a rare direct statement.

VM: "The whole point is, dig yourself. You're not gonna get it from any rock star. You're gonna get it from yourself."

VG: "Are there ever times when you get confused about yourself?"

VM: "Yeah, I went through some *identity* thing, some shit like that, what they call in psychology an identity crisis. It's called *growth*."

Van asks to see the interview before it gets into print, "otherwise things can get bracketed, underlined, added, subtracted, divided, all kinds of things can happen".

This sounds like something out of that televisual symphony of paranoia, *The Prisoner*. In much the same vein, Lester Bangs reports seeing Van on television that summer, singing 'A Cold Wind In August'. He gives a fine, standard reading. "The only trouble is that the whole time he's singing it he paces back and forth in a line on a stage, his eyes tightly shut, his little fireplug body kicking its way upstream against what must be a purgatorial nervousness transferred to the cameraman."

If Van was nervous about his musical past, then he had every right to fear its resurrection. In *Sounds* that September, Chas de Whalley reports that Phonogram have acquired the rights to the Bang material, and reissued it under the title *This Is Where I Came In*. The music is packaged in a hideous sleeve, with a cartoon of Van walking along a New York street, guitar case in one hand, the other clutching his jacket against the chill. It looks like a Woolworth's version of Bob Dylan's *Freewheelin'*, although de Whalley's review suggests a soul mate of Lou Reed. The music here shows Van's mind well on the edge, lurching through a personal hell, and a "thousand backstair drug parties". The collection would walk into "a Top Ten of all-time agonisers, sure as needles is needles and despair is despair".

That scourge of all things hippie, Tony Parsons reviews the album for the *NME* as "My Bang Pages", and compares it favourably with more recent offerings, "as the man himself continues his decline". Like The Stooges' *Funhouse*, or MC5's *Kick Out The Jams*, the album takes on a belated sense of fashionability, music literally before its time. Parsons acts modishly tough. 'He Ain't Give You None' comes "from an area where Morrison excels like no other – that subtle vocal anguish about giving some girl his bleeding heart when anybody else would have broken her legs". Meanwhile, Van's "soulful intensity" stamps its authority on "all the fragmented sources of his inspiration". In November, another part of his musical jigsaw re-emerged from the vinyl scrapyard. WB reissued 'Moondance' as a single: it made Number Ninety-Two in the US Hot Hundred.

Van dropped his pick-up band, Dr John et al. As Goldsmith told Rogan, "Suddenly one day, Van said, 'I don't want to work with this lot anymore, I'm off.'" On the road, Morrison kept to a strict diet, and immediately dismissed anyone found to be taking drugs (which might explain the rapid turnover of his backing musicians). He would phone Goldsmith twice a day, two am and eight am, demanding to know how his new album was selling. Goldsmith now deputed Bill Siddons, one-time manager of Van's old musical friends The Doors, to oversee his American business affairs. The experiment failed, and both were sacked in favour of Bill Graham, Van's old friend from the Fillmore through whom he had met Janet Planet, who began pursuing lost royalties. Van also fell out with Warner Brothers: "I've just been with them too long, it doesn't feel like it felt."

In an interview with Ireland's coming magazine *Hot Press* in March, Van told Dermot Stokes that he should no more be required to discuss his job than any other working man. "I mean, people who go to work from nine to five, how do they do it. Like, nobody stands with a microphone when they come out of the gate and asks, 'How did you do it today?' I mean they just do it. 'How did you work the machine? Was it different from yesterday? Do you do it better when you wear brown overalls than when you wear green overalls?'

"Music to me is spontaneous, writing is spontaneous and it's all based on not trying to do it. From beginning to end, whether it's writing a song, or playing guitar, or a particular chord sequence, or blowing a horn, it's based on improvisation and spontaneity. That's what I keep on trying to get across in interviews, and it's very hard because the process is beyond words."

Meanwhile, Morrison returned to the Manor to record his next album, *Wavelength*. The oracle revealed himself again to Davitt Sigerson in *Sounds* on 1 July. Fresh from the studio, he walks into the Oxford branch of Browns, a spaghetti and salad joint, and orders a large platter of greens. "He isn't annoyed, he just looks that way." As to the new record, "it's all Van Morrison stuff, R&B, soul, folk, whatever. This album is a bit softer, a few more ballad things." Van talks revealingly about his continuing search for Celtic roots. "It's an expression of basic primal survival, it goes back to mythology and whatever, that kind of thing. During that period of time I was very interested in the trip where the Lebanese went to Ireland and the Danes went to Scotland and all that type of stuff. I was born in Northern Ireland, with a Scottish grandmother on my father's side, which puts me in that primal situation."

He is revealed not as a grouch but as a misunderstood leprechaun: "When I'm joking, they take me seriously. I have a dry sense of humour." He talks cogently about mapping out his career in sections. "The way I work is you have a certain set of musicians, you block out a time period, and you just *go* for it. And it comes out the way it comes out."

The new album relied on a musical backbone of Peter Bardens on keyboards, drummer Peter Van Hooke and bassist Mo Foster – who had played together with the reformed Walker Brothers and for the soundtrack of the TV series *Rock Follies*. All three had appeared on the second album by Yellow Dog, and with lead guitarist Bobby Tench – who had earlier played with Jeff Beck and fronted his own band, Hummingbird – this line-up became Van's touring band, fitting him like an old glove. The final piece of the jigsaw, playing rhythm guitar, was Herbie Armstrong, another old musical colleague of Van's. The LP's starring role, though, on accordion, synthesiser and organ belonged to Garth Hudson from The Band. Van himself played saxophone, keyboards and guitar. John Altman remembers going to the Manor with the trumpeter Digby Fairweather "but we waited for six hours and nothing happened".

Wavelength was released in October 1978. The album's cover shot was by photographer Norman Seeff, long associated with Joni Mitchell's svelte sleeves, and he showed Van airbrushed and almost smiling, in tight white trousers, dark T-shirt, and hairy forearms, smoking a cigarette down to the butt. For once Morrison looks like a rock star, or a living James Dean, drugged with mysticism, and behind him are crayon scribbles in blue and purple, as if by a child.

In the States, the album made a rapid ascent to Twenty-Eight, supplemented by a Top Fifty placing for the title track single. Within three months it went gold, and became the fastest selling album of his career. In the UK, 'Bright Side Of The Road' became Van's first solo UK chart single, coming in at Sixty-Three. The album achieved everything that *A Period Of Transition* had failed to, combining a radio friendly sound and hummable songs with an underlying mystical message, there for those who understood.

'Kingdom Hall' goes back to Van's worship with his mother as a Jehovah's Witness, but sexualises it into a potent blend of love and religion. For Dave McCullough, this opening cut "pulls the album together with a strutting, cocksure authority, all fresh upfront breadth". As Van told *Rolling Stone*, "When I started out I was in dance bands, and I wanted to get back into it. I see it as a way of *not* thinking, really. I see dancing as just dancing. When you're really into playing music, the words become irrelevant when you're in that space. And I feel that way about dancing, it goes beyond words." A song about losing yourself.

In 'Checkin' It Out' a love affair runs into the sand, but is rescued by invisible "guides and spirits along the way". Saving a relationship is compared to meditation: both put us in touch with the eternal. For Max Bell, Van sings here with "a voice of crystal sweet reason": for Dave McCullough, the song "winds like a glistening river. Musical enchantment". A song about finding yourself.

'Natalia' divides our two guest critics. Dave McCullough finds "a love song of touching desperation, the contemporary relationship, fleeting and preciously disposable", while Max Bell is more cynical; it is "a song for swinging suckers". Whatever, Van's vocal, the backing riff, the girls' voices and the tune are all gorgeous, like a rich cake, even if the words mean little. We are in the realm of magic again, when two lovers first meet.

'Venice USA' has accordion from Garth Hudson, and a fairground beat like 'Willie And The Hand Jive'. Love again, with tears full of joy, and a finding of one's self that is far more than geographical. A moment of epiphany for Van, the "streets are wet with rain". Of course, they are even wetter in Venice, Italy.

For McCullough, 'Lifetimes' is music "not merely *about* but *is* the very stuff of eternity, inexorable and mighty". Only Morrison and Dylan can give the impression of "by some divine gift actually possessing the complete work deep within them". For Bell, "he turns a worksong into a personal spiritual without resorting to hackneyed sincerity". Two of rock's finest critics have centred independently onto the heart of this song, a holy stillness. This is one of Van's finest songs to the silence, an anthem – an overworked word in pop criticism, but apt here – with tinkling harpsichord, emphasising the feeling of being outside time. "So many lifetimes." The boatman is Charon, ferrying the dead over the River Styx, and there are echoes here of Leonard Cohen's 'Suzanne', Ralph McTell's 'Ferryman', Dylan's 'Watching The River Flow' and Kiki Dee's 'I've Got The Music In Me', all at once. Good vibrations.

If side one constitutes a suite of music, a kind of spiritual rejoinder to Bowie's Ziggy Stardust, then side two is looser, "pivotal modern soul" according to Bell. Its linking theme, as with 'Venice USA' is a series of tributes to American culture, just as Van is about to move back to England. The title track is – all at once – a love song about the mysterious and unspoken communication between a couple, and a fond memory of Van's habit as a boy of tuning into the Voice of America. 'Come Back Baby' refers to Ray Charles, subject of a life long musical love affair. Sex is not the only fruit.

'Santa Fe' was written with Jackie DeShannon, and sees Van giving up some of his much vaunted creative control: it is the first musical collaboration to appear on any of his albums, and is relaxed country rock in the same vein as Cowboy Or England's 'Help Yourself'. A guitar sounding close to tears helps the segue into 'Beautiful Obsession', a song of love to woman or God, which for Max Bell "revisits the undulating terrain of Morrison's timeless mysteries wherein a series of apparently commonplace statements assume a vivid coherence, building on the groove".

More cowboy imagery in 'Hungry For Your Love', with a lovely mellow groove, lots of electric piano from Van, Herbie Armstrong on companionable acoustic guitar and Morrison declaring a love for buckskin. 'Take It Where You Find It' deals with a phrase, "lost dreams and found dreams in America", which had come to mind during a flight from LA to SF. It is a quest song, as with so many of Van's later lyrics, and there is a fourth of July pride to the chorus. Another song about magic, and the search for spiritual illumination, through earthly love. "I'm gonna walk down the street until I see my shining light." This is a view of spiritual consolation which can also take in mutability, "change come over". As Morrison told Chris Welch in the *Melody Maker*, his songs were strong enough to take on a life of their own. "It doesn't worry me if people have different interpretations. Things I've written a long time ago mean different things now. When I'm performing them, they mean totally different things. The songs, the meanings, everything changes constantly."

The reviewers were ecstatic this time around. For Dave McCullough in *Sounds*, here were "statements of strength and passion, a totally fruitful discovery of wavelength". For film maker and novelist Chris Petit, in *Melody Maker*, Van "sounds like a man who has discovered himself". For all that, there was something chilly about the album, "music of a controlled excellence that permits no excess or access". The *NME*'s Max Bell found "a very up and satisfied Van. The best moments come when he transfers his rolling road lines to a meditative, near spiritual quietude. If Van Morrison's new found satisfaction runs to keeping this band on for some live performances then the full renaissance of a genuine talent will be complete."

The same band – without Garth Hudson, but with Katie Kissoon and Anne Peacock on backing vocals – carried out a ten week tour of the USA in early autumn to promote the album, playing dates in major American cities. It was Van's first major tour for four years. He opened in SF's Old Waldorf, storming through a seventy-five minute set. He even told off the audience for clapping.

There is a bootleg CD, taken from a concert from New York's Bottom Line club, distributed at first legitimately on the King Biscuit

Flower Hour in 1989. John Collis attributes this to 15 May 1978, but another source gives the more likely date of 1 November of that same year. Van talks about songs from his new – not his next – album, and five titles are drawn from it. The performance is pleasant, if a little perfunctory. Bardens is the star of the show, adding all kinds of sound colours, but the lack of a horn section leaves a lot of gaps. The compere announces, in a stoned rap, "Star time, show time, the one and only living legend himself Mr Van Morrison", and the opener, 'Moondance', features one verse sung (most appealingly) by Katie Kissoon, and a sax solo presumably by Van himself.

'Into The Mystic' lopes like a wolf, and 'Brown Eyed Girl' replaces the customary horns with the girls' voices. 'Natalia' from the new album is slowed right down at the end, with a new coda, "you don't have to worry bout the motion on the ocean", and the girls sounding like sirens. The show stopper is 'Caravan', at first super relaxed, almost Las Vegas, but Van's soliloquy makes "radio" sound like "radish", delves deep into the song, almost taking it into silence. "They said the coast was clear, baby, the code was jammed." Van is stuck on the phone, between "212" and "415" and an "011441" – he spells these out painstakingly – before leading his band to a triumphant climax.

Sound problems at the New York Palladium led to Van storming off stage early in the set. Concerts in Chicago and Washington were cancelled, and the tour limped to a conclusion in LA, where he was castigated for providing lukewarm entertainment. Sylvie Simmonds, writing for *Sounds*, was convinced that Morrison used the first half of his concerts as a sound check. "For half an hour or more in UCLA's Royce hall, it sounded like someone chewing gum in an aircraft hangar. Two days later in the Long Beach Theatre, it sounded like he was singing through a tea strainer." The audience at the latter kept shouting for the vocals to be turned louder. Simmonds noted five disjointed musicians going through the motions, their solos "as out of place as pigeon droppings on a mink coat". Van seemed to give up just as he was warming up, and "with an acoustic guitar strapped to his podgy front" he was visually reminiscent of Neil Diamond. "Maybe it's a good thing he's been walking out before the end of some of his shows. If he's not careful he'll be racing the audience to the exit."

Justin Pierce, reviewing the same tour for *NME*, found Van "serious, concentrating on a careful performance", but despite the singer's obvious shyness considered that, as usual, "one or two brilliant moments make it all worthwhile". Morrison himself was unrepentant, as he told Chris Welch. "I'm not doing a rock 'n' roll show, you know. I don't come out wearing leather jeans shouting 'Shake it baby'. I did that long ago. The best gig for me on the whole American tour was a small club in Colorado. Bang, it was happening."

On January 1979, *Melody Maker* carried a lead story that "Van's tour Is On", opposite a photo of The Jam, and above a tribute to Charles Mingus. A major British tour was announced, opening with concerts in Cork, Belfast – all tickets sold out in half an hour – and Dublin, and with an augmented band including sax players John Altman and Pat Kyle and Toni Marcus on violin. As to the American debacle, "He was very tired and it was a combination of a health problem and a head problem. He has always had a bit of an unstable character, and he just got freaked out." The man responsible for this prose was rewarded with the sack, and WEA's boss Mo Austin issued a grovelling apology. Van was still furious when he talked to Chris Welch, for the paper that started the controversy and sitting in the Royal Garden Hotel – in the garden, in fact – as a blizzard raged.

Welch found a man of "charm and sensitivity". Joined by Phil Lynott, and dressed in an old fur coat, Crazy Gang style, he laughed a lot. "Yeah, I feel happier in myself. I guess that's because I can balance things out more now." As to punk rock, currently snarling like a mad dog at the heels of sixties superstars like Van – even if most punk figureheads were actually sixties veterans themselves, but let *that* pass – "these punks are pretty smart kids, and they've got a lot of it nailed. But they're losing by the way they're attacking. To be truthful, I don't like punk rock that much." After a sideswipe at journalists – "they look for dirt, so I don't let them interview me" – Van gets down to the real nitty gritty of his art. "Music is like a healing thing, and we're all being healed. I'm being healed. That's what I know, what I feel. People go to a rock 'n' roll show and they come away feeling better."

Welch points out, ironically, given the presence of Lynott who will prove to be yet one more martyr to the lifestyle, that rock 'n' roll is also a force of destruction. Van agrees. "There's too many sensitive people around that don't want to be shattered anymore." Morrison opens up further, revealing that when he was young, "I thought I wasn't going to live very long". So, was 'TB Sheets' wish fulfilment? "I was a complete recluse most of my life, whereas most of my peer group were into having parties and owning a Mary Quant watchstrap...but it's just me. I didn't wake up one morning and invent being into music. I've been into it all my life."

On the opening night of the tour, in Cork, Van played an eighty minute set. He entered to a Mose Allison record playing over the PA, and the band stretched out as their confidence grew, with Tench outstanding on lead guitar, and new sudden death endings to songs and quick tempo changes enlivening the set. Toni Marcos played a pre-Edison stoviola, with horn attached, and Van wore a furry cap, just like a bear.

The two Belfast gigs, at the Whitla Hall, were Van's first home appearance since his blues show with Alexis Korner at Queen's, way before the release of 'Brown Eyed Girl'. Prehistoric times. The show was on the scale of a local Cup derby or Mohammed Ali's last hurrah in Las Vegas. Morrison's presence in an out-of-town hotel provoked a feeding frenzy by the local media. A regional television crew was kept waiting for a promised sentimental walkabout along Hyndford Road; photographers were turned away, and provincial reporters were not even able to blag a complimentary seat for the show. The Troubles were boiling up, and on the day of Van's first gig, the "Shankhill slashers" were about to be sentenced for mass murder.

Van's mother Violet had written a letter to a Belfast paper after her son's previous tour, when he gave his home town a miss. "His father and I pleaded with him not to come, as we had very strong reasons why we did not want him to come home (yes *home*, he still thinks of Belfast as home). He isn't worrying about his own safety, we are." Accompanied by his new girlfriend Brenda, "a tall, shapely, fair haired American", Van gave his all. As local reporter Chris Moore put it, "if his first concert on Tuesday was hot, Wednesday's was a scorcher". This is confirmed by footage preserved in the *Van Morrison In Ireland* video, and by Tony Stewart in the *NME*. "He strides across the stage, a balding short figure dressed in black but stocky, hard and aggressive looking." He looks like a tough pool hall hustler, in a black leather jacket, "pure Cagney". The band display a range of textures reminiscent of The

Caledonia Soul Orchestra, "first with the dark resonance of Toni Marcus's violin, then Pat Kyle's bright sharp tenor sax and finally Bobby Tench's prickly electric guitar". Meanwhile, Morrison's control on stage is ruthless, a pocket general conducting his troops.

They open with 'Moondance', Kissoon taking a verse, then a slightly ponderous 'And It Stoned Me', then flow gracefully into 'Into The Mystic'. As this is not 1970, they then come bang up to date with a rocky 'Wavelength', the "poised blues" of 'Don't Look Back' and a rolling 'Wild Night'. Katie sings 'Crazy Love', "with Kyle's flute circling, dipping and gliding off Peter Bardens' delicate piano phrasing". Van is back for 'Checking It Out', with John Altman on baritone sax, then it's 'Kingdom Hall' and a raft of classics, a jangly and ragged 'Moonshine Whiskey', a controlled 'Tupelo Honey'. On 'St Dominic's Preview', when Van reaches the line about "it's a long way to Belfast city" the crowd explode, as do Van's lungs on 'I've Been Working', blowing the guts out of his harmonica. Indeed, the crowd are part of the performance, adding to the inspiration. They shout fruitlessly for 'Gloria', between a ten minute 'Caravan' and a final encore of 'Cyprus Avenue'. Van laughs, shouts, and falls to the ground. Lights out.

After the Tuesday gig, he jammed back in the hotel, with Phil Coulter on piano. Afterwards, Dylan style, the singer subjected the *NME*'s Tony Stewart – who I have quoted above, obviously in sympathy with Van's music – to a public mauling beneath sweaty arc lights and in front of a film crew. "The whole point of what we're doing tonight is I want to show people *why* I don't do interviews." Published as "When Irish Eyes Are Scowling", there seems little common ground with the inspirational figure on stage, who had the local audience following and cheering his every move. Pete Silverton writes a history of Van's career in *Sounds*, neatly titled "Astral Years", full of reminiscences of Van's lost years in Belfast – managed by Dave Robinson, later of Stiff records and Madness fame, it appears – appearing on stage with a bottle of wine in each pocket, which he would proceed to drink. Silverton reports the Belfast show as a religious ceremony, with 'Gloria' – performed the previous night – as "the final mutual blessing between the performer and audience before each went their separate ways". He then encounters Van backstage, and found a different person. "As I stared into his piggy eyes, he shrank from me, shrivelling into his ageing tweed jacket, his face a mixture of confused terror and embarrassed distaste. He scuttled away like a field mouse, his barrel chest pushed forward, hastening his speed away from the dreaded hack."

The Belfast of Morrison's childhood had been transformed by the normal processes of time as well as by being set in a war zone. The Maritime still stood, but it no longer held Club Rado, while ex-members of Them like Jim Armstrong were still playing R&B in venues like the Harp. From behind his post office counter in County Down, Jim's predecessor, Billy Harrison, was resurfacing with the first of two self-penned albums. In the second, 1980's *Billy Who?*, he'd get a lot off his chest in lyrics referring to Orangefield school and Castlereagh Road, and a song evocatively titled 'Baby Please Don't Go'. Along with Alan Henderson and Eric Wrickson, he had reformed the band for a tour of Germany after 1976's Decca retrospective, *Rock Roots: Them*, had proved a worthwhile exercise. It sold well throughout Europe, indicating a new audience for Them's music, dated but timeless. Indeed, new Ulster bands like Stiff Little Fingers and The Undertones and small town labels like Good Vibrations were recreating the sound of guitars thrashed at speed to machine gun drumming, and a young tearaway on vocals, screaming defiance. Just like the angry young Them, in fact.

The *Van Morrison Live In Ireland* video captures some great live music, especially the show stopper 'Cyprus Avenue' though the colour is grainy and the band look curiously dated in their long hair and seventies clothes. Conversely, the anti-fashion Van looks timeless. There is interesting footage of the band at play, in the hotel, travelling to the gig in a coach, and of Van revisiting the scenes of his childhood. This is intercut with 'St Dominic's Preview', and Van is literally conquered in a car seat as he travels along Cyprus Avenue. Needless to say, it is raining. The video captures some extremely emotional and intimate performances: I admit to being close to tears during 'Tupelo Honey', for no good reason. Here is the very opposite of the truculent Morrison in interview mode, in psychic tune with his band, rocking on his feet and singing with full fury, in a way only Joe Cocker can approach. Toni Marcus is another centre of attention as she bobs and weaves in time to her violin. Even on the tour bus she is practising, playing phantom music in the rain.

John Altman confirms what the video indicates. "They were great shows in Ireland in 1979. I remember there was an *NME* reporter travelling with us between Dublin and Belfast, and a few things went wrong and he just decided to put the knife in. The Johnny Rogan book seemed to be just put together from articles. What you have to remember is these were seminal moments."

That *NME* reporter in question, Tony Stewart, does capture the most symbolic moment of the tour, though, following Van's appearance in Dublin. A solitary punk in the audience has been bellowing insults, during 'Cyprus Avenue' of all things. "When the houselights came up he didn't see the bearded, angry hippie coming for him. He struggled limply as strong, bony hands grasped his throat. They spat fierce curses at each other and crashed into wooden chairs." Hardly Woodstock! "Bouncers separated them, but the punk lost his temper, picked up a chair and threw it into the people leaving the Stadium. He was flattened by five grisly bouncers: punched, kicked and dragged, the panicking punk was out of the hall." A metaphor for two warring rock music generations.

Allan Jones' review for the *Melody Maker* of Van's Hammersmith Odeon gig was titled "Living Legends Die Here". The band, soon to be disbanded, "rumbled with a sluggish disinterest", while Van "just looked totally pissed off". The music was soporific, and lasted only fifty minutes before the encores. Even 'Gloria' was reduced to "an inoffensive little dirge". Jones foresaw "a future in cabaret". Meanwhile, Van was sketching out a more positive direction, talking to John Tobler for the Virgin house magazine *Blank Space*. "We do spontaneous, improvised music now, more poetic music, but we don't do it on gigs." Not yet, anyway. As to the Troubles, which had stopped him revisiting Bangor, the scene of childhood holidays, music could conquer all. "Anybody can understand it. It's not this religion, that religion, black, white, green. Music is universal, it's for every people."

"I had a long conversation with Van the other day," grumbled Steve Winwood in 1981 to the *Times*, "and we found out that we have that in common. He's always been told that *Astral Weeks* is his best record. How's he going to beat that?" Van's past was being recycled by others. 'Gloria' had been radically revamped by Patti Smith, and became a cornerstone of the American new wave. In 1982 Dexy's Midnight

Runners were to follow their number one hit 'Come On, Eileen' with their version of Van's 'Jackie Wilson Said'. (A *Top Of The Pops* appearance featured a large backdrop of darts player Jockie Wilson!) They also invited Morrison to attend a rehearsal in Birmingham, with the view to him becoming their producer. They failed. They adopted his "Reliable Sources" strategy, by announcing that information on future plans would be spread via full page advertisements in the music press, having radically cut down on their press interviews.

Morrison himself again troubled the hit parade, with 'Bright Side Of The Road', the opening track of *Into The Music*, his new album, which itself climbed to Number Twenty-One, his highest since Them. Its lyrics dealt largely with the need for some kind of religious assurance, in increasingly complex and uncertain times. Although the new album was recorded in Sausilito, it was written while Van was staying with Herbie Armstrong in the Cotswold village of Epwell. Its spirit of place is correspondingly strong. Caledonia Soul Orchestra bassist David Marcus was back on board, and there was a new brass section of Pee Wee Ellis – one-time leader of The JBs, James Brown's backing band – and Mark Isham – whose unique sound "fusing jazz and New Age minimalism" would influence Van's own flight into a new sound. As Van told Paul Vincent of KMEL radio in 1981, "the message is getting very, very quiet. When you get really quiet you can actually hear yourself."

Into The Music was released in August 1979 on Van's new label Polydor: its cast list also includes Ry Cooder on slide guitar, and Robin Williamson, once of Celtic musical explorers The Incredible String Band, on penny whistle. In another studio shot by Norman Seef, Van is haloed in blue on the front cover – the colour of religious contemplation, and another link with Joni Mitchell. The same picture has turned sepia on the back, as if with age. Van's eyes are closed in silent contemplation, his wavy hair is starting to recede, and a guitar strap on his left shoulder is the only clue to his profession.

Released in the same week as Dylan's *Slow Train Coming*, a smooth masterpiece of evangelical spite, many saw the album as testimony to Morrison's conversion to what John Collis calls "pantheistic mystical Christianity". Paul Rambali is careful to differentiate this "espousal of the joys of faith" from Dylan's "obsessional baptist fervour", writing not in the *Church Times* but in *NME*. Dylan's conversion was absolute (at the time), a complete redirection of his life and art ushered in by a series of concerts at the Fox Warfield Theatre in San Francisco. There, in some of the greatest concerts of his life, he unveiled a completely new band, set list and persona, and made a bonfire of his sins and most of his audience. *Into The Music* is part of a far gentler and less dogmatic process, carried on from Van's two previous albums. It deliberately echoes the title and spirit of 'Into The Mystic', and God is perceived in music, not the other way round. The record is close in spirit to Richard and Linda Thompson's 1978 album *First Light*, with its participants bathed in healing joy.

As Phil Coulter told Rogan, religion is "one of his great interests outside" – not instead of – "music. I think he's been into everything from mysticism to psychical experiences, through the more organised religions such as Roman Catholicism. Not practising, but studying it." And as Van himself told Steve Turner, "I was born in a Christian environment in a Christian country and I was born after the Christ event, so that makes me a Christian." That said, "sometimes I fluctuate. When you say to me 'Christian', that's got about twenty lights going out." It is as if he is "receiving some sort of inner direction", a process which the singer neither fully comprehends, nor questions.

'Bright Side Of The Road' relies not, as with the new Dylan, on a biblical text but is an answer in song to 'The Dark Side Of The Street', and is wonderfully light, in spirit and texture. Dave McCullough describes its "chirpy pastoral optimism", and it is a love song to a woman – and music – rather than to God, with laughing violin from Toni Marcus. 'Full Force Gale' has the cheerful punch of the best gospel singing, and sees Van "lifted up by the Lord". The experience of being taken out of everyday reality goes back to his childhood, and the epiphanies of *Astral Weeks*: as with Wordsworth, the divine is perceived not through religious teachings but through Nature, the garden of the next song, 'Stepping Out Queen'. "Windfall" here both ties into the previous song, and the notion of a sinner saved, but the thrust of this song is a woman in her full glory – Clapton's 'Wonderful Tonight'. The song is Buddhist, not Christian, if one has to tie it down, with Van's lover working out her "dharma", in the latest of his many songs of rebirth and reincarnation. "Wipe your mirror clean", of the past. Ben Cruikshank suggests that this song is about a transvestite making his face up, Madame George going on the town. Bizarre, but possible.I argued earlier that Van's work is a continuation of the oral tradition, when bards and wandering singers – or indeed itinerant bluesmen – roamed the countryside, and in 'Troubadours' he celebrates that lost world. The music has the weightlessness of Honeybus's 'I Can't Let Maggie Go', where brass and violin soar rather than thump. 'Rolling Hills' is the missing link between *Veedon Fleece* and Van's work with The Chieftains, live in the studio. God is again perceived through the natural world, and though the singer "will read my *Bible* among the rolling hills", it is from the latter that he seems to derive most consolation. The lyrics are a city man's dream of an ideal countryside, a version of pastoral. Here God – "Him" – is found in calm, not the full force gale. John Collis reckoned that "if The Wurzels were a serious group, they might sound like this"!

'You Make Me Feel So Free' switches from Irish folk to soul, but with the same lightness of touch. A strange song, which combines one of Van's best jokes with inner desperation, following his muse through a corrupt and wearying music industry: he looks for salvation in a girlfriend, not a puff of incense. 'Angeliou' is also about earthly love, its hypnotic power, in what Dave McCullough describes as "a typically mystical and floating song that seems to go nowhere but goes everywhere after a few listens". Beautifully arranged, with tinkling piano, soulful violin and comforting brass, this is Caledonia soul music at full power. Van sounds effortlessly sad, revisiting Paris in the springtime and somehow rescuing it from cliche by the sheer honesty of his singing. 'Angeliou' contains the word angel, and the woman here is both flesh and blood – a chance encounter in the street – and ethereal. The half spoken recitation here is deeply seductive.

'And The Healing Has Begun' is the central song here, and perhaps in Morrison's whole career. It starts just like 'Cyprus Avenue', no coincidence as the line about "songs from way back when" hints, and with a walk down the avenue (of dreams), to the sound of a haunted violin. A song of full, blazing sex as well as revelation. The healing here is like that in Arthurian myth, the wounded King restored through the action of the Grail, but it is also through as graphic a seduction, almost, as the original live version of 'Gloria'. Van even names the drinks and musical accompaniment – Muddy Waters of course.

Talking later to Dermot Stokes of *Hot Press*, Van goes into ancient teachings he is resurrecting here: "In the old days if someone was sick, they'd get a harp and play a chord for a certain thing – to heal this affliction or whatever. And these teachings are still floating around in various religious sects. They've been lost but you can still dig them out." Largely due to the work of the likes of Morrison, these ancient techniques are very much part of the contemporary "healing arts" movement. My own local hospital in Southampton now employs a musician to play to sick children, and help their recovery, through sounds of joy.

'It's All In The Game' is a slow and emotional cover version of Tommy Edward's 1957 hit, also covered by The Four Tops. For Dave McCullough, "the tone of bitter tenderness is quite stunning, Morrison uses and stretches the familiar melody and structures of the song to create a mood of hypnotic transcendence". Marcus is again outstanding here, providing a whole sub-text through her violin. In the final surprise of a magnificent album, Van frames the previous song – not his own of course, in 'You Know What They're Writing About' – love which "lifts you up" just like God in 'Full Force Gale'. It is like a Sufi improvisation, and makes McCullough almost gasp. "It's Morrison suddenly walking out of the speakers and telling you what he thinks of that standard, the great love ballad." Van, and the album, ends with a mysterious evocation of two lovers, back on the dark side of the street, meeting "down by the pylons". The music ebbs into silence, with his psychic whisper, and Marcus's spooky violin.

An album like *Into The Music* needs time to grow into, and reviews at the time were mixed. Ian Birch of *Melody Maker* found that "nowadays, people don't so much discover Van Morrison as grow old with him", and the album showed a "depleted imagination", the lyrics "impoverished, recycled cliches". Much like Birch's review, in fact. Paul Rambali, in the *NME*, was open in his hatred for a bland record with slapdash songs. He was not dismayed by Van's refusal here of his greatest gift, to "wring tears from the most commonplace words". That Dave McCullough, in *Sounds*, disagrees can be gauged from the title alone, "Van Is God (Part 617)", and his review really deserves to be reprinted in full. Here is "one of Morrison's most rounded, complete and ordered albums ever", a stimulating celebration of being alive, and a "less diffuse progression from the preceding album's fundamental search for direction". Morrison has always been "far too far ahead of his critics", McCullough excepted.

His conclusion is apt, particularly for the present writer. "I remember somebody once said of Joni Mitchell's *Blue* that it was an album you'd be proud to own for the rest of your life. I think you could say the same about *Into The Music.*"

Van took these new songs on the road, with mixed results. John Altman remembers the Glasgow Apollo show on that tour as a near disaster. "I think Van got vertigo because of the extremely high stage. It's very strange because the night before in Edinburgh he was stupendous. The afternoon before the Edinburgh gig we were all in Henderson's and Van was the life and soul of the party, talking about when he was in Belfast with Herbie and everything." There was a jam in a hotel in Edinburgh, with Altman on piano and Van singing. An American came up to Van and said, "You sound really good, do you do this professionally?"

"Then we got to Glasgow and it was snowing and Van's mood had completely changed. We all thought he was overplaying it, as he kept saying the drop was dangerous and the guy who did the lighting on the show was later killed on a Kate Bush tour when he fell down a trapdoor." At the same gig – "it was one of those nights" – Altman "walked into one of those metal things they have backstage and dented the sax and changed its sound (for the better I must add)". There was lots of humour, to allay the music, serious as your life. One night on the tour bus, Van performed a medley from *The Sound Of Music*. He also had a penchant for George Formby numbers. Perhaps as a result, "by the time we got to Europe it was just myself and the fiddle. I think Herbie had gone and Pete Wingfield replaced Peter Bardens and we did shows all over Europe and at Ingliston for the Edinburgh Festival."

Roy Carr, of the *NME*, met Van at Stockholm's Alexander Club, following a "near faultless concert" in front of five thousand people, with few on stage announcements, but an audience that warms to a performer "for his sheer presence and his ability of communicate on his own terms". Contrary to media myth, Van proves affable and outgoing: "Basically I'm a very simple person. And as such I'm probably far too honest, too blunt when interviewed." He intends at a later date to write his autobiography.

The band reached Edinburgh in late August, for a big open air festival, which combined the best of the old and new waves. John Peel reckoned on air that Van was lucky to be hearing fellow Belfast boys The Undertones. Also on the bill were Brum reggae band Steel Pulse, Squeeze with their original ivory tinkler Jools Holland, the psychodrama of Talking Heads and The Chieftains. There was a Mystery Guest, the aggressively Scottish folksinger Dick Gaughan, whose best work shares Van's fiery intensity, and whose masterpiece *Handful Of Earth* examines exactly the Scotland/Northern Ireland interface of Morrison's Caledonian experiments. The opening track, 'Erin-Go-Bragh' has a native Scots being mistaken for a "Pat", and there is even a Danish tune, 'Randers Hopska', given a Scots lilt.

As Allan Jones reported in his article "A Day At The Races" for *Melody Maker*, The Chieftains preceded Van Morrison. "They sat in a semi-circle and looked like a gaggle of middle aged postmen, teachers and a scout master...which is almost exactly what they are." Van seemed unusually bright and happy, with a new line-up, including his old sparring partner Pete Wingfield. Jones was no fan, however, of the "utterly dreadful Toni Marcus on violin. This horrendous woman is incapable of musical subtlety, she seems to have added flamboyant gypsy dance movements to her usual repertoire of grimaces. This earned her several reproving glances from Mr Morrison. One hears that she will not be with the band for very much longer."

A friend of mine later had a brief affair with Toni in LA, and tells a sad story of her moving for no good reason into a garden shed on her own property. One hopes she is better now, as her talents are far more than Jones gives credit for: a classical prodigy, her violin embroiders *Into The Music* as Scarlet Riviera did Dylan's Rolling Thunder Review. Back to Edinburgh, and Jones reports that 'And The Healing Has Begun' gave Morrison his best vocal showcase, while 'Call Me Up In Dreamland' was a buoyant, unexpected delight, though 'Into The Mystic' was treated with "perfunctory indifference". He played a rare version of 'Here Comes The Night' and ends with 'Brown Eyed Girl' and 'Gloria', both "marred by the vocal contortions of Katie Kissoon, who should be shown the same door as Toni Marcus". Sexist or what.

Van's role in foregrounding women musicians, and giving them an equal profile to men, no more and no less, should be applauded as before its time.

He then brought on The Chieftains to accompany him on 'Rolling Hills' and "a rather sloppy version" of 'Goodnight Irene'. Jones, a professional cynic, and a true comic as a writer, is unimpressed. "The Chieftains plucked, plonked and squawked, Toni Marcus scraped and screeched, Van bellowed and howled. He invited the audience to sing. They, at least, had the distinction of being in tune."

Jones went on to edit *Melody Maker*. Young Manchester new waver Paul Morley, never one to use two words where twenty will do, went on to promote the likes of Frankie Goes To Hollywood, whose T-shirts cornered the market, and whose albums now litter second hand shops on every street corner. While still a humble scribe for *NME*, he reviewed the same day out, his article headed by a photograph of Van being accompanied down some steps by a man holding an umbrella, like a native bearer from the Raj, and the headline "It Didn't Rain On Van But He Pissed All Over Edinburgh".

Later, "the foreboding Van Morrison gloomily led a basic seven piece showband through restrained motions". Back to his roots, The Monarchs' Scottish tour revisited, "his set had a sour sense of pointless functioning, it was sullen and obnoxiously smug". As for Van, "stuffed inelegantly into tight waistcoat and trousers, it seemed as though he was punishing himself out of some secret puritanical ritual". His band worked with unflappable skill and sympathy", but "Morrison's dour intimidation and severely chaste presence lacks dignity; when the voice isn't giving that to him it's a sorry, hollow sight and sound." The band were then joined by The Chieftains for "a mawkish, hymnal finale". The audience, soaked to the skin, drifted away.

There is an anecdote which circulated among Van's band about this same gig, which Morley is viewing through the sourness of new wave sunglasses. Peter Van Hooke sometimes would blank out a number as a joke. When a number was being counted in he would say, "How does it go?" He initially played 'Goodnight Irene' four to the bar, while another musician shouted out "it's a waltz". No wonder it sounded so rough, but from this chance meeting, a mighty collaboration would later grow.

Morrison was always ready to experiment on stage, at least once. John Altman recalls an open air gig in Norway, with Steel Pulse and Nils Lofgren. "He had just put together 'All In The Game'. Pete Wingfield got into a gospel groove during my alto solo and we all got into it, a kind of Ray Charles, Hank Crawford thing. And the crowd loved it, they were really going mad and a lot was made of it afterwards. When Van came off stage Pete Wingfield said to him, 'Great gig'. All Van said was 'No sevenths'. He meant don't take the music into other areas. He wanted the open sound of just the major chords."

A promo LP was released as *Live At The Roxy*, in that same year, but the set – later much bootlegged – is actually from late 1978, judging by the line-up and set list. A good, but not stunning concert until the final track, lacking the extra charge of violin or brass. Bobby Tench is too effacing a player to really cut loose on lead guitar, at least in this context.

The compere announces "Ladies and gentleman, George Ivan Morrison", and we're straight into 'Brown Eyed Girl' with a synthesiser like a penny whistle. 'Crazy Love' is sung by Katie Kissoon, but the real musical treat comes with the final encore, 'Cyprus Avenue'. It is a sad and thoughtful take, with lots of ad libs from Van. "It seems like 'Last Year In Marienbad', and a Fellini movie too" is just one. The phantom lover is addressed thus, "you came walking down in the wind and the rain, when the snow was on the ground, when the sun shone through the trees, and you were standing there", then more jaw droppingly as "in all your sanctified, vaginal Baptist revelation". I've listened dozens of times, and I'm sure I'm not mishearing "virginal" here. The song seems to stop on the word "revelation" and Van roars, like a man possessed. "I woke up this morning, and said…it's too late to stop now." And it is.

His journey into the mystic continued with his new band. A black and white video shot at the Capitol Theatre, Passaic, New Jersey, in October 1979 features a transitional line-up still with Toni Marcus and Katie Kissoon, along with Pee Wee Ellis, Mark Isham, and the return of Pete Wingfield and John Platania. On 'Tupelo Honey', Van puffs at a cigarette and swigs from a beer bottle between verses. Stimulated by far more than alcohol and tobacco, he uses the song to talk in tongues, producing two voices in dialogue, just like the actor Jonathan Pryce playing both Hamlet and his father's ghost. There are also new, improvised lyrics: "King James *Bible*, read it on the balcony". An instinctive Christianity has began to pervade his music. Old friend Herbie Armstrong was "born again", a subject which pervades Van's work, and on his album *Back Against The Wall*, thanked Christ for entering his art, playing music "for pure love of every day". He hoped to persuade his old friend likewise, though pointing out that Van "certainly knew about the Lord long before I did". Van, in turn, claimed just to be "groping in the dark for a little more light". This theme engulfs *Common One*, his next album.

Meanwhile, the *Sugar Was Tough* bootleg captures a live gig at Berkeley in early 1980. The compere announces "welcome back home to San Francisco", and Van had indeed moved back there from Brentwood. The set list features 'Bright Side Of The Road', 'Angeliou' and 'Full Force Gale' from his latest record, alongside old chestnuts like an anthemic, cheerful 'Here Comes The Night' – robbed of all its anguish – and 'Moondance', 'Tupelo Honey' even 'Brown Eyed Girl'. The line-up is as at new Jersey, all girly chorus and sweet brass, further sweetened by violin. Toni Marcus is still in the band. In July, Van played the Montreux Jazz Festival, with a slimmed down band which included another name from his past, John Allair, on keyboards. A stunning video exists of 'Ballerina', with Platania embroidering the song with long, gnarled hands which play over his guitar like a spider. Van seems to be lost in a dream. Two new songs were featured, 'Summertime In England' and 'Haunts Of Ancient Peace', both from the next album.

In February, Van and his full band – including Allair and lead guitarist Mick Cox – had travelled over to Super Bear studios in the south of France, for an intense week of recording. The album was mixed back in California, rather than the Albion which inspired its songs. Joni Mitchell's engineer Henry Lewy received a namecheck for production work. Jeff Labes returned, as musical arranger, with Toni Marcus replaced by an anonymous string orchestra. The whole gang sound like a wide screen Caledonia Soul Orchestra, the full monte.

Common One was released in September 1980, though the record company were unable to find a single from the album. The front cover, a photograph by the possibly pseudonymous Rudy Legname, shows a lonely figure walking high on a ridgetop, silhouetted by the sky. With stick in hand, he picks his way over a rough terrain, which on closer inspection is studded with prehistoric tumuli, arranged like a sleeping dragon. The serpent paths of Avebury. This could easily be the ploughman, homeward plodding his weary way, of Thomas Gray's 'Elegy Written In A Country Churchyard' – who "leaves the world to darkness and to me". Or it could be one of Wordsworth's idiot peasants, full of native wisdom. The graphics, by John Paul Jones – one presumes not the Led Zeppelin bassist – are straight out of Robert Graves' grammar of poetic myth, *The White Goddess*, a hart caught in the thicket.

The album put Van back in cult corner, reaching Number Fifty-Three in the UK album charts, and Seventy-Three in the States. Allair reports that Van's method in the studio was to run down a new song on acoustic guitar, and record as soon as the musicians learned the changes. "Right off the top, the raw stuff – that's what he wants. He's pretty non-verbal. He wouldn't tell you what to play, but he'd tell you if he didn't like it." *Common One* has just this spontaneity of sound, and a freshness all its own.

'Haunts Of Ancient Peace' is like a slowed down Traffic, a search for the grail down in Avalon on a quiet Sunday morning. Van seeks "love and light", thus setting out the object of his quest. Allan Jones talks of "a slow jostling of trumpets and saxophones", and the music drifts between the speakers, druidic, egoless, heading for a dying fall and a whisper. "Be still" is the musical direction hereabouts.

'Summertime In England' is seventeen minutes long, set to the same rhythm as Lou Reed's 'Walk On The Wild Side', but the very opposite of that celebration of narcissism and cross dressing. The song divides into a triptych of movements, like one of Roy Harper's epics: it lacks the verbal architecture of, say, 'Me And My Woman'. Jones describes Van's voice as "both tough and smooth, like a well oiled muscle". The radio is a source of angelic voices, the "ether" which brought the young Van the blues, and here unites him and his "common one" with the poets. This is less bathetic than some critics have discerned: Wordsworth and Coleridge are "smokin" with poetry, not spliffs. After all, opium was the chosen drug of the latter. The song moves towards its conclusion with frightening self assurance, Labes' wonderful arrangements following every twist and turn of Van's mind.

The song ends in silence and in light. It also leaves most classical rock fusions dead in the water.

'Satisfied' is back to the boys in the band, a funk concerto. Van namechecks JD Salinger, chronicler of adolescent angst, and by implication Wordsworth. Like 'Daffodils', mountain wildness can lift the spirit – the karma even – in the big city. This is a song of being sometimes "completely in the dark", the same yin/yang dichotomy of The Grateful Dead's 'Truckin''. "Sometimes the light is shining on me/other times I can barely see." Morrison sees spiritual poverty all around, but he has to change himself first, "on the inside".

'Wild Honey' is built on a pun, and recalls the sweetness of 'Tupelo Honey'. Morrison's voice is set full on gorgeousness, crooning yet another anthem to fulfilled love. A symphony of brass. The refrain repeats over and over again, uniting the natural and the spiritual spheres, "when the light comes shining through".

'Spirit', the shortest track here and still clocking in at over five minutes, is a song of darkness set to a bounce beat. The melody line rises upwards, suggesting hope, and the chorus comes back down again, but with new resolution. The angel here is both ethereal and mortal, the ideal girlfriend of 'Angeliou' and Dylan's 'You Angel You'. In a bizarre interpretation, John Collis imagines Van manning the Samaritans' switchboard here. It is certainly a good song to play anyone contemplating suicide, though Van is light on reasons to believe. It is a song which consoles itself, for no given reason.

'When Heart Is Open' is music that has almost come to a dead halt, New Age sounds before their time. It flows between key images, with – as Allan Jones describes it – "the easy tempo of a dream". The opening is gently reminiscent of Richard Strauss as purloined by *2001*, or the sound of whales singing, or the start of 'Flute Song' which opened Richard Thompson's "Sufi" 1977 concerts. Van starts wordlessly, then makes time stop with a series of slow instructions. He becomes Dai Greatcoat, David Jones' First World War soldier going down to the woods where he will meet his death. The song is infused with the White Goddess, a lover who is also the world. That is my interpretation, anyway, of a song which everyone can bring themselves to, and bathe in their own reflection. It is interesting, therefore, that John Collis finds the song "frankly impossible to listen to", and Paul Du Noyer hears an asthmatic Van moaning "like a man in the throes of terminal constipation".

Writing for the *NME* Du Noyer finds the whole album "colossally smug and cosmically dull; an interminable, vacuous and drearily egotistical stab at spirituality. Into the muzak." Well, everyone is allowed an opinion, it's just that some people have blocked ears. Allan Jones in *Melody Maker* is closer to the mark, finding "an album of spiritual and musical rejuvenation". It moves into areas not touched since Tim Buckley's *Starsailor*: "He doesn't preach, he guides the listener through the seductive, melodic textures of his hymns (there really isn't another word to describe them)." Jones adapts the singer's favourite metaphor, that of rebirth. "Just when you thought his corpse was growing cold, it's time to take Van Morrison into your arms again."

Dave McCullough in *Sounds* says everything in the title of his review, "I Wandered Lonely As A Clod". He undoes all the good work of his review of *Into The Music*, regarding this "irrefutably as a bad record", whimsically pastoral, "unlistenably slow and sluggish". The late, great critic Steve Burgess, in *Dark Star*, agrees with McCullough that this is not rock music in anything but the loosest sense, but regards this as a blessing, not a curse. A master of the rock pun, Burgess describes the album as blarney stoned, "a private dervish dance, a worthy, if static, focus of Van's soul".

The debate still rages, over possibly the most controversial item in Van's whole discography. For the professorial Greil Marcus, it offers "a Van Morrison with nothing to say and a limitless interest in getting it across – to himself". Johnny Rogan drones on in his usual heretical fashion, that this is at best fourth form poetry. Morrison has "adapted the mantle of the John Clare of rock music" – a "peasant poet", who died in a Northampton mental asylum, having produced some of the greatest nature lyrics in the language – "though his lyrics were probably closer to Ambrose 'Namby Pamby' Phillips". A poet with whom even I am unfamiliar. Rogan does admit that *Common One* represents a great work unrealised, and that in a later interview, Morrison admitted that his original concept was even more esoteric than what appeared. The album has proved rich and inspirational, and it is perhaps no coincidence that one of the most important bodies currently helping to restore and protect the English countryside is called Common Ground.

As David Hayes told the *Van Morrison Newsletter*, "*Common One* is one that stands alone by itself. It was very worldly and was a high point. I remember on 'Summertime In England' that Pee Wee did the call/response one night off the cuff and it just stuck."

Van was recreating England in his imagination, like John Cowper Powys, writing huge and meticulous novels of Dorset life (and the cosmos) while criss-crossing America by train, giving public lectures, just as Van played rock clubs. Morrison had made a new home in Mill Valley, a settlement of a few streets just over the bridge from San Francisco, overlooking the Bay and close to his daughter Shana. He joked to friends about how both were "running parallel", experiencing teenage and mid-life traumas respectively. Shana had begun to study classical piano and was taking singing lessons.

Nevertheless, Van was beginning to feel homesick, as he confessed to John Tobler: "I'm not really an American. I talk the language and I know what's going on, but at the same time I need to integrate the other parts of myself – because, when it comes down to it, I was born in these islands. I couldn't really leave America because there's too much happening, but at the same time, I don't want to leave this, so I'm making a compromise in between – a bit of both to be happy with the situation." His parents had by now returned home to Belfast, and Van began house hunting. He considered a mansion in Berkshire just vacated by the pop group Five Star, but rejected its rolling acres because it was "too near the road".

He also investigated a house in the Oxford village of Stadhampton. Its owner told John Collis that "sometimes when we weren't going to be away he would come and stay in the house during the day time and then go back to his hotel. We'd go out to work and he'd move in. He always had a girl with him. Often a different girl." She found Van terribly shy, but inquisitive about his Celtic heritage. "He'd get into quite deep discussions about things like Stonehenge. Questions rather than answers." She would often find bits of paper covered with notes, which she threw away. Van eventually bought the house, and kept it for some years, though he was to move back to London, close to his old haunts in Notting Hill.

Appropriately, 'Summertime In England' is a highlight of a Dutch TV concert recorded in Rotterdam in 1981. Mick Cox and Herbie

Armstrong play guitars, Pete Wingfield's curly head is back on board, and Pee Wee Ellis – who looks a little too dignified for this sort of thing – joins in on backing vocals as Van in dark shades ad libs about when "Auden and Isherwood split" (in Berlin) and summons up Ginsberg in Saint Louis, and Ferlinghetti's City Lights books publishing Colin Wilson. A Beat manifesto?

Talking to Paul Vincent on KMEL radio, back in California, Van said: "I don't really think of myself as a 'songwriter'. I know songwriters and I'm not one. A songwriter's a guy that can come in at nine-thirty in the morning and write a song on demand, and I've never been able to do that. I'm an inspirational writer. *A poet*. I write when I'm inspired." On a different register, he also talks of playing 'Mechanical Bliss' to Dudley Moore "and he flipped over it. He really loved it." But humour plays no part in what he is currently trying to do on stage. "What I'm doing is playing the music, and I have to concentrate on that. I have to build the energy and I have to put a spell on it, so to speak. I don't want to talk because it breaks the spell. Music is what I'm saying." The whole point of what he is doing is "to make people listen to *themselves*". A noble aim, worthy of the greatest art, to locate the hidden sense of the mystic inside us all.

CHAPTER EIGHT

Irish Heartbeat

Van had a new girlfriend, Ulla Munch, from Vanlos in Copenhagen. 'Listen To The Lion', made flesh. Ulla's influence on Van's reborn sense of Celtic mysteries infused *Beautiful Vision*, completed in California towards the end of 1981. Three tracks were written with Hugh Murphy, an old acquaintance from Decca, and producer of Gerry Rafferty's 'Baker Street'.

New musicians included Chris Michie on guitar, Tom Donlinger on drums and Mr Dire Straits himself, Mark Knopfler. Recording took place at the Record Plant, Sausilito. The album was released in February 1982, and reached Number Thirty-One in Britain, and Forty-Four in the States. The avant-garde cover is set in a starry night sky, a la Van Gogh. At its centre is a moon-like crescent of light – from which an aged hand appears – which acts as a prism through which a rainbow of light emerges. This "Beautiful Vision" is slick rather than beautiful, inept rather than visionary. Much better to have used Julia Margaret Cameron's photograph of the same title, in which Julia Stephen – Virginia Woolf's mother – stares into the camera, eyes blazing, an image of mystical womanhood.

Some of the lyrics derive from *Glamour – A World Problem* by the mystical writer Alice Bayley, aided by a mysterious Tibetan. Closer to earth, the album is heavily themed on Belfast memories, and Sean Fulsom plays pipes on two of the songs. Talking to Johnny Rogan, Phil Coulter confirmed this new sense of Irish roots. "I think he's a lot happier." Van had found an Irish bar in San Francisco that played traditional music. "He has this thing about the evolution of the Celtic tradition and Celtic culture." One night he played Coulter an album of gaelic chants from the Shetlands. "It was very primeval and he was fascinated by that."

The opening song, 'Celtic Ray', deals with this ancient culture, though in the absence of a lyric sheet it is not always possible to tell exactly what words Van is saying. Production difficulties which saw much of the original vinyl pressings cut off-centre added to the shoddy packaging to suggest a lack of quality control, though this does not extend to the music. The concept in the opening song is that of 'Wavelength', with messages coming through the ether from Mother Ireland. The Celtic ray, like something from a children's comic, or Saturday morning pictures, is a kind of motherlode to a man who has been "away too long", an antidote to madness and "the corporate man". In a form of controlled schizophrenia, Van can hear "the voices calling". He mimes this other-worldliness with the way he sings "children", in a way to lift the hairs at the back of your neck. The backing breaks into a jig, and Van fades out, moaning wordlessly.

'Northern Muse (Solid Ground)' combines the state of Ireland with a young woman, in County Down (which stars in the opening track of *Irish Heartbeat*). Again, there is a ballad-like lilt to proceedings. As Van told the Irish magazine *Hot Press*, "Some of the material, when it started, was more traditional. 'Solid Ground' and 'Celtic Ray' started basically as folk-oriented stuff."

'Dweller On The Threshold' is straight out of HP Lovecraft, but jaunty. Van still stands in darkness, like Christ in Holman Hunt's painting *The Light Of The World*, waiting to enter in. The angel here is corporeal, female. Here is Van's first reference to a "burning ground", and the music of the spheres, whose perfect harmony is mimed by his musicians. Mark Isham sounds Beatle-ish, bubbling with joy.

'Beautiful Vision' has simple, repeated lyrics, and the vision could either be heavenly or of his new girlfriend, or both, though the music drags a tad. 'She Gives Me Religion' is a counterpart to 'Covenant Woman', one of Dylan's finest songs, thanking a woman rather than slagging her off for a change. Van travels further along the mystic avenue – made of Cyprus, perhaps – with his tenderness of voice sparked off by Isham's "hieratic sound". Robert Redford, for whom he was to score *A River Runs Through It*, spoke of "the emotional depth of his work, very simple, almost minimal at times but it still has power to it". Before meeting Morrison, Mark had experimented with synthesiser music, and played trumpet with acts as diverse as The Sons Of Champlin, Pharaoh Sanders and The Oakland Symphony Orchestra. He was later to record *Vapor Drawings*, the first electronic album for Windham Hill, and to work with cutting edge artists like XTC, Was (Not Was) and David Sylvian.

'Cleaning Windows' is a breath of fresh air, embroidered by dancing guitar like Jerry Garcia at his most playful. The song is structured around the panel game 'What's My Line'. Remember how Van once named his favourite artist as its resident toff, Lady Isobel Barnett (a woman who didn't have to work!)? Van thinks he might have been happier in his first chosen profession, amid a chugging beat. This is a Keatsian exercise in nostalgia, with taste and smell and sound. Even here, Van is at the bottom of the ladder, concerned with doing a good job. He calls out the numbers of the houses to clean, like a bingo caller.

Woven into all this is his story of early enthusiasms, on the street that he was born: Jimmy Rodgers and Muddy Waters and Christmas Humphreys, country and blues and buddhism, and his love for Jack Kerouac. Despite the jokey reference at the end to going on the dole, Van was soon to leave these childhood streets, to go on the road. The five Woodbines, beside being a slice of social history, remind us of a still younger Morrison, going for cigarettes and matches in the shops.

'Vanlose Stairway' is a song of new love, in which he asks Ulla to send him both her photo, her pillow – drenched in perfume presumably – her guitar and a *Bible*. It is clear who he was addressing in 'She Gives Me Religion'. Like the opening song, this is about forms of communication unknown to the Post Office or British Airways. "Hold it," Van says, and plays uncredited harmonica, groaning through it like a bull.

'Aryan Mist' huffs and puffs like a train, even if the first word of the title is still too tarnished by associations with the Nazis to sit comfortably. It is like that ancient symbol of healing, the swastika, which they first appropriated, then reversed. Hitler was also a nature mystic, a man of visions. "Gurus from the east and west lift you up": Van is yet to throw them away. Mist is half air, half water, and both are crossed in the next song, 'Across The Bridge Where Angels Dwell'. It is best explained literally; Shana and her mother then lived in San Mateo, literally across the bridge from Van's house in Mill Valley. Finally all words are spent, and the album ends with 'Scandinavia', an instrumental. Van plays untutored piano, in what sounds like a variation of 'Chopsticks', to Mark Isham's synth, with a drum thumping like a heartbeat. For Lester Bangs, it "points Van towards the snowpeaks that melt into those sunpale pools Brian Eno cultivates so assiduously". For me, the chords are reminiscent of 'Little Drummer Boy', as performed by David Bowie and Bing Crosby.

The Dorset poet David Caddy has written about "auras" as energies which in medieval times were believed to emanate from people, stones, trees, the whole material world in fact, like an inner fire. It is just this sense of a hidden universe of energies that Van Morrison reveals in *Beautiful Vision*: it lies at the heart of his mystery. Caddy has compared the old belief in auras – still used in psychic healing – with more recent experiments by modern American poets like William Carlos Williams, George Oppen and Charles Bukowski. They similarly attempt to delineate in words the unyielding texture of the everyday. "No ideas, but in things." This is the very quality that these songs lack, and which was so omnipresent in *Astral Weeks* or even *Common Ground*. Minute particularities. After all, even William Blake needed a grain of sand through which to see heaven.

Maxim Jakubowski speaks of "a quiet, spiritual grace" behind Van's new music. British rock critics of the time, cynics all, were surprisingly enthusiastic. For *Sounds*, "Morrison is sorting his mind out in a kind of semi restful glory, as if preparing his huge, biographical, Yeatsian music for the final sorting out". *NME* found that "religious feeling moves through this album, supplying a quiet strength", while *Melody Maker* praised "a feeling, hugging melange of folk, gospel, rock and his own impassioned blues". American reviewers were less convinced, *Creem* considering that too many songs "celebrate those vague bromides favoured by Dylan in recent years", and *Trouser Press* asking instead for another *Wavelength*. The most extraordinary volte-face was by Lester Bangs in *Village Voice*.

He had at first dismissed the previous album through the eyes of his friend Greil Marcus, "Van *acting the part of* the mystic poet", but had come back to the album to find holy music, "rapturous quarter of an hours which pass like vast moments", like Miles Davis' work on *In A*

Silent Way. Geoff Wall has sensibly pointed out that all of Van's later albums need time to grow into, and that they give up their mysteries slowly. *Beautiful Vision* is "true soul music", but the lyrics here are Hallmark card stuff, "safe and self conscious in a way that ultimately drains off the passion and merely lulls".

Passion was fully in evidence on a Rockpalast special, recorded in Essen, Germany in April 1982, and later reshown on the BBC. Eighteen songs are immaculately played and recorded. Some of the more vapid songs on the new album blossom in live performance, with Van crouched at an electric piano, a jovial bearded giant on bass, Chris Michie on guitar and the Ellis/Isham brass section. There are now three girl singers, much like the gospel chorus who gradually drowned out Dylan in the early eighties. Highlights included a ten minute 'Summertime In England' and 'She Gives Me Religion', with a trumpet solo from Mark Isham as clear and penetrating as a bell.

Van seems far more content and secure. As Phil Coulter told Rogan, "He's not angry anymore; he's very mellow. He's straightened himself out. His hang up now is coffee." No more dope or alcohol. "He leads a very simple and straight life. He has a live-in lady and last September he had his kid staying with him during the summer holidays." He was self assured enough to turn down the chance to write the score for Francis Ford Coppola's *One From The Heart*, a disastrous movie shot entirely in the studio, and attempting to recreate the weird magic of Powell and Pressburger, but missing the target completely. "I just thought it was out of my ball park, you know. I'm not particularly fond of Las Vegas. I didn't feel like I could be *true* doing that kind of music, though I like Coppola a lot. I think he's a great film maker."

In late March, Van had undertaken a four night sell out engagement at the Dominion Theatre in Tottenham Court Road. It could have been titled *Apocalypse Now*, Van delving deep into his soul, and bringing it all back home. One reviewer even noticed a leather jacketed customer with "Van Is God" studded on his back. Following an acoustic set from Herbie Armstrong – who cheekily updated an emotional version of 'Friday's Child' with the injunction "it's too late to stop now" – Van was mesmeric, playing a full ninety minute set. Gavin Martin in *NME* described him as "singing with more passion than anyone alive", still hungry and back with a vengeance. He had learnt Dylan's trick of giving new life to old songs. "Songs are recoloured, re-vibed and re-interpreted. It's as if he has subsumed all his old strengths and scopes and crystallised them." Diamonds from coal. Martin picks out as highlights the duet with Pee Wee Ellis on 'It's All In The Game', the "splintered funk" of 'I'm Satisfied' and 'Cyprus Avenue' as almost a new song, "sparse rhythm and new vivid lyrics".

In June, Van performed at the annual Glastonbury Festival, down in Avalon. *NME* pictured the resulting mudbath, with a caption beneath Van's photo, "warm love in a cool climate". Recent and as yet unrecorded songs like 'Real Real Gone' made up the bulk of the set, as the tour continued on to Europe and Ireland. At the intimate and friendly Gaiety Theatre, Dublin, Martin again reported back to the *NME*, on a band that were "fine and rich, hot and tight, sassy and jazzy", like an older, wiser version of James Brown's Famous Flames. A highlight was "the chilling emotional exposition of 'It's All In The Game' – "a classic performance which makes you melt with its delicious aching shudders and leaves you drained and exulted after its climactic crescendo". Better than sex? The gig ended like a party, all the old truculence was gone. For Barry McIlheney, here was a rediscovered old master, largely due to Dexy's Midnight Runners, "looking more like an East Belfast pool hall king than ever before", a working man in his prime. By the time the tour wound down in North America, the show had come to include a large slice of vintage R&B covers.

When the lure of Albion proved too strong, and Van relocated to Holland Park, he found the rough R&B of his youth still vibrant, and back in fashion. The Pretty Things, reuniting Phil May and Dick Taylor, were playing at the Bridge House in Little Venice. Morrison was frequently seen in the audience there and elsewhere, shopping in Notting Hill, in Ladbroke Grove pubs, or sitting quietly in Holland Park. He also enrolled at the Tottenham Court Road HQ of the Scientology movement, to whom he had been introduced by Robin Williamson. Reports of him grabbing unwary passersby remain unconfirmed. The leader of this controversial cult, former SF writer L Ron Hubbard received "special thanks" on the sleeve of Van's next album, *Inarticulate Speech Of The Heart*.

Released in March 1983, the album was recorded in Sausilito, Dublin and London. The line-up is much as before, with the addition of two Irish musicians from the traditional music firmament, Arty McGlynn on acoustic guitar, and Moving Hearts' Davey Spillane on uillean pipes and flute. As on *Common Ground*, the cover is bisected diagonally by the horizon, but this is a hi-tech graphic design, as befits the smooth sheen of the music inside. The divide here is between deep space and a featureless red planet. Streaming off into infinity, like a "girdle around the earth", is a stave of music, on which hearts have replaced the notes. To counteract this ethereal image, Morrison gives namechecks to his new business manager Paul Charles and to his accountant. The album reached Morrison's highest ever chart placing in the UK at Number Fourteen, while racking up his lowest US chart placing – One Hundred And Sixteen – since *Blowin' Your Mind*.

Again there is no lyric sheet, and this seems intentional: with one major exception – a spoken poem – the words are often used merely to give extra colouring to the music. Isham has largely put aside his trumpet for a synthesiser and here is New Age music in all its emotionless glory. The album flows together as an easy listening experience, with Celtic colouring. Almost half the record is instrumental, 'Connswater', named after a Belfast canal, is a slow Irish dance, 'Celtic Swing' starts slowly, then struts along in dance band style, with Van playing saxophone, blowing into it like the sea heard through a shell. The title track is based on simple chords repeated slowly, with woodblock percussion straight out of *Pet Sounds*: it returns with a vocal line, the same phrases over and over again, like a mantra. 'September Night' is reminiscent of parts of *Dark Side Of The Moon*, wordless moanings set to a slow beat.

What lyrics there are sound inspired by Scientology, an upbeat faith which preaches the overcoming of inner mental blocks, and the removal of "engrams", knots in the psyche. The problem is that by removing personal road-blocks you can also amputate creativity. This was exampled by The Incredible String Band's descent from a spiky mix of stoned mythological tales, and odd wisdoms, to a blanded out, charmless whimsy. Who wants to be totally happy anyway?

'Higher Than The World' puts the cover picture to music, but how can you be higher than a flower, or live in a sound. Van sounds convinced, anyway. In 'River Of Time' heart and soul meet, as if on a butcher's slab, but the music thrills and Morrison's voice blends in nicely with the synth and girly chorus. 'Irish Heartbeat' is slow and sentimental, one of those anthems Van seems to be able to pluck from the air. "Won't you stay, with your own ones" doesn't look much in print, but his singing turns it into an aching lament for one's native land. Billy Connolly took it back to Caledonia when he used it as the theme tune for *Billy's World Tour Of Scotland*. 'Cry For Home' is a more cheerful call home. It would make a good theme song for Van's favourite soccer team, whomever they might be. 'The Street Only Knew Your Name' is set back in the Belfast of his youth, with a synth riff, teenagers hanging out at night. Were I to be pernickety, the word "only" should come at the beginning of the title here, as Van is gently boasting about the fact that every street in the world now knows who he is. But then, how can a street know even its own name?

Moving swiftly on, Van made his first commercial video for 'Celtic Swing'. It was typically perverse to make a video for an instrumental, and the results are charming, set in Ireland where a grumpy Van with his saxophone becomes a reluctant pied piper, followed wherever he goes by a young boy, who is presumably his young self. It all looks like something from the French new wave.

The major song on the album is in fact a poem – yes, a real one, recited, though Morrison cannot stop himself breaking into song, and a slow saxophone ends the proceedings. 'Rave On, John Donne' sounds like a Ginsberg rant of joy, with the metaphysical Elizabethan and other dead poets brought up to date, as beacons of light. Walt Whitman, Omar Khayam, WB Yeats as well: an Open University reading list of visionaries. David Hayes confirms that a forty-five minute version was recorded live in the studio. "It filled two reels of twenty-four track tape. There was a gap in the middle where the engineer frantically put the next tape on. It was some session, it was like being in a church."

Reviews of *Inarticulate Speech Of The Heart* were mixed. The most enthusiastic was by Niall Stokes in the *Hot Press* – "an oceanic depth" – opposite a similarly heartfelt endorsement of Clannad's *Magical Ring*, another work to combine Celtic roots and synthesisers. Van "has pared his language back to nothing, in the hope of, even just once, expressing that everything, that wholeness, that oneness, which, at the end of it all, defies meaning and fulfils it". Yes, well...As Adam Sweeting in *Melody Maker* writes, "don't talk about it, listen to it". More downbeat are *Sounds* – "his third appalling album on the very rapid trot" – and *Record Mirror* – "he gets more wishy-washy album by album. This is the worst so far." Maxim Jakubowski invokes Eric Satie and John Coltrane, and "a light jazzy groove, as sharp as a ray of sunshine". *Music World* think the album sounds great if the sun is shining, but not so good if it is raining. Gavin Martin thinks that "it's not what he sings, it's the way he sings". Writing in the *NME*, he also points out the sheer oddness of the instrumentals here, with Van playing saxophone like "an aboriginal or African blow pipe". As he points out, "It's a sad state of affairs when the new sheer strength and vision of the latest incarnation of The Van Morrison Band should be enjoyed by an audience that is predominately middle class and middle aged."

Ironically, with this band in tow, Van told Radio Ulster in February that he had cut live gigs to a minimum. "It's a matter of moving on into other creative areas. Part of the problem with performing is this expectancy that you're going to do stuff you did five years ago. You're not there any more. You're going backwards." He spoke of a renewed interest in Irish literature, and that he had "been listening to Celtic folk music. Various – music from Brittany, England, Scotland, Wales, Ireland. The blues is 'their' music. You can play it but it doesn't belong to you." The Breton harpist Alan Stivell was a particular favourite: he too was taking traditional music into the age of electronics. Van had found another outlet for his creativity. "I'm writing a book at the moment. It's not really an autobiography. Fact, fiction, philosophy, mysticism. My experience." Meanwhile, Howard DeWitt, a professor of popular culture, published *The Mystic's Music*, a short biography full of tiny anecdotes, like Van renting a Mercedes car with personalised number plates "R'N'B".

The Spring 1983 promotional tour for the new album saw Van's latest homecoming. The Manor's mobile recording studio was shipped over to record the best of four nights in early March at Belfast's Grand Opera House, though the resulting album restricted itself to material drawn from his last four albums.

With much the same band as of late, except that Tom Donlinger had replaced Peter Van Hooke on drums, Van gave a fiery display. Highlights included 'It's All In The Game', the audience held rapt in attention, and

'Danny Boy', of all things. Barry McIlheney in *Melody Maker* reported a version of 'Summertime In England' which namechecked Seamus Heaney, Dylan Thomas and DH Lawrence, a 'Full Force Gale' that lifted the heart, and finally 'Gloria'. "Morrison, looking every bit his age, stood motionless belting out this standard for showbands, rock bands and punk bands throughout the ages, and the circle had been neatly and finally completed." Just as at his previous home concerts in 1979, Van was able to lift the collective spirit of a divided nation, testifying to his music like Billy Graham to God.

In March, Van performed 'Cry For Hours' live on Irish TV's *Late Late Show*. Talking to Bill Flanagan of *Musician* he explained that, while living in so many places had given him "a broader perspective on life in general", there was still "a big part of me that's just strictly involved with the island of Ireland". He refused to become involved politically, however. Talking to Irish journalist Dermot Stokes, he wished instead "ideally to induce states of meditation and ecstasy, as well as make people think". Through books like Cyril Scott's 1937 opus *Music: Its Secret Influence Through The Ages*, he was exploring the transforming power of his art. "I was trying to do meditation at the Fillmore East, if you know what I mean!" So that's why he stormed off stage.

In a May *NME*, Gavin Martin found a man "upright, smart and sober", pacing around the Scientology centre, reading aloud from the works of L Ron Hubbard. Meeting in the Tara hotel – where else? – Morrison refuses to talk about either scientology or the past, which leaves a lot of gaps in the conversation. Van is highly nervous, dressed in black, looking like someone who has wandered into the wrong funeral service. He munches steak and chips while responding tersely to Martin's polite queries. "I went through the R&B thing but I transcended that. I transcended folk, transcended every medium. So now I'm just myself."

Van went through a quiet period, again reassessing his career, and emerged at the start of 1984 with a new band and newly targeted creativity. He was about to record a trilogy of albums of blazing rock poetry. In January, Rockpalast recorded fourteen songs at the "Midem" beanfeast in Cannes. The set was much as it had been in Belfast, but the musicians accompanying him now included baby faced guitarist Arty McGlynn, bearded keyboard player Kenny Craddock – a well respected session man who had played with Lindisfarne and the Paul Brady band – Martin Drover on trumpet, Richard Buckley on saxophone and backing vocals, black bassist Jerome Rimson and power drummer Terry Popple, with two girl singers. Van himself played keyboards.

February saw the release of *Live At The Grand Opera House, Belfast*, a wake for the old band, which reached Number Forty-Four in the British album charts, though it did not trouble the US Hot Hundred. As so often, an official live album sounds weedy and skimps on running time compared with bootlegged delights from Europe, which the BPI pursue as if they were class "A" drugs. Most of the songs sound better airbrushed on the original albums, and the selection policy restricts Van's past to a few bars of 'Into The Mystic' at the start. Worthy additions include a startling break in 'Haunts Of Peace' and a part two added to 'Rave On, John Donne': "tonight you will understand the oneness".

Sandy Robertson's review in *Sounds* was subbed as "Morrison Minor". It was rather ungracious, Van was "overweight…just like the music", and went on and on and on. The cover version of 'It's All In The Game' is "an insult to whatever greatness he ever had". 'Rave On, John Donne' sounds like a parody by The Two Ronnies. For Christopher Hill, Morrison "welds the hazy gleam of occult poetry to the heat of R&B", but *Record Mirror* found "a record as ponderous as the title, really". The front cover shows the Opera House illuminated, like a wedding cake, all portholes and stained glass. A poster for Van's concert tour is up. This is set on an impressionistic background which could be grass, or slate, or rock, or the dark side of the moon.

In the *NME*, David Quantick found the album a useful compilation of Van's Mercury years. Van now completely cut his links with WB, who had still been distributing his work in the USA. This provoked a rumour, amplified by *Rolling Stone*, that he had been dropped. Speaking to the same magazine, Morrison angrily put the record straight. "I heard about it secondhand. I think they dropped a lot of people, and I was the biggest name on there. I figured that somebody thought I was in Timbuktoo sleeping under a hedge. Sy Waronker was extremely embarrassed. He said he'd apologise…he said we were in negotiation and we weren't negotiating. My next move was to give up my US rights to Polygram because they'd been representing me for six years everywhere else. Just a natural follow up." Is that clear, now?

The same line-up appeared at the Montreux Jazz Festival in July, playing a wide ranging set which included a medley of Them's three greatest hits, Mose Allison's 'If Only You Knew', and retreads of 'Jackie Wilson Said', 'St Dominic's Preview', 'Hard Nose The Highway' and 'Ballerina', a particular treat. A thirteen minute instrumental, called 'Jazz Session' ensued with "real" jazzers Joe Henderson on saxophone, drummer Billy Hart, and trumpeter Freddie Hubbard. "I've known about this young man for a long time and he's told me today that he likes jazz, and we're going to have a jam session, because I want to go to Ireland, because I'm Irish, old Hubbard. This is a gas, that we can all play together." Proceedings finished with Ray Charles' 'What Would I Do?'. The whole thing is captured on the *I Can't Go On...But I'll Go On* CD bootleg.

Other musical collaborations included jamming with The Chieftains in Edinburgh, reprising *The Last Waltz* – as a B movie – with a reformed Band at an outdoor event in the Midlands, and playing 'Moondance' with The Gil Evans Orchestra. A private tape of a 22 June gig at Southampton Gaumont is infinitely superior to the *Live In Belfast* album, with a tight band, an interesting set list, and a growling, aggressive Morrison in full control. This is particularly laudatory, as an Irish voice announces at the start of the concert that "Mr Morrison has hurt his leg, and is doing this set on a stool, just in case you wonder why he's not moving around". Before the interval, his band play a twenty minute set of almost avant-garde jazz. After it, the same voice announces a man who for twenty years has written "with inarticulate speech of the heart", which sounds unintentionally insulting.

Van's set starts chronologically, with the trio of Them hits, 'Brown Eyed Girl', and two from *Astral Weeks*, 'Young Lovers Do' and the title track. This is particularly effective, with just guitar, drums and organ. The static Van is still in good voice, and brings things up to date with 'I Will Be There' and 'You Win Again', before plunging back into the past for 'Jackie Wilson Said' and 'St Dominic's Preview', with a good new guitar riff. Other delights include a driven 'Hard Nose The Highway', 'I'm Not Working' during which Van groans like a dying man and the audience clap along wildly, and an epochal 'Haunts Of Ancient Peace'.

Ideal entertainment for a summer's night, even in Southampton. Next up, to everyone's amazement, is a cortege slow 'Madame George'. The drums sound like an Orange parade, McGlynn plays arpeggios on his guitar, and the stricken Van puts everything into his voice, infinitely sad and caring. Stately keyboards enter the equation and the (electric) bass rumbles. Van almost spits out the line about "have mercy it's the cops", then scats the final verse, getting stuck on the "loves to love" line like a gramophone needle. He whispers "say goodbye" as the music dies away, and then stutters out consonants, breaking down the words to their atoms. A stunned audience, aware they are in the rare presence of genius, pause for a moment, then somebody whoops, and everyone applauds wildly.

Hardly a pause – there is no way this tape is edited – and we're straight into 'Like A Ballerina', with organ straight out of *Highway 61 Revisited*, and Spanish guitar. The musicians bring out the swaying dance at the heart of the song, which conveys its subject. Without wishing on Van the horrible accident that befell Robert Wyatt, he really should sit down on stage more, if this is what results. His vocals are slurred and regal, as the band sway from chord to stately chord, and everything comes to a gentle close. A short flourish on the drums and we're into an upbeat 'Summertime In England', which sounds all of a piece with the wonders that have just unfolded, but with added brass.

On 7 July, Morrison joined Bob Dylan on stage at Wembley, on an encore of 'It's All Over Now Baby Blue', alongside Eric Clapton, Chrissie Hynde and Carlos Santana. It was the first time that I had ever myself seen Morrison in real life, and he looked almost too everyday to be on stage, until he opened his mouth, and wild honey poured out. They repeated the exercise at Slane Castle, on the water meadows of the Boyne. The two strummed guitars and shared a microphone, a la Everly Brothers. A young Bono interviewed the two elder statesmen of rock backstage. Van praises Bono's journalistic skills, and they talk shop, about recording techniques. Van remembers when "you were in the room, they turned the tape on. After about eight hours or so they'd say 'Okay, tea break, it's over'."

Van was now as at home in TV studios as he once had been in tiny clubs. In August, he performed 'Northern Muse' on *The Mary O'Hara Show*, bringing it all back home to the middle of the road. In October, he played two numbers with Caledonian folk rebels, The Battlefield Band. He also sang two songs as part of a celebration of sixty years of BBC broadcasts from Ulster, introduced by his old friend Phil Coulter. November saw Van live in the *Old Grey Whistle Test*'s cramped studio, in front of that ludicrous man kicking a star. He previewed 'A Sense Of Wonder' from his forthcoming album, like a man desperate to share a secret.

Dexy's Midnight Runners were rerunning Van's past, at speed. The reformed band recorded a debut LP called *The Celtic Soul Brothers* and added the Emerald Express string section for their second album *Too-Rye-Ay*. Van and his band were touring Australia: while there he recorded two songs live for TV, 'Tore Down A La Rimbaud', and the title track of his new album, *A Sense Of Wonder*, released in February 1985.

It reached Number Twenty-Five in the British charts, and Sixty-One in the States. Original pressings had to be recalled when the estate supervising WB Yeats' literary archive forced the withdrawal of Van's musical version of his poem 'Crazy Jane On God' from the album. Peter Bellamy had much the same problem, initially, in recording Rudyard Kipling's poems, reuniting them with the English folk tunes which he realised had inspired them in the first place, and un-censoring them by restoring the earthy language that Kipling would have used had he dared. Bellamy was later elected vice-president of the Kipling Society, and Morrison's pioneering work later inspired a whole album of rock settings of Yeats' lyrics. Meanwhile, Van admitted temporary defeat, substituted Mose Allison's 'If You Only Knew', and told Stephen Davis "I thought, okay, fine. I thought I was doing them a favour. My songs are better than Yeats!"

On the new album, Bob Doll replaces Mark Isham on trumpet, removing the music's focal point. Otherwise, the band used is largely that with which Van had recently dispensed as a touring unit. Front and back are photographs of Van, reappearing as a sales point, after all those new age, airbrushed images, but there is far more to it than that. After three albums in which he tried to hide himself, become anonymous, drop himself from the lyrics, this is a wonderfully egotistical effort. It is as if Van's personality – and his poetic individuality – have emerged from Celtic mists into sharp sunlight.

The cover is very much part of the album's message, as is the short story about Boffyflow and Spike. Van peers through a circle of leaves, like a birdwatcher gazing from his hide, just as Boffy "is covered with leaves completely, the buckijit". His eyes and mouth are set in an unmistakable and unforced smile, rather than his more characteristic scowl, or look of mystic rapture. On the back cover he is unsmiling yet somehow impish: he wears the same Spanish style hat, and a cloak – the "greatcoat" of the song – buttoned at the top with a silver clasp. The whole ensemble covers a shirt, unbuttoned at the neck, which rather undermines the effect, and thus becomes faintly ludicrous, but that is presumably all part of the plot. The inner sleeve of the vinyl release intersperses lyrics and dying leaves.

The short story also printed on the sleeve has a similar gnomic wit to Dylan's effort on the back of *John Wesley Harding*, John Lennon's cod surrealism, or some of that other punster Robyn Hitchcock's Secret Island tales. Literary parallels are, most strongly, the mad whimsy of Flann O'Brien – though lacking the vein of sheer terror running through his best work – or Spike Milligan's novel *Puckoon*. The "Spike" here is also surely Milligan, one of the masters to whom the album pays homage. Van has learned to lighten up, and his character Boffyflow is a right 'idjiot', a trickster, a court jester, who freezes the leaves while waiting for his dole cheque. He (mis)reads his own lyric sheet, and even pours fun at his "Belfast Cowboy" nickname.

> "You're terrible, you are. You blurt." He put away six
> doubles of Jameson from the bar and sank into a deep
> apathetic slumber, mumbling "Blinkin' Cowboys,
> Blinkin' Cowboys".

The music inside likewise carries a serious message lightly. 'Tore Down A La Rimbaud', which took eight years to write, deals with a creative block: after all, Rimbaud abandoned poetry and went off to Africa to live a life of adventure. As Van told Stephen Boston, "I'd been reading Rimbaud when I got the original idea. The idea is ten or twelve years old, and I just rewrote it. I wasn't writing anything at all and I really don't understand why. Sometimes I get over a block by just sitting down at a typewriter and typing what I've just done. Got up, had breakfast. Sometimes I get out of it that way. Sometimes not." There is more still, for the song is one of thanks, to a mentor. Madame George, perhaps. The music is full of joyful brass and women's voices, close – as are the lyrics to 'Bright Side Of The Road', another song of hope with which to open proceedings.

More jaunty sounds introduce 'Ancient Of Days', which could equally well be taken slow, as a hymn. God, again, in Nature. Van hums and tickles the piano keys on the gentle, rather plodding instrumental 'Evening Meditation'. The guitar strum at the end is pure Roy Harper, whose odd blend of mellifluousness, sarcasm and anger seems to be an influence here. No shame in that, Jethro Tull and mid-period Led Zeppelin both took over his inspiration wholesale. Harper is, of course, fanatically anti-God, so one should not take the parallel too far. The subject of devotion in 'The Master's Eyes' could be God, or L Ron Hubbard, or even William Blake.

As John Collis points out, "If Morrison's questions were ever to be answered, his career would be over." For the same reason, he is careful never to explain his songs, leaving them to expand in the minds of his listeners, like flowers in water. By the same token, his cover version of Ray Charles' 'What Would I Do?' is given a double focus, missing a girlfriend and missing God, maybe missing his lyric gifts as well, if any of them were to be taken away.

'A Sense Of Wonder' is hymnal, written for friends' children, and goes back to Van's own youthful translation into eternity, "the eternal presence, in the presence of the flame". He calls his love "Philosophy", just like that odd stray Them track. "Told you, darling, all along, I was right and you were wrong". Van returns to the rich specifics of his childhood, which he can somehow make seem like our own. The details change, but the glow of recollection is universal. "The man who played the saw outside the city hall. Pasty suppers down at Davy's Chipper, gravy rings, barnbracks, wagon wheels, showballs. A Sense Of Wonder." Similarly wondrous is the backing by Moving Hearts, the electric counterpart to Planxty, with Donal Lunny and Christy Moore its original twin pilots. Van Morrison and Moving Hearts in concert, now there's a thought. They recombine for an instrumental, 'Boffyflow And Spike', which is as Irish as the foam on real Guinness or soft rain.

Mose Allison's 'If You Only Knew' is as sardonic as only Americans can be, prefiguring a whole stream of Van's own songs about the shabby compromises of the record industry. It cuts deeper still, in its implied threat of "what could happen to a man for telling the truth", and this leads in beautifully to the words of William Blake as selected by the poet Adrian Mitchell in 'Let The Slave', the hard and bitter search for wisdom. It is certainly not to be found in record company receptions. Morrison follows closely the arrangement on *The Westbrook Blake* album, while somehow failing to recapture Phil Minton's desperate, screamed vocal, or Westbrook's rhythmic discipline. I respect Morrison's reading, by turns hammy and clipped, but the original chills my soul. Jah Wobble's more recent excursions into Blake capture the same barrow boy exuberance.

The final song, 'A New Kind Of Man', was "named after a book on William Blake. The book stresses that Blake was very New Age and that maybe this could develop now. I think it's a possibility but I think it would be very difficult, because at the present time you have your Future Shock, and it's very difficult to deal with that and have your New Age at the same time." The song is strongly reminiscent of Blake's painting 'Bright Day', Adam reborn. This is the song of a survivor, and Van sings it with rightful pride.

The press release accompanying the album mentions eleven sold out nights at the Dominion Theatre, and announces with some amazement that "the world's most reluctant rock-star (next to JJ Cale) is now prepared to help promote his records and career by doing press interviews, live shows, photo sessions and even television!" The exclamation mark is theirs. For the first time since *Wavelength*, "Van has consented to having his picture on the front cover". The release was obviously written by a fan, who annotates the title track as "luxurious, warm and glowing. A soulful performance to send shivers down your spine. Over seven minutes of heaven." 'Boffyflow And Spike' is "very jolly", and 'A New Kind Of Man' is "how I feel after listening to this forty-five minute album".

The WB Yeats poem 'Crazy Jane On God' is still in place at this point. It would further have embroidered the album's theme, with its chorus "all things remain in God". Jane recounts two hauntings, all part of the sense of wonder. Even the title of the collection in which this poem appears seems to be relevant, *Words For Music Perhaps*. Perhaps not, until the Yeats estate later relented.

Reviews were mixed. Hardened reggae expert Penny Reel in the *NME* found that "the greatest white soul voice since Elvis Presley" was still let down by his material, and had yet to recapture his early "careless grace". Reel – as his pen name hints – prefers the instrumentals, of which 'Boffyflow And Spike' is "quite possibly The John Barry Seven possessed by the Da Danaan". Elsewhere, he thinks that Van sounds like Georgie Fame, a prescient observation. No such doubts from Barry McIlheney in *Melody Maker*, despite the awful headline "In Transit Van", who captures the album's strangeness, and the "truly immense" nature of its title track. The album as a whole is a "sort of homecoming".

In March, Van appeared on *The Tube*, that cauldron of live rock from Newcastle, and gave his all for three songs from the new album, in blue woolly pullover and truculent air, filmed from below, and playing a big sparkly guitar. His tour band played their socks off, and Van shared lead duties with Arty McGlynn.

Van had attended a centre in Hampshire, a kind of secular church devoted to the native American seer White Eagle, who was revered as a "realised master". He could even be the model for 'The Master's Eyes'. Morrison's spiritual search was still in full flight, like a football fanatic determined to visit every Football League ground. He also made contact with the Wrekin Trust, set up by Sir George Trevelyan to "awaken the vision of the spiritual nature of man and the universe, and to help people to develop themselves as vehicles for channelling spiritual energies into society". Even more germane to his music was his Trevelyan's niece Katherine, who in *Fool In Love*, published in 1962, outlined her "sense of unimaginable wonder". Longing for God took possession of her, and "the sun shone with a new light, as though translucent gold were at its heart. I saw not only the physical sun but the spiritual sun also, which poured down on me as I walked in the garden." (The Trust researched "near death" experiences.)

Wrekin Trust director Malcolm Lazarus had already organised a conference on "The Power Of Music To Change Consciousness" a subject close to Van's heart. As Lazarus told Steve Turner, "I think that it was in 1985 that Mick Brown, a writer from the *Sunday Times*, got in touch with me and said that Van was looking for a spiritual dimension for his music. I was doing a conference in Winchester and Van came down, and although he found it a bit heavy going he got something out of it. He then decided he wanted to do something of his own." Van's interest was that of an outsider, and he refused to participate in workshops where students learned to raise their own consciousness through music. "He knew that there was something valuable there, yet like a lot of artists he was afraid to do anything to the creative process. It's a reasonable fear." Nevertheless, Van's inspiration and commitment seem to be reborn around this time. Who better to help effect this than a man called Lazarus.

In May, Van talked to Stephen Davis of the esoteric magazine *New Age* for an article eventually titled "The Mystic". Morrison had just flown in to his old home town of Cambridge, and had checked into a hotel hugely up-market from his original apartment. He had recently met Allen Ginsberg, and found a common purpose. "Ginsberg explains his own visionary experience, not on drugs, and it sounds like the same as mine." He agrees to having read Robert Graves' *White Goddess* – "I find identity there…that's my lineage, musical or otherwise" – and talks of how his work unites black R&B and Irish folk, though the latter was "buried temporarily". All kinds of odd facts come tumbling out. In his first showband he did comedy routines, the favourite being a version of Charlie Drake's 'My Boomerang Won't Come Back'. He prefers coffee to hashish as a spur to creativity. Bruce Springsteen has "definitely ripped me off, my movements off as well. My seventies movements, you know what I mean. This stuff" – he demonstrates by stomping across the floor. Shana, now fourteen, is into U2. The circle is complete.

Van worked on the score for the movie *Lamb*, set in Ireland, a tragic tale of the friendship between a young boy and a Catholic priest. During the summer and autumn, he toured the UK, Europe and America, promoting the album. In *Melody Maker* that October, Tom Morton reviewed his appearance at the Edinburgh Playhouse. There are lots of empty seats. Van comes on "clutching a big electric guitar, balder than before, more squat, but *stalking* on, shoulders back. Down to business." He has a six piece band but no backing singers.

The concert gets going about half way through, with a stunning 'It's All In The Game'. "The sprawling, improvised 'Help Me' grooved into a sublime R&B orgasm of vocal and instrumental soloing, while 'She

Gives Me Religion', an *immense* song – saw Van at the piano and hearts in every throat." The concert peaks with 'Astral Weeks' and 'Sweet Thing'. After ten minutes of crowd mania, the band return, for 'Send In The Clowns', of all things. "'Send in the clowns…don't bother, they're *here*!' And he walks off. A wizard, a true star."

A private recording of a gig that same month at Southampton Gaumont reveals much the same, a rumbustious affair, with a sound like The Stranglers with added brass. It is almost too energetic, and the best moments are when quietness reigns, like the organ in 'It's All In The Game' which slows everything down almost to silence, or when 'Solid Ground' segues into 'Wild Mountain Thyme'. Best of all is 'Sweet Thing', slow and regretful with piercing harmonica, and flute, which segues into 'No Going Back' with Van almost in a trance. Other oddities are thrown in, like 'Heathrow Shuffle' and 'Dimples', but there is little of the holy quiet of the last year's gig at the same venue, and 'Summertime In England' is just a song, this time around. The concert has all the excitement of watching a man run full pelt into a brick wall.

Next stop was Belfast. In an interview with Seamus Creagh of the *Hot Press* he said, "I'm not doing anything special. The pace has been too much this year, so I'm taking a long holiday. In fact I've no idea when I'll be back on the road. There's nothing I'd like more than to have a blow with a few boys but you can't do that without touring. I like to play but I hate the road. And that's the price you have to pay. I can't think of any other way to play unless I owned a club, but I don't like that environment. I don't drink and I don't see myself as an impresario." In May 1985, a gossip column in the *Daily Mirror* claimed that Van had begun to attend Alcoholics Anonymous meetings in Chelsea.

"Besides, I couldn't go into a club like Ronnie Scott's, because there would be a couple of thousand people in the street." Give it a few years, Van. "It's difficult to get a few boys together just for a rehearsal – I'm dealing with professional musicians. They just want a cheque. The people I'm dealing with are employees who get paid for what they do. If I could do a couple of gigs every six weeks that would be enough."

Van broke his creative silence on 17 May 1986, when he joined U2, Elvis Costello, Clannad, Rory Gallagher and The Pogues for Dublin's "Self Aid", nicknamed "Paddy Aid" by all concerned. Following the example of fellow Irishman (Sir) Bob Geldof's Live Aid, employers pledged jobs over the telephone, and funds raised for work creation schemes. Van was introduced on stage with the words "if Van Morrison was a gunslinger, he'd shoot copycats", an example of job creation in action.

Melody Maker reckoned that Van "is rapidly turning into Blarney Hotspur. In the picture we ran of him at the Self Aid launch at the Irish embassy, he looked rather like he'd turned up to empty the dustbins or sweep the floor." No matter, when "he can still sing the wings off angels" and he played three songs, all new: 'Thanks For The Information', 'Here Comes The (K)night' and 'A Town Called Paradise'. Neil Drinkwater on keyboards was added to his tour band, and played his part in an unforgettable performance.

Meanwhile, Van entered Ronnie Scott's club – the crowds lying in wait for him seeming to have suddenly dematerialised – and laid down a version of 'Send In The Clowns' with trumpeter Chet Baker. He entered another lion's den of popular culture in June, and performed 'Ivory Tower' on fellow Irishman Terry Wogan's TV show. The following month, he played the Greek Theatre, Berkeley, with a new set list. 'Moondance' and 'Into The Mystic' were back, along with 'Rave On, John Donne'. 'Cyprus Avenue' was followed by 'In The Garden', a devastating combination, and 'Send In The Clouds' was now established as the tongue-in-cheek encore.

Most beguiling were the boys in the (new) band, an American dominated line-up largely from Van's past, with Platania and Hayes, Jeff Labes and Dahaud Shaar, of all people. Pee Wee Ellis was back on saxophone, and Bob Doll on trumpet, with Terry Adams on violin, a good mix of old lags and new faces. This was also largely the band who helped Van record his new album, *No Guru, No Method, No Teacher*, another career highlight.

Recorded at Sausilito and the London Townhouse, Labes, Platania and Hayes were back on board, with Baba Trunde on drums and Kate St John – from Dream Academy – on cor anglais and oboe. Richie Buckley and Martin Drover survived from Van's usual tour band. The title was a conscious rebuttal of media attempts to cast him as enslaved to Scientology or any other one creed. He had made this equally clear in his interview for *New Age*.

As he told Anthony Denselow of the *Observer*, "There have been many lies put out about me and this finally states my position. I have never joined any organisation, nor plan to. I am not affiliated to any guru, don't subscribe to any method and, for those people who don't know what a guru is, I don't have a teacher either." None, other than himself.

His new interest in how music can be used to heal the divide between mind and body was mirrored by what came to be titled "New Age" performers, who used sound patterns to "relax, inspire and uplift". 1975's *In Search Of The Turtle's Navel* by William Ackerman was self released on the artist's own Windham Hill label, named after his Californian construction firm, and hit a common chord. It was the first of many such, matching the music with suitably calm and pastoral covers. Alongside New York's Vital Body Marketing, specialising in acoustic, "low stress" music, such gentle, calming sounds fitted perfectly as a background to meditation, improvised movement, and group therapy. New Age's reference points included the trance music of Can, Tangerine Dream's synthesiser dreams and the ambient sounds leaking out from Eno's Obscure record label. Music for the better class of airports; VIP lounge music for old hippies. The new names disguised old practitioners: Stairway was a front for Jim McCarty, veteran of Keith Relf's classical fusion band Renaissance, whom I saw in a small club in 1969, building just such stairways to heaven.

There were cutting edge parallels in the work of 4AD bands like The Cocteau Twins and Dead Can Dance, and in world music exotica like the cunningly marketed Le Mystere Des Voix Bulgares. Celtic mysticism – twinned with the subtle use of synthesisers – was explored in remote Donegal by Gaelic speakers Clannad, and their young relative Enya. Even if now dulled through familiarity, the shock value of this was like an Atlantic storm, and their music proved ideal material for TV and film soundtracks. It is virtually interchangeable with Morrison instrumentals like 'Scandinavia' and 'Evening Meditation', and the whole concept was given a recent kick up the backside by the Afro-Celt Sound System, a sparkling combination of dance floor rhythms and a string quartet, uillean pipes and sintars, Celtic harp and koras, bongos and talking drums. Davey Spillane is in place, as he was on *Inarticulate Speech Of The Heart*.

A long preamble, but *No Guru, No Method, No Teacher* grows out of this ground, and contains a genuine holiness, for want of a better word, and musical freshness that needs to be set in context to be understood. The facts are simple. Released in July 1986, the album peaked at Number Twenty-Seven in the UK album charts, and Number Seventy in America. The front cover is tinged with purple, as Van, with an open neck white shirt, black sweatshirt just peeping out, and dark jacket stands next to a carved Eastern deity, its face eroded with the centuries. A before and after shot perhaps, Van foretelling his decay, or a spiritual symmetry. Van is his own Buddha. The back shot is dark and obscure, but seems to counter-balance carved stone with leaves. Ars longa, vita brevis. This alone could fuel years of thought.

As Van tells Mick Brown on the *Interview Album*, a Mercury promo release also from 1986, talking specifically about the song 'In The Garden': "I take you through a definite meditation process which is a form of transcendental meditation. It's not TM, forget about that. You should have some degree of tranquillity by the time you get to the end. It only takes about ten minutes to do this process. So then you ask yourself why make albums, why tour. It's very difficult to do this. The bigger the audience is then the harder it is to put across what you're doing. When you've got intimacy you've got more of a chance of taking people through this experientially. So this is really it. This is what I'm doing in this song. I used to do this quite a bit. For instance, when I did this in the sixties, we'd get to a place where there's a meditative part, say at the end of 'Cyprus Avenue'. The whole 'Cyprus Avenue' was just a build-up to bring it to a point where we could go into meditation."

The trouble was that in those hedonistic times, some took this process seriously, and others "thought that it was a chance to say 'right on' or something". Too much else was going on in those kaleidoscope days, "politically, and drug wise. People couldn't really relate on that level." The world of rock 'n' roll, with its heavy emphasis on youth culture, and its endless manipulations behind the scenes is not set up for such things, though one could argue back that exactly the same applies to all organised religions. Rock music is "set up to stimulate. It's got to be exciting. That's got nothing to do with the meditation process, which is what I'm about and what ultimately the songs and everything else are all about. At some point I'll have to make the split from rock 'n' roll. You don't have to have an album out to do this, you don't have to be in the charts or necessarily be famous." Van was later to deny that he had ever been a rock star.

The opening song 'Got To Go Back' opens with Kate St John's haunting tones, and memories of school back in Belfast, with the music of Ray Charles. Van needs to go back to that sense of wonder, his early feelings of being lifted up and filled by "that love that was within me". It is the present, not the past, that is another country, and Van is in exile, hinting at a dependence on booze. This is another song searching for "The Healing", and here it is unambiguously located in childhood. Mind you, Dennis Potter's play *Blue Remembered Hills* was a chilling assessment – adults literally acting as children – as to how power relations in adult life start in the playground. Perhaps there is really no escape at all, except into second childhood, at the final end.

'Oh, The Warm Feeling' is a second hopeful song in a row, with love rekindling these childhood feelings, the safety of family life, and again love "healed my emotions". Saxophone – I presume – mirrors Van's voice as it bubbles away, warmly happy.

The beginning to 'Foreign Window' always makes me want to cry, so critical discernment goes out of the window here. There is a grace and majesty here which I have experienced from little else in rock music, though Mighty Baby's virtually unknown album *A Jug Of Love* comes close, and Platania here has a touch of Martin Stone's driven acoustic guitar on that epic. Both records deal with the need to continue, whatever the handicaps, and both are deeply consoling, healing even. The words deal with some kind of self imposed therapy, perhaps fighting addiction of some kind. Again we are in a haunted world of "masters" and the Lord and decadent poets. Byron died, despite his countless dissipations, in the fight for Greek freedom. There is something painterly about this song, and an odd reference to Calvin, that puritan monster, founding his kingdom of the elect in Geneva.

'A Town Called Paradise', in turn, recalls Bunyon, his pilgrim's progress past the false prophets who would lead him into the slough of despond, and on to Jerusalem. Indeed a snatch of the song of that name, using Blake's poem, surfaces briefly. The love object here is called child, perhaps Shana, perhaps the infant Jesus. Van talks about jumping for joy, and the music does just that.

'In The Garden' takes us back to Hyndford Street, and the world of *Astral Weeks*, and on to Eden. Here, as in the next song, gardens are wet with rain, and a childlike vision comes into view. Van recreates the trances of his youth, going into a meditation in which he meets the Holy Trinity in a suburban garden, while sitting at ease with his own family. Forget the critics, this is great poetry – "you were a creature all in rapture/you had the key to your soul" – and Van's awed vocals and the way the tune and piano meander round each other merely add to the silence. I too shiver with emotion, whenever I hear this song.

'Tir Na Nog' is the Irish mythological land of eternal youth, another kind of garden. Through love, one recaptures the child within. There is another echo of *Astral Weeks*, the line about "you kissed mine eyes", along with a soulful cello. A strange song which gets odder the closer you look at it, with all kinds of faiths and mythologies packed in. It is like one of those pilgrimages that Seamus Heaney writes about in 'Station Island', climbing a mountain on one's knees.

'Here Comes The Knight' is a great pun, and quotes from Yeats' epitaph. A gorgeous tune in which it is Van who is now accused, of "truth and alchemy". Plead guilty, I reckon. 'Thanks For The Information' hits back. Van is cheerfully bitter, and twists the cliches of business life into a trap, which he carefully sidesteps. A comic version of 'Let The Slave'. 'One Irish Rover' is a little bit of self glory, gloriously melancholy, while 'Ivory Tower' is another echo of Yeats, who actually lived in one. For John Wilde this song is "delicately jaunty", and breaks the "mood of solemn, serene reflection". For another reviewer, Van is either copying Tom Waits here, or he has a sore throat. I put it down to sheer emotion. He addresses himself, with Them-like lead guitar and harp.

Most reviewers praised Van's return to form. In *Sounds*, John Wilde found that "the crescendos here are never dampened by their subtle nature, and never fall short of blinding". The whole album aches with "a steady stream of sorrow". Barry McIlheney in *Melody Maker* made more direct sense. "Van Morrison is old enough to be my dad, he's fat and bald and he wipes the floor with the best of them. No contest." Writing for the *NME*, Sean O'Hagan was a little less convinced. "He no longer takes the breath away", and as a musician he has been content to age with dignity.

In an interview with Anthony Denselow in the *Observer* of 3 August 1986, Morrison said, "This is my job, and all that other bullshit is not my responsibility. The whole thing of being famous is an illusion and I pay no attention to illusions. I was once in the business where I played rock and R&B, but now I'm as far removed as night is from day. I'm forced to do music part-time now; ninety-five per cent of my time is taken up with the business of getting the music out. The record company does nothing except distribution. I book the musicians and in most cases I pay for it. I book the sessions. I have to go through a major record company for distribution, so I'm forced into this game. I'm not fond of playing games. Sometimes it feels as though I will never do another album and I've no idea of what may happen next. I enjoy playing the music. The rest is complete nonsense."

He amplified this point to Mick Brown on the *Interview Album*. "I think there's a lot of illusions in this world. The man in the street knows that it's nonsense but it's perpetuated. Why? Because a lot of people are making a lot of money out of it. It's not happening for artistic reasons. The record business is not artistic. The film business is not artistic. They're money businesses." He had decided to wind down, and this would be his last tour in the rock 'n' roll arena. "It's not working for me any more. Maybe people can come and see me under different circumstances. In different places that aren't rock 'n' roll places. I certainly don't want to do this album-tour bit any more."

Jeff Labes tells some interesting anecdotes behind the scenes. Chrissie Hynde of The Pretenders came in to do some vocals "but she couldn't cut it. She was a nervous wreck." Van wanted a less intense album, repeating over and over to the drummer "brushes, brushes, brushes". Van had brought Ry Cooder to play some slide guitar, rather like bringing in Michelangelo to paint the bathroom ceiling. Morrison had seen his album entitled *Jazz*. "He hired Ry and he starts one song, Ry plays through with it, Van didn't say a thing. He did it for every song, Van didn't say one word. At the end he says, 'Thanks, see you.' When Ry is gone he turned to Mick Glossop and says, 'I thought he played Jazz.'"

Morrison then toured Europe, promoting his new album. The Dusseldorf gig survives intact on the *Rave On* bootleg double album. It presents a career overview from the last decade – only 'Moondance', 'Domino' and 'Gloria' predate his mid seventies hiatus. The concert is well played and sung, but it seems to rush along, refusing its audience the expected release. Van sounds like a man in a hurry. His band is back to the usual touring combo, with a brass section of Richie Buckley and Martin Drover, and Neil Drinkwater replacing John Allair on keyboards. This is the band that will play on *Poetic Champions Compose*, and they turn 'In The Garden' into a shattering experience, busking at first, Drinkwater's piano a tinkling fountain, then Van quietens things almost to a whisper, like the last words of a dying man.

The tour to promote *No Guru* took in gigs in London with The Blues Band, and in Belfast, fronting the big band of the Northern Ireland Music Association. Van's Hammersmith Odeon appearance was reviewed by Len Brown in the *NME* as "flickering with light". The gig is an "almost religious ceremony", its highlight the devotional undercurrent to 'In The Garden'. "That Van increasingly looks like a struggling insurance man turned hellfire preacher merely adds a comic nature to his mysticism." Allan Jones in *Melody Maker* saw Van continuing to deconstruct the myths surrounding him, and strike into new territory, just like his contemporary Lou Reed. There is an underlying aggression to his approach, almost punk-like. Earlier songs are stripped of their original grandeur, "played and sung with pugnacious urgency". Morrison sings with bravado, chilling in his intensity. He cuts out 'Full Force Gale' in mid phrase, and is back in the dressing room before the audience can quite realise what has hit them, felled by a sucker punch.

The January edition of *Q* magazine carries an interview with "the irascible seer of Holland Park – Kensington, actually – in which he agrees with Jung that his concentration on creativity has meant "I'm not a salesman, and I'm very bad at selling things. If I had to do that for a living, I'd probably be completely broke." To say this in the middle of a decade when everything had a price and nothing had value was a brave thing indeed. Chris Salewicz describes a man who is the very antithesis of designer cool, in food stained jumper and broad flared trousers, a "curious cove" of whom "the unfortunate squashed down effect of his body suggests something primal, almost swamp-like" or a character from Tolkein, or Toad of Toad Hall, "grumpy, irascible". But lovable, a word that he omits.

Salewicz does catalogue a series of survival measures, like the good luck superstitions footballers employ before a big match. Van takes a personal chef on tour, who makes a sandwich with its crusts cut off and a small fruit salad each night, neither of which Morrison ever touches.

He needs to see a seat plan before he will enter a restaurant, and must sit with his back to the wall, and hidden away from the public. No one backstage must smoke or drink in his presence, and he arrives one minute before due on stage, leaving ten minutes after the encore, to stay in a different hotel to everyone else. Signs more of shyness than hauteur, and apparently he is at his happiest sitting in Holland Park, feeding the birds. In the garden.

Down to business. Van sees music as only one aspect of the spiritual quest which he perceives as his life's work. "It's like trying to clear yourself of these layers of experience, like peeling an onion" – Peer Gynt, anyone – "getting all that stuff off and being yourself. For me the spiritual thing in a nutshell is simply being yourself." To get into the "contented state" in which he can create new music, Van uses meditation, something he has done naturally for years, "stopping the mind". You don't need a mantra, indeed his own music will do. His entire artistic output is aimed at establishing a meditative state within the listener. "Transcendent moments."

Van himself gets the same feeling from the music of Debussy, or the poetry of William Blake, with whom he feels a great affinity: "I don't know if that comes from reincarnation, or what." He laughs. "I don't remember what it is I remember. But I just know that feeling." As to his sense of fitting into a Celtic tradition, definitely yes, but "'Celtic' is a loaded word nowadays, it's politically loaded. Many people do not want to acknowledge the broad Celtic vision."

In February, Van flew to Copenhagen to perform with the Danish Radio Big Band, giving an epic grandeur to the likes of 'Vanlose Stairway' – of course – and Celtic statements like 'Listen To The Lion' and 'Haunts Of Ancient Peace'. His appearance that June in Avalon, or at least the Glastonbury Festival, is a spirited and rocky affair, with lots of harmonica from the Man. The two new backing singers add a soothing layer of sound, floating above and counterpointing his deep growl. There is some fine churchy organ on 'Solid Ground', with Van testifying the gospel of love. There are particularly fine versions of 'Foreign Window' and 'In The Garden', still factory fresh.

In July, a Polydor promo video was released, with an interview and a live performance from the Hammersmith Odeon of 'Did Ye Get Healed?'. Van, in a shiny jacket, sings and plays sax, almost at the same time. Sweaty with intensity, he slows things down at the end, but the coup de grace comes from one of his backing singers, possibly June Boyce. "Did he get healed?" she asks, salaciously. So *that's* what the song is about!

This question was not merely rhetorical. Van was soon to put his mission to find how music can work towards "healing and uplifting the soul" into practice. On a September weekend in Loughborough, he organised and helped fund a conference for the Wrekin Trust, entitled "The Secret Heart Of Music". A poster described it as "An Exploration Into The Power Of Music To Change Consciousness". The introductory brochure explained further. "Music can form a bridge between the spiritual and material worlds. This unique gathering has been arranged to help restore music to a central place in our culture as a unifying and transcendent force." *Not* the Eurovision Song Contest, then, and available at a cost of one hundred and sixty-four pounds for the weekend.

Bob Kennedy recorded the proceedings for the *Van Morrison Newsletter*. The event opened with Malcolm Lazarus introducing Van and reading aloud from 'The Mystery' from the new LP. A short set followed from Van, Robin Williamson, Clive Culberson and harpist Derek Bell, playing soothing versions of 'Tir Na Nog', 'The Healing Has Begun', 'Celtic Ray' and 'In The Garden', interspersed with spoken passages from Irish folk tales, and Van and Robin duetting on the latter's 'Mr Thomas', later released on a Van B-side.

On Saturday morning, seminars swung into action on subjects like "Music As A Force In Spiritual Development", "The Effect Of Music Upon Hormonal Secretions In The Endocrine Gland" and "Music, Magic And Mysticism". Among musicians providing the sounds of transformation were Per Vilayayt Khan, spiritual leader of the Sufi Order of the West and also a pupil of Pablo Casals, the Indian musician Nishat Khan and the Consort of Music. Most crucial for Van's own future direction was the presence Derek Bell, from The Chieftains. The programme notes on Morrison indicated his own immersion in Irish culture, as part of "his struggle to reconcile the mythic, almost otherworldly vision of the Celts, and his own search for spiritual satisfaction, with the apparent hedonism of blues and soul music, has produced many inspired and visionary performances".

One such was given that night, when Van and his band played music largely from his new album. The following morning, saw an Open Forum, with comments from the delegates. A teacher of handicapped children told how she had used music to bring about mood changes in the children, and help them communicate. Morrison diffused some quasi-political comments, and as a finale the Anthony Rooley ensemble sang some Renaissance choral work, then were joined by Van for a light hearted 'Greensleeves'.

Talking later to Kennedy, Malcolm Lazarus said the project would have continued further had he not left the Trust the following year, ironically through ill health, to be replaced by people who "didn't have the grasp". It was ever thus. Lazarus felt that Van's lyrics continued this quest, "making his spiritual ideas tangible to the listener". He himself had been "using music to help people to enter into altered states of consciousness; transformational journeys". In just the same way, Morrison can create on stage what is akin to a religious experience. "He becomes a channel. In a concert hall, he becomes part of a mass psyche as it were, and he channels something into it."

The same month saw the release of *Poetic Champions Compose*. Recorded in London and Bath, it features Van's British musicians solely, with a solid core of Neil Drinkwater on piano, bassist Steve Pearce and Roy Jones on drums. Driving on top are Martin Drover on trumpet and flugelhorn, guitarist Mick Cox and the Dublin based Fiachra Trench, who arranged the string and woodwind parts and plays organ on 'Give Me My Rapture'. Paul Ridout is thanked for synthesiser programming, and June Boyce provides gentle background vocals.

"I started off making a jazz album, but after three numbers I thought I should put some words in," said Van. The album reached Twenty-Six in the UK and Ninety in the United States. On the front cover, Van, windswept and with a leather collar tight to his neck, stares coldly at the viewer as if from around a corner. The background is hazy, but dominated by two parallel lines behind his head, like massive barbed wire. On his left are cartoons of a piano, sax and guitar. On the back cover, these have become real, and Van is playing all three, in a state of rapture and with microphones and a palm tree behind him.

The album is Van's third masterpiece on a roll, as different from *No Guru* as that album was from *A Sense Of Wonder*, but taking its most transcendent moments, and extending them to a whole album. There are few comparisons in the whole of "rock" music with *Poetic Champions Compose*; it has a wholeness and a sense of poise all its own. John Martyn's *One World* or Ijahman's inspirational reggae come closest in spirit; healing music, which bodies forth what Van was trying to intellectualise at the Loughborough conference. As John Munro points out, the album plays games with the listener. "There are jaunty snatches of melody here that could be echoes from 'Brown Eyed Girl', while 'Someone Like You' could be the contented conclusion to the search begun on 'Listen To The Lion'."

Each side opens with an instrumental, and the album closes on one: all have a healing, beneficial feel. 'Spanish Steps', presumably those in Rome, sets Van's saxophone against a string section and gentle piano chords, a tune as calm as a millpond. Its title and shadings are similar to Miles Davis' *Sketches Of Spain*, and the guitar concertos of Rodriguez. 'The Mystery' is a song of consolation and hope, alchemical, turning dirt to gold. It could well be a message to Van's daughter, 'Hey Jude' style: "You know you've got so many charms, it's just begun." Violins take the place of the accustomed brass section here. The arrangement could equally fit in on Roy Harper's most underrated album, *Come Out Fighting, Ghengis Smith*, which also contains its fair share of word poetry, or early work by Al Stewart or Cat Stevens. A boy, his guitar, and an orchestra. Van's harmonica is sweet as honey, though there is something harshly patriarchal about the lines "trust what I say and do what you're told".

Some critics discerned that these songs could equally be to a woman or to God, love songs in whichever context, and 'Queen Of The Slipstream' places a new girlfriend in a sacred setting, haloed with light. It also places Van clearly in the bardic tradition, where "poetic champions compose". The Celtic harp is not accidental, here. Van's vocal, though, sounds a little disconnected. 'I Forgot That Love Existed' is also about "beginning to see the light", as Lou Reed put it. Van certainly sounds committed here, choked with emotion, but then he's singing about himself. Socrates and Plato are dragged in to praise love, and this is less crass than it at first sounds. The song is about uniting thought and emotion, a heart that can think and a brain that can feel.

The traditional blues 'Sometimes I Feel Like A Motherless Child' closes the side with a lament. Its subject is a man waiting for the Kingdom of God. Sung as straight gospel on the soundtrack of Pasolini's film *The Gospel According To St Matthew*, this imports a further dimension to the album, the starkness and beauty of that everyday account of miracles. How John Collis could call this version "perfunctory" is beyond me. It is Mother Ireland whom Van is missing, "so far from home", and his world weary vocals are like sobs of pain.

Appropriately, then, the next track is the instrumental 'Celtic Excavation', with Van's saxophone like a lonely soul traversing the ocean. "I've been searching a long time" is the opening line to 'Someone Like You', too, and its slow sadness follows on perfectly. Another song about waiting for the light, with sumptuous strings, the combination of melancholy and melody close to what that haunted troubadour Nick Drake achieved during his brief life. The song's title echoes a line from 'Reason To Believe', written by Tim Hardin, another lost soul, dead before his time.

'Alan Watts Blues' is dedicated to the American seeker after Eastern wisdom, a Beat who turned to Zen. Heights have always been associated with spiritual wisdom – Moses coming down with the tablets, the sermon on the mount, Christ ascending – and Van sits in his car, high on a mountain top, quoting Steinbeck and looking down on the rat race below. Maybe it's the lack of any real tune, but he sounds trapped rather than freed in this song. Watts' biographer called him a "genuine fake".

'Give Me My Rapture' opens merrily, rapturously indeed, and has the inner swing of the best gospel. For all that, Van seems a little selfish, asking for "my" rapture today, like a prize. Funny, I thought that the essence of Christianity lay in helping others, with rapture as a by-product. To add to the confusion, the keyboard combination has the rich lustre of The Band or Procol Harum, and the organ sound is straight out of Dylan's 'Positively Fourth Street', a song of the utmost hatred for an ex-girlfriend.

In 'Did Ye Get Healed?', Van turns his attention outwards, though Collis discerns "an almost voyeuristic curiosity about the faith of another, unnamed convert" here. This is a little unfair, as it is a song of joy, with June Boyce's voice matching Van's saxophone note for note, and Van genuinely trying to extend his feeling of inner certainty to another, and to heal her inner conflict. "Sometimes when the spirit moves me, I can do many wondrous things." Back to the theme of the Loughborough conference. 'Allow Me' is the third saxophone led instrumental, one too many for those listeners who can take only so much plangency at one sitting. An alternative view is that the album leaves words behind at its most intense moments, entering the silence. Martin Drover's trumpet is straight out of late fifties period Miles Davis, which would make Morrison John Coltrane.

Van talked on a Polygram promo disc about his love for improvised music, and his refusal ever to perform a song the same way twice. "I came in with the jazz people." His music is a continuing process of work, "the whole smorgasbord", right from *Astral Weeks*, "the most spiritually lyrical album I've ever done". His journey continues. Indeed, "all music is spiritual. Is it just a couple of strings on a fret board, or is it piano wire. What is it? It's not just a piece of wood. Of course all music is spiritual. It couldn't be anything else."

This belief feeds into *Poetic Champions Compose*, an album which is more than the sum of its parts, exuding an overall sense of calm and optimism. In *NME*, John Munro found it to be "a collection of deep devotion and powerful inspiration". Van deals with the mysteries of Heaven and Earth, no less, and transcends despair. He continues to reach out towards something else, "a vision that he and his listener alike see only in partial glances". Mat Snow in *Sounds* thinks that Van's cover shot looks as if "he'd sooner fill you in than sing a song". But this is one of his prettiest and most accessible offerings. "In the sweetly rolling moodscape of his tunes you hear the universal harmony with which he strives to become as one."

In *Q*, Paul Du Noyer finds "the same old magnificent thing", a trance like stream of words and sound. "He still sings as if in residence of some higher state of consciousness. One imagines his people having to shake him awake at the end of each day's recording, telling him it's over, time to go home."

With 1987's *Poetic Champions Compose* Van Morrison's contract with Mercury Records was indeed over, and his new contract with Polydor stipulated that marketing campaigns for future "product" be non aggressive, and not intrude on his privacy. Or his mystique.

On the promo LP, he indicates his own future direction. He has come to his Celtic crossroads. "A lot of serious musicians are either in the folk field or heading that way. The truth now lies in the traditional forms of music." Jack O'Neill, reviewing a December 1987 gig at Belfast City Hall for the *NME* found too that Morrison is making music "not above or beyond but outside his time". O'Neill comes as close as anyone to defining the essential Van.

"A little piece of rock that is forever poetry, Morrison moves in a world of writers and relics, mysticism and music, chapter *and* verse. An electric guitar does not hang easily on his shoulder; his playing is uncomfortable, self conscious and usually done with the thumb. His voice is restless, striving – always searching for newer, *deeper*, more fundamental perspectives".

Bringing It All Back Home, a TV series produced in collaboration by the BBC and RTE, was a five hour exploration of "the Celtic roots of rock 'n' roll". Musicians taking part, from both sides of the Atlantic, included The Everly Brothers, Christy Moore, The Pogues, Emmylou Harris, Clannad, The Waterboys, Hothouse Flowers, Pete Seeger, Cowboy Jack Clement, Elvis Costello and Van Morrison.

He was intent on delving back into his own Celtic roots, and his collaborators at the Edinburgh rock festival years before were now to prove crucial. The Chieftains had long been admired by rock musicians like The Grateful Dead. Their career already stretched back two decades, having emerged in 1963 from Sean O'Riada's folk ensemble Coeltiori Cualann – about the same time Van was touring Germany – though by 1988 only two original members remained, Paddy Moloney on uillean pipes and tin whistle and Martin Fay on fiddle. They played in Phoenix Park, Dublin to a crowd of one and a third million assembled for a Papal Mass, with the line-up that was to collaborate with Van, including violinist Sean Keane, ex BBC Symphony Orchestra harpist Derek Bell, vocalist Kevin Conneff and flautist Matt Molloy from The Bothy Band and a later incarnation of Planxty.

The Chieftains had a comfortable niche somewhere between classical and traditional music. Following a Top Forty album in 1986 with Irish pop flautist James Galway, some long term fans accused them of emasculating their art, which was to miss the point entirely. The whole glory of The Chieftains was their stylistic inclusiveness: The

Rolling Stones and Frank Zappa were later collaborators. Indeed, it was through their flexibility of style and attitude that a synthesis of Celtic music and rock would reach an audience previously biased against one or the other.

The Chieftains rejoined Van on stage at Belfast during the *No Guru* tour. Afterwards, Van and pixie lookalike Paddy Moloney discussed recording an entire album together, pacing St Stephen's Green deep in conversation. Both had specific short lists of songs, and Morrison was adamant that there should be no lengthy instrumental sections. A consensus was hammered out, to cover two previously released Morrison songs (including the title track) and draw the rest from traditional sources. From September to the following January they spent time at Windmill Lane Studios in Dublin, recording a joint album, *Irish Heartbeat*.

During this process, on 29 October 1987, Van joined The Chieftains before a live audience at Balmoral Studio in Belfast. They performed Patrick Kavanagh's 'Raglan Road', two traditional songs – 'Star Of The County Down' and 'My Lagan Love' – and a Van Morrison original, 'Celtic Ray'. The studio was decked out in Celtic emblems, Van wears a green shirt for the occasion, and his performance is mesmeric but bizarre, meatily beating at a drum kit with brushes, or strumming his guitar. He hums, fills his lungs and roars, moans like an old bluesman, and whispers: it is all too much for one violinist, who cannot prevent a grin breaking out. Van's commitment to this music is certain: he sounds drunk with inspiration. Appropriately, the concert was broadcast by the BBC on St Patrick's Day, 17 March 1988.

Meanwhile, an *NME* poll in January named *Astral Weeks* Number Six in the *NME* readers' all time one hundred albums poll, behind two albums by The Smiths, *Psychocandy* by The Jesus And Mary Chain, Joy Division's *Unknown Pleasures* and the first Velvet Underground album. It comfortably outpaced anything by The Beatles, Dylan, Sex Pistols, Marvin Gaye or The Clash. The master tapes of material issued by Warner Brothers came back under the control of Van's own Exile Productions, as did all new work. In February, hoping to set up some kind of psychic centre near Avalon, Morrison relocated to Bath, close to his favourite Woolhall Studios.

Morrison also made a guest appearance at a *Late Late Show* tribute to The Chieftains, again broadcast in March, joining with them on 'Star

Of The County Down' and 'Marie's Wedding', the last with Christy Moore, Gary Moore and Paul Brady. Morrison made "explicit what had long been implicit", according to – of all people – Bill Graham in *Hot Press*. Symbolic stuff. It is as if Van's San Franciscan mentor is reborn as a journalist on the leading Irish music paper. A coincidence, but according to Jung all coincidences have their hidden purpose.

Irish Heartbeat was released in June 1988. In Bobby Harvey's photograph Van and The Chieftains stand on a granite ledge, with a headless statue behind Derek Bell. It is winter, and most of The Chieftains have their hands in their pocket. Van stands in a vaguely simian pose, hands in black mittens, blue jeans and black overcoat, hair untidy and thinning, unsmiling and looking out of shot, as do all but two of The Chieftains. A green Celtic knot design reappears on the inner bag, superimposed over the lyrics. The album reached Number Eighteen in Great Britain, though only One Hundred And Two in the States, despite *Rolling Stone*'s confidence in its "splendour and intense beauty". A single of 'I'll Tell Me Ma' failed to follow the Top Ten progress of The Pogues' 'Fairytale Of New York', which also mined Irish culture, combining love with bitterness.

The hidden agenda here was more honourable, though Shane McGowan is one of the few other genuine poets in rock. Even if Morrison makes few political statements, this was certainly a call for unity, to those in the know. Irish folk music has long been seen by many as "Catholic" fare. As moderate an old hippy as Christie Moore performed some (extremely good) songs by hunger striker Bobby Sands, as a political act, while less subtle bands like The Wolfetones concentrate almost exclusively on the music's "rebel" constituent. For an Ulster protestant to sing along was, in some eyes, a sacrilege.

'Star Of The County Down' was originally associated with John McCormack. Van's playful vocal is sweetened by harp, pipes and violins, and all join in roughly for the chorus. A duet with June Boyce on 'Irish Heartbeat' from *Inarticulate Speech Of The Heart* sounds almost like Gram Parsons and Emmylou Harris, the gruff and the heavenly, with country flecked fiddle. Van's wordless vocals at the end, with soft accompaniment, could be spliced from *Astral Weeks*. On 'Ta Mo Chleamhnas Deanta', Kevin Conneff supplies the Gaelic, Van and Mary Black the English translation. The harpsichord and gentle lilt could be from Kubrick's amoral masterpiece *Barry Lyndon*, in which time seems to stop.

John Wilde describes The Chieftains' work on 'Raglan Road' as inspiring Morrison into "a rapture that truly borders on the demonic. This is some fierce tremble, this is a worship that chokes. You can smell the tears." On the other hand, the *Belfast Telegraph* reckoned that if Patrick Kavanagh had lived to hear this interpretation there would have been "trouble in the Dublin pubs". Slow and stately at first, Van certainly works himself and his drum kit up into a right old lather.

'She Moved Through The Fair' was one of Fairport's first ventures into traditional folk, although there is a literary edge to the words, and Padraic Colum laid claim to them. David Cavanagh describes "a slow seduction by violin". The way Sandy Denny sings the final verse suggests that the bride-to-be has passed over, "my dead lover came", and will never see her wedding day, an interpretation which Van's hushed, repeated vocal – "not be long" again and again – and his near death rattle at the very end at least hints at. Or it could just be the eagerness of young love. A rapid contrast comes with the children's street song 'I'll Tell Me Ma', with urgent percussion, and the ambience of a marching band. The ensemble slyly – or bravely – insert snatches from a Republican rebel song and an Orange anthem, 'The Sash', "spontaneous fun" in Moloney's words. Van admits that he once skipped to this song, or at least skipped school. "Did you wear black stockings?" Moloney responds, with a chuckle.

Denis Campbell describes 'Carrickfergus' as "a melancholic air worthy of Otis Redding" – Celtic crossroads indeed – and though it is difficult to think of anyone, Engelbert Humperdinck even, ruining this, Van's singing is more tender and emotional than anyone dare expect. There is just enough tartness to rob the performance of false sentiment. The song undercuts itself anyway in the line "I'll sing no more now till I get a drink", and Van sounds wickedly thirsty, suddenly. The funereal end is matched by his pause before the last phrase, judged to perfection.

'Celtic Ray' first appeared on *Beautiful Vision*, but the printed words emphasise the subtlety of this song, combining the Celtic outposts with representative figures, Lewellen, McManus, the coalbrick man – Cornwall or Brittany – and Jimmy. Van and the musicians swing here, with a lilt. The opening to 'My Lagan Love' is inexpressibly lovely as only

The Chieftains can be, and Van's vocal soothes and strains just where it should, going into a weird effusion at the end. The *Belfast Telegraph* churlishly complained that were Morrison to sing this at a Belfast party, "people would leave early". Well, more fool them. 'Marie's Wedding' is a hectic Scottish reel, with Maura O'Connell, Mary Black and June Boyce joining in the celebrations. This is probably the song that Richard Thompson subverted with typical low cunning into the bitter 'Nobody's Wedding', and then chopped most of the words out, so that nobody would know what he was singing about! Van sings it straight. As Ben Cruikshank commented, it completes an album so listener friendly, "that it just has to be replayed from the start a second time".

Apart from Robert Sandall in *Q*, typically sniffy – "is the mystical old codger, you wonder, trying to cheer himself up" – the reviews were ecstatic. As Gavin Martin later observed, Van's career has long been marked by his ability "to constantly turn new, tantalising variations on the hybrid he formulated out of American R&B and Irish traditional – Celtic Soul". Here, he has simply upped the traditional element. In the *NME*, beneath a pencil drawing of Van good enough for an album sleeve, and under the headline "Celtic Champions Compose", Denis Campbell found the infectious enthusiasm of The Chieftains had rubbed off on Morrison, "who has responded with a warmth worthy of the tunes".

John Wilde in *Melody Maker* – "Emerald Aisles" was the heading here – finds Morrison as if struck by lightning. "You have to delve back before the giddy days of *Astral Weeks* to find him quite so *let* go." The collaboration has awoken his roisterous spirit. In *Sounds*, David Cavanagh finds some of the "most haunting, rousing, downright *friendly* music of the year". It says more about Ireland than a thousand tourist brochures. "This record bears a golden glow." In the *NME*'s end-of-year round up, the album came second in a critics' poll, between Public Enemy and REM.

In April, Van played at the Riverside, Coleraine, for the University of Ulster Literary Society. The evening was filmed, and broadcast on Ulster TV that July, as "Van The Man". In between an interview and discussion, Van went unplugged, with only Clive Culbertson on bass and that formal-looking imp, Derek Bell on piano. He revisited his American years for a reborn 'T For Texas' and Leadbelly's 'When I Was A Cowboy'. 'A Sense Of

Wonder' is tender, 'Celtic Ray' wistful, and 'In The Garden' classically beautiful. Van sings about petals falling down, and Bell plays downward notes: as Van sings about the breeze blowing "against your face", Bell imitates the scene with an arpeggio. A career highlight. 'Raglan Road' stirs the blood. Morrison, one presumes, plays a guitar break that almost talks, against the flowing tide of Bell's keyboards.

Even before the release of *Irish Heartbeat*, a joint tour of Britain and Europe with The Chieftains was underway, and Van began visibly to enter the spirit of things. Like Guinness, The Chieftains were good for him. Morrison even mingled with audiences before the show, chatting freely, swapping banter and responding to requests on and off stage. At one show, he burst into fits of giggles, necessitating a second take on 'Carrickfergus'.

The *Irish Heartbeat* tour opened at Aberdeen in late April 1988, and reached London's Riverside arts centre a fortnight later. Microdisney's Sean O'Hagan, writing for the *NME*, described proceedings. "Tonight genius has his legs bent, his arms spread and his face contorted in creative exorcism. The music is pouring down over his shoulders and Van Morrison is way out there – beyond words and meaning. Something has happened to the most uncomfortable of live performers and I'd bet it hinges on his proximity to the sheer joyousness of The Chieftains' work in motion. He's smiling, laughing, cracking the odd off mike joke and trading sarcasm with court jester Paddy Moloney."

Morrison's own set opens with him playing saxophone with a six piece band, including Derek Bell on keyboards, on a Celtic tinged instrumental, which merges into 'Vanlose Stairway'. "He sustains this celestial mood throughout, pursuing the gospel of poetic wholeness and metaphysical quest that has been a mainstay of his music for a long time now." 'In The Garden' is sung as if in a trance, as the band "move with his every nuance".

The Chieftains enter, and the augmented band smash into 'The Star Of The County Down', Morrison's grin matched only by that of his bassist. 'She Moved Through The Fair' literally "takes the audience's breath away, Morrison repeating his dredged up exorcism to invoke the heroine's violent death". 'My Lagan Love' collides with a Pogues-like 'Marie's Wedding' and suddenly "all and sundry are on their feet tearing the roof off the once sedate Riverside". "Awesome," O'Hagan concludes.

The *Melody Maker* considered "you left transformed. You have just watched genius culminate, pass the utmost. A wondrous sight."

An audience tape of that same concert confirms the new crackle in Van's live act, and a whooping, ecstatic audience, even before The Chieftains come on stage. There is a full set with Van's band, including a driven version of 'Common One', and a version of 'Did Ye Get Healed?' where even the sax solo has a Celtic wildness. 'Solid Ground' has a harp part tonight, and The Chieftains give a full sound, and an energy that explodes from the stage, and is partly captured even on tape, laced with delicacy and restraint where they're needed.

In "Heart For Art's Sake", David Cavanagh spoke with Derek Bell who puts the first move in this collaboration down to Van's manager, who set up a meeting on Paddy Moloney's home ground. Morrison – helpless laughter here – "got locked in the bathroom of the Wicklow hotel. They had to fetch a pick axe to get him out." The Chieftains' keyboard player later told him about his own 1979 masterwork, *Derek Bell Plays With Himself*, and Van nearly had to be taken away in an ambulance, he was so cracked up. Indeed, Bell confirms that Morrison is deeply humorous, and "all the funnier because he's got this deadpan serious face with a permanent frown on it". I still don't reckon that Nicky Horne would see the joke, though. Bell even hints at a future collaboration, recording a whole album of Van's own songs. A dream that is still not yet reality.

Talking to the *Hot Press*, Bell reveals that it was his recordings of the British mystic composer Cyril Scott which drew Van to him: "He was looking for some sort of a spiritual answer to things." Van had already read around three thousand books on mysticism, "during a period of period crisis". Another point of contact was a mutual love of good ice cream. He will ring up and say "Coming for a scoop? I'm here." Their profiles confirm this secret addiction (touchingly innocent in the world of live music). "All flavours, but especially chocolate."

Van performed 'Marie's Wedding' as part of "Fife Aid" in St Andrews in July, and is the undoubted star of the resulting video. A more serious concert, musically at least, was filmed at the Ulster Hall, Belfast in September, and broadcast on Channel 4 early the next year. The hour long show opens with three songs from Van's latest band – Arty McGlynn, Clive Culbertson, Dave Early, Richie Buckley and June Boyce – along with special guest Derek Bell, no longer playing only with himself.

By now, McGlynn was also moonlighting in the severely underrated Patrick Street, with Andy Irvine. The band kick into spirited versions of 'Tore Down A La Rimbaud', 'In The Garden' and 'Rave On, John Donne', before being joined by the might of The Chieftains for a full set. Wonderful is the only word. The aural evidence surfaced on the *Dark Knight Of The Soul* bootleg. Delights included 'Boffyflow And Spike' and encores of 'Goodnight Irene' and 'Moondance'.

In October 1988, Morrison and The Chieftains were back in London, at the Royal Albert Hall, but the old troubled Van Morrison seemed to be back in charge. As *Melody Maker* put it, "when he is not in touch with the muse that drives him, Morrison has often down the years been inclined to give up, retreat behind routine readings of his devotional hymns". For all that, Eric Clapton, joined in the general merriment and so forgot his dignity as to leap on stage to dance an impromptu jig, before being shooed back to his seat.

Gavin Martin interviewed Van and Paddy in tandem, and declared "I want a pint of whatever these two are on". A fellow called Micky the Muck, who's a pig, attended the recording sessions, apparently. Van thinks that Paddy is at least one hundred years old, while he's only twenty-six. Paddy thinks they should both take a shuttle to Mars: "We'd be the first musicians to play there and anybody that wants can come up and join us."

Martin completes the hilarity with an apocryphal guide to Van Morrison, some of which might even be true. He eats up to nine full meals a day. At a gig with Elvis Costello and The Confederates he pushed guitar legend James Burton out of the way and did the honours himself. A planned book of prose and poetry was turned down by a leading publisher at the last moment, since when live versions of 'Summertime In England' have been augmented with the cryptic lines "Faber and Faber – we lost a few". All part of the mythology.

Paddy Moloney told the *Hot Press* that "the press certainly seemed to love that album. But I don't think it really had much effect on people. We certainly didn't notice any great difference in our audiences. I was very doubtful originally, but it worked out all right." Could we expect *Irish Heartbeat II* any day now? "Well, maybe not quite that soon."

The magazine asked him to name his top ten humorous moments with Van, and his reply speaks volumes. "I don't want this to be libellous." Nor me, Paddy, nor me! He finally settles on Van describing a small stage with a metal barrier around it as being like a cage – "Van's just so quick" – then more hesitation. Finally, at point eight, "oh yeah, the time Paul Durcan got his cue to go on stage at The Point and the trumpet went on by mistake. We all cracked up at that...and Van saw the funny side of it afterwards." The emphasis being on the last word. Finally, Paddy concludes that "the main thing about Van is that he's a very creative person. You have to ignore all the things people tend to talk about. Life's too short for looking at people's bad side."

The two have much in common, not least a reputation for being occasionally bull headed, and their love of Goon-like humour. Moloney was so close to Peter Sellers that he swears to having seen him at the foot of his bed, smiling, at the very hour when he later heard on the radio that Sellers had died. Van would talk to him about anything but music, and left Paddy to get the arrangements – or "shapes" – together for the album. Talking to *Q*, Moloney reckoned that Van is so tight wound that it is only on stage that he can cut loose. "He's in a cage otherwise."

Stories later emerged of Paddy and Van refusing to speak to one another, and pouring a bottle of wine (each) over each other's heads. On The Chieftains' in-concert LP, *An Irish Evening*, Roger Daltrey of The Who has replaced Van at the mike, for a version of 'Raglan Road'. Peace later broke out, and Van joined The Chieftains on his instrumental 'Boffyflow And Spike' on 1990's *Celebration* CD. At the end, instruments crash to the ground, and Van shouts out "Cosmic", then "we've got to do some aerobics". Paddy kept this in, though even he was bemused. One thing is clear. For Van, "everything else is a distraction from the music". Morrison sang 'Have I Told You Lately' on their 1995 album *The Long Black Veil*, alongside guests who included Sting, Sinead O'Connor and Marianne Faithfull.

In a later interview, for BBC radio, Paddy reckons that Van's vocal technique is close to a style of singing that can still be heard in remote pockets of Connemara and Donegal. "At the end of a song, he just rattles on. You don't know when he's going to stop, he doesn't know when he's going to stop, depends what's in him at the time." Once Moloney asked him to give them the "billy" when he was coming to the end of his vocal extravagances, meaning a nod of the head. "We went into it, comes up near the end, 'Billy, Billy', he shouts out."

CHAPTER NINE

Years Of Fame

Van's subsequent live gigs were regularly attended by Georgie Fame, an old friend from the sixties. Since The Blue Flames burnt out, Fame had toured with Alan Price, starred in his own BBC2 series, and recorded an album of Hoagy Carmichael songs with jazz vocalist Annie Ross. He was to find in Van a generous front man, who never failed to introduce the members of his band, and direct audience response towards them. During an appearance at the 1989 Glastonbury Festival, Fame took lead vocals during a short solo set with Van's band, drawing mass applause for old warhorses like 'Yeah Yeah' and 'Get Away', hits twenty years before, when most of the audience were hardly born. In turn, Van was to find Georgie a constant and encouraging presence, a wonderful organ player and backing singer, who could also direct the band while Van concentrated on his own vocals. A safe pair of hands, just like Simon Nicol has been through thirty years of Fairport's varied line-ups.

As another band member was to notice, "Georgie's very open and he probably takes the pressure off him as far as the limelight is concerned. The band improvises sixty per cent of the time, and we'd rarely go through a play list. Van is into another aspect of music."

Fame made his presence felt on *Avalon Sunset*, and was part of the band who previewed the album at a private gig at Ronnie Scott's club on 24 May 1989. Footage of five earlier songs surfaced on *One Irish Rover*, almost two years later. Pee Wee Ellis and Haji Ahkba were passing through: the other musicians settled into place, and were still all on board for the Beacon Theatre gig in November, since issued on video. Drummer Dave Early, the brass section of Richie Buckley and

Steve Gregory and pianist Neil Drinkwater were all old lags by now. New to the Morrison experience were Fame, Brian Odgers on bass and Bernie Holland on guitar, who had been around since Bluesology, and specialised in coming in to prop up fading groups: Jody Grind, Back Door ....

By now, Morrison was signed to Polydor in Britain, and Mercury in the United States. *Avalon Sunset* was released in June 1989, and broke into the UK Top Twenty – at Number Thirteen – while reaching a disappointing Ninety-One in the USA. Its cover has a New Age feel to it. After two appearances as Mr Grumpy, Van's face is again in purdah, and instead there is the far more relaxing image of a swan gliding over water reddened by the setting sun. On the back, the river is empty, fringed by reeds. Between the two words of the title is a mystical insignia in violet, which comprises Van's initials, entwined around each other like a couple making love. *Ivan* Morrison acts as producer.

The album was recorded in London and Bath, not that far from Avalon, Arthur's mythic kingdom, lost now among the Somerset levels. Sunset suggests a coming darkness, just as the album's final track suggests not so much summer as its ending. For all Van's new Christian zeal, the album presents a vision of glories passing. There will be scattered tracks in the future which pursue a mythic quest – 'Avalon Of The Heart', on the next album, for one – but there will never again be the concentrated invention of the great run of albums to which *Avalon Sunset* provides the coda. In future, one will look for isolated glories.

Van restricts himself to guitar. Fiachra Trench is again responsible for string and brass arrangements, and thus dominates the album. Katie Kissoon is back on backing vocals. The great jazz trumpeter Henry Lowther joins the fray on one track, leading a brass section of Cliff Hardie on trombone, Stan Sultzman on alto sax, and Alan Barnes on baritone sax. Between them they have concocted one of those rare albums which is perfectly rounded, its sum somehow more than its parts.

The main debate at the time centred around Van's spiritual pilgrimage, and with which faith or sect he now identified. Asked at Loughborough whether he was a practising Catholic, he answered, "No, the nearest I got was the Church of Ireland. But I'm pathless at the moment. I'm trying to find a path." However, according to Derek Bell, "after he teamed up with Cliff Richard, he went back to Hallelujah

Christianity again". This held little appeal for Bell, but "Van likes to keep changing his concepts. He always says, 'I need to go in a new direction.' We no longer share an interest on that level, but we still get on very well as people."

Herbie Armstrong, another musician who was also a personal friend of Van's, had joined a Pentecostal church in Notting Hill Gate, of all places. As he told the Van Morrison fanzine of the time, "I now play music for pure love and love of every day, and it's through Jesus Christ. He's put something back into me and I pray that one day Van will find the Lord, because Van is checking it out and he certainly knew the Lord long before I did." Rather like Bob Dylan, who was singing songs rich with biblical imagery and with a black and white morality, long before he converted. Van's is a less judgemental Christianity than Dylan's, quicker to praise and slower to point the finger of scorn. If one thinks of how Cat Stevens, of all people, re-emerged as something akin to an English Ayatollah, then the new Van is moderation personified. As he told Gavin Martin, "I'm into it all, orthodox or otherwise. I'm just groping in the dark for a bit more light."

'Whenever God Shines His Light' is certainly open in its Christian message, naming Jesus for a start, and accompanied by happy, clappy Cliff Richard for seconds. Actually, Cliff is dreadfully underrated by smart critics, a great singer within his own chosen limits, and his duet with Van is genuinely thrilling, rather like mixing mild and bitter. The words are darker than the cheery backing suggests: Van is singing out of confusion, despair and loneliness. It is God now who gets the healing done.

'Contacting My Angel' is less biblically correct, as this angel is a woman, and very much alive. Van gets messages from her without the help of BT – maybe they are using the Celtic Ray – but the music swirls and a bass guitar booms, and he sounds transformed, so the results are real enough. All the usual themes are there: water from a mountain stream, which heals, love's power to transform. Then, in an odd twist, Van meets a real angelic presence, "the youth of eternal summers".

On 'I'd Love To Write Another Song', a full throated jazz band back his return to basics, his need to write a love song to "make some money, pay the bills". There is again a darker side to all this, as if such writing blocks make life not worth living, and it is only through his art

– not life – that he can "feel things bright and new". There's a good joke though; he offers to "rhyme", but by pairing it with "mind" doesn't, quite.

The response is one of the finest love songs of the century, which I remember devastated me when I first heard it, as it seemed both something never quite said before, and yet a song I felt I had known forever. I hope it paid Van's bills for a few months. Fiachra Trench's arrangement is lush but not mawkish. Acoustic piano and guitar play against rich strings, but any sickliness is counteracted by Van's low growl. Earthly love transmutes into that for God, just like in Dante, "there's a love that's divine, and it's yours and it's mine". The morning sun has set by the end of the song, suggesting love shading into death, but subtly.

Autumn sunshine lights 'Coney Island', which begins at dawn, the dawn of creation perhaps. A perfect day, just like Lou Reed once sang about, and Van sets paradise firmly in Ulster, as if the Troubles were gone. "Wouldn't it be nice if it could be like this all the time." By speaking this soliloquy, he seems to be in the room, by turns matter of fact, ecstatic, loving and wistful. On this showing, Van would have made a superb actor, and he certainly gives a boost to the Northern Ireland Tourist Board.

In 1996, the Radio 4 programme *Going Places* tried to trace this day out as if Van was reciting from his diary, rather than imagining perfection. The route zigzags from the coast of County Down up to Belfast, and it is decided that Morrison would never make a good tourist guide. There is a more famous Coney Island, just south of Brooklyn. During the programme, a proud Ulsterman lays claim to this a having taken its name from the County Down landmark.

A TV advert for Bass stole the idea, but left out the poetry:

> Came down at the coast near the harbour
> and had fish fresh off the boat for lunch.
> Beautiful, the sunshine streaming onto the water.
> But the best part of the day was in the bar later on,
> it was grand to warm up by the fire and talk it over again.
> Wish every day could be like that.

Van's voice and the orchestra end together, in a heart stopping moment, then the strings pick up, seemingly to continue the same piece, but instead we're into 'I'm Tired Joey Boy'. Night again, the darkness just before dawn, which is always the worst. Van is back in his depression, and makes a rare overt comment on the Troubles: "I've no time for schism." Written to a friend from school, who became a farmer, he seems to regret his past ambitions, which distanced him forever from such a simple life. Joey probably also has the odd sleepless night, wishing he was Van. Like Dylan in 'Watching The River Flow', Morrison sits by running water, and ponders. Literally lifted up, as in the opening song, Van finds peace in mountain heights – as ever – and not so much in God, but in silence. The same thing, really.

'When Will I Ever Live To Live In God' deals with just this sense of doubt, after the certainty of 'Whenever God Shines His Light On Me'. On the other hand, it is precisely such doubts that make us continue to listen: if Van ever grew certain in one of his religious paths we would begin to lose interest, just as Richard Thompson's songwriting seems to have closed down – except in fitful flashes – since his immersion in Islam.

A sweep of harp strings, melancholy piano and Van infinitely sad. The sun sets on Avalon, or at least Bristol docks, and Morrison babbles about angels and William Blake, incoherently. The second verse is plainer. He is introduced by his new lover to the glories of Christian architecture, but it fails to move his soul. Heavenly organ from Fame, and Van realises you have to do things your own way. We're back in the last song, a mountain and a shepherd, the green glory of Ireland. Through such childhood landscapes, Van does indeed learn to live in God. He even invokes "a sense of wonder" to remind us of past raptures. The final chorus is not so much a question as an answer.

In 'Orangefield' we're back in the territory of *Astral Weeks*, in both historical and psychic terms. It is a bright autumn day. Van is back at school, falling in love for the first time and forever. She was the apple of his eye – both fruitful (like the name of his school) and Eve tempting him to sin – and her beauty becomes like the sun, or God. "It lit up our lives." It is not merely fanciful to compare this vision to that of Beatrice in the *Divine Comedy*. Everything is both symbolic and factual, all at once. She even stands by flowing water, "by the riverside".

'Daring Night' might invoke the lord of the dance, as in Sydney Carter's hymn, but it deals with full, blazing sex, whatever its churchy organ and gentle lilt might suggest. "The bodies move and we sweat and have our being." It is night time again, but bright with stars and the moon. Love too brings its own light, and the lovers seem to be up there with the heavenly bodies (pun intended), "in the firmament we move". Hardly a Christian song, with The Great Goddess of the Eternal Wisdom overlooking proceedings, but uplifting in just about every sense.

'These Are The Days' ends the album in "endless summer". Human love turns divine, as in 'Have I Told You Lately', transmuting from his girlfriend to the magician who turned water into wine. Van's lover is like a grown up version of the girl in 'Orangefield'. Appropriately, the lovers walk again by a sparkling river, and the bitter regrets of 'I'm Tired Joey Boy' have vanished with the light. The paradise glimpsed so briefly on 'Coney Island' is now here and forever, no past, nor future. If this is not a vision of paradise, then I don't know what is.

Reviewers at the time were nonplussed. In Q, Mark Cooper was, as usual, the clearest sighted, hearing a "warmly relaxing R&B stew" and music "sometimes trance-like in its ability to deepen a mood of religious calm". In Sounds, David Cavanagh found that "if Morrison is to attain peace of mind – like all of history's wracked comedians and artists – he also risks losing the previous torment of his muse".

Talking with fellow musician Sean O'Hagan in the NME, Van agrees with Jung: "That's the closest explanation I can find for my work. Writing songs comes from the collective unconscious or my own unconscious or both." His music is a search for transcendent moments, though he can rarely reach them on stage. "It's where you switch off the mechanism, switch off what's referred to as *the constant voice*." He also ties himself into a literary tradition. "Basically Irish writers, and I include myself here, are writing about the same things, energy and about when things felt better. Either that, or sadness. And that's it."

O'Hagan notices how, on stage, Van was "a man gone beyond language, words failing him in a positive way". He accurately predicts how Van is looking towards another Irish writer, Samuel Beckett, the "poet of silence". Van agrees: "Language is a way of going back, I suppose. He's saying, 'I can't go on. But, I'll go on.' That's what it's all about. 'Fail better,' he's saying, *'fail better.'*"

On 18 June, near to the Summer solstice, Van played Nijmegen with Fame and the boys. According to a fanzine article, he launched straight into a pumping 'Did Ye Get Healed?', and a full bore performance took on "an almost religious glow". During 'Cleaning Windows', Van demonstrated the proper arm motion when polishing glass with a chamois: "You go up, left, right, down, left, up, centre, all the way down." He even told the doubtless bemused Dutch audience how to climb the ladder so as not to drop the bucket.

During a hymn-like 'Northern Muse', Van gives another kind of instruction manual, for life this time. "When the heart is open you will change. Just like a flower slowly opening. Give, give, give more, five better. When you're completely empty and you're completely drained, and you can't go on anymore, you have to give, give again, give more, give better. When you're down, depressed, despondent, pissed off, fucked off, you have to give, give more, give again, give better. When the heart is open."

On stage, Van thanked Georgie Fame, The Blue Flames and The Van Morrison Band – who merge into one another – three in one, just like the Holy Trinity. He told O'Hagan in a later interview about how he had begun to lose interest in life on the road. "I started touring very young. I spent years living out of a suitcase from about fifteen to twenty-two. I was living in hotels for years. That was my tolerance level. I don't want to waste my life touring, because I did that early on. It's just one day at a time. Some days are good, some are bad. That's life, I'm just taking it as it comes." On the other hand, as he confided to Paul Jones on Radio Two, since hooking up with Georgie Fame, "It's a whole new thing. Before this for six or seven years I was really bored with performing." Dublin saxophonist Richie Buckley had noticed this new found enthusiasm following some well received concerts at the Dublin Stadium in 1989.

Back in Nijmegen, Van reads the Lord's Prayer, after the following improvisation, in the middle of 'Summertime In England'. "Picture yourself in the middle of a field, in Somerset. Just picture yourself in the middle of a field about half past four. It's June, summer solstice, and you can hear a brass band from across the field. Play."

Van did just this himself, that same week, when he topped the bill at the 1989 Glastonbury Festival. Fellow musicians told the *NME* how Van's music had affected their own work. Bono envies Cliff Richard for singing with him. He produces "beneath the skin music". For The Proclaimers, "he's an Ulsterman who sings soul music without insulting black people by mimicking them".

David McComb burst into tears during 'Raglan Road' at the Albert Hall and continued crying for the rest of the concert. *Astral Weeks* "disintegrates your whole body, soul and life". Van is a good painkiller. Boy George's favourite song is 'Moondance', and envies him his Johnson's leather jacket, that and his large reproductive equipment (I paraphrase). Mike Scott regards 'Summertime In England' as "just the highest music I've ever heard". For Shane MacGowan, "he's brilliant and inspiring, a natural Irish soul singer – always uplifting". His favourite song is 'My Lonely Sad Eyes', his favourite album *Astral Weeks*, "because there's no bullshit on it".

Gavin Friday remembers a free open air Millennium concert with Van and The Chieftains, "as tight as a knot in a nun's knickers". Jazzer Andy Sheppard likes his voice because it sounds like a tenor sax, and for Joby from Energy Orchard, he is a "medicine man". Edwyn Collins has a Scots word for him, "carnaptious", a man unwilling to compromise or co-operate.

The *NME*'s Danny Kenny noted how, following on from The Bhundu Boys, the day was dominated by the vast shadow of Van Morrison. "Not for nothing does he have the reputation (and something of the look of) an extremely disgruntled pig, but his presence on the site caused an instant upping of the in-air electricity level, a tangible throb of expectation." *Sounds* saw him coaxing his band to heights of improvised beauty. "At one stage he engaged in a phenomenal bout of call and response singing with the saxophone; at another he floated entirely free of the song with a burst of inspirational scat that defied cold analysis. This was ecstasy for the ears."

Van's live schedule was punishing. At the Montreux Jazz Festival on 17 July, he performed with Georgie Fame and The Dallas Jazz Orchestra, including 'Listen To The Lion' and 'Here Comes The Night' in his set. Two days later, he played two songs at the Prince's Trust 1989 Rock Gala, at Birmingham NEC. Other acts included Phil Collins, Level

42 and Jeff Beck. More importantly, the musical director was George Martin, conducting The City Of Birmingham Symphony Orchestra, and they combined with Van on a spine chilling, wide screen version of 'Orangefield'. At the Eco Rock Festival for a Greener Future, held in St Andrews a week later, Van was filmed performing three songs: 'A Sense Of Wonder', 'Marie's Wedding', and 'Cleaning Windows'.

'Have I Told You Lately' was a minor hit for Van himself in July 1989, when it made Number Seventy-Four. Rod Stewart's 1993 version became a million seller. The "easy" generation were treated to an instrumental arrangement by Richard Clayderman with The James Last Orchestra. An earlier song of the same name was associated principally with Tony Bennett, and a US hit for Ricky Nelson.

In August, Van took some time off from all this activity to meet his long time hero Spike Milligan, through the good offices of *Q* magazine. Van remembers Sunday mornings from his childhood, "The Goons, then *Round The Horne*, Jimmy Clitheroe, they seemed to be all on a Sunday. The Goons were huge in Ireland: kids I grew up with talked like that all the time." He invokes Spike's name at a gig that night, during a bizarre, as yet unrecorded boogie called 'Max Wall'. When asked whether he is Protestant or Catholic, Van at first sidesteps, "I'm not really anything", then admits to being "theoretically Church of Ireland". "A Proddy," Milligan retorts.

Spike hardly allows Van a word in edgeways, but gets in some telling points. "You're basically a very serious person. You are different, Van, you're a very strange man." He also thinks that Van is too modest by far, though "you have a very strange charisma. I don't feel quite comfortable in your presence. A sense of menace. There's a sense of abandonment in your singing. I thought, he doesn't think, he just does it." Milligan compares this to his own time spent as a jazz musician: "When I was playing that trumpet I couldn't think about the rates, the rent. It was liberation, self therapy. And you can induce that therapy in other people".

Van admits that he uses the blues as drama: "That's what I picked it up from. You make things more than they really are, to get it across, I find. It's fantasy, illusion." Interesting how, when he relaxes his guard with a fellow performer, Van's interviews suddenly make such blinding sense. In late August, he played the Belfast Opera House again, one night in a pair of Raybans, after someone jokily said they made him look like Roy Orbison.

David Cavanagh in *Sounds* finds the Georgie Fame led band "a jazz combo by any other name", and take some time to settle. 'Raglan Road', however, is "hoarse and hurt", and 'Gloria' the best spelling lesson he has ever had. In 'Summertime In England' the vocal duel with Richie Buckley lasts a full minute on the phrase "Mr Lawrence". The lights come up the moment that the last chord of a charged 'She Moves Through The Fair' dies away. "I think that they sensed nothing musical, physical or spiritual could follow it."

Polydor had snapped up the rights to twelve of his previous albums, and rush released seven of them in September. Robert Sandall in *Q* found "some of the most inspired, least convincing and less well known moves of his inexorably slow burning career". In November, Van appeared with Jerry Lee Lewis at the Hammersmith Odeon, performing two songs, 'Goodnight Irene' and 'What'd I Say'. On the first of these, Lewis looks half stuffed, stiff backed and trading phrases with Van, who badly needs a haircut, but drives the old rock 'n' roller on. Lewis's stubby fingers can still coax magic out of his grand piano.

Later that same month, Van was joined on stage by John Lee Hooker at the Beacon Theatre, New York, performing 'Boom Boom' and 'It Serves Me Right To Suffer'. The gig's importance was indicated by its title when later released on video: "The Concert". As if there had been no others! The packaging is almost identical to *The Best Of* CD, advertised on the back. Shots of the city alternate with Irish mountains, and a swan landing: Van sings standing on a red carpet, tightly squeezed into a blue suit, and taking the Bobby Charlton route to concealing impending baldness. As all who have tried it know, it doesn't work!

There are four songs each from *Irish Heartbeat* – given a jazz swing – and from the new album. 'Moondance' segues into 'Fever', and Mose Allison appears for one song, his own 'Thank God For Self Love', tossed between him, Fame and Van. The band is stripped down to the two keyboard players, of whom Fame looks enviably slim and poised, Neil Drinkwater boyish and formal, Buckley – in a bowler hat – and Gregory on brass, Early on drums and Odgers in a psychedelic skull cap on bass, with Bernie Holland on guitar. Van goes into an impromptu rap about walking the green fields. 'Summertime In England' starts at a cracking pace, a cross between an Irish jig and Frank Zappa.

Then things get really strange. "Professor Heaney, I read your book. *Preoccupations*. Tom Paulin, we lost a few." Paulin is a professional Irishman born and part raised in Yorkshire, who wrote some wonderful early poems, then declined into incomprehensible doggerel – stiff with Belfast slang – and ended as a mean eyed cultural critic on BBC2. Georgie now plays some formal organ chords, and Van shouts out "Mystic church", and introduces the Rev Fame. Morrison is suddenly taking a "long, long" (much repeated) drive to paradise (again much repeated), with every syllable echoed by Buckley. "Squealing feeling," Van shouts, and Buckley switches to his saxophone, dragging out all kinds of weird and wonderful sounds. Then we're back to the vocal duet, "way back" and "previous" over and over again, with Georgie Fame cracking up with laughter. Now Bernie Holland gets into the act, imitating Morrison's vocal riffs on guitar. Van and Buckley trade "Mr Lawrence" back and forth, Van introduces his band and leaves the stage, only for Holland to shimmy across the stage, and Fame to repeat "Mr Morrison" endlessly, then "Mr Hi-Fidelity". He returns, to wild applause.

The next song, 'Caravan' is if anything more extraordinary, with Van going into a burst of vocal improvisation about "the radio station plays", when the band plays in turn light classical, a drop dead imitation of Weather Report, and soul. Van shouts out "rain check", then goes into a brief snatch of 'In The Midnight Hour'. The band shout out, as if in unison, "it's Ivan", and he comes in without a second's pause for a supercharged 'Moondance'. Drinkwater quotes from 'Greensleeves', and Bernie Holland makes his guitar strings dance during a solo fast and brief as a streaker. Flute and accordion introduce 'Star Of The County Down', with hand signals from Fame, who spins right round on his stool. 'In The Garden' opens with a chorus of another Irish anthem, 'Danny Boy', and Van repeats "born again" seven times and "you fell" at least twelve, to point up the Christian message. He thanks the band – definitely called The Blue Flames – and they respond with what sounds like a peal of bells. 'Have I Told You Lately' is sung straight, a secular hymn. Van watches Drinkwater's piano solo, comments quietly "isn't that perfect" – it is – and roars like a lion.

'Gloria' is restored as a celebration: Van throws in a snatch of 'Smokestack Lightning', howling like a werewolf, and dedicates the next part of the show to John Lee Hooker, who "ain't nothing but a stranger in this world, don't turn him from your door", and there he is, in suit, tie, shades and hat, a Texas star on his lapel. Hooker has the gift of intense stillness on stage, unsmiling. Van watches him like a proud son, and was later to clone his costume and demeanour. They duet like a pair of voodoo priests, and the song develops into 'TB Sheets'. Goose bump time. "Serve me right to suffer, serve me right to be alone. Living in memories of days gone by."

"John Lee, the king of the blues," Van exclaims. Hooker leads off on 'Boom Boom', which closes all kinds of circles, a staple of the R&B boom, hell it even gave it a name. Van and John Lee lock guitars, like two rutting bulls. Van grins a baby grin, suddenly overawed. He leads the applause afterwards, and Hooker even takes off his shades, a king among his subjects. The concert ends with haunted saxophone, doubled with flute, an eerie sound indeed, and we're into 'She Moved Through The Fair'. Credits roll over Van, eyes closed, singing in the aftermath of passion. The two guitarists patrol the stage, like sentries. Van repeats "be long" over and over, then goes into a wordless moan, with saxophone wails and even Georgie Fame yowling. Storming drums, and then silence. Shouts and howls from the audience, then fade to silence.

One mystery remains: what did the woman credited with "hair and make-up" actually do? In a review at the time, Geoff Wall describes the video, which should still be available, as "ecstasy for the ears", and it is a tonic for the eyes as well. A surprise and a delight.

On 1 December 1989, Morrison guested with Georgie Fame on NBC TV's *Late Night With David Letterman*. Van's ten minute appearance was his first on American TV since 1978. He was also about to hit British TV screens, with a hit single. Two years before, Van had begun dedicating 'Gloria' on stage to Cliff Richard, whose 'Mistletoe And Wine' became 1988's biggest selling British single. Their duet on on 'Whenever God Shines His Light' was released as a Christmas single, and they made a promotional appearance on Terry Wogan's BBC1 chat show. Van looked small and tubby next to the ageless Cliff, who gyrated around the stage like a schoolboy. When their single hit the Top Twenty, they were invited onto *Top Of The Pops*, Van's first appearance on the show since 'Here Comes The Night'. He looked smarter and more animated, as they sang live to a backing tape.

Van also appeared on *Slim Galliard's Civilisation*, a series on BBC2. They jammed together on 'Arabian Boogie' and Van read extracts from Jack Kerouac's *On The Road*, his bible, to Galliard's piano accompaniment. Comedian Lenny Henry, who began his professional life as a mimic on the execrable *Black And White Minstrel Show*, told an anecdote about Morrison on the *Late Late Show*. Henry had been performing at a New York club in late 1989. During his routine, Van shouted out, "Do Norman Wisdom." Wisdom was a rubber jointed comedian, popular in the early sixties for his pathos and his appearance of stupidity. An English Jerry Lee Lewis, he had appeared with Van's friends The Pretty Things in the film *Goose For The Gander*: they appear in a psychedelic dungeon, wild haired and manic, with Twink predominant. Finally, Lenny obliged, to the bemusement of his American audience. Morrison collapsed in hysterics, and remained silent for the rest of the set.

What follows is close to a modern miracle, down by Avalon, an extraordinary story first researched by John Collis. Andy Lock was a local teacher, who got married in the parish church of St Stogumber. He wrote to Van's record company to ask permission to use his music during the ceremony. His bride entered to the strains of 'Connswater'. During the reception there was a phone call to say that Van himself would be shortly arriving. His then girlfriend, Cathy McGhee, had persuaded him to attend. They thought it was a hoax, but sure enough Van arrived, "very shy and nervous", and stayed for an hour or so, turning up a few weeks later for a Saturday night chat. Emboldened, Lock asked him to play a concert in the church, for expenses, and he said yes.

On 17 January 1990, Van and his band – now featuring Haji Ahkba on trumpet – played one of their most memorable concerts. Tickets, priced at ten pounds and limited to three hundred only, sold out by word of mouth. During the interval, Van "walked out with the audience and walked back with them. That's how good a mood he was in. Afterwards he said it was the best concert he'd ever done. You could literally hear a pin drop in there." This was despite an altercation outside with a local television crew. Proceeds went towards the restoration of a medieval wall painting. As Lock told John Collis, "I was looking through the visitor's book in the church, and I found an entry for New Year's Day 1990 'Van Morrison, Belfast and London, looking forward to the gig', so he must have come down on his own, looked around the church, didn't talk to anybody, went away again." He saw Van as being on a "higher plane than basic Christianity. I don't even think he's particularly religious. At Stogumber he was trying to get a sense of meditation, of relaxation, over the audience."

This is confirmed by the bootleg CD, *The Church Of Our Lady St Mary*, which, despite the strictures of the fanatically accurate Clinton Heylin in his book *The Great White Wonders*, is extremely listenable. Any sonic distortion comes from the setting, which adds a haunting distance to the music. As Van comments, it's the first time he has ever played in a church. In the opening song, 'Did Ye Get Healed?', the brass section wavers in the air, like slightly rackety celestial trumpets. Though not credited on the bootleg, it is surely Georgie Fame on (electric) organ and backing choir.

Van had attained his heart's desire, to take his holy music into a consecrated setting, and chose his material carefully. Next up is 'Whenever God Shines His Light', suitably humble, and 'It's All In The Game', with churchy organ. 'Orangefield' is pedestrian, but 'When Will I Ever Learn' picks up the ancient vibes, with an organ solo like a peal of bells. Van testifies to the Lord in 'Full Force Gale', and digs deep in his soul on 'Vanlose Stairway', again with wonderful organ playing, straight out of Percy Sledge. This is English gospel music, no problem. The slower the song the better in this context, and Van has never sounded so like a preacher, terrifying his flock. It's a surprise that he didn't climb into the altar for some of these songs.

'Give Me My Rapture' has the joy of Pentecost, while 'So Quiet In Here' takes on added meaning, "so peaceful", and Van whispers reverentially to an acoustic backing. The audience silently concurs with the line "this must be paradise". Mose Allison's tongue-in-cheek 'Thank God For Self Love' – a musical ancestor to Randy Newman – is a daring choice in this context, and if that isn't Georgie Fame on second vocal, he must have beamed in on the Celtic Ray. 'Into The Mystic' finds its true home here, even if the drums do boom around the pews. Van is warming to his task. 'She Gives Me Religion' would convert a heathen, and a long slow organ intro to 'Northern Muse' – this is not generally a concert where musicians wish to stretch out on solos – gives way to Van at his most tender, hymning "a salt of the earth type lady from County Down", in Gavin Martin's words. In this context, a female deity in a male bastion. The organ swings into a snatch of 'Auld Lang Syne', and Van into 'When Heart Is Open". The pacifist anthem 'Down By The Riverside' concludes this musical service, and the audience happily claps along, doubtless infuriating any traditionalists in the congregation. "Ain't gonna study war no more", military or ecclesiastical. Van should end up in stained glass, on this showing.

Later that month, he treated Milan to an acoustic 'Wonderful Remark' and a re-run of 'Buona Sera'. In February, he filmed a session with the twenty piece Danish Radio Big Band, described by Bobby Surf in the *NME* as "a short night of good tempered confusion". Van idly fingered his Telecaster during an amateurish sax solo, and only 'Got To Get Back' chimed in with his sense of discomfort. Georgie Fame came on, like a knight riding to the rescue, and contributed to a spine tingling 'Vanlose Stairway', but the musical format of this "marriage of convenience" was too strict to allow Morrison really to soar. Not quite as constricted as the San Remo Festival, where he sang 'Have I Told You Lately' to a pre-recorded backing track.

In March, he performed on Channel 4's *Rock Steady Special*, with Mose Allison, shot in the ornate setting of St George Church Hall, Bristol. Enjoyable in itself, this is also a pointer to the future, with Alec Dankworth on bass and Alan Skidmore on tenor sax. There is a spiffing version of 'Baby Please Don't Go'. On St Patrick's Day, Van was filmed at the Joker Club, Belfast, and interviewed by Gerry Anderson, a man who was later to infuriate Radio Four listeners with his blarney. Radio Two's Paul Jones chatted to Van about their shared past on air, later that month. Two fine blues harp players, they swap favourite tracks, and anecdotes. Van tells how John Lee Hooker stole 'TB Sheets' from him, and Jones comments that "most of us fans steal our songs from people like Hooker", so it evens things up a little.

Van talks of jamming with Little Walter in a London pub, and gaining harmonica tips over Chinese takeaways. Jones admits to envying Van at the time: "You came from that little bit nearer to America than we did."

Van explains his vocal style, original from the start, as due to his "phrasing like a horn. I think a lot of it came from that, from saxophone." He greatly admires Ray Charles, for all kinds of reasons, but partly for his saxophone playing: "In fact I think he should play more." Jones comments that Van is very into phrasing: "It's the backbone of your own style." Morrison grunts assent. "Uh huh, yeah."

In April, *The Best Of Van Morrison*, a Polydor anthology agreed to but not selected by Van – "I don't have time to do that sort of thing" – hit Number Four in the UK. It only grazed the US Top Fifty, but eventually earned Morrison his second platinum disc, having logged three years in the charts. Only one song from *Astral Weeks*, but three tracks from Them, 'Brown Eyed Girl' and a good career summary. The CD adds 'Wonderful Remark', featuring Nicky Hopkins and Jim Keltner. Written around the time of *Moondance*, it first surfaced on Robbie Robertson's soundtrack for that bitter movie *The King Of Comedy*.

Polydor released a promo interview disc, with Sean O'Hagan, which *Select* magazine padded out into a feature article. Van opens up a little more than usual, and there are some good anecdotes. Dick Rowe came up to a young Van in the vocal booth at Decca, and said, "Can you really shout, make it aggressive." The Jimmy Page conundrum is cleared up at last. He played a "sort of bass guitar part, but it was on lead guitar" on 'Baby Please Don't Go', and contributed rhythm guitar to 'Here Comes The Night'. Van had first seen him playing Spanish acoustic guitar with Marianne Faithfull. Van writes few songs that are directly autobiographical: "Some part of your experience you'll write into your songs, and the rest you'll make up." 'Brown Eyed Girl', for example, began with a calypso rhythm, and then Van took a couple of names from Lewis Carroll's *Sylvie And Bruno*, an extremely obscure sequel to *Alice In Wonderland*, sort of. "A song comes from all sorts of things. It can come from this teacup. A lot of them come from various fragments of ideas, and then it's a case of pulling the fragments together."

Astral Weeks was crucial here, a transitional stage, in which Van's writing deepened, "more getting in touch with the unconscious, I reckon". Then things became a treadmill: "I used to just finish a record and then I'd just walk into the studio and start cutting tracks again." Reviewing the fruits of this labour in *NME*, Stuart Maconie reckons here is where Kevin Rowland and Tanita Tikaram got their ideas. The latter could hardly fail to, being managed by Van's ex-business director, and using musicians from his past bands. Maconie describes the young Van as exuding lechery "like an over heated ferret", and the mature one writing songs that "even got an old agnostic like me whistling".

Holland's "Pink Pop" Festival, held on 4 June, adds saxophonist Candy Dulfer to the band. She had first met Van at a jazz festival there – "he was very friendly and unassuming" – and also introduced her to Guinness. "He said it was good for my health." A month later, Van played the Montreux Jazz Festival, opening with Georgie Fame's party piece, 'Yeh Yeh'. A good, standard set, which majors on 'Sweet Thing', slowed down and emotional, a duet with Fame which leads into Steve Gregory's flute solo – dancing from note to note, just like Jimmy Hastings' work with Caravan (the band, not Van's song). The song then merges into 'Astral Weeks', a particular delight. A synthesiser whirs, and Fame comes in with a lightness of touch close to, again, Caravan's shy genius Dave Sinclair. Van sounds so much older now, and the return of 'Sweet Thing' like a lament for lost dreams. He cracks up on the following song, 'Star Of The County Down', so all is well. "No prima donna," he repeats endlessly during 'When Heart Is Open', and he's absolutely right.

Later in July, Van appeared in the waking nightmare of Roger Waters' bleak epic *The Wall: Live In Berlin*. Van's one time manager Harvey Goldsmith had brought together all manner of celebrities, alongside a symphony orchestra, a marching band and a choir, and the ego of Waters himself, no mean thing alone. Bryan Adams, Marianne Faithfull, Sinead O'Connor, Thomas Dolby and Joni Mitchell joined Irish flautist James Galway and actors Albert Finney and Tim Curry. But this was to prove no *Rocky Horror Show*. A horror show, perhaps…The setting was Potzdamer Platz, the former no man's land between East and West, and site of the *Fuhrerbunker*. The recently demolished Berlin Wall was rebuilt in polystyrene, and then again demolished, with help from the German army. God knows what Morrison thought of all this, sandwiched between giant inflatables and a firework display, but – as *NME* reported – it was left to him to carry the event. "His unmistakable voice cuts over the technological babble on 'Comfortably Numb' and the encore of 'The Tide Is Turning'."

Having appeared at that year's Fleadh in Finsbury Park, Morrison completed the double by taking part in Feile Ninety, bringing it all back home to Ireland. Stephen Wynne wrote about a lifetime highlight, 'Moondance' beneath a Tipperary moon. 'Orangefield' was sparser and quicker than on the album, with brass "as tight as the maestro's waistband". 'Summertime In England' is driven by boogy woogy piano, with new words, as ever, in the middle, "spending a shitload of money on a Saturday afternoon and coming back with a smile on your face". 'Caravan' includes an injunction to meditate three times a day, and an observation as to how boring snooker is on the TV. Alex Higgins, come back. In August, David Wild interviewed Van for *Rolling Stone*.

"What do people want – blood? What I do is work. It's not magic mirrors. It's real hard work." He remembers a time before TV, when "the only stars I knew were in the sky". Or on the radio. MTV is "crap". So why did he later make video promos, to show on it?

On 27 August, he performed before a sell out crowd of 13,589 at the Grandstand, Toronto, and went on to play large venues in the United States. Concert reports flowed back to the *Van Morrison Newsletter*, like match reports for a major sports team. The Spectrum, Philadelphia is a large hockey arena, half full tonight, but Van shrinks it to the size of his living room. He grins, and yodels on 'Cleaning Windows', ending with a joyous incantation of Little Richard song titles. He even sings Dylan's 'Just Like A Woman'. In Lake Compounce Park, Van is greeted with 'Happy Birthday', which the musicians follow with a salsa flavoured version of the same song.

In early October, *NME* announced the release of a new album and a UK tour to back it up. *Enlightenment* reached Number Five in the UK – part of his musical resurgence – and Sixty-Five in the States. Its cover is an abstract photograph, which seems to be the petals of a flower (although it could be liquid in motion) emerging from some kind of abyss, which on closer inspection turns out to be two open hands. They proffer this gift directly to the viewer.

The recording dates spanned smart London studios and the Real World, in Box. 'So Quiet In Here' was taped at the Kirk, Rode, Somerset which could either be a church, or a studio, or both. Fiachra Trench again provides arrangements, with Irish maestro Michael O'Suilleabhain on piano. No Neil Drinkwater this time, replaced by Alex Gifford, though Georgie Fame, Bernie Holland and the usual rhythm suspects are in place. The brass section is like a roll call of the new wave of British jazz from the late sixties: Frank Ricotti, Henry Lowther, Malcolm Griffiths.

Enlightenment at first sight seems to be just what its title suggests, a happy and spiritually fulfilled Morrison, celebrating his luck. It is a very appealing record, the best kind of public entertainment. The opening song, 'Real Real Gone', deals with Cupid's arrow striking home, but it is also a cry of need – "don't you know I need your help". Love is mediated through the poets of soul music, Sam Cooke et al. Van certainly sounds happy enough, fronting up a fat brass section.

'Enlightenment' is actually the opposite of what it sounds: it is full of doubt, not affirmation. "I'm meditating and still I'm suffering." He seems to be saying that everything is a state of mind, you can either choose to live in heaven or hell. A choir hum what is almost 'A Whiter Shade Of Pale' and Van spits out the words, bitter sounding, still unsure of himself. He blows some nice harmonica, though. 'So Quiet In Here' is a direct continuation of 'Into The Mystic', even opening with foghorns blowing and much the same riff, but there is a rapture here unmatched even in that song. Van's vocal is that of a man totally sure of himself. Love and companionship are the answer, as humans float towards the "other shore" of their demise. The great change in his more recent songs is that rather than looking for the light, he is now more intent on entering the silence. "You can hear, it's so quiet."

'Avalon Of The Heart' contains two of Van's most obvious quotes from himself, the title of his previous album and "the viaducts of my dreams" from 'Astral Weeks'. That song is specific as a laser beam. This is soft focus stuff, "the enchanted vale", a fuzzy version of Tennyson's 'Lady Of Shalott', with the aptly named Ambrosian singers cooing in the background. Mood music. A full orchestra crashes in and Van fights them for precedence, but the result is all sound and fury, signifying very little.

'See Me Through' starts with violins as they should be, mysterious and slightly menacing, with a piercing harmonica adding tension. Van sings as if to himself, "sad and forlorn". He quotes from that terrifying nineteenth century hymn 'The Old Rugged Cross' but we don't hear much about Jesus on this album. The possible saviour is a woman. The guitar break is clunky, like early Them, and Van mentions "baby please don't go". For a slicker artist, this would be post-modernism, like

Bowie updating Major Tom in 'Ashes To Ashes', but for Van it's something far more powerful, digging back into himself. He is suddenly into free association, in love with a childhood sweetheart who once "used to love my tie", and is tied to him now in an all accomplishing desire. "Set my soul on fire."

Soul returns in 'Youth Of A Thousand Summers', another picture in words of Blake's *Bright Day* painting, a golden youth who is also an angel, maybe Christ – "ancient of days" – but despite the great organ break and Van sounding like it all means something, it doesn't really, and nears self parody. 'In The Days Before Rock 'N' Roll', on the other hand, is unique enough to be bizarre, a collaboration with Irish poet Paul Durcan, who fractures his spoken monologue here as if he is reading it word by word from idiot boards, or totally banjaxed with drink.

Here is a new take on Van's obsession with old time radio, and one can picture the brown bakelite set on a lounge table, a Telefunken model with foreign stations inscribed on its dial. He adds a further twist with memories of betting on Lester Piggott, and letting goldfish won at a fairground go free. Into a mountain stream, of course. Elvis is the first prophet of a new sound, and Durcan reads out a list of blues and rock 'n' roll singers, like old testament prophets. It is not coincidence that Ray Charles is called the "high priest" of this new musical order. The strings sound like something from *Children's Favourites With Uncle Mac*, and much remains unexplained. Who is Justin, for example? Durcan, a "real" poet, adds a surrealistic tinge here, and his own work is full of such sly wit.

He recalled to Harry Browne of the *Irish Times* "four very intense days of work". Four people were cloistered in the studio: himself, Van singing and playing piano, bassist Steve Pearce and drummer Dave Early. "We'd been locked up together for four days, everyone giving to everyone else. Everyone was playing to the other." One thinks of the penultimate episode of *The Prisoner*, where McGoohan and Leo McKern were locked into one take, a psychological battle to the death, after the filming of which McKern took to his trailer, and called for a therapist. Rather like Number Six in his willed loneliness, Van was, according to Durcan, "lost in the music – totally and utterly unreachable, except through music". Van's final "come aboard" is spoken as if to a child, and the track ends with some studio chat. "There's certainly some beautiful things in there," Durcan says.

In 'Start All Over Again', we're back with sunsets and a whole year survived. A soul tinge here, and Van tries to resurrect an old love affair. "There's horizons yet to see." A feminist song, in that he leaves it to his woman to decide, giving her the time and "your own mind". 'She's A Baby' is perhaps not so politically correct – how would Van like to be addressed thus, especially at his age – but this song contains real heartache. He is off his food with love, and in a lovely pun doesn't have "egg on my face", literally. Even at his local cafe. His yearning vocal here has been compared to Smokey Robinson, and the lyrics too have the lead Miracle's sense of word play, masking a deep sadness. After all, no less than Dylan once called Smokey one of America's greatest poets. Morrison seems to be singing about more than just love here: the picture of lows and highs sounds like clinical depression.

'Memories' is similarly bitter sweet. These reminiscences are "precious" and yet also unrecoverable: the song predates the death of Van's father George in Belfast that winter, but acts as a beautiful memorial. An accordion wafts, and a guitar imitates a harp, or the other way round. Simple words, but the meaning resides in Van's vocal, developing subtly through a mood spectrum. A song at the end of love, closing an album which began with young love. Perhaps the underlying meaning comes, half hidden, in Van's moaned outro to 'See Me Through'. "Please yourself", the lyric sheet reads, but to me it sounds more like "pray for yourself". No method, no guru, no teacher.

Ann Scanlon found Van's music "more full of life, love and joy than ever", though her review in *Sounds* was subbed "The daze after rock 'n' roll". The *NME*'s Stephen Dalton thought it was his most accessible album since *Wavelength*. Enough for almost any other singer, but "we know and *he* knows that he can do better". In *Melody Maker*, Carol Clerk compared Morrison's heightened work rate with his peers, Dylan – a croaky prophet on *Oh Mercy* – and Neil Young, also undergoing some kind of renaissance, having rejoined Crazy Horse for *Ragged Glory*. For all that, *Enlightenment* was "far from illuminating".

Van certainly lit up the venues he played that autumn. The emphasis was very much on the last two albums, but with sly glances back to his past career, and influences. In Doncaster, 'Cleaning

Windows' incorporated part of "The Story Of Them", and alluded to George Formby, simply by changing the way he pronounced the second word of the title. Formby's songs are stiff with voyeurism, for those intent on finding some kind of psycho-sexual key to Morrison's muse. Van incanted "Can you feel the silence" as one by one his musicians left the stage.

Soul veteran Andy Fairweather-Low, formerly of Cardiff's Amen Corner, played support. A *Sounds* review of a Wolverhampton gig compared the evening with a similar concert twelve months before. Then, Van had prowled the stage "like a caged beast", and discovered a storming set. Now he seems back to the cantankerous worst, too often "hurried and perfunctory", when not being downright weird. He has lights trained on the crowd, and instructs them to "meditate to the karma". Nevertheless, Morrison might look like "a gnarled and bloated road digger", but his voice remains rich as plum pudding.

By and large, though, the tour was notable for the good spirits on stage, which beamed across into the audience. At Wembley, Lonnie Donegan turned up during the encores. Van dresses like a dustman, with an old knitted shirt and trainers, and fronts a series of "tacky backdrops", but is still breathtaking. At Liverpool, he wears a baseball hat, so the rest of the band also adapt headwear, with Georgie Fame in a stetson. He hides behind his organ at one point, like a naughty schoolboy. In Preston, for an encore Van goes way back to cover 'It's All Over Now Baby Blue'. In Exeter, audience members talk of a Phil Spector-like wall of sound. At Bristol, he tells the audience that even he doesn't know who Justin is, and changes the name Lester Piggott to Scobie Breasley in the same song. A good time guaranteed for all.

That fine interrogator of popular culture, Melvyn Bragg, introduced *Clear Cool Crystal Streams*, an hour's programme on Van's work. Across the Atlantic, Van appeared live in a Los Angeles studio, along with jazz maestros Herbie Hancock, Chick Corea, Freddie Hubbard and Larry Carlton, and the ever faithful Georgie Fame. Talking to *Into The Music*, Fame reveals that the contact with Van came through his son, a recording engineer, who let him know that Morrison wanted a word. "I was doing a week at Ronnie Scott's doing a jazz thing and Van came down a couple of nights and we started talking and we decided to do it, to tour together." Making music as a form of seduction. He explains how his organ part on 'The Days Before Rock 'N' Roll' was morse code, three dots and three dashes. "You always used to get that morse code interference on the radio when you'd be trying to tune it in, you'd pick up the ships. It was all completely out of time, but it fitted." The same trick as on the theme music to *Inspector Morse*. Van and Georgie played in tandem on BBC2's *Late Show* in November, playing three songs from the new album, live in the studio.

One of the best insights into Van comes with Gavin Martin's article "Teenage Van Club" in the *NME*. It is Christmas in Belfast and Van has arrived for a series of concerts in his home town, amid bomb scares and all night drinking sessions. He has shed his latest manager Chris O'Donnell, and is organising his own affairs now. The young Belfast band Energy Orchard are playing support, and their recently departed vocalist Brian Kennedy will play a large part in his own later career. Van has talked about setting up a studio in Belfast, and took a brief interest in the Dylanesque singer-songwriter Andy White. He also plans a musical workshop for the unemployed in Bangor. This has not led to any reciprocity with Energy Orchard, a band whose record sales were never to match their potential. "He gave me this cold fish handshake and there was an embarrassed silence." Also on the bill, at Van's insistence is comedian John McBlane, who caricatures local politicians.

Van himself plays for well over two hours, a frenetic concert which ends with 'See Me Through'. "It resolves into a close to the bone mantra. Morrison builds the incantation up gradually, then just when he's reaching an exasperated and tense peak, the music breaks open leaving just a sparkling piano melody to cast a spell, like sunlight coming through rain clouds." Without missing a beat, Van whispers a release from the torment, "wake up, it's a new day". Before the show, he has surrounded himself with monitor speakers, "five round his feet, and two behind him" so that in concert he can "latch on to a lick of guitar, a blast of horn or a piano refrain and draw it out, use it to take him and the audience to a new realm". During Energy Orchard's own soundcheck, he is seen, a rotund figure in a Santa hat, dancing at the side of the stage.

There is a further odd little insight. One of the band accidentally strays into the private area backstage where Van prepares himself for his performance, a no go area as carefully patrolled as any in Ulster. He is met with Van's flailing arms, and two security guards hustle him away.

Meanwhile, in the film *Sleeping With The Enemy*, Julia Roberts adopts 'Brown Eyed Girl' and the BBC play *Out Of The Blue* – in which Catherine Zeta Jones appeared nude – used Van's recent music as a soundtrack. Van became musically involved with Welsh heart-throb Tom Jones, writing four songs for his album *Carrying A Torch* and playing guitar, as well as choosing the band. "It was the most hectic session I've worked on in a long time," the engineer commented. Jones added that "it was the best feeling I've had on a recording session since the early days". Both singers had played the Top Rank circuit in the early sixties, both recorded for Decca, and both were deeply influenced by soul. A promo video shows both men miming in the studio, looking like (male) beauty and the beast, until Van grins like a pixie, and sparks of affection fly between him and Tom. Magic.

Van also recorded a video promo with The Chieftains, unseen in public. Of greater importance was Channel 4's *Coney Island Of The Mind*, a half hour special. Filmed mainly in County Wicklow, at the home of Garech De Brun, of Claddagh records, Van talks with some leading Irish poets of the printed page: Seamus Deane, Michael Longley and John Montague, author of 'The Rough Field', an epic poem which goes right to the heart of the Ulster Troubles through history. They compare the way that their native landscape has defined their art. For Van, this was at first an "unconscious" move, and he only later was to discover his own tradition. "You find out that what you are writing about you already are." Being in the countryside gives him a certain amount of mental space, "in which to receive". Montague talks about the redemptive powers of art, quoting Patrick Kavanagh's 'Shancoduff' and his own 'The Hill Of Silence'. Seamus Deane, an academic who has compiled a whole encyclopedia of Irish writing, likens it to a way of "singing the universe". Landscape can bring unity to a broken land, and unity, which through art can "repossess something imaginatively might be a way out of belonging to something fractured, discontinuous. One can cross all the borders of time and place and find some imaginative locale in which one can say, here we are in possession again. An Ireland which represents a healing unity."

As if to prove the point, Van reads part of 'I'm Tired Joey Boy', which started life as a poem in the tradition of the Antrim school. Longley, whose own work has deepened with age, finds that he shares a Belfast childhood, and swap the names of youthful haunts, like incantations. "He knows his place," Van comments, with no pun intended. He also praises Longley for the soothing quality of his reading voice. Gerald Dawe talks to Van on a hill above Belfast, and joking about a former woodwork teacher at Orangefield, who rubbed wood potions into his head to make it shine, Van laughs so much that he falls back out of the camera's path of vision. Symbolic, or what. Here, Van gives something back to the muse, and generously acknowledges his peers.

Following hard on the heels of this wonderful programme was BBC2's *One Irish Rover*, a career overview. It opens with Van and Bob Dylan singing a duet above Athens, sitting high on the Hill of the Muses. The *Independent* described "the Irish singer flanked by Bob Dylan and the Acropolis: all three of them legendary, all looking their age, and all a waste of time talking to with a microphone in your hand. Dylan appeared never to have heard the songs, and his customary diffidence seemed to increase with his visible realisation that he was not the main attraction." What I see is two great poets and singers, gazing shyly at each other, in mutual respect. Poetic Champions Compose. There are further collaborations, all carefully tied to their place. John Lee Hooker sits on a jetty in Mississippi. The Chieftains join Van in Belfast, the Danish Big Band in Copenhagen, and Georgie Fame at Ronnie Scott's. The real star, and influence, though is the landscape of Ulster, shot at its most timeless and peaceful, as if the Troubles had never existed. By ignoring them, this brace of television shows – which indicates what the medium can do when imagination and thought are given due precedence – disprove Van's theory that television is inherently crass. As inspiring as those sounds filtering through Van's radio.

It seems a world away from the sweaty, frantic world of the *Soul Labyrinth* bootleg, recorded – whatever the packaging says – in the Hague in March 1991. The record opens with some soul and R&B covers, including Bo Diddley's 'Who Do You Love', then Van storms into his own musical poems, ending with a charged version of 'Moondance'. The *Pagan Streams* double bootleg CD is even better, also recorded on a night in Holland, with Van's band coming on like The Grateful Dead. Operating almost by telepathy, the weave between songs, building them up in new combinations, putting Van's own work into a framework of rock and soul and jazz, just as the *Coney Island* documentary located him in a native tradition of words.

The sound is somehow intensely alive in the way that good bootlegs always are as compared to their official counterparts: just compare the Stones' *Liver Than You'll Ever Be* with *Get Your Ya Ya's Out*, the difference between brown and white bread. The key performance is an eighteen minute version of 'Summertime In England', with Van shouting with and at his band, quoting from 'I Believe' of all things, then 'Astral Weeks', as the music slows down and speeds up, as if by instinct. "If you listen, you can hear the brass band blowing from across the field", and his wind section obliges.

Van gets lost, "where are we now", and then goes into a rap about the Swedenberg Church in Notting Hill Gate. "I felt the silence, and his mystic grace." Further along, Van lists his favourite gospel singers, then a snatch of 'Jack And Jill Go Up The Hill'. He reiterates "going across the sheuoch", which starts another detour into a list of the routes across the Irish sea, and then a chorus of "what time is it, it's hustle time". Ridiculous in print, but even with just the sound to enthrall, music that lifts you up into the stratosphere. Van name checks the band, which now includes Georgie Fame on "organs, vocals, everything else", Candy Dulfer, Nicky Scott, Steve Gregory, Ronnie Johnson, and Haji Ahkba – it sounds like Ozzy Osbourne at first, a truly bizarre thought. 'Caravan' has an odd section, where Van urges meditation, and a long "om" comes from one of the instruments. "Bring it up a little bit," Van instructs, and his musical helpers oblige.

In early June, The Van Morrison Band opened three concerts for Bob Dylan, in Rome, Bologna and Milan, at the last of which Dylan joined him on stage. He stood to Van's right, a couple of paces behind, improvising a harmonica break to 'Whenever God Shines His Light'. He stayed for 'Enlightenment', sitting on the drum podium.

In August, Van and his red hot band took part in Feile Ninety-One in Tipperary with The Pogues and Nanci Griffith. The *NME* reported that "it's impossible not to be uplifted by Van's tidal wave of joy. He leaves the stage screaming 'SOUL! SOUL! SOUL!' and I'm left making a mental note that trance music isn't the exclusive preserve of Acid House." Van also made a triumphal return to Edinburgh for a Celtic Rock showcase, with The Chieftains, Shetland violin wizard Aly Bain and Runrig, part of a new Scots pride. It was the first rock concert to be officially part of the Edinburgh Festival, and *The Scotsman* reported in suitably apocalyptic terms. Morrison "moaned ecstatically, eyes closed and oblivious to the floodlit ramparts of the castle. His performance was restless, searching for some kind of peace of mind. His songs are hymns to his continued survival, his voice devotional and spiritual. For the audience his finale, 'Moondance', was a prayer answered."

Van had also taken to performing in a pub, the King's Head in Newport: "Van just rung up and asked if he could play on Sunday. He's bringing a brand new band." He also gave an interview to the *Now Dig This* rock 'n' roll magazine. The first single he bought was Bill Haley's 'Razzle Dazzle'. Van drops the names of rockers like Sil Austin and Jimmy Giuffre. "If ever there's anyone who was a footnote or an asterisk it was him, he's my main influence on saxophone." He looks back with nostalgia to the Maritime Hotel. "I think I'm at my best in a club situation, but it's difficult for me now. It's not so readily available."

Van's new guitarist Ronnie Johnson was also interviewed, for *Guitar Magazine* and reveals worryingly muso tastes, such as The Mahavishnu Orchestra's *Inner Mounting Flame*: "I thought it was wild, and quite elite too." As to punk, it "just pissed me off to high heaven". Given that Morrison could make Johnny Rotten look like an altar boy, perhaps he did not know quite what he was getting into here.

The most extraordinary track on the *Pagan Streams* bootleg reflected this manic side of Van, the Keith Moon inside. He introduces 'Send In The Clowns' almost straight – "I learned this from Shirley Bassey" – then changes "clowns" to "clones". A falsetto backing singer (male) takes over, thus robbing Van of his customary joke, about entering "in his usual flares", but he gets the vocal back, and hammers the line "bring 'em all in", seemingly forever. We are back with Van even before Them, putting on a turn. The whole band crack up, and the song veers into Bonzo Dog Band parody. Later, in the middle of 'Gloria', he goes into an odd narrative about seeing art students from Queens – the audience laugh – and becoming a beatnik, and moving to Wardour Street and seeing Georgie Fame at the Flamingo, and about how Johnny Kidd And The Pirates were the first British Beat group. He then leads an elocution lesson on the original song. Van as raconteur, and manic wit.

It is a side of Van missing from his next album, a double, *Hymns To The Silence*, issued in September 1991. It hit its peak at Number Five in the UK. On the front cover, Van sits on a park bench, pensive and unsmiling, framed by leaves. On the back is the urban wasteland of Hyndford Street, Van's birthplace. The street sign is vandalised, and there is graffiti on an adjacent wall, with cars parked up against the pavement and no one in sight. The inner sleeve has another shot of Hyndford Street, under grey skies and with a "for sale" sign further down. Opposite is 'On Hyndford Street', a poem of the utmost beauty, which Morrison recites inside in a hushed voice over a synthesiser drone, as if in deep hypnosis. In these mean back streets, the young Van could feel "wondrous and lit up inside".

Missing in action, again, was WB Yeats' poem 'Before The World Was Made'. His work was now out of copyright, and Van could issue his version at long last, unimpeded by the law. Unfortunately, the sound engineer "had a fever the day we mixed it, and I'm damned if I can remember where I put it". *Hymns To The Silence* is a vast, sprawling affair, easier to respect than to love, but at its heart are two of Morrison's greatest songs, the title track and 'Take Me Back'. Here is Van's clearest evocation of childhood revelations among an "avenue of trees", when he could enter eternity just like Yeats' poem. The irony of that poem is that the dreamer seems vain and unresponsive in the everyday world. Similarly, Van's insistence here on the pains of being a professional musician seem to me like an actor showing us his make-up box. The spell is broken.

Stephen McGlynn sensibly divides the album into three movements. First up are work songs, "someone – part Van, part everyman – trying to produce the goods in an increasingly complex world". Next comes a detailed foray into Van's Belfast roots, and the album ends with some tender love songs. Some found the album patchy and preachy: for Andy Gill, "this is getting too like Sunday School for fun". The reasons are more to do with the music than the lyrics, somehow lacking passion and drive. The way that he can subvert the Christian hymn, 'Just A Closer Walk With Thee', into an evocation of childhood Sunday afternoons is probably heretical, but then in the following song he turns things back again, so that "Sonny Boy, blow your harp" takes us back to heaven. *NME*'s Gavin Martin got things about right. Van might look like the Terminator on the sleeve, and parts of the album are humdrum, but it can also transport the listener "into a world beyond music".

When he played Dublin's Point Depot in November, Morrison had virtually a brand new band, young and eager, and largely unknown. The focal points were Tina Lyle on vibes and Kate St John on sax. Ronnie Johnson's guitar led a rhythm section of John Miller's keyboards, Nicky Scott's bass and Paul Robinson's drums. Van played sax and guitar, and sang, as Tom Noone reported, "like a man possessed". The two hour set moved at a breakneck pace; 'Into The Mystic' featured a saxophone duel between Morrison and Kate St John, and in 'Sweet Thing' his harmonica set against vibes, guitar and keyboards, before he comes back in to sing "when the meditation is right, when the motivation is right". Songs from the new album jostled out the likes of 'Summertime In England' and 'Full Force Gale' from the set list.

It was as if Van was wiping the slate clean. When Buddy Guy – hero of Eric Clapton's Albert Hall blues nights – unveiled a plaque at Van's birthplace on Boxing Day, through the good offices of the Belfast Blues Appreciation Society, he responded by describing this as an "invasion of privacy". It wasn't as if he still lived there. *Private Eye* ran a cartoon captioned "Van Morrison was miserable here". A decade earlier, the same magazine had carried a scurrilous story about him supposedly climbing onto a bus and giving away armfuls of his new album. It is part of the kind of media picture which Van attacks on *Hymns To The Silence*. John Collis quotes Cliff Richard's comment that Van is "filled with self loathing". Not on the evidence of his music.

In December 1991, Morrison appeared on a spoken word cassette issued by a small independent label, Moles Of Bath. Recorded in 1989 and mixed in 1990, it dramatises the story of Cuchulain, one of the greatest hero figures in Irish myth. The version here was written by Bob Stewart, a folk musician who has also published widely in the occult field. Both Yeats and Lady Gregory had used the Cuchulain myth as a creative springboard, and Van gives a wonderfully spiky reading, full of anger and violence, which must have proved cathartic. He sounds like Ian Paisley on Sunday morning, or Father Jack. Though the project is humour free, Stuart Baillie in the *NME* thought that Van's method acting bellowings made him "come across as a bit of an eejit, actually".The cassette is a reminder that "stormy words, hyperbole and stadium sized emotion" were already part of Irish culture, in the days before rock 'n' roll. Back to the Celtic Ray.

The Cuchulain saga mythologises a great battle between Ulster and Connaught for the sacred soil of Ireland, though this retelling fails to open up any contemporary parallels. It all sounds a little forced. Out of costume and early in 1992, Van opened up to Victoria Clarke of the *Irish Post*. At school, "there wasn't one book by any Irish writer", so he had to discover Joyce and Yeats for himself. "I was making unconscious connections, you see…from the air or the ground." In the sixties, unlike now, it was uncool to be Irish, "then it was very American". His first local heroes were the McPeake family who'd "already played Carnegie Hall before I ever came out of Belfast".

He seems bitter, and Clarke describes him as suffering an increasingly obvious backlash in the music press. "I'm not a celebrity. I don't want to be a celebrity." His music deals with a "struggle for survival. It's got nothing to do with making me happy. It's just a job. Does anybody's job make them happy? I don't know."

He kept on doing it, though, and in April interrupted a vacation in the US to play selected gigs. Reports filtered back home. In Berkeley he was so eager that he had to be restrained from going on stage half an hour before showtime, and once there hardly paused between songs, like a chain smoker, though he "spoke not a word the entire night and didn't smile or acknowledge the audience". Joyce Millman of the *San Francisco Examiner* describes him leaving the stage chanting "I'm still on a chain gang" over and over into a hand held microphone, a guitar slung over his back. "If this is a life sentence, Morrison isn't pushing too hard for parole." During 'In The Garden' the audience is on its feet, but "as Van whispers low there is not a sound in the house. It is hypnotic, mystical, beyond physical reality."

He also made a sentimental return to Marin County's Great American Music Hall, tiny despite its name, where he had so often performed in the early seventies. One night, his only spoken words were an attack on a journalist who had misread one of his lyrics, which said he launched into a blistering 'I'm Not Feeling It Anymore', "lit red hot with disgust".

Back in Britain, he played the Scottish Fleadh on a wind swept night at Glasgow Green, and included a rock 'n' roll medley, and Fleadh Ninety-Three at Finsbury Park: a video shows him in shades and suede waistcoat, singing 'I'll Take Care Of You' and playing harmonica one handed. Pee Wee Ellis is back in the band, alongside Kate St John on brass, and although the organ player is hidden behind a pillar – the amateur cameraman tries to focus on him, and takes the viewer for a hilarious roller coaster ride as a result – it certainly *isn't* Georgie Fame. Also in June, Van played Glastonbury, opening with 'On Hyndford Street', which magically breaks into 'Baby Please Don't Go'. There is a fierce guitar solo on 'Ordinary Life', and Van sounds Dylanesque. In fact, the songs from *Hymns To The Silence* take on new life on stage, with Van adding a sense of passion sometimes missing in the studio.

A book could, and will, be written about Van's career in the nineties alone. In the time and space left to me, I am forced to pick out some plums for the reader to chew on, and refer anyone wanting more background information to *Wavelength*, the excellent Van fanzine, put together with fanaticism and love, as these things so often are. Since he met Fame, really, Van has been engaged in his own version of Dylan's "Neverending tour", as a whole slew of concerts, press reports and bootlegs attest. As he told *Q* in early 1997, in the old days his career was more centred around specific recordings. "But the live thing is more where I'm at now. Maybe I've always been there and not known it."

This partially explains why his most recent records have seemed to be a kind of pot pourri of earlier songs and themes, as if they had been mixed in a blender, and reshaped. It also explains the critical backlash, for critics who want endless newness, and fail to understand that this is how great artists tend to work. The days of blazing creativity are behind him. Van's job now is to rub at the Philosopher's Stone, just as Neil Young has been doing over much the same period, and to re-order and revisit his past, engaging in side projects – with Mose Allison or a jazz big band – while always looking to move forward in his own career. Not that this is a humourless enterprise. In July, Bob Geldof arrived at a Radio One roadshow in Bangor, spectacularly dishevelled, even for him, and blamed it on a late night drinking binge with Van the previous evening. They had given an impromptu jam in a North Down bar. "Van Morrison just walked casually across the dance floor, and started to perform. Then there was this guy who did impressions of us. He did Van, then he did me. Then he did Paisley. It was hilarious."

That same month, Van gave a fine impression of an academic, turning up in Coleraine in grey suit, gold tasselled cap and red silk gown to receive an honorary Doctorate of Letters. The citation spoke of a "refusal to admit commercial compromise which has its roots – like his music – in the Ulster soil from which he springs". Arise Dr Morrison, who later expressed an interest in taking up a post as a philosophy lecturer at Belfast University.

At Point Depot, Dublin in August, Van was in a flashy designer shirt and shades, but his most important fashion accessory was Georgie Fame, back on keyboards and vocals, and as bandleader. The band looked amazingly tight as Georgie watched their every move and Teena Lyle and Kate St John play a "duelling banjos" type duel on recorder and oboe during 'Haunts Of Ancient Peace'. Richie Buckley joins on sax for the second encore, to show that there are no hard feelings. In Belfast, Fame opened with a jazz instrumental by Lester Young, and Van announced "you have gathered by now we don't talk, we just play music", culminating with 'Gloria'; "this one got me arrested".

Fame outlined his week for the *Guardian*. On Saturday, he leaves house guest Alan Price to set off for Dublin, and his first gig with Van for a year. "I'm completely immersed in the music and am pleased to report very few mistakes considering my long absence." Sunday is Belfast: "the concert is dynamic, pure soul." Monday: "to Edinburgh by hook or by crook." Drummer Alan Morris has been sacked, or resigned, and Geoff Dunn takes over in extremis. The band switch airports, and planes. "It's Morrison's birthday to boot, and he produces yet another memorable performance." Tuesday. All change. Georgie grabs some rest, phones his oldest son who is producing a Swedish heavy rock band, has a siesta, "shower, shave, put on my best King Kong suit, smile" and reunites with Carol Kydd's rhythm section, with whom he is playing tonight. They set off for the Queen's Hall, "swinging and avoiding the recession".

That October, Van himself played a one off concert in Aberdeen, with Maceo Parker and the JB horns, including Pee Wee Ellis. Parker called his band Two Per Cent Jazz And Ninety-Eight Per Cent Funk though Van's own set began quietly, even playing a snatch from 'Tupelo Honey'. Candy Dulfer was back as main soloist, and Van even quoted from *Oklahoma* on 'A Town From Paradise'. The horns joined him on stage, then just as things were hotting up a bomb scare cleared the hall. Van, in leather jacket and flying helmet, joined the audience outside. Most went home, but about two hundred stayed to see Van restart his set with an astonishing slowed down reading of 'Vanlose Stairway' with much emphasis on the part about "the pillow where my baby used to lay". The JB horns returned for 'Gloria', Van singing "just about midnight" exactly on time. Van played on, though, into the early hours, with a tribute to Dylan and 'Have I Told You Lately'.

Van reunited with The JB horns over four nights at the Masonic Auditorium in San Francisco that December, adding a definitive version of 'Sweet Thing' one night to a set list that included 'Moondance', 'In The Garden' and 'Cleaning Windows'. He spent Christmas in California, recording at the Record Plant, Sausilito, where he was re-united with pianist John Allair. Planning a blues album, he was joined by Robert Cray's backing musicians, and John Lee Hooker, with whom he cut an update of 'Gloria'. He also played a tribute gig dedicated to Joel Selvin – a rock journalist, of all things – alongside Chris Isaak and Todd Rundgren, and joined Maria Muldaur on stage at a Harvey Mandel club gig. More formally, he and his band played the Mystic Theatre at Petaluma, a small theatre with standing room only – always the best for live music – for no more than six hundred people. He would be back there a year later, to record yet another definitive live album, showing just how it should be done.

But Van failed to turn up at the eighth annual Rock And Roll Hall Of Fame induction dinner held on 12 January 1993 at the Century Plaza Hotel, LA, which doesn't seem too big a deal, except that everyone was there to celebrate him. The award was accepted for him by his friend Robbie Robertson. Van was busy recording his new album back in England, and playing gigs. At that legendary rock playground Gloucester Leisure Centre, on 22 January, he confessed during 'See Me Through' to "having money in the bank, a car in the driveway, a colour TV and a mobile phone" but no spiritual ease! Pee Wee Ellis was back on board, and the trumpet playing was so good on 'Lonely Avenue' that

Van stood back in amazement, picked up a box of paper tissues, and threw them at the player concerned. The next night, at Bristol's Colston Hall – one of the venerable theatres scorched by Dylan in 1966 – Van played for more than three hours, taking songs from throughout his whole career, including a new arrangement of 'Brown Eyed Girl'. By Dublin in February, he had dropped virtually everything from *Hymns To The Silence* and was reunited with Richie Buckley and Haji Ahkba. As a dig at the Hall Of Fame debacle, Van mentioned that Johnny Kidd received no awards, but he certainly knew how to play rock 'n' roll. For 'Gloria', Van was joined on stage by an extraordinary line-up, almost a roll call of rock: Bob Dylan, Bono, Elvis Costello, Steve Winwood, Chrissie Hynde, Nanci Griffith and Kris Kristofferson. Judge a man by his friends. It was as if Van was wilfully shaking the kaleidoscope of his past, into endless new patterns. The previous night, at a gig held at Tullynally Castle – home of battling peer Lord Longford – to raise funds against the planning felling of an ancient forest, Van had played an acoustic set with Arty McGlynn. Longford had met Van at a formal dinner at Leixlip Castle, the home of a Guinness heiress. These were the circles that Van now moved in, literally in the presence of the Lord.

In March, Van closed another ancestral pile, the Town and Country Club in London, where he had been asked to perform the final rites. Gavin Martin found it "a rapacious feast of wonderment, endlessly tying up his preoccupations and song stories". Here was the most autobiographical man in showbusiness. Exactly, and I hope that the present study has indicated just that, despite the frequent protests from the man himself, like a songbird trying to lead predators away from his hidden nest! Here was "at least the tenth great band he has had in as many years", with Brian Kennedy on second vocals. Van ends by roaring "you give me nothing" into the night, seemingly endlessly. The weirdest thing in the show is one of his thrown away asides, "sometimes I feel like Phil Spector, sometimes I feel like Howard Hughes".

Meanwhile, record buyers made a second journey through Van's past with *The Best Of Van Morrison Vol 2*, which just stopped outside the UK Top Thirty. There were two Them songs, 'It's All Over Now Baby Blue' and (oddly) 'Don't Look Back', but nothing from the Bang sessions, or *Astral Weeks*. The selection concentrated on Van's career in the eighties. Peter Paphides described it as "an essential purchase only for the very lazy or the very nervous", and the period in question as "one long existential crisis". For Patrick Humphries, it was "a pointless exercise", with nothing previously unreleased on show. Real fans wanted a three CD box set of lost work, right now.

Van returned to San Francisco that spring, for more gigs. One highlight was a supercharged 'Domino', and on 'Vanlose Stairway' he quoted Ray Charles about crying so hard that you gave the blues to your neighbour. 'In The Garden' brought the audience to the point of tears. Van kept the houselights up for the weekend's gigs at the Masonic Hall, so that he could see the audience, while – in his shades – they could not really see him. Neat.

Van was back in London for the Fleadh, playing a set drawn from his upcoming album, although his descents into near silence – so devastating indoors, were drowned out by diesel generators, burger vans and fans chatting. He joined Bob Dylan – given Irish citizenship for the night – on 'One Irish Rover'. Flash bulbs popped madly as rock's grumpy brothers seemed to be singing in different keys, even more hit and miss – as Andy Gill dryly observed – than Bob's duet with Johnny Cash. A closer harmony was in evidence back in Dublin, where Van was beginning to be seen walking out with his new girlfriend, Michelle Rocca.

Morrison and Hooker's double act on 'Gloria' had just missed the Top Thirty as a taster for Van's new album, again a vinyl double, *Too Long In Exile*. Georgie Fame was back, as was Candy Duffer. The album is a relaxed, tuneful affair, which looks back to Van's R&B heritage, and finds space for songs by Sonny Boy Williamson, Doc Pomus – whose death was commemorated in Lou Reed's bleak album *Magic And Loss* – Ray Charles, James Moody, South Carolina soulman Brook Benton… and WB Yeats. Released in June, its cover is a symphony in blue, with a lonely figure standing upright but dwarfed by an urban landscape, straight out of *Eraserhead*. Curiously dated, the walkways and tower blocks look like a giant Meccano set, and Van – if it is he – gazes towards a "To Let" sign above the "Shamrock Bar and Grill". This is the world of The Pogues' 'Fairytale Of New York', of the Irish diaspora.

Inside, Van in hat and coat stands on an urban street by dirty parked cars. A sign on the side of a blank building has a quote from Ron

Hubbard, "Buy It, Read It, Use It", so perhaps Scientology is still part of Van's world view. More likely, it's all part of the tease. Jonn Savannah takes on the role of second vocalist, which Brian Kennedy is soon to make his own on record, as well as on stage. The musicians largely comprise Van's touring band. The album came straight in at its Number Four peak in the UK, and also hit the US Top Thirty, just.

The album's mood is generally "up", though the opening title track contains some sombre lyrics – "you can never go home again". Even here, Van – living in self imposed exile near Bath – sings in a sprightly manner, and the backing music is joyful and upbeat. Exile doesn't sound too bad here. Yeats, Beckett and Oscar Wilde all died abroad, and Van brings in two modern heroes, with all too human flaws, George Best and Alex Higgins. 'Bigtime Operators' follows, Van's finest song about being ripped off by the music business, words which tie in with the vaguely Mafioso atmosphere of the cover, and of his subsequent dress code. He plays some great lead guitar on a Chicago style blues, genuinely bitter here, his voice choked with distaste, but also with a dark humour. "They looked like politicians, but they acted like thugs" is a little naive, though. I thought the two were interchangeable. 'Lonely Avenue' is a lovely, steady rolling blues, with Van blowing hard on harmonica and saxophone, and Georgie Fame getting every note just right.

Later on the album, Van sings one of his finest slices of sexual healing, 'Till We Get The Healing Done', where the unnamed saviour must stay all night, and not just for prayer. Even 'Gloria' has added words now, in which she becomes a "natural born soul sender". 'In The Forest' ties in nicely with Van's new ecological awareness: these ancient roads are themselves now in peril. He is moving towards the big band jazz of later albums, instant nostalgia, and 'Moody's Mood For Love' is half straight, half affectionate parody here.

Those intent on finding traces of paedophilia in Van's work could example 'Good Morning Little Schoolgirl' here, except that it is merely part of the blues tradition he is mining, and the object of desire certainly post-pubescent. Innocence is the real quest, as in Yeats' Poem 'Before The World Was Made'. The real exile here is from the safety of a childhood spent in Mother Ireland. The quote "time and space" is an example of Van's tracing back his own words into the Irish tradition, as the phrase also surfaces on *Astral Weeks*. The very opposite of plagiarism, finding correspondences later.

Critics responded to the overall joyousness contained here. Peter Paphides reckoned that "never has one man's regression therapy sounded *this* exhilarating". Gavin Martin told those who had found the previous album too mellow that here Van has rediscovered his "earthy, elemental fire". He is still "the foremost blues auteur". Even that newspaper for old and young fogeys everywhere, the *Daily Telegraph* found a "vivid reappraisal of his blues and jazz roots". David Hepworth in *Q* supports my theory – before I had even thought it up – that whereas Van once toured to publicise new albums (sometimes with extreme reluctance), he now released albums "to justify and underwrite his touring". Hepworth is less than convinced by the current offering, with 'In The Forest' – beautiful, actually – "summoning up the risible vision of our hero tripping across a babbling brook and making sheep noises in the direction of his lady love in the Arthurian nightie". Well, okay, Van does make a baaing sound, but it's meant to convey contentment, not a desire for wool. It was Roy Harper, not Van, who contracted a serious illness through kissing a pedigree sheep, or at least that was what his publicist told the world.

Van played Glastonbury again, a gig saved by his "trembling, gravelly voice" and "his new grittier, bluesier material", or so a young whippersnapper reckons in the *NME*. He also played a no frills, daytime set at Slane Castle, watched side-stage by Neil Young. A new interview with Victoria Clarke for Exile Productions – total control – was passed on to *Q*, like a fifth gospel. Van does not care what people think of him, he says, and on being told that at least he is not dead or a junkie, he talks – "I'm revealing too much here" – about having lived on the edge: "I've got close to the flame, and been burned a few times."

He makes a rare reference to the greatest new songwriter of the eighties, and his near namesake, also of Irish parentage. "My songs are not open in the same way that Morrissey is open. He doesn't really talk that much either." They also share an aversion to pop videos (and to Johnny Rogan, who has written biographies of them both, Morrissey going so far as to hope he dies in a car crash). Van namechecks The Pogues, "they didn't have any preoccupations about Irish music. They were the spearhead of the attack on all that bullshit that's been going on for so long. They cracked it because they were London Irish." Van in turn had felt as if he were the musical equivalent of a sex object. The British need stars, because of a "huge emptiness inside". So what would make him happiest in the world? Shirley Bassey. Why? "She's a great singer. She's Celtic, which is close to my heart. End of interview."

In August, Van topped the bill at a WOMAD concert held at the Cornwall Coliseum, St Austell. Brian Kennedy again joined proceedings for 'Crazy Love', and according to one reviewer he stole the show. Van played 'Celtic Ray', "because we're in a Celtic country", and the evening ended with Kennedy taking the John Lee Hooker part in 'Gloria', fed the words line by line by Van, standing a few steps behind him, who stopped in the second verse, with a twinkle in his eye, "leaving a hapless Kennedy dumbfounded at the mike". The next evening, Van played near home ground at the Wiltshire Festival, held at Lydiard Park, singing to the setting sun.

His private life was becoming public. Since Janet Planet and possibly Jackie DeShannon, Van had chosen girlfriends who fought shy of fame, and by and large they were left alone by the media. When Van began going out with a former Miss Ireland, the difference in perceived seriousness, beauty and age had the hacks foaming in their beer. We are not talking here just about the tabloids. Van was broadsheet material, nowadays.

Typical was a *Sunday Independent* article that September. "The lust free liaison between Van Morrison and his escort Michelle Rocca continues to boggle the mind of close friends and confidants alike. A post-Curragh do at Rathsallagh was last week's setting for the passionless peccadilloes. A lively and intriguing affair by all accounts. Keith Richards and Paul Brady made it lively, while the intrigue was added by the Platonic Pairing. Luckily the couple did not frighten the horses and Van at his first race backed three winners." We're talking about a horse race, by the way. "It's the best fun I've had since 1968," declared Van. With wonderful ineptitude, the paper connects this date to the Woodstock Festival (actually 1969) in the Summer of Love (1967). One needs to take their other "facts" with a pinch of salt. Van was buying a house for "my fiancee". The journalist notices that Michelle slaps Morrison sharply on the wrist when he dares to look at another pretty woman.

The autumn publication of Steve Turner's fully illustrated biography *Too Late To Stop Now*, including photos of Ms Rocca, provoked Van to a state of outrage. "Lies, exaggerations and innuendo," he thundered to the *Belfast Telegraph*. "The fact that I may be successful at what I do does not mean that I accept that anyone can come along and publish details of my private life for other people to read purely for their own enjoyment." He sent the author a list of thirty-six alleged inaccuracies, claiming to *Today* "that book is about someone else". Turner replied that two thirds of these were simply opinions he didn't agree with, and that Morrison's management team had made enquiries about buying up the entire print run. "Of course it was out of the question. It would have been an admission of guilt." Turner then rather twists the knife. "The truth was far worse than I actually wrote. There were some very wild stories that I left out." If you are reading this current tome in a bookshop, grab it and buy it while you can, before a representative of the artist impounds it. Like Salman Rushdie, I might have to spend the rest of my life in hiding, from a Celtic fatwah. Stuart Baillie in the *NME* thought that Turner failed to explain Van's music, and why his work was "so strange, so dreamy and sexually bizarre".

Van did seem troubled at this time. John Collis quotes a gig at the King's Hotel, Newport when Morrison supposedly lambasted his audience for their ignorance. Here is a censored version: read Collis's book for the whole, unbelievable rant. "'Brown Eyed Girl' was lunchtime. This is dinnertime. It's an affliction of somebody's imagination. Which means in other words the Yanks, you know. I'm talking about soul. I'm a soul singer, I sing soul songs. Blues. Fuck the pop charts. I don't want to play 'Brown Eyed Girl'. Because I don't have to. If I had to I'd commit suicide."

Paul Lewis, writing for *Bluesline*, puts the record straight. This small Welsh hotel was a place where Van has developed his music over the previous few years. "Being present at one of these gigs is like watching rock history being made." Occasionally, Van has just wanted to play the blues. On this occasion, he is "blooding" Brian Kennedy, first sending him out to play a solo set in front of Van's band, and then using him as second vocalist, running through songs from Van's past. "Van's current group is really a child of the King's, since it has been in this room that they have really developed into the unbeatable unit they are today."

Van stopped the show one night to say that they were the best band he ever had. The show during which he delivered his diatribe was "unruly, tormented and nearly three hours long". With the next night's offering, sharper, more contained, and including a reference to Turner as a "parasite scumbag", these were "the wildest Van Morrison shows I've ever seen, the very epitome of great rock 'n' roll theatre".

Only a genius could then switch to a gig at Derry's Festival of Literature, interviewed on stage by Nik Cohn, author of *Saturday Night Fever*. Van then played a relaxed set with a stripped down band, combining his songs with poems by Patrick Kavanagh and Yeats. "Like good reciting poets, he seemed to find the applause hard to handle," thwarting a lone clapper by running his tunes into medleys. A method which was to bear amazing fruit on *A Night In San Francisco*. Van had also run into one of the greatest of living poets, Allen Ginsberg, having seen him on an RTE chat show. Van simply phoned up the TV station to invite him out for a late night drink. Fame might be an imposition, but it does enable you to meet the heroes of your youth, on equal terms.

As in the previous year, Morrison played some gigs in the weeks leading up to Christmas in San Francisco. At the Mystic Theatre, he was accompanied by Jim Hunter from Howling Wilf and The VJs, with whom Van had toured in 1991, then Jimmy Witherspoon and Junior Wells joined the on stage fun. Brian Kennedy was now very much part of the band, taking the strain off Van, and even singing some of his songs, though it was really Georgie Fame who held it all together. Some low key gigs at the Berkeley Theatre earlier that week had seen people phone up afterwards, complaining that there was not enough Van. A charge increasingly to be laid against his live shows, though showing a complete misunderstanding of what he was now trying to do. At the Nob Hill Masonic Auditorium, though, Van "played his sax as if he was testifying to his maker". Another review described him as looking like "an undercover police officer", and roaming the stage, staring at his musicians during their extensive solos.

Here, again, we see the influence of the wonderfully eccentric Mike Westbrook. During a recent concert tour of his big band, Westbrook spent great swathes of his time pacing around like a short sighted professor, closely studying each soloist in turn, with head bowed and a mysterious smile on his face. Every now and then he would pace back to his grand piano, to play with massive skill and sensitivity. It's called being in control. Joel Selvin noted how Van took one of his most incidental pieces, 'See Me Through', and "blew the number into epic proportions, calling signals to the band and taking the piece into breathtaking turns and twists, rummaging through its nooks and crannies for corners he could open to the light. The kind of remarkable examination that only a gifted artist would attempt – and Morrison made it shine."

Drawn from these concerts, though remixed back in England, *One Night In San Francisco*, is Morrison's third in-concert album, and some contend the best. While it lacks the drop dead majesty of *It's Too Late To Stop Now*, the range both musically and in emotions is immense. The albums seem to go on forever, encompassing an ocean of music. Van mixes in his own songs – often radically updated – with all kinds of influences and brief quotes. The only thing really missing, both from the record and from the concerts it draws on, is Van's own early work, although Kennedy sings a sweeter than sweet 'Tupelo Honey', and there is a spirited 'Moondance'.

I'm certainly not going to attempt a track by track analysis, or we'd be here all night! Just listen to 'In The Garden', which starts like a Bruce Springsteen epic, with Hollywood piano, then into a brief snatch of 'Danny Boy', and a supercharged version of the song. Urgency has replaced awe, and woodwind eddies around Van's scene setting. As he enters the song, it begins to slow, and his voice to grow deeper. Some percussive piano, Van enters the mystic for another verse, then some asthmatic harmonica, and he is by now almost beyond speech, "taking his own wife, to be ill again". He's listening to Sam Cooke on the radio "and the night is filled with space", and Shana comes in with the chorus of "You Send Me". Van responds with the "no guru" mantra, and the band pick up urgency again, strict drumming and a typhoon of voices. Ahkba toasts Van Morrison, who has just left the stage, and the audience demand him back as the band play a peal of bells.

The band have settled to a series of double acts: a rhythm nucleus of bassist Nicky Scott and drummer Geoff Dunn, guitarists Ronnie Johnson and James Hunter, Teena Lyle on vibes and recorder and Kate St John on sax and oboe. Keyboards were also twinned between Georgie Fame and Jonn Savannah. Haji Ahkba returned on flugelhorn

315

and as master of ceremonies, while Candy Dulfer guested on alto sax. No strings, but otherwise a flexible unit, that could handle just about anything. Van was helped out on vocals by Brian Kennedy and his daughter Shana, self assured and already taller than her father. A band and street choir to storm heaven.

A Night In San Francisco was released in May. A night shot of the "Port Of San Francisco" is picked out in lights, while picked out in red type over the track listings are the words "ballads", "blues", "soul", "funk" and "jazz". For such a mighty offering, the album charted in the US at a lowly Number One Hundred And Twenty-Five. The *NME*'s Stuart Baillie thinks the "crud" here could have been edited down, especially the first twenty minutes of supper club routines, although in my own eyes this would destroy the organic growth of the whole, like a perfect night's entertainment. The final twenty minutes are majestic, "his band are blamming away, stellar, involved and the quiet bits are almost holy – not dim and autumnal, like before. John Lee Hooker steps out for 'Gloria', and everybody goes rightly, outrageously mad."

Peter Paphides finds a "portly middle-aged path" being followed here. After twenty-five years, his jelly roll must have "moulded beyond all recognition". In *Q*, Dave Henderson hears a "tour-de-force in the style of a larger than life R&B revue". Barry Egan felt that "the band play so close they're almost in each other's minds", and fellow Irish reviewer Oliver Sweeney discerns "a series of musical nods to his Gods". For *Elle*, it is ideal music for "late nights on the beach". As Van says on stage, in homage to Ronnie Scott, "you've made a happy man very old".

On Valentine's Day, Morrison received a Brit award, presented by former hostage John McCarthy, who had been helped through his ordeal by Van's songs. There were video tributes by the likes of Sting, for whom Van was "a musical mentor and a spiritual mentor", and Elvis Costello, who looked forward to listening to Van's work "when I'm an old man". Bono made noises, pulled faces, then declared, "Van – you're The Man." Peter Gabriel said that he had shown rock artists "what it means not to compromise", while Bob Dylan scatted "God bless you Van – blah, blah, blah, blah, blah, blah, blah, blah". Most heartfelt was John Lee Hooker's "I love you, man". Morrison gave a brief, emotionless series of thank yous, then duetted with his daughter on 'Have I Told You Lately', before being joined by Brian Kennedy and

Shane MacGowan on a shambolic 'Gloria'. MacGowan also confirmed to the *Hot Press* that his own next album would be a set of covers of Them songs, produced by Van: "We were just having a drink, and the idea came up." Which is what it has stayed as, bar room talk.

In February, Van undertook an eight date UK tour, with Georgie Fame guesting on most gigs, and Michelle Rocca reciting Irish poetry during 'Gloria', to the incredulity of Van's audience. The *My Name Is Raincheck* double bootleg – from the Manchester Apollo – captures a lower key version of the SF gigs, deeply boring at times, or maybe it's just the tape quality. The highlight is the fine new song of its title, but reviews were mixed. Ian Gittins saw the Oxford gig, and noted "a gruesome vision of poodle perms, slacks and gormless grins". And that was just the band. Van looks like Arthur Lowe (from *Dad's Army*) in Raybans, and "his grumpy fervour gets to me". Despite the meat and potatoes R&B, he bellows through 'My Funny Valentine' like a man calling in the cows.

During 'In The Garden', Van "becomes a victim of his muse", responding to his band's every nervous tic and twitch. "I've only ever seen Al Green testify more sweetly." But he should shoot his band. *Mojo* goes to Exeter Great Hall, to find Van trading jokes with James Hunter, and coasting from song to song. During 'Gloria', he has a mock argument with Kennedy about what street she lives on, though again Black feels the band need to lighten up. In Dublin, Van insists to Bob Geldof that aliens exist, and joins him for a breakfast of porridge and red wine. As Geldof says, after Van has gone, "The spirit of Flann O'Brien is alive and well." When fans compared notes, this self styled "Rhythm & Blues & Soul Revue" – shades of Rolling Thunder – played much the same set much the same way every night.

Strange, then, that Van should felt compelled to write to Dublin's *Sunday Independent*, to declare "I'm Not A Rock Star". "What I am is a singer and songwriter who does blues, jazz, soul etc. I made my reputation as a blues singer in Belfast on the R&B scene, which I started in that city. On the one hand I am quite flattered by the sudden attention of the rock star mythology, but on the other hand I do not need or want the attention, having spent most of my life living the role of an anti-hero and getting on with my job, so I tip my hat to the gods and goddesses of the media and say thanks, but no thanks." This was sent from Van Morrison, Chiswick, London W4, presumably a company address.

Although debatable whether Van was still a rock star, it became certain that actor Richard Gere never would be. In June, Van played at Grosvenor House, for Gere's Tibetan Aid charity, jamming with Sting on 'When The World Is Running Down', and with Gere himself on "blues guitar". *Hello*, not *Mojo*, reported *this* gig, and noted an audience including the likes of Koo Stark and Marie Helvin.

Van also found time to play at a Literature Festival in Galway, appearing alongside writers Roddy Doyle, Derek Walcott and Linton Kwezi Johnson. Now that would be a band. After gigs in Sweden, he flew his band out to the Montreux Jazz Festival, where a fine 'Ain't That Loving You Baby' is captured on video. Van was in the audience, alongside Robert Plant, at a Bobby Blue Bland gig at his home from home, the King's Hotel, Newport, and was eventually persuaded up on stage. In August, this non rock star was accompanied by The RTE Symphony Orchestra for the "Celebration Of USA 1994". He played five songs, opening with 'Carrickfergus' and ending with the definitive rock opus, 'Gloria'.

Following a lead set by Imaginary Records, it became fashionable for contemporary bands to elaborate – or simply copy – songs by such half living legends as Syd Barrett, Captain Beefheart and Peter Green. The original purpose was to celebrate the work of artists underrated by a mass audience, through the use of star names from the current rock universe, but the idea was soon taken up to apply to just about any artist of a certain level. Not to have one was the equivalent of not having been interviewed by *Q*, or not having your vinyl back catalogue released on CD.

Most of these tributes were unsolicited by the artist concerned – indeed this was part of the point of the thing – but Van Morrison himself commissioned 1994's *No Prima Donna*, a patchy affair. Although generally pleasant, with lots of Phil Coulter orchestrations, only Marianne Faithfull's croaky 'Madame George' and Elvis Costello's 'Full Force Gale', accompanied by the three strong Voice Squad, and like a wild religious chant, really stood out. Released in August 1994, it featured a black and white shot of Michelle Rocca, haloed in light, and laughing, showing a full mouth of gleaming teeth, eyes closed and heavily made up. She is dressed in white, with a double string of pearls around her neck, the image of *Hello* style sophistication.

Andy Gill carried out a full page autopsy of the album for *Q*, showing how the underlying joy of Van's music had been excised to leave "the stilted musical equivalent of an awards ceremony". Why not ask Dylan to cover 'Into The Mystic', or Dr John 'The Bright Side Of The Road'. Or Elton John, for that matter. Patrick Humphries felt that it was all too respectful. "It should have been recorded in a smoky bar off Grafton Street."

The idea for the album had come from sessions Van had with Brian Kennedy to re-record some of his old songs for a new Irish film called, appropriately, *Moondance*, and starring Ruadhri Connor and Marianne Faithfull. Perhaps it should have been left like that, as a movie soundtrack. Even Oscar nominated actor Liam Neeson could add nothing to Van's original 'Coney Island', though Neeson and his family are serious Morrison fanatics. At their wedding reception, the new Mrs Neeson sang a song by Van rather than make a speech.

The other star, Michelle Rocca, had met Van at a charity dinner. Already famous in her own right, she presented the Eurovision Song Contest from Dublin one year, and hosted her own TV show. Talking to the Irish *RTE Guide*, she said, "I've heard I'm a prima donna as well, but the people who say these things, who've dumped on me, have never met me." This sounds shockingly like a female Van, so at least the two could compare chips when they rubbed shoulders. She also sounds extremely fond of the man, and a little in awe. "I've tried to teach him a little bit. But how can you teach a guru?" He has encouraged her to read work by Shelley – Van's favourite – Tom Paulin and Yeats at his concerts.

Writing a profile of Van in the *Sunday Independent* Michelle reveals that he once briefly enrolled in Alcoholics Anonymous, but found that the last thing it was was anonymous. The private Van is "honest, mordant and funny. He loves watching Basil on *Fawlty Towers*, enjoys Spike Milligan, and has a child-like sense of humour." Example: what is small and brown, and comes out of the ground at one hundred miles an hour? The answer is a mole on a motorbike! He – Van, not the mole – enjoys performing, but "not all the time". He is not driven in a way that journalists endlessly write about. She says this, then adds that he "writes, records and tours almost constantly". It is something he is "compelled to do", from inside. Michelle compares him to a medieval troubadour, "singing his songs like some driven Puritan". Work is easier than play, but "I'd rather work than talk about the work, okay?".

When Michelle told him that Paul Durcan had called him the greatest Irish poet since Patrick Kavanagh, Van calmly agrees, and adds that Durcan himself is the only Irish poet "that is doing it today". Though a little unfair on the likes of Michael Longley, or indeed Heaney, this is a wonderful rejoinder to the kind of poet lauded by pretentious English critics. The nonsensical whimsy of Paul Muldoon, unutterable crap which is treated with the hugest admiration by the likes of the *Poetry Review* is indeed like a burp, next to Van's typhoon of words.

Michelle thinks that Van is "on a constant quest for spiritual release". He enjoys getting drunk every now and then with his old mate Bob Dylan. "We talk about music, songs. Just ordinary things." Rocca asks, in her professional capacity, about whether he can be romantic. He laughs. "I am sometimes. I can be." Best to leave them there.

In September, Van's song 'Wild Night' was a US Number Three hit for John Mellencamp. The man himself was touring Europe, playing "The Irish Heartbeat" Festival in Italy, with The Saw Doctors and The Cranberries. Van's set included a brief snatch of 'TB Sheets' in a medley. Five horn players and a full band enlivened his late September gig at Utrecht, including a snatch of Gene Vincent's 'Be Bop A Lula'.

Michelle Rocca accompanied him to a BMI awards ceremony at London's Dorchester Hotel on 23 October, where an ebullient Van sang 'Gloria' and 'Have I Told You Lately', for which he had just racked up one million US airplays. In early 1995, he appeared on *A River Of Sound*, singing 'My Lagan Love' to piano backing by an old friend, the pianist Michael O'Suilleabhain, as part of his TV series tracing "The Changing Course Of Irish Traditional Music". A CD drawn from the series, with contributions by Christy Moore, Brendan Power and Donal Lunny, contained sleeve notes which could also stand as a footnote to Van's career. "Our music is a water of life, whiskey of passion. It uplifts us, releases us, marks our joy and sadness. It is a music to live for and to die for. The great hero of early Ireland, Fionn MacCumhaill, is said to have expressed a preference above all music for 'the music of what happens'."

Also happening, in February, was the release of John Lee Hooker's *Chill Out*, including a stunning duet with Van on 'Serves Me Right To Suffer'. The two great, dark voices intersected over an organ backing by Booker T Jones, who himself had recently shared some cataclysmic concerts with Neil Young. As Van enters the song, Hooker laughs wickedly and they take a musical excursion that could easily have lasted for the whole album. Only Elvis Costello, perhaps, would be equally at home on Irish traditional folk and bayou blues.

Van was now engaged to Michelle, and the secret spilled over into his performance at the IRMA awards. The rendering of 'Have I Told You Lately' with Sinead O'Connor and Paul Brady was dedicated to Michelle. As Ireland's *Sunday Independent* reported, "Michelle had swapped her old diamond solitaire for Van's Celtic designed gold band. When Van and Michelle left their table to pose for photographs (when has Van ever before left a table to pose for anyone?) he was cheerful and relaxed. 'I'm very happy,' he told me. The couple have been friends and business partners for over three years. No wedding date is set, but a long engagement is not envisaged."

There is certainly a charge to the Cambridge Corn Exchange gig of 14 April 1995, faithfully captured on the *Lost In A Fugitive's Dream* double bootleg, and which rivals *A Night In San Francisco*. It opens with Brian Kennedy's highly romantic take on 'Sweet Thing', out of the Marty Balin Valentine stakes. New guitarist Alan Darby has a more pleasing style than his predecessor, and there is also a new brass section of Matt Holland and Leo Green, joining Georgie Fame and Teena Lyle, and the established rhythm section. The only cause for dissent, given the high ticket costs was, as Scotland's *Daily Record* put it, that "at eighteen pounds a head you expect Van the Man – not Van's other man".

A different band completely – with Fame the only common denominator – recorded *How Long Has This Been Going On* on 3 May at Ronnie Scott's for Christmas release. Later that month, Van appeared on *Letterman In London*, duetting with Sinead O'Connor on 'Have I Told You Lately', with backing from The Chieftains. The result sounds like early Incredible String Band, amateurish in the very finest sense. Van laughs, O'Connor sings like a bird. Michelle Rocca did not sound so sweet in an article in the *Sunday Independent*, saying that

"Letterman hasn't a word to throw at a dog. This was a muttering neurotic and no ways about it." Thank God Van never appeared on Channel 4's *The Word*, then. "My Well Known Singer Friend", as she terms Van, thought "there's more craic in a morgue. He looks like Bugs Bunny."

The couple were often to be seen at Bad Bob's, a Dublin country and western club, along with the likes of Shane McGowan and Jim Capaldi. In June, Van played the Fleadh, but Stephen Dalton of the *NME* was not impressed. Come back, David Letterman. "During his flaccid set, the stench is overbearing. Van Morrison is an overrated old donkey, crippling generation after generation of potentially interesting Irish musicians." How? "It is time to admit that there is no fun in hearing Morrison's *'Pebble Mill'* band dribble out yet another lukewarm trickle of watery bilge while that famous scat-soul voice mimics the sound of a goat farting into a paper bag." He doesn't actually say what Van played, but that's far less fun than a good mindless critical kicking.

Van, taking off time from destroying the Irish musical heritage, was meanwhile jamming with Junior Wells down in Newport. In May, he had joined Dylan on stage in Dublin, for a version of 'Real Real Gone', which probably describes Zimmerman's voice by that time. Morrison also found time to release a new album, *Days Like This*, in June.

The front cover is a monochrome shot of Van, dark clothes and shades, like one of the sinister "Men In Black", Government agents who turn up and hassle anyone who has had an alien encounter. A henchman of the cigarette smoking man in *The X Files*. With him is Michelle, elegantly dressed in a white ball gown, and both are being dragged along by a muzzled greyhound in a suburban alleyway, the kind from which a teenage gang could emerge at any moment. They'd probably run a mile from this strange couple. Nobody would buy the album on the strength of the cover alone: it is like a deconstruction of *Veedon Fleece* where the dogs have shrunk, Van has lost his mystique, and the landscape has been built over, and turned into slums.

Van sings and plays harmonica. No Georgie Fame, but adult returners include Ronnie Johnson, Arty McGlynn, Phil Coulter, Kate St John, and Pee Wee Ellis. Shana is credited for her first studio album with dad, and the song 'You Don't Know Me' appears to describe their long period apart. The album reached Number Five in the UK, and debuted at Thirty-Three in the States. An unkind critic (me) would take some lines from 'No Religion' – "and there's no mystery, and there's nothing hidden" – as symptomatic. That was my initial impression, and then I began listening carefully to 'Ancient Highway', a nine minute evocation of pagan streams, autumn days, and a town called paradise, Van's world in a nutshell, and all set to a Spanish tune. That old black magic, seeping through, an *Astral Weeks* strum, and you're enraptured all over again.

Michelle interviewed Van on a promo album issued by Polygram. The lyrics had come first, which was unusual for Van. 'Ancient Highway' is about escaping the rat race, and it relates to a painting of Ray Charles in the book *Rock Dreams*, driving a car through the desert. Van comes back, as ever, to the blues. "I was born with the blues. I mean a lot more races than black people have been oppressed in the world. So it's got nothing to do with black, white. Junior Wells says, 'I don't care if you're white, I don't want to fight.' I don't care if you're purple, green, lavender, turquoise. People are people, you know."

In *Q*, David Sinclair argues that the album is a "glorious return to form". Michelle has stirred something in the old curmudgeon, and "the result is a collection of songs in his classical Celtic soul vein, suffused with a spirit of romantic optimism". Morrison set out for a world tour, playing the United States and Montreux. Michelle again interviewed her fiancee, for *Q*, in August. He thinks he has "run out of steam" on his mystical approach to songwriting. He is not seen as a poet because "the academics wanted the monopoly on it. And you get these anthologies of poetry and they don't want any songs on them. They want to keep it safe, so they draw a line. There's no advantage to being a poet nowadays."

The next major development in Van's music was on show at his appearance at the Royal Festival Hall on 12 July. Billed as "Van Morrison and Georgie Fame", as part of the Capitol Radio Jazz Parade, it was the first public performance of the material which had been recorded at Ronnie Scott's in May. As Georgie told the audience, "This is the first public performance of a lot of new, and old, material that Van and myself have been toying with since our schooldays." He then introduces Alan Skidmore on tenor sax – who had played with Van and Mose Allison on the Channel 4 Bristol recording – Guy Barker on piano, Robin Aspland on piano, Alec Dankworth on bass and Ralph Salmins. The last two had played on Kate St John's album, so musical contacts had already been made.

Of the fourteen songs previewed that night – including 'Moondance' and 'Vanlose Stairway' – nine were retained for Van's appearance with The BBC Big Band at the Edinburgh International Festival in August, along with 'Haunts Of Ancient Peace', 'Days Like This' and a selection of jazz standards. The concert was broadcast on BBC2, though the constraints of working with a big band led, in the *Guardian's* view, to there being "no smoulder, no slip sliding into vocal improvisations and a definite air of containment". A few days earlier, Van had appeared at the Helsingor Jazz Festival with The Danish Big Band, with a more interesting set list, including 'Here Comes The Knight', 'Listen To The Lion' and 'Orangefield'.

The group previewed at the Festival Hall went out on tour that autumn. At the Cork Jazz Festival, in late October, they played as Van Morrison and The Jazz Set. At some of the gigs on the tour, some of the audience walked out, annoyed at the new direction, as Van began to stretch out in this new musical context. The double *Stepping On A Dream* bootleg captures a gig at Bournemouth, along with some of the Big Band tracks from Helsingor. Georgie Fame's organ is the glue that holds everything together, Van apologises for singing so many new songs, and for being so "baffling", though he has rarely sounded so lively and in such a good mood. He even makes his musicians play wrong notes on 'That's Life' and there are magnificent versions of 'In The Garden' and 'Have I Told You Lately', among much else. "Thank you for your company," he says at the end of the proceedings. The band crack like a whip, and Van's older songs breathe again in this new musical context. The string bass even brings back memories of *Astral Weeks*. The jazz tour was an acquired taste, but one worth acquiring, and superior musically to the album recorded at Ronnie Scott's. Had that been released earlier, the audience might have been more understanding of what was going on here, though there is nothing but applause on the bootleg recording. Michelle Rocca acts as Van's Yoko Ono. "Isn't he great, what do you think? He has no one to explain to." Except her, presumably.

On 30 November, Van played to sixty thousand people in Belfast city centre as a preview to Bill Clinton's appearance. Swingin' Bill, himself a keen saxophonist, had at first wanted to get in on the act, literally, until advised otherwise by security advisors. Van sang 'Days Like This', which had become the official anthem of the peace movement, and the theme music for a television advert licensed by the Northern Ireland Office. He was becoming respectable, in the eyes of people who had once seen him as an outlaw, and this acceptance was underlined by his being voted best songwriter at the annual *Q* awards.

He also appeared at an event in Swansea, as part of the UK Year Of Literature, talking again to Gerald Dawe about the literary influences behind his work. Influences which he only discovered after he had written the songs, so the chat petered out, and Van came back after the interval doing what he was best at, singing his songs.

A sadder event in Van's diary was his attendance at the memorial service to Rory Gallagher, who had died in June. Their friendship stretched back to showband days, and Rory was hugely missed, as a kind of national ambassador of the blues, right from the days of Taste. For me, and so many others, he will now be forever young and in blue denim, strutting the boards of the 1970 Isle of Wight Festival, testifying to the blues, just like Van. There is a lovely tribute to Rory on Christy Moore's *Graffiti Tongue*.

How Long Has This Been Going On? appeared shortly before Christmas 1995 on Polygram's Verve/Polygram Jazz imprint. Besides Van's current band, Pee Wee Ellis was back, both as arranger and saxophonist, Annie Ross sang on 'Blues Backstage', and the set list, largely not written by Van, included Edison and Hendricks' 'Centrepiece', also covered by Joni Mitchell. 'Moondance' is updated, and there is an unexpected recall for 'Heathrow Shuffle'.

The front cover is dominated by a photo of Van and Georgie Fame – both in hats usually seen on a racecourse. They gaze up, as if in awe, at an awning on which the name of Ronnie Scott's club appears. On the back cover and the picture CD is the mouth of a saxophone. Inside, the two pose with Ronnie Scott himself who, like so many genuinely funny men, also had a hidden well of loneliness, and was to take his own life a year later. Van's song 'Melancholia', from his previous album, would prove a fitting epic for this visionary jazzman, who built up virtually single handed one of the best jazz clubs in the world. Back in happier times, the three sit outside at an outdoor pavement cafe, also in London if the copy of *Time Out* is to be believed.

The sleeve note quotes Mose Allison as recorded by Ben Sidran, two participants on Van's next album, as it happens. Allison, two of whose songs appear here, praises Van's direct musical approach. "I mean, there's no showbiz, there's no outrageous acts or uniforms or costumes. And there are no antics on the stage. He strictly just goes out and plays, and he has a real good band."

John Fordham interviewed Van on a promo CD, and he talked about listening to his father's jazz collection as a child: "To me, it was like breathing." Perhaps this whole project is a secret tribute to the man who first infused his son with such a profound love of music. Morrison is currently listening to tenor players like John Coltrane, "the ballad stuff" and, as ever, Ray Charles. The album took an afternoon to record, four hours maybe five, just like the early days of Them. They chose Ronnie Scott's "for the vibe". Reviews of the album were mixed. Caspar Llewellyn Smith, writing for the *Telegraph* – what else – is the most dismissive: "Van huffs and puffs where he should whisper." On the other hand, the *Manchester Evening News* thought "he was crooning his heart out". American critics generally took the second option, "the feel of a relaxed jazz session". Stephen Phillips in Cleveland's *Plain Dealer* sums up my own view, that "Morrison's tone is occasionally off and his range isn't particularly wide. But Morrison's having a blast and his sense of swing is impeccable. Recommended."

In January 1996, Van appeared on BBC2's *Later*, with Georgie Fame and the jazz line-up, and looked like the invisible man, both mysterious and menacing, swathed in a uniform of black hat, dark glasses and black suit. A cross between a Mafia sidekick and one of The Blues Brothers. Behind the disguise, he was entering yet another phase in his career, one which had its genesis at Swansea. If a muffled and distorted sound system there had rendered the discussion with Dawe virtually inaudible – and little was revealed anyway, other than that 'Mystic Eyes' was inspired by a line from *Great Expectations* – the second half has set Van on a new course. Backed by Fame and four others from the jazz tour, the ninety minute performance was virtually acoustic, and included songs which Van rarely now performed, but counted among his most intense, and poetic work. Where better to give them rebirth but at a Festival of Literature.

An incredulous audience was treated to 'Ballerina', 'Slim Slo Slider' and 'Madame George', 'St Dominic's Preview' and 'On Hyndford Street'. He also previewed a brand new song called 'The Healing Game'. In early December, Van used a low key Irish tour to virtually rewrite his career; in Waterford he seemed to be making up the set list as he went along. 'Madame George' contained snatches of two earlier songs, 'Who Drove The Red Spots Car' and 'TB Sheets'. The absence of a lead guitarist – this was still basically the jazz band – forced Morrison to play lots of acoustic guitar, and thus revisit his folk roots, to devastating effect.

By the time he played a 17 December 1995 gig at Dublin's Point, later broadcast on RTE and thus captured in perfect sound on the *The Night Is Full Of Space* bootleg, Van was motoring through heaven. The concert includes superb readings of the new *Astral Weeks* trinity of 'Ballerina', 'Madame George' and 'Slim Slo Slider', and what sounds like a set list from a Morrison fan's dream. In fact, having bought and listened to this album, the first thing I did the next morning was check it was still on my CD pile, and not some kind of deranged vision, as a result of immersing myself too deeply in writing this book!

The music is staggering, in which new songs like 'Days Like This' and 'Melancholia' live and breathe in live performance, jostling for attention with the cream of the past, 'Listen To The Lion', 'Irish Heartbeat', 'In The Garden', 'Have I Told You Lately', and even 'Brown Eyed Girl', a song which Van had so recently vowed he would never again sing. His voice belies his age, or rather graces it, a deep and subtle musical instrument which wrings every ounce of meaning and poetry out of these songs, and soars above his band like a great bird of prey, circling the skies. A different, more aching take on 'Slim Slo Slider', can be seen on amateur footage of a January 1996 gig from the Royal Concert Hall, Glasgow. Van, in his new uniform looking and sounding like an ex-gangster making his final confession, attacks his guitar like a young punk, and moans the words as if coughing up blood. The camera follows him like the barrel of a gun.

At this concert, part of a month long "Celtic Connections" celebration, Van appeared with a stripped down band, reintroducing Ronnie Johnson on guitar, with Nicky Scott on bass and Geoff Dunn on drums. Leo Green played tenor sax and Matt Holland trumpet, with Georgie Fame acting as music master. John Williamson reported for the local paper, like a man who had seen heaven: "The band is stripped down to an eight piece, with Brian Kennedy used as a backing vocalist rather than as a much employed substitute for Morrison's own vocals. With his voice in such fine fettle, the band playing so well, and his sense of humour evident, even the festival organisers could not have hoped for such value for money from their last minute coup." Nor the audience.

It was as if the relaxed jazz tour, and then Van's appearance in Swansea, had triggered off some internal switch – the one labelled "genius" – and unnoticed by the general musical press, he was flying high again, making music as good as anything in his whole career. In Spring 1996, he set out for dates in Spain and then an American tour with a kind of superband. The Glasgow line-up was now augmented by Haji Ahkba, Robin Aspland on grand piano, Alec Dankworth on string bass, Ralph Salmins on drums, and Pee Wee Ellis, giving a kind of double group effect, with two drums, two basses and two keyboards as well as a large brass section.

The ensemble crashed the studios of David Letterman in New York, indeed Van virtually fell on stage, and played a joyous 'Moondance'. On the surviving video – which seems to burn out the cathode rays of the TV with its sheer joie de vivre – Morrison is animated and cheery, smiling and jokey with Fame, and burning with enthusiasm. Letterman, having forgiven the treatment meted out to him in London, quite obviously cannot believe his luck, and embraces Van like a beanpole wrapping itself around a small, plump and lively puppy. It is as if someone has taken the band which performed so respectably in the *Later* studio, and doubled their number, halved their age, and injected them with helium. Startling.

This zest for life carried over into four nights in late April at New York's "Supper Club", the same small and intimate venue where Bob Dylan had so recently revived his own faltering career, gaining in the process a new, sad majesty on stage, and breathing new life into some of his greatest songs. Van delivered a four hour set, which Dan Murray reported back to an incredulous *Wavelength*. Van had just climbed up onto Ralph Salmins' drum riser, as if he was back at the Whiskey: "Van has his back to the audience and his hand on his hip, and is doing bumps and grinds as he screams over and over into his hand held mike; 'Don't let me breakdown! Don't let me breakdown!' A roadie rushes out to help the singer back down to the stage. Flugelhorn player Haji Ahkba heads for the stand-up mike to give Van his send off. But the performer is not yet spent. Grabbing Ahkba in a virtual headlock, Van continues his exorcism, 'Don't let me breakdown'. At least fifty repetitions of the plea pummel the audience until finally he takes his leave."

Van has an eleven strong band, and on the first night played a "meandering, tension filled" fifty minute 'Man's World'. All four concerts opened with a suite of songs from the new album. 'Who Can I Turn To' was dedicated to Michelle, and the brass section pumped "like pistons, Van's vocal flights like a magic carpet ride". During 'Lonely Avenue', he talked about calling up Lou Reed – who had ECT as a youth – to tell him about the noises and voices the singer said he hears in his head. Just like a shaman. On the second night, Van refers to himself as "the artist formerly known as Van Morrison", and 'In The Afternoon' takes flight on stage, with the singer "talking all out of his mind". The third night, Van stomps around the stage as if it was 1970, and knocks the mike stand over, *on purpose*, during 'The Healing Game'. Next stop, The Who.

"My patience is wearing thin," Van says during 'Have I Told You Lately' and members of the audience agree. This is the only tired performance of the four nights, and probably due to his earlier appearance on *David Letterman* show. On night four, Michelle Rocca was by his side, and Richard Gere jams on 'Vanlose Highway', and made a short speech about the healing power of music. A girl shouts out "I love you" in Gaelic, and Van asks her "are you sure you're in the right place". After the show, old friend Robert De Niro whisks Van away for supper.

The band move on to New Orleans, then Memphis, where Van sings an elongated version of 'See Me Through', including The Hollies' line "he ain't heavy, he's my brother". Talking about De Niro? On a humid night and before a massive festival crowd, Van goes into a strange rap about "we don't need strings, we don't need bullshit, we don't need people...all we need is...". The sentence is never finished, but somehow I don't think the final word is "love". At New Orleans before Memphis, the highlight again was a virtually acoustic 'Slim Slo Slider', sung as BP Fallon recently observed "with the gravitas of a gravedigger". Van kissed Michelle on stage during the encore of 'Have I Told You'.

Van then flew back to Amsterdam for a ninety minute set, short by his current standards, debuting a new song 'Fire In The Belly' and 'Boppin' The Blues', one of the tracks he had recently recorded with primal rocker Carl Perkins. In June, he played four dates at Wembley, doubling up at last with his long time hero Ray Charles. Gavin Martin in the *NME* reported that these were his first support slots in twenty years. "Easing into the performance with a lugubrious slipping funk work of 'Satisfied', the highlight of the set was 'The Healing Game', which Van introduced as 'a song about East Belfast, back in the days before everything got fucked up'." Martin describes it as "a sad anthem, a beautifully modulated act of soulful hope, useful nostalgia". Van then joined Ray Charles for an encore of 'I Believe To My Soul'.

There were reports in the gutter press that Michelle had been having an affair behind Van's back with a wealthy horse trainer. This from the *Mirror*, which John Pilger has recently taken to task for its steep descent – begun under Robert Maxwell before his last swim – from a campaigning newspaper with a heart to a second rate *Sun*. After protests about this gross invasion of privacy, Van himself became the object of the same journalists, the real muck raking thing after all his years lambasting poor rock scribes. They pursued him to a Warminster love nest, and claimed, without proof, that he was taking resort with ladies of the night. All rather touchingly innocent, and so what? The situation with Rocca was soon resolved, and there are currently unconfirmed rumours that a quiet wedding has taken place. Long may she inspire his muse. The *Sunday Times* revealed, less contentiously, that Morrison had offered music for Michael Flatley's *Lord Of The Dance*, a multi-media show retelling Celtic folk tales, and centred on high-tech displays of step-dancing, in the wake of *Riverdance*, but the music was never used.

Towards the end of the year, *Tell Me Something* appeared, a CD devoted to the songs of Mose Allison, and featuring Allison, Fame, Morrison and Dr Ben Sidran, once of The Steve Miller Band, and creator of a series of pleasurable jazz piano albums. Other musicians were drawn from Van's jazz band, and Pee Wee Ellis again arranged the charts. The album is an interesting sideline. On its orange front cover appear four small photos of Allison, in jumper and rustic hat, Fame at the microphone, Sidran resting his hand on his cheek, and Van with eyes closed behind dark glasses. Piano keys decorate the back cover and the CD booklet. Sidran's sleeve notes mention that "Van rates Mose as one of the greatest songwriters of our century. He really does speak the modern blues better than anyone before or since. The sessions were fast and clean, all live performances and first or second takes."

"I've wanted to make this record for a long time," Van explained. "There are so many Mose songs that I admire, this album contains maybe a tenth of them." The whole recording was done in a day. "We've practised thirty years for this opportunity," added Sidran. "This thing has haunted our heads for so long; it's almost a part of our musical vocabulary." In *Q*, Mark Cooper reckons less is more in Allison's knowing, laconic style, which has been gracing and unnerving the world's nightclubs for the past forty years. Jazz's answer to JJ Cale, though those who miss Van's spiritual side here must remember that Allison specialises "not in the mystic but in knowing the score", which can make him either brilliant or insufferably smug.

Van even attracted one Paul Lloyd, a plasterer from Merthyr Tydfil, as a professional imitator. He appeared on *Stars In Their Eyes*, singing 'Brown Eyed Girl', which was reckoned to be Van's biggest hit, though he went, appearance wise, for Van in the mid seventies, and was beaten on the night by "Dinah Washington". In a more lasting form of public acclaim, following in the footsteps of old mates Eric Clapton *MBE*, Harvey Goldsmith *CBE* and *Sir* Cliff Richard, Van – the original white soul rebel – received the award of the Order of the British Empire for "services to music". Morrison had reached his mansion on the hill.

CHAPTER TEN

The Healing Game

1997 saw Brian Kennedy's *A Better Man* CD – better than the man? – at the top of the Irish charts. Kennedy grew up on the Falls Road, one of six children, before moving to London. As he told *Q*, "When I first began performing with Van, people assumed I had a record deal. He's been dead supportive of me and I've only missed two nights in four years with him because of my solo career." *Q* mentions Brian's girlish voice, and lyrics which – like Morrissey's – refuse to be gender specific. "Some men hear it, big rugby players, and they think it's all right to fumble up to me and visit a possibly new side of themselves. My songs could be about men or women, but they're not about sex, it's more longing and love. I know in my mind I'm a man."

The same month, Michael Eavis told *Mojo* about his plans for the next Glastonbury Festival. One name was pencilled in already. "Van Morrison goes on all the time; no matter what's happening in the outside world, he's always there with me and always will be. He comes back fresh as a daisy every year for me." The same issue ran a superb retrospective on The Pretty Things, a formative influence on Them. The process was two way, and for Phil May, Van is still "the dog's bollocks. When you meet him now he's like a bloke who really knows where he is and doesn't take any bullshit."

On the cover of *The Healing Game* a threatening Van walks across the shot, along with what looks like one of his minders, aka Pee Wee Ellis. The album was recorded in Dublin, and released in March 1997. Morrison, dressed and photographed in monochrome, looks like he could damage rather than heal you, The Guvnor coming to pay you a call. It is as if all that youth and hope, the beauty and desire of *Astral Weeks*, has been leeched away, a kaleidoscope of colour corroded to black and white. Alternatively, he could be a dead man, walking. The album is dominated by Georgie Fame's superb organ playing, Brian Kennedy's backing vocals, and what is largely Van's jazz band from the Ronnie Scott sessions. Also returning to the fold are Haji Ahkba and Katie Kissoon – adding "fiery, soulful vocals".

The opening song, 'Rough God Goes Riding', sets the tone for the whole album, as dark as its cover. Van's voice is as bleak as Leonard Cohen on his album *The Future* – basically there isn't one – or Dylan's wracked vocals on his last decent album *Oh Mercy*. Everything is broken. Van's album begins with "mud splattered victims" on the TV, WB Yeats' "rough god" – a figure from the Apocalypse and his poem 'The Second Coming', and Van being staked out by the tabloid press. Ellis's saxophone solo is masterful, the same slow scream as Van's throaty shout. Van asks for a *Bible*.

The rest of the album somehow hangs together in a way that *Days Like This* didn't, and is listener friendly, however bleak its subject matter. It plays further games with Van's stock subjects: in 'Fire In The Belly' he listens to the radio, and a woman is like a "high flying cloud", as in 'Beside You'. At one point he imitates John Lee Hooker.

'This Weight' is almost The Band's most famous song, about being freed, but is actually about slavery, the underlying motif of the whole album. As the *Guardian* states, "Pee Wee Ellis's baritone sax solo against a misty backdrop of tenor, trumpet and flugelhorn is a joy." Just like Van's American band and Street Choir of twenty-five years before. The combination of bitter vocal with Kennedy's youthful echo is like father and son, and the song does not so much end as be abandoned. It sounds like time slowing down.

In 'Waiting Game', Van is wonderfully world weary, his aeons deep voice counterpointed by Kissoon's lullabying soprano. He is "the brother of the snake", both in Eden and in the mythology of long lost friend and namesake Jim Morrison. Except that this "lizard" is not sexual but poisonous.

Even more startling is the mysterious 'Piper At The Gates Of Dawn', taken almost straight from *The Wind In The Willows*, with Paddy Moloney's uillean pipes and Phil Coulter's stately piano revisiting past glories. The tragedy of Kenneth Grahame was that he never truly grew up, despite being forced by his parents into a serious job in the Bank of England. Van sounds infinitely sad, lost back in his own childhood. It cannot have escaped his notice that the title is shared by The Pink Floyd's first album. More importantly, the song resolves itself in silence.

'Burning Ground' has been attacked for its "ludicrous spoken playlet about the burning of jute", though Morrison is relating a scene from his childhood – jute was shipped to Belfast from India – and sounds particularly like a hellfire preacher here, which is appropriate. The song has a similar tone to Dylan's late masterpiece 'Blind Willie McTell'. 'It Once Was My Life' starts with drunken, happy conversation, then a gospel choir backs Van's sour picture of disillusion. "Trials and tribulations", which one could again lay at the feet of the *Sunday Mirror*. The background voices turn nightmarish. Musically, we are back with the Bang sessions. Acoustic bass, then 'Sometimes We Cry' quotes Johnny Ray, but these are real tears, not faked. Van's voice was never more saxophone-like, full throated, bellowing pain. 'If You Love Me' is a touching duet, but cliched, like a slowed down Bonzos. Fifties pop, echoing down the years. 'Have I Told You' mark two this is *not*. Good harmonica, though, set to a wordless chorus, and the four chord trick.

The title song of *The Healing Game* deals with Belfast street singing. As Van later told *Q*, "People find it incredible when I tell them that people used to sing and play music in the street. I think there's a whole oral tradition that's disappeared." One localised on the Hyndford Street district. The song is about when people used to sing on the streets: "It came from America, where they had all the doo-wop groups. That's the general idea of the song: you've never really moved from this position. You took a lot of detours but you're still back on the corner." The final culmination of the long abandoned 'Street Choir' project, here is a doo-wop chorus and church organ, straight out of Procol Harum. Van is like the protagonists in Yeats' play *Purgatorial*, condemned to eternal recurrence, "here I am again", back with the "backstreet jelly roll". The orgasmic sax solo, and the typhoon of a final chorus do suggest an escape from the hell sketched out on this album. Only music can assuage.

Reviewers could not fail to compare this album with the week's other release, U2's *Pop*. The Dublin band started with an evangelistic faith in rock music, and seemed to follow at first in Van's footsteps, even recording a (different) song called 'Gloria'. Next they turned, like

Van, to soundscapes, sculpted by Eno. Then the *Zooropa* tour embraced multi-media and post-modernism: when they wanted a deep voice of authority they turned to Johnny Cash, not Van. Their new CD embraced all kinds of new popular music, bass and drums and techno, while Van was seemingly turning backwards, into the down-the-line R&B of his youth.

Under the different surfaces, both Van and Bono – who he once described a nice kid, who hadn't grown up yet – were dealing with matters of faith and desperation. Most reviewers failed to dig that deep. *Mojo*'s David Hepworth, thought that since 1980, Morrison had made eleven albums which have exhibited a lack of ambition unparalleled among his contemporaries; I would argue the direct opposite here. "All the shades of delight and wonder of his younger music" had now been blanketed by a "peevish fog of injured innocence". Fine, until you realise that Van's early songs could be even more peevish and damaged. 'He Ain't Give You None' is hardly 'Woodstock'. In *Q*, Lucy O'Brien considered Morrison to be "on classic form, both ruminative realist and nostalgic dreamer". For the *Guardian*, "the disc pivots on Morrison's rapport with his excellent band", imparting "moments of sublime musicianship". The *NME*'s John Muvey was not so charitable. "Where once he soared, now he plods. Trudges. Lumbers. Grunts a bit." Morrison has landed on the riverbank, "with a resounding flop".

'The Healing Game' also appears on John Lee Hooker's new CD, *Don't Look Back*, which Van also produced. It had taken years for them to get together long enough to make a whole album, although the *Observer* heard only "the sound of two men on artistic auto-pilot". Hooker, though, told *Q* that, "I don't know any young guys who play the true blues like me and BB and Van. They play sophisticated blues, but no one plays the deep, deep blues like we do." What did they talk about on the phone? "Women."

'The Healing Game' is the title track of two CD singles by Van and the boys. Both front covers show Hyndford Street, empty of traffic, with Morrison and Kennedy standing by a lamp post (*not* like George Formby) with the rest of the band – or gang – walking towards you with slow menace. Van looks grim and solid, almost as if stuffed. He has changed his shirt between the two shots. The second CD contains a brassy update of 'Full Force Gale' and two new songs. The Dylanesque

'Look What The Good People Done' seems to be about another misunderstood Ulsterman, George Best, who could do with a football what Van does with words, and who was given the nearest thing to a public crucifixion on the *Wogan* TV show. 'Celtic Spring' has Paddy Moloney on whistle, and the repeated refrain, about going "to the regions again". Van is once more setting out for his Celtic crossroads.

Yet to see an official release – though now scheduled for November 1997 – is an even more exciting package, *The Philosopher's Stone*. A double CD set, this was subtitled "The Unreleased Tapes Volume One", and although it did not appear on its advertised release date of 15 July 1996, some promo copies were issued. I have listed the proposed tracks in my discography, with comments on each track by Simon Gee. "I wouldn't call them out-takes because that suggests that these tracks were somehow secondary. They're not, these are just really good songs that weren't released at the time," one source close to the project told *Ice*.

The title is drawn from alchemy, turning dross into gold. One hopes this project – or the ones that its subtitle presumes will follow – will not go the way of Neil Young's long threatened ten CD box set of out-takes and live recordings. Dylan's three volume *Bootleg Series* only scratched the surface of that artist's back pages when released, and had the unfortunate effect of rather showing up his current releases. As Van told *Q*, "It's hard to work out why you didn't put something out at the time. Usually it felt like it didn't fit. When I was with Warner Brothers, they were very minimalist. They always said that they didn't want more than twenty minutes on a side, because of recording levels."

Also newly released at the time of writing, March 1997, is *New York Sessions 67*, a repackaging of the Bang material, and the one minute bursts of "song" designed to free Van from his contract. For Martin Aston of *Q*, these represent "a musical revenge job of unparalleled contempt". Peter Doggett of *Record Collector*, who also wrote an excellent three part survey of Van's career for that magazine, found that isolating the deliberately unusable fragments "emphasises both their idiocy and their wicked humour". Van is seen in photographs with Bert Berns, with "not a trace of outrage or resentment on his face".

Another album released in early 1997 was *Now And In Time To Be: A Musical Celebration Of The Works Of WB Yeats*. Put together by two travel journalists, who had been driving round Sligo with Van's music on the car stereo, and heard his setting of 'Before The World Was Made'. This same version appears on the album, along with new settings of Yeats' poems by Christy Moore, The Waterboys, The Cranberries, Shane MacGowan, as well as readings by Richard Harris, and an archive recording of Yeats himself. "Irish poets learn your trade/sing whatever is well made."

The final piece in this glut of new Van related material was *The Van Morrison Songbook*, which brings together covers of Van's work already out on record, by acts as diverse as Energy Orchard ('Madame George'), Steel Pulse ('Brown Eyed Girl'), Goldie Hawn ('I Wanna Roo You') and Billy Connolly ('Irish Heartbeat'). A great improvement on *No Prima Donna*.

Morrison has influenced everybody from Graham Parker to Tanita Tikaram. One outstanding cover of his work is the live version of 'The Way Young Lovers Do' which Jeff Buckley has recorded live twice, on *Live At Sin-e* and *Live From The Bataclan*. Both versions outlast ten minutes, and Jeff uses his father's exuberant style, like a blissed out angel, to take the song into brave new worlds. It is repaying a debt, as there is a definite Tim Buckley influence on Van's own live reading of 'Vanlose Stairway', particularly on the under recorded 'My Name Is Raincheck' Manchester bootleg. Jeff embroiders the song, develops it to tell his own narrative, bends it and squeezes it out of shape.

Maybe Shana will later do the same, deconstructing and re-enhancing her father's myth. *Wavelength*'s Thomas C Palmer Jr reports a gig of hers in Boston which features such secret delights as her father's 'Twilight Zone', along with the traditional song 'The Blacksmith', and her own songs, one co-written with her mother. Back home in San Francisco, "We have a really big following where we live. A mailing list." Her backing musicians also play with Claddagh, which she describes as an Irish showband. The circle is unbroken.

Van's influence on other musicians remains a fascinating one, for them and for us. His recent collaborator James Hunter, aka Howling Wilf, tells of how Morrison told him "there's a tendency to get onto one thing and really burn it out quickly by overplaying it. I think he wants to do it sparingly so it'll last a bit longer." For Elton John, "he's usually on Planet Van anyway". Trip-hopper and the deeply weird Tricky, whose work approaches the menace of Van's early days, grudgingly admits "he's consistent". More expansive is Mike Pickering from dance magicians M People: "He's one of my all time heroes." Even noted grouch Woody Allen, who acts a bit when not playing in his weekly jazz band, admits that he "used to like listening to *A Sense Of Wonder* on Sundays". Noel Gallagher first reckoned that "he's a miserable old **** really, and his music is just not my generation" but then adds, with something close to graciousness, "yet he means it and I respect him for that".

As I write, rumours circulate about a joint tour of Britain by Morrison and Dylan in early summer. Both share(d) the same accountant. As the story goes, he once invited them to dinner. Neither said a word, either to him or each other. When Dylan had gone, Van leaned over to his host, with a twinkle in his eye, and said, "I thought he was on pretty good form tonight, didn't you."

A clue to Van's own methods comes from the passage from Kerouac's *On The Road*, which he read on the TV tribute to Slim Galliard, about whom it was written. "Great crowds of young semi intellectuals sat at his feet. When he gets warmed up he takes off his shirt and undershirt and really goes. He does and says anything that comes into his head. He'll slow down the beat and brood…everybody leans forward breathlessly to hear. He goes right on, for as long as an hour." Galliard then recites the same phrase, over and over, "for fifteen minutes, his voice getting softer and softer till you can't hear". Dean Moriarty comments, his hands clasped together in prayer, that "Slim knows time, he knows time". Galliard tells Van that the "slow time" described here is "real authentic Cuban rhythm".

Contemporary writers have been as entranced by Van as Kerouac was by Galliard. In Hanif Kureishi's story *With Your Tongue Down My Throat*, published in *Granta Twenty-Two*, the hero takes a bus ride east, to Holland Park, where the rich people live. "For example? Van Morrison in a big overcoat is hurrying towards somewhere in a nervous mood. 'Hiya, Van! Won't you even say hello?' I scream across the street. At my words Van the Man accelerates like a dog with a winklepicker up its anus." This compares to an anecdote Jackie Leven recently told on stage, about seeing Van almost mown down by a bus, having walked into its path, and the heated exchange between himself and the driver.

In *Three Amerikanische LPs*, an early German language film by director Wim Wenders, the narrator holds up a copy of *Astral Weeks*, and then 'Slim Slo Slider' comes onto the soundtrack, while a girl stands on a balcony, smoking a cigarette. Wenders, director of *Paris, Texas* and much else, hopes one day to work with Morrison. "I only saw him once in San Francisco and he did the whole show with his back to the audience. Maybe he's just shy." In his book *Emotion Pictures*, he says of Van's work, "I know of no music that is clearer or more full of feeling or more perceptible to my senses than this." It gives a feeling of what cinema could be like at its greatest pitch, "*perception* that doesn't always jump blindly at meanings and assertions, but rather lets your senses extend further and further".

The German novelist Peter Handke is a long time Van fan, quoting from 'Coney Island' in 'Attempt At A Successful Day', and admitting to having based one of the leading characters – a singer – in his 1994 blockbuster *Mein Jahr In Der Niemandsbucht* (My Year In Nobody's Bay) on Morrison. Burnt out from recording his new album, the singer escapes to the hills of Inverness, and looks back over his long career. Ulgich Buehring translates a key passage for *Wavelength*. "'Being in the song' was for him the original source." He felt as if "inside himself something started to heal, something which he didn't want to heal, although he had sung about it again and again".

Jurgen Rank translates from another of Handke's books, where the protagonist, Sorger, attends a concert which can only be by Van the Man. "The singer was a short, square man who seemed to be extremely robust and totally lost in thought. His voice was mighty from the beginning without the need to get loud. It did not come from within the chest but started at first as if independent. It made itself heard as the sound of one who, after a long, miserable, unspeakable breeding suddenly started to sing. Each of his songs assembled itself by a quick, sometimes stuttering and repetitive sequence of cutting, embittering, threatening (in any case never relieving) cries of pain." The concert goes on, with the singer never smiling, searching as if deep into himself.

"For a long time he seemed as a living dead banned in his own 'machinery, but carried little by little this vibrating undertone to his voice which, berserking, broke through to an all common hymn. Sorger was a witness of what 'hymns' could be, and understood the disproportioned and anonymous looking man on stage as a reluctant singer of freedom."

Roddy Doyle's novel *The Woman Who Walked Into Doors* has its protagonist cleaning a client's house, to the sound of 'Tupelo Honey', which takes her back to happier times. "I love Van Morrison," she declares to herself. "Van's my man." One positive thing about her wretched life: "It has a great soundtrack."

Wavelength contains a moving poem, 'Morning Ritual' by Chris Murray, a recovering alcoholic, about how songs like 'Melancholia' can console the lonely:

> & all the better for having Van by my side
> making morning easier to face up to.

British poetry, meanwhile, or that officially sanctioned by the Poetry Society and the posh Sundays, has become tricksy, post-modernist, anti-realist; work that is icily cold at its heart. Concepts like beauty or truth telling are rigorously resisted. There is a small cultural industry devoted to pushing this stuff, generally a load of old twaddle, which the foolish and pretentious somehow believe must somehow be good for them as they can't understand it. One of the heavily marketed "Best Of Young British Poets" is Don Paterson, who is far better than most, and earns his crust as a freelance musician. In a notorious piece for the *Observer*, he praises Van's songs, then spoils it all by writing, with appalling condescension: "Can we get this straight – Van doesn't and can't write poems." Another poem by Chris Murray – *not* on any Arts Council approved list – adds, sensibly:

> This sounds like sour grapes.
> Van at his worst
> is better than Paterson at his best.

Tom Paulin, much quoted during Van's live renditions of 'Summertime In England', praises "the terrific way he has of building in bits of Belfast speech into the songs or playing that speech against the song". Morrison takes his native accent "and then he's putting this American charge into it, so he's picking up blues and making this kind of transatlantic bridgehead". Paulin compares this mastery of rhythm to the American recluse Emily Dickinson. Another maverick, the poet Paul Durcan, who of course has recorded with Van, places him in the "age-old oral and placename tradition known in Irish as the *dindsenchas*".

For cultural critic par excellence, Greil Marcus, "Morrison is heir to a tradition of mysteries, and he knows it. He's a Celt and at least a spiritual descendant of St Brendan, who set out from Ireland fifteen hundred years ago and who, according to legend, reached America. So Morrison...can understand that there are no divisions, that all parts of himself are somehow linked. Yet this is not a belief, it is a possibility, and the tension remains, driving the urge to wholeness."

That theory is translated into reality in Paul Du Noyer's "The Big Man", for *Q*, Van's first major (independent) interview for eight years; and he's got flu. Van is out to puncture the myths surrounding his career. He never believed in the sixties' utopian dream. "To me, everything's always been hard so I never had that pie-in-the-sky thing." He never intended to live in America, but was completely broke after the Bert Berns saga, "commercial suicide". This ties in with an earlier interview with Gavin Martin, which speaks of him surfacing in Boston "still obviously downhearted, still drinking heavily (at one point reportedly close to the big abyss). He would often phone up DJs on the all night radio stations making requests for John Lee Hooker records in an indecipherable drunken Irish harangue." Whatever the truth of that, Van left the USA as soon as his daughter Shana became a teenager.

Morrison resists interpretations of his work: "When you're drugged up you can read anything into anything." People over analyse him. "They blow it out of all proportion, the reason being they want to make themselves look better, or more intellectual." (Guilty as charged, I'll come quietly, officer.) Most of his songs are fictional. He most enjoys live performance, the rapport with his band, but it is hard work. "What's going on there is very complex, and if somebody does something wrong and the concentration goes...I mean, there's a lot of cues. I'm putting forth the music and it's very intense, there's no let-up and everybody's on their toes all the time, from the minute they walk on stage till they come off."

As to music, "sure it's magic, I think it is". Van used to talk about getting people into a meditative state, but people take it out of context, so now he prefers not to. He has never really left his home town of Belfast. "Basically I'm still there. In my head. I'm still hanging out with the corner boys." He has just rediscovered *Astral Weeks*. "It made me just sit up. There was a lot of stuff going on here that was definitely off the wall and out there. And it was good. I felt an affinity."

What fellow practitioners most admire is his ability to completely lose himself in his music. Natalie Merchant told *Hot Press* that she had seen Morrison on stage, "in almost like a shamanistic state, a trance state, when he's really 'on'. It can't happen like that every time, but it happens." For the spooky Dr John: "Van is a deep cat. That poetry that comes out of him is like automatic writing or just spiritual flows. It's so hip, man." The more down to earth Paul Jones remembers him turning up to jam with The Blues Band, and then how he "scurried" back into the dressing room, and how Jones had to dig him out, like a mole. A "most extraordinary man, but isn't he wonderful".

As Van told Davitt Sigerson in 1978, "I've been around for quite a while. Picture the situation. Put yourself through working in showbands, touring in buses with seven or eight people, sleeping in parks, having no money. Put yourself through working the clubs in Germany, up on to when the R&B movement thing was happening in the sixties. The thing that has carried me through is the time I put in when I was absolutely nobody. When I was in Them, it was anti-climactic. 'All right, so I'm a star, but I don't want it.' So I gave it back. 'I don't want to be on *Top Of The Pops* every week. I don't want to be a star.' I just do my music."

I asked the poet Elli McCarthy what Van's music had meant in her life. "When I fell in love, we did it to *Moondance*. Later, through an eleven year marriage which took us to Crete, India and the ownership of a tiny croft in the Shetlands where our daughter Tao was born, Van and his music was always with us. Things move on – marriages wax and wane – but old festival goers never change, and though the children grow, we continue to go, dragging them with us! And now the skinny Irish gypsy we once knew as 'Van the Man' plays for one hundred thousand people. Only the first utterance of passionate rage lets you know that he's somewhere in the star studded line up. Is that Georgie

Fame on dual keyboards, hell Linda where's the binoculars? He sings his lyrics for himself, it's the only way he knows how to live. He still adores women, he's met the banshee in his sea gypsy days. He is middle aged, overweight, far too short for me, yet when he sings 'I ain't tired, I just feel like lying down', I'd go down with him! What is he – God only knows. But when he sings we dance – we hold our children high, we sweat it down in the fields of Avalon."

Legendary publicist BP Fallon, who has seen just about everything, reckons "sometimes he has an aura of unease; you can see him suffering daggers of discomfort. He's at his happiest on stage, that's probably his oasis. Something happens there, something spiritual." As he told Fallon, Morrison's spiritual search continues: "At one point I took courses in Scientology over a period of eighteen months but I'm not a joiner. I've done rolfing, it's a bit like shiatsu. I've also investigated Buddhism, Hinduism…esoteric Christianity. I don't believe in myths anymore. If I could find a religion that works."

Phil Coulter thinks that Morrison sometimes makes life difficult for himself, as if on purpose. It is this that drives him on. As Coulter told Johnny Rogan, "He's very restless – physically, emotionally and creatively. He's totally unpredictable." In one interview, Van turns to Michelle and says, "I'm not a nice guy. I never said I was." She disagrees, but then love is blind.

I will end by returning to the words of long time musical collaborator David Hayes. "Van is the only person I have ever met in the music business that, if all the elements are right and everything is in place, he can take the music into a totally different realm, where you kind of melt into it. It is very rare and anybody who works with Van and experiences that is lucky." The same applies to those of us who see Morrison in concert, or listen to his records. We might at times be aggravated, bored, surprised, elated, lifted up. On a good night, devastated by a mighty torrent of words and music, and their creator, we are truly blessed. Did ye get healed?

Discography

All listings are original UK issue, unless otherwise mentioned. I have tried to cut my way through the minefield, and list only essential items. For a fuller listing, see the indispensable Record Collector *issues 178-180, and the exhaustive listings in* Wavelength, *and Michael Hayward's information placed on the Internet. Video information comes courtesy of Andy Nieurzla's Videography in* Wavelength. *All information checked by Simon Gee of* Wavelength.

● with GEORGIE AND THE MONARCHS

GERMAN AND DUTCH 7 INCH SINGLE

CBS
1307   Boozoo Hully Gully/Twingy Baby – 1962

● with THEM

UK 7 INCH SINGLES

DECCA
F11973   Don't Start Crying Now/One Two Brown Eyes – September 1964
F12018   Baby Please Don't Go/Gloria – November 1964
F12094   Here Comes The Night/All For Myself – March 1965
F12175   One More Time/How Long Baby? – June 1965
F12215   (It Won't Hurt) Half As Much/I'm Gonna Dress In Black – August 1975
F12281   Mystic Eyes/If You And I Could Be As Two – November 1975
F12355   Call My Name/Bring 'Em On In – March 1966
F12403   Richard Cory/Don't You Know – May 1966
MAJOR MINOR
MM509   Gloria/Friday's Child – July 1967 MM513
          The Story Of Them Pt 1/The Story Of Them Pt 2 – September 1967

US 7 INCH SINGLES

PARROT

9702	Don't Start Crying/One Two Brown Eyes – 1964	
9727	Gloria/Baby Please Don't Go – 1965	
9749	Here Comes The Night/All For Myself – 1965	
9784	I'm Gonna Dress In Black/(It Won't Hurt) Half As Much – 1965	
9796	Mystic Eyes/If You And I Could Be As Two – 1965	
9819	Call My Name/Bring 'Em On In – 1966	
3003	Richard Cory/Don't You Know – 1965	
3006	I Can Only Give You Everything/Don't Start Crying Now – 1966	
365	Gloria/If You And I Could Be As Two – August 1972	
	credited to Van Morrison & Them	

UK EPs

DECCA

DFE 8612 THEM – February 1965
Philosophy/Baby Please Don't Go/
One Two Brown Eyes/Don't Start Crying Now

DUTCH EPs

UNTITLED – 1967
Times Getting Tougher Than Tough/Stormy Monday
Baby What You Want Me To Do/Friday's Child

UK/US ALBUMS

THEM *Side One:* Mystic Eyes/If You And I Could Be As Two/Little Girl/
Just A Little Bit/I Gave My Love A Diamond/Gloria/
You Just Can't Win
Side Two: Go On Home Baby/Don't Look Back/I Like It Like That/
I'm Gonna Dress In Black/Bright Lights Big City/
My Little Baby/(Get Your Kicks On) Route 66

LP: Decca 4700 – June 1965

LP: Parrot PS 6100 5 (mono)/PAS71005 (stereo) – July 1965
US Issue of first album, omitting 'My Little Baby', 'Bright Lights Big City',
'Just A Little Bit', 'I Gave My Love A Diamond' and 'You Just Can't Win'.
Adds 'Here Comes The Night', 'One More Time' and 'One Two Brown Eyes'
CD: London 820 563-2 – 1988

THEM AGAIN

>*Side One:* Could You Would You/Something You Got/Call My Name/
>Turn On Your Love Light/I Put A Spell On You/
>I Can Only Give You Everything/My Lonely Sad Eyes/
>I Got A Woman
>*Side Two:* Out Of Sight/It's All Over Now Baby Blue/Bad Or Good/
>How Long Baby/Hello Josephine/Don't You Know/Bring 'Em On In

LP: Decca LK 4751 – January 1966
LP: Parrot PS 61008 (mono)/PAS 71008 (stereo) – April 1966
>*US issue of second album, omitting 'Hello Josephine', 'I Put A Spell On You', 'Hey Girl' and 'I Got A Woman'*
CD: London 820 564-2 – 1989
>*adds 'One More Time'*

COMPILATIONS

THE WORLD OF THEM

>*Side One:* Here Comes The Night/Baby Please Don't Go/
>I'm Gonna Dress In Black/Richard Cory/
>I Put A Spell On You/Bring 'Em On In
>*Side Two* Gloria/Mystic Eyes/Turn On Your Love Light/
>It's All Over Now Baby Blue/One Two Brown Eyes
>Don't Start Crying Now

LP: Decca SPA 86 – October 1970
>*featured alternate takes*

THEM FEATURING VAN MORRISON, LEAD SINGER
Double LP: Decca DPA 3001/2 – October 1973

BACKTRACKIN'
London APS 639 *US issue* – 1974

THE STORY OF THEM FEATURING VAN MORRISON
London LC 50001 *US issue* – 1977

THEM – ROCK ROOTS

>Don't Start Crying Now/I'm Gonna Dress In Black/Route 66/How Long Baby/
>Bright Lights Big City/Don't You Know/Call My Name
>The Story Of Them Parts 1 And 2/Mighty Like A Rose/Times Getting Tougher
>Than Tough/Stormy Monday/Baby What You Want Me To Do/Friday's Child
Decca ROOTS 3 – 1976

THEM

>Don't Start Crying Now/Baby Please Don't Go/Here Comes The Night/One

More Time/(It Won't Hurt) Half As Much/Mystic Eyes/Call My Name/Richard
Cory/Gloria/The Story Of Them Part 1
One Two Brown Eyes/Philosophy/All For Myself/How Long Baby/I'm Gonna
Dress In Black/If You And I Could Be As Two/Bring 'Em On In/Don't You
Know/Friday's Child/The Story Of Them Part 2

See For Miles SEE 31 – 1984

THE THEM COLLECTION
Double LP: Castle CCSLP 131 – April 1986

THEM FEATURING VAN MORRISON: THE COLLECTION

Baby Please Don't Go/Bright Lights Big City/I Put A Spell On You/
Hello Josephine/Turn On Your Love Light/Don't Start Crying Now/
Gloria/The Story Of Them/It's All Over Now Baby Blue/I Got A Woman/
My Little Baby/How Long Baby/Here Comes The Night/Stormy Monday/
I Like It Like That/Go On Home Baby/Out Of Sight/
Baby What You Want Me To Do/Route 66/Friday's Child/Little Girl/
Hey Girl/Call My Name/Mystic Eyes

CD: Castle CCSCD 131 – 1992
sleeve notes by Michael Heatley

THEM FEATURING VAN MORRISON

Gloria/The Story Of Them/Stormy Monday/Mystic Eyes/Hey Girl/
Baby Please Don't Go/Here Comes The Night/My Lonely Sad Eyes/
Richard Cory/(It Won't Hurt) Half As Much/Turn On Your Love Light/
I Put A Spell On You/Don't Look Back

Castle – 1982

● VAN MORRISON

UK SINGLES

LONDON
HLZ 10150 Brown Eyed Girl/Goodbye Baby (Baby Goodbye) – July 1967

WARNER BROTHERS
WB 7383	Come Running/Crazy Love – May 1970
WB 7434	Domino/Sweet Jannie – December 1970
WB 7462	Blue Money/Call Me Up In Dreamland – June 1971
K 16120	Wild Night/When The Evening Sun Comes Down – November 1971
K 16210	Jackie Wilson Said/You've Got The Power – August 1972
K 16299	Warm Love/I Will Be There – August 1973
K 16392	Caledonia/What's Up Crazy Pup – May 1974
K 16486	Bulbs/Who Was That Masked Man – November 1974
K 16939	Eternal Kansas City/Joyous Sound – May 1977

K 16986   Joyous Sound/Mechanical Bliss – July 1977
K 17254   Wavelength/Checkin' It Out – October 1978
K 17322   Natalia/Lifetimes – February 1979
            *None of the above come in picture sleeves. All the seven inch and twelve inch
            releases that follow do*

MERCURY
6001121   Bright Side Of The Road/Rolling Hills – September 1979
MER 99   Cleaning Windows/It's All In The Game – March 1982
MER 110   Dweller On The Threshold/Scandinavia – June 1982
MER 132   Cry For Home/Summertime In England (live) – February 1983
MERX 132   Cry For Home/Summertime In England (live)/
            All Saints Day twelve inch – February 1983
MER 141   Celtic Swing/Mr Thomas – May 1983
MERX 141   Celtic Swing/Mr Thomas/Rave On, John Donne twelve inch – May 1983
MER 159   Dweller On The Threshold (live)/ Northern Muse(Solid Ground)
            – April 1984
MER 178   A Sense Of Wonder/Haunts Of Ancient Peace (live) – October 1984
MERX 178   A Sense Of Wonder/Haunts Of Ancient Peace (live) twelve inch – October 1984
MER 223   Ivory Tower/New Kind Of Man – 1986
MERX 223   Ivory Tower/New Kind Of Man/A Sense Of Wonder/Cleaning Windows twelve
            inch – August 1987
MER 231   Got To Go Back/In The Garden – August 1986
MER 254   Did Ye Get Healed?/Allow Me – August 1987
MER 258   Someone Like You/Celtic Excavation – November 1987
MER 261   Queen Of The Slipstream/Spanish Steps – April 1988
MER 262   I'll Tell Me Ma/Ta Mo Chleamhnas Deanta – June 1988
            with The Chieftains
MERX 262   I'll Tell Me Ma/Ta Mo Chleamhnas Deanta/Carrickfergus twelve inch – June 1988
            with The Chieftains

POLYDOR/POLYGRAM
VANS I   Have I Told You Lately That I Love You/ Contacting My Angel – June 1989
VANX 1   Have I Told You Lately That I Love You/Contacting My Angel/Listen To The
            Lion twelve inch – June 1989
VANCD 1   Have I Told You Lately That I Love You/Contacting My Angel/Irish Heartbeat
            CD – June 1989
VANS 2   Whenever God Shines His Light/I'd Love To Write Another Song
            – November 1989
            track one with Cliff Richard
VANX 2   Whenever God Shines His Light/ I'd Love To Write Another Song/Cry For
            Home twelve inch – November 1989
            track one with Cliff Richard
VANCD 2   Whenever God Shines His Light/ I'd Love To Write Another Song/Cry For
            Home/Whenever God Shines His Light (unedited) CD – November 1989
            track one with Cliff Richard

VANS 3   Orangefield/These Are The Days – December 1989
VANX 3   Orangefield/These Are The Days/And The Healing Has Begun twelve inch
          – December 1989
VANCD 3   Orangefield/These Are The Days/And The Healing Has Begun/Coney Island
          CD – December 1989
VANS 4   Coney Island/Have I Told You Lately That I Love You – January 1990
VANX 4   Coney Island/Have I Told You Lately That I Love You/A Sense Of Wonder
          twelve inch – January 1990
VANCD 4   Coney Island/Have I Told You Lately That
          I Love You/A Sense Of Wonder/Spirit CD – January 1990
VANS 5   Gloria/Rave On, John Donne – July 1990
VANX 5   Gloria/Rave On, John Donne/Vanlose Stairway twelve inch – July 1990
VANCD 5   Gloria/Rave On,John Donne/Vanlose Stairway/Bright Side Of The Road
          CD – July 1990
VANS 6   Real Real Gone/Start All Over Again – September 1990
VANX 6   Real Real Gone/Start All Over Again/Cleaning Windows twelve inch
          – September 1990
VANCD 6   Real Real Gone/Start All Over Again/Cleaning Windows twelve inch CD
          – September 1990
VANS 7   In The Days Before Rock 'N' Roll/I'd Love To Write Another Song twelve inch
          November 1990
VANX 7   In The Days Before Rock 'N' Roll/I'd Love To Write Another Song/
          Coney Island twelve inch – November 1990
VANCD 7   In The Days Before Rock 'N' Roll/I'd Love To Write Another Song/
          Coney Island CD – November 1990
VANS 8   Enlightenment/Avalon Of The Heart – February 1991
VANX 8   Enlightenment/Avalon Of The Heart/ Jackie Wilson Said twelve inch
          – February 1991
VANCD 8   Enlightenment/Avalon Of The Heart/Jackie Wilson Said CD – February 1991
VANS 9   I Can't Stop Loving You/All Saints Day – May 1991
          with The Chieftains
VANX 9   I Can't Stop Loving You/All Saints Day/Carrying A Torch twelve inch – May 1991
          with The Chieftains
VANCD 9   I Can't Stop Loving You/All Saints Day/Carrying A Torch CD – May 1991
          with The Chieftains
VANS 10   Why Must I Always Explain/So Complicated – September 1991
VANX 10   Why Must I Always Explain/So Complicated/Enlightenment twelve inch
          – September 1991
VANCD 10 Why Must I Always Explain/So Complicated/Enlightenment CD
          – September 1991
VANS 11   Gloria/It Must Be You (live) – May 1993
          track one with John Lee Hooker
VANCD 11 Gloria/It Must Be You (live)/And The Healing Has Begun (live)/See Me
          Through (live) CD (1 of 2) – May 1993
          track one with John Lee Hooker
VANDR 11 Gloria/Whenever God Shines His Light (live)/It Fills You Up (live)/

Star Of The County Down (live) CD (2 of 2) – May 1993
track one with John Lee Hooker
VANCD 12 Days Like This/I Don't Want To Go On Without You/That Old Black Magic/Yo
CD – May 1995
All but title track previously unreleased
74321271702 Have I Told You Lately/Love Is Teasin'/Fenny Hill (instrumental) – 1995
with The Chieftains; Van on first track only CD
5770152 Perfect Fit/Raincheck/Cleaning Windows (live) CD – September 1995
5774892 No Religion/Whenever God Shines His Light/Have I Told You Lately/Gloria
CD – November 1995
5775792 No Religion/Days Like This/Raincheck CD Digipack – November 1995

VERVE/EXILE
5762052 That's Life(live)/Moondance/That's Life
with Georgie Fame & Friends CD – February 1996

POLYDOR/EXILE
573-391-2 The Healing Game/Have I Told You Lately/
Whenever God Shines His Light/Gloria – February 1997

573-393-2 The Healing Game/Full Force Gale 96/
Look What The Good People Done/Celtic Spring – February 1997

DOVER
ROJ 12 Carrying A Torch/Walk Tall (Valley Of The Shadows) – March 1991
track one with Tom Jones, track two Tom Jones only
ROJ X12 Carrying A Torch/Walk Tall (Valley Of The Shadows) twelve inch – March 1991
track one with Tom Jones, track two Tom Jones only
ROJ CD12 Carrying A Torch/Walk Tall (Valley Of The Shadows) CD – March 1991
track one with Tom Jones, track two Tom Jones only

US SINGLES (Where not duplicated by UK release)

BANG
545 Brown Eyed Girl/Goodbye Baby/(Baby Goodbye) – July 1967
552 Ro Ro Rosey/Chick A Boom – 1967
585 Spanish Rose/Midnight Rose – 1968

HIP POCKET
16 Brown Eyed Girl/Midnight Special – 1968
four inch flexidisc, in picture sleeve

WARNER BROTHERS
7383 Come Running/Crazy Love – March 1970
7434 Domino/Sweet Jannie – October 1970

7462	Blue Money/Sweet Thing – May 1971
7488	Call Me Up In Dreamland/Street Choir – April 1971
7518	Wild Night/When The Evening Sun Goes Down – August 1971
7543	Tupelo Honey/Starting A New Life – December 1971
7573	Like A Cannonball/Old Old Woodstock – March 1972
7616	Jackie Wilson Said/You've Got The Power – August 1972
7638	Redwood Tree/St Dominic's Preview – October 1972
7665	Gypsy/St Dominic's Preview – January 1973
7706	Warm Love/I Will Be There – June 1973
7744	Green/Wild Children – September 1973
7797	Ain't Nothing You Can Do/Wild Children – February 1974
8029	Bulbs/Cul De Sac – July 1974
8450	Moondance/Cold Wind In August – 1977
8805	Kingdom Hall/Checkin' It Out – 1979
49162	Full Force Gale/You Make Me Feel So Free – 1979
50031	Cleaning Windows/Scandinavia – 1982

DUTCH SINGLES (where not duplicated by UK or US release)

WARNER BROTHERS
> Full Force Gale/Bright Side Of The Road – 1979
> Full Force Gale/Troubadours – 1979

GERMAN SINGLES (where not duplicated by UK or US release)

WARNER BROTHERS
> Redwood Tree/Jackie Wilson Said – 1972
> Gloria/Warm Love – 1974

SPANISH SINGLES (where not duplicated by UK or US release)

MERCURY
> Cleaning Windows/Aryan Mist – 1982

ALBUMS

Bang material: songs have been shuffled between successive albums

BLOWIN' YOUR MIND
> *Side One:* Brown Eyed Girl/He Ain't Give You None/TB Sheets
> *Side Two:* Spanish Rose/Goodbye Baby (Baby Goodbye)/Ro Ro Rosey

Who Drove The Red Sports Car/Midnight Special

LP: BANG BLP (S) 218 *US issue* – September 1967
  Some copies include the censored version of 'Brown Eyed Girl'
LP: LONDON HAZ 8346 – February 1968
CD: Sony Gold Mastersound 4804212 – February 1995
  remastered, adds alternate takes of 'Spanish Rose',
  'Ro Ro Rosey', 'Goodbye Baby (Baby Goodbye)', 'Who Drove The Red Sports
  Car' and 'Midnight Special'

THE BEST OF VAN MORRISON

Spanish Rose/It's All Right/Send Your Mind/The Smile You Smile/The Back
Room/Brown Eyed Girl/Goodbye Baby (Baby Goodbye)/Ro Ro Rosey/
He Ain't Give You None/Joe Harper Saturday Morning

LP: BANG BLPS 222 *US issue* – 1970
LP: PRESIDENT PTLS 1045 – May 1971

TB SHEETS

He Ain't Give You None/Beside You/It's All Right/Madame George
TB Sheets/Who Drove The Red Sports Car/Ro Ro Rosey/
Brown Eyed Girl

LP: BANG BLPS 400 *US issue* – January 1974
LP: LONDON HSM 5008 – March 1974
CD: SONY 4678272

THIS IS WHERE I CAME IN

Spanish Rose/Goodbye Baby (Baby Goodbye)/He Ain't Give You None/
Beside You/Madame George/TB Sheets/Brown Eyed Girl/Send Your Mind/
The Smile You Smile/The Back Room/Ro Ro Rosey/
Who Drove The Red Sports Car/It's All Right/
Joe Harper Saturday Morning/Midnight Special

LP: BANG 6467 625 – September 1977

BANG MASTERS

Brown Eyed Girl/Spanish Rose (with extra verse)/
Goodbye Baby (Baby Goodbye)/Chick A Boom/It's All Right/
Send Your Mind/The Smile You Smile/The Back Room/
Midnight Special/TB Sheets/He Ain't Give You None/
Who Drove The Red Sports Car/Beside You/
Joe Harper Saturday Morning (with extra verse)/Madame George/
Brown Eyed Girl (alternate take)/

I Love You (The Smile You Smile) (previously unreleased)

CD: COLUMBIA 4683092 – 1991

> *'Ro Ro Rosey' is omitted due to technical difficulties, though present on American issue. The sleeve notes by Bill Flanagan are a masterly overview of the original sessions. The tracks are all remixed from original master tapes*

THE LOST TAPES

CD: Movieplay Gold 74012/3 – January 1993

> *Portugal issue only. Contain all of the hitherto unissued contractual obligation tracks for Bang Records, mixed in with previously released tracks, despite the division in title between 'The Bang Masters' and 'Previously Unreleased Takes'. This collection was imported into the UK via Prism*

PAYIN' DUES

CD1: Brown Eyed Girl/He Ain't Give You None/TB Sheets/Spanish Rose/ Goodbye Baby (Baby Goodbye)/Ro Ro Rosey/Who Drove The Red Sports Car/Midnight Special/Beside You/It's All Right/Madame George/ Send Your Mind/The Smile You Smile/The Back Room/Joe Harper Saturday Morning/Chick A Boom/I Love You (The Smile You Smile)/ Brown Eyed Girl (alternative take)

CD2: Twist And Shake/Shake And Roll/Stomp And Scream/Scream And Holler/ Jump And Thump/Drivin' Wheel/Just Ball/Shake It Mable/Hold On George/The Big Royalty Check/Ring Worm/Savoy Hollywood/ Freaky If You Get This Far/Up Your Mind/Thirty Two/All The Bits/You Say France And I Whistle/Blow In Your Nose/Nose In Your Blow/La Mambo/Go For Yourself/Want A Danish/Here Comes Dumb George/Chickee Coo/Do It/Hang On Groovy/Goodbye George/Dum Dum George/Walk And Talk/The Wobble/Wobble And Ball

CD: Charly CD8035-2 – 1994

NEW YORK SESSIONS '67

2CD set: Burning Airlines PILOT 6 – 1997

Post Bang Material:

ASTRAL WEEKS

> *Side One: Part One: In The Beginning*
> Astral Weeks/Beside You/Sweet Thing/Cyprus Avenue
> *Side Two: Part Two: Afterwards*
> Young Lovers Do/Madame George/Ballerina/
> Slim Slo Slider

LP: Warner Brothers K 46024 *US issue* – November 1968
LP: Warner Brothers WS 1768 – September 1969
CD: Warner Brothers K 246024 – May 1987

MOONDANCE

Side One: And It Stoned Me/Moondance/Crazy Love/Caravan/
Into The Mystic
Side Two: Come Running/These Dreams Of You/Brand New Day/
Everyone/Glad Tidings

LP: Warner Brothers K 46040 *US issue, gatefold sleeve* – February 1970
LP: Warner Brothers WS 1835 *UK issue, single sleeve* – March 1970
CD: Warner Brothers K 246040 – January 1986

VAN MORRISON, HIS BAND AND THE STREET CHOIR

Side One: Domino/Crazy Face/Give Me A Kiss/I've Been Working/
Call Me Up In Dreamland/I'll Be Your Lover Too
Side Two: Blue Money/Virgo Clowns/Gypsy Queen/Sweet Jannie/
If I Ever Needed Someone/Street Choir

LP: Warner Brothers WS 1884 *US issue* – December 1970
LP: Warner Brothers WS 1884 – January 1971
CD: Warner Brothers 7599-27188-2 *German issue; UK available*

TUPELO HONEY

Side One: Wild Night/(Straight To Your Heart) Like A Cannonball/
Starting A New Life/You're My Woman
Side Two: Tupelo Honey/I Wanna Roo You (Scottish Derivative)/
When That Evening Sun Goes Down/Moonshine Whiskey

LP: Warner Brothers WS 1950 *US issue* – October 1971
LP: Warner Brothers K 46114 – November 1971
CD: Polydor 839 161-2 – 1988

ST DOMINIC'S PREVIEW

Side One: Jackie Wilson Said (I'm In Heaven When You Smile)/
Gypsy/I Will Be There/Listen To The Lion/
Side Two: St Dominic's Preview/Redwood Tree/
Almost Independence Day

LP: Warner Brothers 2633 *US issue* – July 1972
LP: Warner Brothers K 46172 – August 1972
CD: Polydor 839 162-2 – 1988

HARD NOSE THE HIGHWAY

> *Side One:* Snow In San Anselmo/Warm Love/Hard Nose The Highway/
> Wild Children/The Great Deception
> *Side Two:* Green/Autumn Song/Purple Heather

LP: Warner Brothers K 46242 – July 1973
LP: Warner Brothers WS 2712 *US issue* – October 1973
CD: Polydor 839 163-2 – 1988

IT'S TOO LATE TO STOP NOW: A TWO RECORD SET RECORDED LIVE IN
CONCERT LOS ANGELES AND LONDON SUMMER 1973

> *Side One:* Ain't Nothing You Can Do/Warm Love/Into The Mystic/
> These Dreams Of You/I Believe To My Soul
> *Side Two:* I've Been Working/Help Me/Wild Children/Domino/
> I Just Wanna Make Love To You
> *Side Three:* Bring It On Home/St Dominic's Preview/
> Take Your Hand Out Of My Pocket/Listen To The Lion
> *Side Four:* Here Comes The Night/Gloria/Caravan/Cyprus Avenue

LP: Warner Brothers K 86007 *gatefold sleeve* – February 1974
LP: Warner Brothers WS 2760 *US issue, triple gatefold* – March 1974
CD: Polydor 839 166-2 – 1988

VEEDON FLEECE

> *Side One:* Fair Play/Linden Arlen Stole The Highlights/
> Who Was That Masked Man/Streets Of Arklow
> You Don't Pull No Punches, But You Don't Push The River
> *Side Two:* Bulbs/Cul De Sac/Comfort You/Come Here My Love/
> Country Fair

LP: Warner Brothers WS 2805 *US issue* – August 1974
LP: Warner Brothers K 56068 – October 1974
CD: Polydor 839 164-2 – 1988

TWO ORIGINALS OF VAN MORRISON
LP: Warner Brothers K 86009 – October 1975

> *re-release in gatefold sleeve of* His Band And Street Choir *and* Tupelo
> Honey

A PERIOD OF TRANSITION

> *Side One:* You Gotta Make It Through The World/It Fills You Up/
> Eternal Kansas City
> *Side Two:* Joyous Sound/Flamingos Fly/Heavy Connection/
> Cold Wind In August

LP: Warner Brothers K 56322 – April 1977
CD: Polydor 839165-2 – 1988
with Mac Rebennack

WAVELENGTH

Side One: Kingdom Hall/Checking It Out/Natalia/Venice USA/
Lifetimes
Side Two: Wavelength/Santa Fe/Beautiful Obsession/
Hungry For Your Love/Take It Where You Find It

LP: Warner Brothers K 56526 – November 1978
CD: Polydor 839169-2 – 1988

INTO THE MUSIC

Side One: Bright Side Of The Road/Full Force Gale/
Stepping Out/Troubadours/Rolling Hills/
You Make Me Feel So Free
Side Two: Angeliou/And The Healing Has Begun/
It's All In The Game/You Know What They're Writing About

LP: Mercury 9102 852 – August 1979
CD: Mercury 800 057-2 – 1986
CD: Polydor 839603-2 – August 1989

COMMON ONE

Side One: Haunts Of Ancient Peace/Summertime In England/Satisfied
Side Two: Wild Honey/Spirit/When Heart Is Open

LP: Mercury 6302 021 – September 1980
CD: Mercury 800 043-2 – 1986
CD: Polydor 839600-2 – August 1989

BEAUTIFUL VISION

Side One: Celtic Ray/Northern Muse (Solid Ground)/
Dweller On The Threshold/Beautiful Vision/
She Gives Me Religion
Side Two: Cleaning Windows/Vanlose Stairway/Aryan Mist/
Across The Bridge Where Angels Dwell/Scandinavia

LP: Mercury 6302 021 – February 1982
CD: Mercury 800 036-2 – 1986
CD: Polydor 839601-2 – August 1989

INARTICULATE SPEECH OF THE HEART

Side One: Higher Than The World/Connswater/River Of Time/

Celtic Swing/Rave On, John Donne
Side Two: Inarticulate Speech Of The Heart No 1/
Irish Heartbeat/The Street Only Knew Your Name/
Cry For Home/Inarticulate Speech Of The Heart No 2/
September Night

LP: Mercury MERL 16 – March 1983
CD: Mercury 811 140-2 – 1986
CD: Polydor 839604-2 – August 1989

LIVE AT THE GRAND OPERA HOUSE, BELFAST

Side One: Introduction/Into The Mystic (instrumental)/
Inarticulate Speech Of The Heart/Dweller On The Threshold/
It's All In The Game/You Know What They're Writing About/
She Gives Me Religion/Haunts Of Ancient Peace/
Full Force Gale
Side Two: Beautiful Vision/Vanlose Stairway/Rave On, John Donne/
Rave On Part Two/Northern Muse (Solid Ground)/
Cleaning Windows

LP: Mercury MERL 36 – February 1984
CD: Mercury 818 336-2 – 1986
CD: Polydor 839602-2 – August 1989
Recorded at the Grand Opera House, 11-12 March 1983

A SENSE OF WONDER

Side One: Tore Down A La Rimbaud/Ancient Of Days/Evening Meditation/
The Master's Eyes/What Would I Do
Side Two: A Sense Of Wonder/Boffyflow And Spike/If You Only Knew/
Let The Slave incorporating The Price Of Experience/
A New Kind Of Man

LP: Mercury MERH 54 – January 1985
CD: Mercury 822 895-2 – February 1985
CD: Polydor 843116-2 – May 1990
*Some early sleeves list the banned WB Yeats poem 'Crazy Jane On God' in
the place of 'If You Only Knew' which appeared on test pressings*

NO GURU, NO METHOD, NO TEACHER

Side One: Got To Go Back/Oh The Warm Feeling/Foreign Window/
A Town Called Paradise/In The Garden
Side Two: Tir Na Nog/Here Comes The Knight/Thanks For The Information
One Irish Rover/Ivory Tower

LP: Mercury MERH 94 – July 1986
CD: Mercury 830 077-2 – July 1986

CD: Polydor 849619-2 – August 1991

POETIC CHAMPIONS COMPOSE

> *Side One:* Spanish Steps/The Mystery/Queen Of The Slipstream/
> I Forget That Love Existed/
> Sometimes I Feel Like A Motherless Child
> *Side Two:* Celtic Excavation/Someone Like You/Alan Watts Blues/
> Give Me My Rapture/Did Ye Get Healed?/Allow Me

LP: Mercury MERH 110 – September 1987
CD: Mercury 832 585-2 – September 1987
CD: Polydor 517217-2 – 1992

IRISH HEARTBEAT

> *Side One:* Star Of The County Down/Irish Heartbeat/
> Ta Mo Chleamhnas Deanta/Raglan Road/
> She Moved Through The Fair
> *Side Two:* I'll Tell Me Ma/Carrickfergus/Celtic Ray/
> My Lagan Love/Marie's Wedding

LP: Mercury MERH 124 – June 1988
CD: Mercury 834 496-2 – June 1988
> *with The Chieftains*

AVALON SUNSET

> *Side One:* Whenever God Shines His Light/Contacting My Angel/
> I'd Love To Write Another Song/Have I Told You Lately/
> Coney Island/I'm Tired Joey Boy
> *Side Two:* When Will I Ever Learn To Live In God/Orangefield/
> Daring Night/These Are The Days

LP: Polydor 839262-1 – June 1989
CD: Polydor 839262-2 – June 1989

THE BEST OF VAN MORRISON

> *Side One:* Bright Side Of The Road/Gloria/Moondance/
> Baby Please Don't Go/Have I Told You Lately/
> Brown Eyed Girl/Sweet Thing/Warm Love/
> *Side Two:* Jackie Wilson Said/And It Stoned Me/Here Comes
> The Night/Domino/Did Ye Get Healed?/Wild Night/Cleaning
> Windows/Whenever God Shines His Light

> CD adds 'Wonderful Remark', 'Full Force Gale', 'Queen Of The
> Slipstream', and 'Dweller On The Threshold'

LP: Polydor 841970-1 – March 1990

CELTIC CROSSROADS – THE ART OF VAN MORRISON

CD: Polydor 841970-2 – March 1990

ENLIGHTENMENT

Side One: Real Real Gone/Enlightenment/So Quiet In Here/
Avalon Of The Heart/See Me Through
Side Two: Youth Of 1,000 Summers/In The Days Before Rock 'N' Roll/
Start All Over Again/She's My Baby/Memories

LP: Polydor 847100-1 – October 1990
CD: Polydor 847100-2 – October 1990

HYMNS TO THE SILENCE

Side One: Professional Jealousy/I'm Not Feeling It Anymore/
Ordinary Life/Some Peace Of Mind/So Complicated
Side Two: I Can't Stop Loving You/Why Must I Always Explain?/
Village Idiot/See Through Me Part II (Just A Closer
Walk With Thee)/Take Me Back
Side Three: By His Grace/All Saints Day/Hymns To The Silence/
On Hyndford Street/Be Thou My Vision
Side Four: Carrying A Torch/Green Mansions/Pagan Streams/
Quality Street/It Must Be You/I Need Your Kind Of Loving

LP: Polydor 849026-1 – September 1991
CD: Polydor 849026-2 – September 1991

THE BEST OF VAN MORRISON: VOLUME TWO

Real Real Gone/When Will I Ever Learn To Live In God/
Sometimes I Feel Like A Motherless Child/In The Garden/
A Sense Of Wonder/I'll Tell Me Ma/Coney Island/Enlightenment/
Rave On, John Donne/Rave On Part Two (live)/Don't Look Back/
It's All Over Now Baby Blue/One Irish Rover/The Mystery/
Hymns To The Silence/Evening Meditation

LP: Polydor 517760-1 – January 1993
CD: Polydor 517760-2 – January 1993

TOO LONG IN EXILE

Side One: Too Long In Exile/Big Time/Lonely Avenue
Side Two: Ball And Chain/In The Forest/
Till We Get The Healing Done
Side Three Gloria/Good Morning Little Schoolgirl/
Wasted Years/Lonesome Road/Moody's Mood For Love
Side Four: Close Enough for Jazz/Before The World Was Made/
I'll Take Care Of You/Instrumental/Tell Me What You Want

LP: Polydor 519219-1 – June 1993

CD: Polydor 519219-2 – June 1993

A NIGHT IN SAN FRANCISCO

CD1: Did Ye Get Healed?/It's All In The Game/Make It Real One More Time/I've Been Working/I Forgot That Love Existed/Vanlose Stairway/Trans-Euro Train/Fool For You/You Make Me Feel So Free/ Beautiful Vision/See Me Through/Soldier Of Fortune/ Thank You Falettinme Be Mice Elf Again/Ain't That Loving You Baby?/Stormy Monday/Have You Ever Loved A Woman?/No Rollin' Blues/Help Me/Good Morning Little Schoolgirl/Tupelo Honey/ Moondance/My Funny Valentine

CD2: Jumpin' With Symphony Sid/It Fills You Up/I'll Take Care Of You/It's A Man's Man's World/Lonely Avenue/4 O'Clock In The Morning/So Quiet In Here/That's Where It's At/In The Garden/ You Send Me/Allegheny/Have I Told You Lately/Shakin' All Over/ Gloria

CD: Polydor 521290-2 – April 1994

Masonic Auditorium, San Francisco 18 December 1993 and The Mystic Theatre, Petaluma 12 December 1993

DAYS LIKE THIS

Side One: Perfect Fit/Russian Roulette/You Don't Know Me/ No Religion/Underlying Depression
Side Two: Songwriter/Days Like This/I'll Never Be Free/ Melancholia/Ancient Highway/In the Afternoon

LP: Polydor/Exile 527307-1 – June 1995
CD: Polydor/Exile 527307-2 – June 1995

HOW LONG HAS THIS BEEN GOING ON?

Side One: I Will Be There/The New Symphony Sid/Early In the Morning/Who Can I Turn To?/Sack Of Woe/Moondance/Centrepiece
Side Two: How Long Has This Been Goin On?/Your Mind Is On Vacation/All Saint's Day/Blues In The Night/Don't Worry About A Thing/ That's Life/Heathrow Shuffle

LP: Polygram/Exile 529 136-1 – February 1996
CD: Polygram/Exile 529 136-2 – February 1996

TELL ME SOMETHING: THE SONGS OF MOSE ALLISON

One Of These Days/You Can Count On Me (To Do My Part)/If You Live/Was/Look Here/City Home/No Trouble Livin'/Benediction/Back On The Corner/Tell Me Something/I Don't Want Much/News Nightclub/Perfect Moment

CD: Polygram/Exile 533 203-2 – December 1996

THE HEALING GAME
Rough God Goes Riding/Fire In The Belly/This Weight/Waiting Game/Piper At The Gates Of Dawn/Burning Ground/It Once Was My Life/Sometimes We Cry/If You Love Me/The Healing Game

CD: Polydor/Exile 5371012 – March 1997
LP: Polydor/Exile 5371011 (ltd edition) – March 1997

CASSETTE ONLY RELEASE

CUCHULAINN
Spoken word retelling of Irish saga
Cassette: Moles MRILC 012 – 1991

TRACKS BY VAN MORRISON ON OTHER COLLECTIONS

'Hungry For Your Love' (An Officer And A Gentleman, Polygram 1982)
'Wonderful Remark' (King Of Comedy 1983)
'Here Comes The Knight' (live) (Live for Ireland, MCA 1987, from Self Aid)
'Boffyflow And Spike' (A Chieftains Celebration, RCA 1989)
'Brown Eyed Girl' (The Wonder Years, Warner Brothers 1989)
'Wonderful Remark' (Nobody's Child, Warner Brothers 1990)
'TB Sheets' (Dogfight, Nouveau 1991)
'Someone Like You' (Only The Lonely, Varese 1991)
'Jackie Wilson Said (I'm In Heaven When You Smile)' (Queen's Logic, Columbia 1991)
'Brown Eyed Girl' (Sleeping With The Enemy, Columbia 1991)
'That's Where It's At' (A Week Or Two In the Real World, Real World Records 1994) *Sam Cooke's song with The Holmes Brothers*

GUEST APPEARANCES ON OTHER ARTISTS' ALBUMS

Chet Baker, Live At Ronnie Scott's, London (Hendring/Wadham) 1987
The Band, Cahoots (Capitol) 1971
The Band, The Last Waltz (Warner Brothers) 1978
Jim Capaldi, Fierce Heart (Warner Brothers) 1983
The Chieftains, The Long Black Veil (BMG) 1995
Mick Cox, Compose Yerself (SBM) 1990
Georgie Fame, Cool Cat Blues (Bluemoon) 1990
John Lee Hooker, Never Get Out Of These Blues Alive (Crescendo) 1972
John Lee Hooker, Born In Mississippi, Raised Up In Tennessee (ABC) 1973

John Lee Hooker, Mr Lucky (Silvertone) 1992
John Lee Hooker, Chill Out (Pointblank) 1995
James Hunter, Believe What I Say (Ace) 1996
Tom Jones, Carrying A Torch
Roger Waters, The Wall: Live In Berlin 1990 (Mercury) 1990
Bill Wyman, Stone Alone (Rolling Stones) 1976

SINGLES PRODUCED BY VAN MORRISON FOR OTHER ARTISTS

Jackie DeShannon, Sweet Sixteen, Atlantic 1973
Herbie Armstrong, Real Real Gone, Avatar, 1980
Tom Jones, Carrying A Torch, Dover, 1991

SONGS BY VAN MORRISON RECORDED BY OTHER ARTISTS

Across The Bridge Where Angels: Dolores Keane (Lion In A Cage)
And It Stoned Me: Pride (Mind Candy)
And The Healing Has Begun: Waterboys (A Golden Day bootleg)
Angeliou: Deacon Blue ('Riches' CD single) (VMS)
Bayou Doll: Buckwheat Zydeco (Five Card Stud)
Bit By Bit: Roy Head
Brand New Day: Dorothy Morrison (single)
        Esther Phillips (single)
        Frankie Laine
Bright Side Of The Road: Hothouse Flowers (No Prima Donna)
Brown Eyed Girl: Del Amitri (twelve inch)
        Jimmy Buffet (One Particular Harbour)
        El Chicano (Viva: Their Best)
        Tommy Graham (Planet Earth)
        Iain Matthews (Go For Broke)
        Moody Brothers (Cotton Eye Joe)
        Henry Paul Band (Anytime)
        Johnny Rivers (LA Reggae)
        The Senators (Hopes and Bodies)
        Steel Pulse (VMS)
        Texas Mavericks (Who Are These Masked Men)
Caravan: Deodato (The Big Cuckoo)
Carrying A Torch: Evangeline (Evangeline)
        Tom Jones (Carrying A Torch)
Cleaning Windows: Pee Wee Ellis (Sepia Tonality)
        Barrence Whitfield & Tom Russell (Hillbilly Voodoo) (VMS)
Come Here My Love: This Mortal Coil (Filigree And Shadow)
Come Running: The Joy (The Joy)

Comfort You: Pumpkinhead (Pumpkinhead)
Coney Island: Phil Coulter Orchestra (CD single)
        Liam Neeson (No Prima Donna)
Could You, Would You: Willy De Ville (Miracle)
Crazy Love: John Anderson: (You Can't Keep A Good Memory Down)
        Vikki Carr (Superstar)
        PJ Colt (PJ Colt)
        Isley Brothers (Shout And Twist)
        Brian Kennedy ('Intuition' CD single)
        Esther Phillips (single)
        Nolan Porter (Nolan)
        Maxi Priest (Intentions)
        Helen Reddy (Very Best Of)
        Sanne Salomonsen (Where Blue Night Begins)
        Cassandra Wilson (No Prima Donna)
Domino   Buddy Rich
        Swingle II
Fairplay: Robyn Hitchcock ('Oceanside' promo twelve inch)
Feedback On Highway 101: Johnny Winter (Saints And Sinners)
Flamingos Fly: Sammy Hagar (Nine On A Scale Of Ten)
Friday's Child: Herbie Armstrong (Back Against The Wall)
        Lisa Stansfield (No Prima Donna)
Full Force Gale: Elvis Costello & The Voice Squad (No Prima Donna)
Gloria: Boots (Here Are The Boots)
        David Bowie (Die Bowie bootleg)
        Elvis Costello (Bone Of The Attractions bootleg)
        Definition Of Sound (CD single)
        Doors (The Matrix Tapes bootleg CD)
        Eddie And The Hot Rods (The End Of the Beginning) (VMS)
        Jimi Hendrix (The Singles Album)
        Alan Lancaster (Life After Quo)
        101ers (Elgin Avenue Breakdown)
        Iggy Pop (Nightclubbing bootleg)
        Santa Esmeralda (Don't Let Me Be Misunderstood)
        Shadows Of Knight (single)
        Patti Smith (Horses)
        13th Floor Elevators (Demos Everywhere bootleg)
        Johnny Thunders & Hanoi Rocks (single)
        The Wheels (single)
        Frank Zappa (Frank Zappa vs Tooth Fairy)
Have I Told You Lately:
        The Chieftains (Long Black Veil)
        Emilio (Life is Good) (VMS)
        Rene Frogen (Live In Concert)

Laura Fygi (Turn Out The Lamplight)
Dolores Keane (An Drolchead Beag)
James Last & Richard Clayderman (In Harmony)
Mighty Clouds Of Joy
Rebekah Ryan ('You Lift Me Up' single)
Rod Stewart (Vagabond Heart/Unplugged And Seated)
He Ain't Give You None: Jerry Garcia (Garcia)
I Can Only Give You Everything: Richard Hell & Voidoids (Destiny Street)
MC 5 (single)
I'm Not Feeling It Anymore: Tom Jones (Carrying A Torch)
I'm Tired Joey Boy: Tom Petty (Too Good To Be True)
Into The Mystic: Icicle Works (Seven Singles Deep)
Esther Phillips (You've Come A Long Way Baby)
Johnny Rivers (Slim Slo Slider)
Irish Heartbeat: The Burns Sisters (Close To Home)
Billy Connolly (CD single) (VMS)
Brian Kennedy & Shana Morrison (No Prima Donna)
I Shall Sing: Art Garfunkel (Angel Clare) (VMS)
Miriam Makeba (The Queen Of African Music)
Toots And The Maytals (Reggae Got Soul)
It Must Be You: Tom Jones (Carrying A Torch)
I've Been Working: Bo Diddley (Portrait)
Orphan (More Orphan Than Not)
Bob Seger (Live Bullet)
I Wanna Roo You: Jackie De Shannon
Goldie Hawn (VMS)
Jackie Wilson Said: Dexy's Midnight Runners (Too-Rye-Ay) (VMS)
Linden Arden Stole The Highlights: Robyn Hitchcock (Oceanside twelve inch)
Madame George: Energy Orchard (Shinola) (VMS)
Marianne Faithfull (No Prima Donna)
Moondance: Joan Armatrading (Show Some Emotion)
Peter Corry (Live At The Grand Opera House)
Georgie Fame (Coll Cat Blues)
Terry Garthwaite (Hand In Glove)
Bobby McFerrin (Bobby McFerrin CD) (VMS)
Nana Mouskouri (Nana)
Rupert Parker (Songs From The Harp)
Pele ('The Celtic Rumour' CD single)
Irene Reid (single)
Show Of Hands (Formerly Anthrax)
Grady Tate (Bag Of Goodies)
Vinx (The Storyteller)
My Lonely Sad Eyes: Maria McKee (You Gotta Sin To Get Saved) (VMS)
Mystic Eyes: The Crawdaddys (Crawdaddy's Power)
Stackwaddy (Stackwaddy)

One Two Brown Eyes: Energy Orchard (Energy Orchard)
        Iggy Pop (Nightclubbing bootleg)
Queen Of The Slipstream: Brian Kennedy (No Prima Donna)
Real Real Gone: Herbie Armstrong (single)
        Tom Fogerty (Deal It Out)
Ro Ro Rosey: Charlie Brown
Slim Slo Slider: Johnny Rivers (Slim Slo Slider)
Some Peace Of Mind: Tom Jones (Carrying A Torch)
Sunday Night Yap: Pierce Turner (Now Is Heaven)
Sweet Sixteen: Jackie DeShannon (single 1980)
Sweet Thing: Flower Pornoes (Ich & Ich)
        Waterboys (Fisherman's Blues) (VMS)
TB Sheets: John Lee Hooker (Never Get Out Of These Blues Alive)
Tell Me All About Your Love: Brian Kennedy ('Intuition' CD single)
These Were The Days: Elisabeth Von Trapp (Wishful Thinking)
Tupelo Honey: Blackfoot (After The Reign)
        Phil Coulter Orchestra (No Prima Donna)
        Richie Havens (Live On Stage)
        Dusty Springfield (Cameo) VMS
        Wayne Toups (Zyda Cajun Blast From The Bayou)
Vanlose Stairway: Georgie Fame (Three Line Whip)
Vanlose Stairway/Mercy, Mercy, Mercy: Georgie Fame (VMS)
Warm Love: Johnny Coppin (Roll On Dreamer)
Wild Night: Amazing Rhythm Aces
        Polly Brown (Super 20 Disco Specials And Love Songs)
        Richie Havens (The End Of The Beginning)
        Martha And The Vandellas
        John Mellencamp (Dance Naked)
        Martha Reeves (Thelma And Louise)
        Johnny Rivers (Wild Night)
You Make Me Feel So Free: Sinead O'Connor (No Prima Donna)
You Move Me: Tom Fogerty (Deal It Out)
You've Got The Power: Roy Head
Young Lovers Do: Jeff Buckley (Live At Sin-e)
     Maria McKee (You've Got To Sin To Get Saved)
     Shusha (This is The Day)

NO PRIMA DONNA: THE SONGS OF VAN MORRISON
CD: Polydor/Exile 523368-2 – 1994

THE VAN MORRISON SONGBOOK
CD: Connoisseur VSOP CD 233 – 1997
When first announced, this was to comprise 18 tracks, but the release includes only 15, missing out the pre-advertised Joan Armatrading, 'Warm Love', and John Lee Hooker, 'TB Sheets'.

Readers of *Wavelength* bear witness to live versions of Van's songs by – among many others – David Bowie, Counting Crows, Bob Dylan, Bob Geldof, Gary Glitter, The Grateful Dead, REM, Southside Johnnie, Bruce Springsteen and U2.

They also provide details of foreign language versions of 'Brown Eyed Girl' in Catalan(*Ulls de Mel*), 'Have I Told You Lately' in Norwegian (*Har Jeg Sagt Deg Alt Jeg Burde Si Deg*) and 'Bright Side Of The Road' in Spanish (*A Este Lada De La Carretera*).

PROMO ITEMS AND RADIO STATION BROADCASTS

BOTTOM LINE, NEW YORK 15 May 1978
CD: King Biscuit Flower Hour, DIR Broadcasting – 1989

VAN MORRISON LIVE AT THE ROXY
Brown Eyed Girl/Wavelength/And It Stoned Me/Checkin' It/Hungry For Your Love/Kingdom Hall/Crazy Love/Tupelo Honey/Caravan/Cyprus Avenue

LP: WBMS 102 Warner Brothers Music Show: Promotional Release – 1979

THE INTERVIEW ALBUM
Interview with Mick Brown, as part of promotion for *No Guru, No Method, No Teacher*
LP: Mercury 830 222-1 – 1986

ST PATTY'S DAY SPECIAL: TURN UP YOUR RADIO – AN EVENING WITH VAN MORRISON
Greek Theatre, Berkeley 25 July 1986, with tracks from *It's Too Late To Stop Now* and spoken word appearances by Graham Nash, Robbie Robertson and Huey Lewis.
2CDs: Radio Today Entertainment (New York) – 1989

DAYS LIKE THIS
Interview with Michelle Rocca, talking about some of the songs
CD: Polygram – 1995

HOW LONG HAS THIS BEEN GOING ON?
Interview with John Fordham, talking about some of the songs
CD: Polygram – 1995

THE PHILOSOPHER'S STONE
Promo only – Summer 1996 (comments by Pete Howard and Bill Levinson)
Disc One   1) Really Don't Know
                     Recorded in 1971. "A really stunning piece of music, very powerful"
                     2) Ordinary People
                     Also recorded in 1971. "A great blues song"

3) Wonderful Remark
Eight minute performance recorded in San Anselmo, California in 1973. The
original version of the song that Morrison later contributed to the
soundtrack of *King Of Comedy*. "Very pretty and ethereal, with Ronnie
Montrose on guitar and background vocals"
4) Not Supposed To Break Down
Recorded at Caledonia Studios in Fairfax, California in 1973
5) Laughing In The Wind
Caledonia Studios, 1973. Jackie DeShannon on background vocals. "A very
catchy, strong song with lots of horns, vintage early seventies Morrison"
6) Madame Joy
Caledonia Studios, 1973. "Really spectacular." This was supposedly the
original title for 'Madame George', so the mind boggles
7) Contemplation Rose
Caledonia Studios, 1973. "A beautiful song with allusions to Harlem"
8) Don't Worry About Tomorrow
Caledonia Studios, 1973
9) Try For Sleep
Caledonia Studios, 1973. Co-written with John Platania. "A very slow tempo
song, sung by Van in falsetto. The mood is set by the song's first words, 'It's
four o'clock in the morning'"
10) Lover's Prayer
Caledonia Studios, 1973. "Very beautiful, in the tradition of Van's love
songs"
11) Drumshabo Hustle
Caledonia Studios, 1973. "A fascinating, entertaining song about the music
business and record companies"
12) Twilight Zone
A legendary performance, lasting eight minutes. Recorded in Holland in 1974,
and mixed at the Record Plant in Sausilito, California the same year. "A very
slow, bluesy, late night song that would fit right in on *Veedon Fleece*. Van
performed it on tour in 1975"
13) Foggy Mountain Top
Like the previous track, recorded in Holland, and remixed in Sausilito. "A
slow, piano driven blues number, with a soulful harmonica break"
14) Naked In The Jungle
Recorded at the Record Plant in 1975. "A very energetic, keyboard driven
tune with effective scat singing by Van"
15) There There Child
Co-written with John Platania. Recorded at Caledonia Studios, 1976

Disc Two   1) When I Deliver
           Record Plant 1975
           2) John Henry

Traditional song, Record Plant 1977
3) John Brown's Body
Also a traditional song, Record Plant 1979
4) I Have Finally Come To Realise
Record Plant, 1975
5) Flamingoes Fly
A new spelling, and a different version from that which appeared on
Period Of Transition. Recorded in Holland in 1974, with Pete
Wingfield on piano. Mixed at the Record Plant
6) Stepping Out Queen Part II
Recorded at the Record Plant in 1979. A sequel to the track which appears
on *Into The Music*
7) Bright Side Of The Road
Different version to the official take
8) I'm Ready
Recorded at the Record Plant, 1979
9) Street Theory
Recorded in France in 1980. "A rapidly paced, piano driven song...
a cross between 'Turn On Your Lovelight' and 'Come
Running'. Features Mark Isham on synthesiser
10) Real Real Gone
Original version, recorded in 1980, and once played by a San
Franciscan radio station. Ten years later, a new version appeared on
Enlightenment. Pee Wee Ellis on saxophone
11) Showbusiness
Nine minute song, recorded in London 1982
12) For Mr Thomas
Recorded in 1983. Van performs a song written by
Robin Williamson, a long time musical colleague, and co-founder
of The Incredible String Band
13) Crazy Jane On God
Recorded in 1984 in England and California. "A very pretty song" with
additional vocals by Irish folk rockers Moving Hearts. At   the time the
estate of poet WB Yeats refused their permission for Van to use
this poem on LP
14) Song Of Being A Child
Recorded in 1987 in Bath. A collaboration between Van (music)
and Peter Hudke (lyrics)
15) High Spirits
Recorded in 1988 in Northern Ireland. Co-written with Paddy Moloney
of The Chieftains, who perform here

A two CD compilation of unreleased songs, initially agreed by Van Morrison and due for release 16 July 1996, but yet to appear. It was to contain a booklet with track by track annotation. The information here comes courtesy of the Internet and Simon Gee.

The June 1996 *Ice* newsletter gives fuller details. Having turned down the idea of a box set of old material, Morrison himself selected thirty previously unreleased performances from his archives. All but four are previously unheard songs. A source close to Morrison told *Ice* that, "I wouldn't call them out-takes, because that suggests that these tracks are somewhat secondary. They're not, these are just really good songs that weren't released at the time." The set contains material often between albums. Like Neil Young, Morrison was very prolific, often abandoning album projects half way through, or later.

A subtitle on test pressings states that this is only "Volume One", and judging by songs already in circulation – like 'I Shall Sing', 'Feedback On Highway 101', 'And The Streets Only Knew Her Name', 'Don't Change On Me' and 'Grits Ain't Groceries' – there is quite enough good material for further compilations, or a box set. "Basically, they went in to do the box, and found out he had so much unreleased material, that instead of trying to figure out how to work all of the unreleased material into the box, they're going to lead with this package. Then perhaps there'll be a box set."

IMPORTANT BOOTLEGS

Bootlegs are the ultimate expression of the free market, and their number and quality tend to reflect the cultural importance of the artist concerned. In a century's time, the best of such items will be an important tool towards understanding some of history's greatest poets and musicians in performance.

There are a huge number of Van Morrison related items, reflecting a fanatical interest in his live performances which no official release programme could or would ever satisfy. Morrison once himself bootlegged the bootlegger, by including live tracks from Pagan Streams *on two CD singles. There is a comprehensive survey of such items in John Collis's huge discography – I append here a brief chronology of the illicit CD and tape delights not on offer at your local music megastore.*

Early radio sessions and rare singles by Them and The Monarchs

BLUESOLOGY 1963-73
Studio demos, 1969-71 **GETS HIS CHANCE TO WAIL/LAUGHING IN THE WIND/NAKED IN THE JUNGLE**
Fillmore West, 26 April 1970 **ROCKS HIS SOUL/INTO THE MAN/MOONLIGHT SERENADE/LIVE IN SAN FRANCISCO**
Pacific High Studios, 19 September 1971 **DESERT LAND/INTO THE MYSTIC/THE INNER MYSTIC/THIS IS VAN MORRISON**
Aquarius Theatre 1972
San Anselmo 15 February 1973 **STORMY WEATHER IN SAN ANSELMO**
Los Angeles Troubadour 26 May 1973/World Tour 1974.

out-takes from a proposed third album of It's Too Late To Stop Now **IT AIN'T WHY, IT JUST IS/IT'S NEVER TOO LATE**
Cowtown Palace 17 January 1974
Cambridge, Massachusetts 11 March 1974
Vara Studios, Amsterdam 24 June 1974, *with Dr John* **AMSTERDAM'S TAPES**
Montreux Jazz Festival, 30 June 1974 **IF YOU DON'T LIKE IT GO FUCK YOURSELF/PURE**
The Orphanage 29 July 1974
Studio demos, 1974-75 **LAUGHING IN THE WIND/NAKED IN THE JUNGLE**
Vara Studios 22.6.74
Mechanical Bliss, 1975 out-takes
The Last Waltz: rough-mix masters 25 November 1976 **FRIENDS AND OTHER STRANGERS**
King Biscuit Hour, Bottom Line Club NY, 15 May 1978 **GOSPELS FOR THE OCEAN/IRISH SOUL**
Bottom Line 1 November 1978
Roxy Theatre, LA 26 November 1978 **LIVE AT THE ROXY**
Hammersmith Odeon 27 February 1979
Rockpalast TV Special, Essen Germany, 3 April 1982 **CAN YOU FEEL THE SILENCE/LIVE IN ESSEN**
Bob Dylan, Paris, 1 July 1984: 1 encore **LES TEMPS CHANGENT**
Bob Dylan, Slane Castle 8 July 1984: 2 encores **FROM THE COAST OF BARCELONA**
Cannes 1984
Montreux Jazz Festival, 11 July 1984 **HAUNTS OF ANCIENT PEACE/I CAN'T GO ON...BUT I'LL GO ON**
Frankfurt 1986 **COPYCATS RIPPED OFF MY SOUL**
Ronnie Scott's Club 6 June 1986, *with Chet Baker* **DARK KNIGHT OF THE SOUL**
Greek Theatre, Berkeley 25 July 1986 **SOUNDING IN THE CLOUDS/ST PATRICK'S DAY**
Edinburgh Playhouse 1986 **LIVE IN EDINBURGH AT THE PLAYHOUSE**
Danish Radio Big Band, Copenhagen, 28 February 1987 **LISTEN TO THE LION**
Glastonbury 1987
Coleraine University 20 April 1988, *with Derek Bell* **DARK KNIGHT OF THE SOUL**
Hammersmith Odeon 10 May 1988
Ulster Hall, Belfast 15 September 1988, *with The Chieftains* **DARK KNIGHT OF THE SOUL**
Church of Our Lady St Mary, Stogumber, Somerset 17 January 1990 **THE CHURCH OF OUR LADY ST MARY**
Montreux Festival, July 1990 *with Georgie Fame* **LIVE IN MONTREUX**
BBC TV soundtrack, *One Irish Rover* broadcast 16 March 1991 **VAN MORRISON MEETS BOB DYLAN AND JOHN LEE HOOKER**
Concertgebouw, the Hague, Holland 31 March 1991
Some bootlegs claim incorrectly that the performances come instead from the Fleadh, Finsbury Park and Feile, Dublin 1991 **SOUL LABYRINTH**

Utrecht/Vredenburg, Holland 1 April 1991 **PAGAN STREAMS**
Glastonbury Festival 28 June 1992 **VAN THE MAN**
Bristol, 23 January 1993 **WILD NIGHT**
The Point, Dublin 6 February 1993 **LIVE IN EDINBURGH AT THE PLAYHOUSE**
Hammersmith Apollo, 22 March 1993 **WILD NIGHT**
Manchester Apollo, 4 March 1994 **MY NAME IS RAINCHECK**
EMA Awards, Belfast 13 April 1995 **LOST IN A FUGITIVE'S DREAM**
Cambridge Corn Exchange 14 April 1995 **LOST IN A FUGITIVE'S DREAM**
Danish Radio Big Band, Helsingor Jazz Festival 5 August 1995 **STEPPIN' ON A DREAM**
Edinburgh 1995 International Jazz Festival, with BBC Big Band **EDINBURGH CASTLE**
Bournemouth LEC, 16 September 1995 **STEPPIN' ON A DREAM**
Mercury Music Awards 1995 **STEPPIN' ON A DREAM**
The Point, Dublin, 17th December 1995 **THE NIGHT WAS FULL OF SPACES**

Filmography

Some of the items below capture something of Morrison's grace and danger on stage. He has not willingly embraced the MTV age, though, or its obsessions with flashy director's videos, the very antithesis of Van's work. See Wavelength *for fuller listings, and updates.*

GLIDE

A German B/W movie, rumoured to have been made in 1962, while Van was touring with The Monarchs. *Wavelength* magazine are certain it does not exist.

READY STEADY GO

ORIGINAL PERFORMANCES (VOL I) includes Them performing 'Baby Please Don't Go' in 1964. In 1994, Ulster TV also broadcast a November 1964 interview, in which a young Van talks about a scuffle which broke out among the audience during a local Them gig.

WHERE THE ACTION IS

Three promos, of 'Call My Name', 'Mystic Eyes' and 'Brown Eyed Girl' made for US TV. The first two, paradoxically, feature Them on London bridge. The third is Van alone in a New York studio.

TOPPOP GOLD, DUTCH TV 1967

Mimes 'Mystic Eyes' with Cuby and the Blizzards, in a garden (though not 'misty wet with rain'). Rebroadcast on 'Toppop Gold' in 1990.

RANDALL'S ISLAND POP FESTIVAL, 17th July 1970

Four minute 'Come Running', later shown on US TV

FILLMORE EAST, NEW YORK, October 1970

'Cyprus Avenue'

DON KIRSCHNER'S IN CONCERT, April 1973

Four songs in colour, 'I've Been Working' , 'Caravan', 'Gloria' and a nine minute 'Cyprus Avenue. With The Caledonia Soul Orchestra in top

form, and Van in a black stetson hat, this US TV
broadcast is legendary among Van fanatics. Rightly so.

OLD GREY WHISTLE TEST, 23 July 1973
"Whispering" Bob Harris interviews Van and two members of his band, John
Platania and David Hayes.

RAINBOW THEATRE, 24 July 1973
The first BBC simultaneous broadcast of rock music on TV and in stereo on
Radio One, on the *Old Grey Whistle Test*. Anne Nightingale introduces eleven
songs with The Caledonia Soul Orchestra, culminating with a near ten
minute 'Cyprus Avenue', during which a ten-year-old Shana is seen on stage.
A future star is born. On the following day, Irish TV broadcast four more
songs, ending with 'Gloria'.

TALK ABOUT POP, RTE, 11 September 1973
Interview with Donall Corvin, plus five live songs played solo, including a
savagely curtailed 'Autumn Song' and 'Drumshanbo Hustle'.

WINTERLAND, SAN FRANCISCO, 2 February 1974
A medley of '4 O'Clock in the Morning' and 'Family Affair' on bootleg video.

HAMMERSMITH ODEON, Spring 1974
BBC TV broadcast

MONTREUX JAZZ FESTIVAL, 30 June 1974
Four live tracks from the lost years, including the instrumental 'Heathrow
Shuffle' – with Van blowing saxophone – and 'Naked In The Jungle'.

MUSIKLADEN, Bremen 10 July 1974
Four tracks, opening with 'Heathrow Shuffle'. All four were reprised on ITV
in 1988. 'Bulbs', a rare public performance of a song from *Veedon Fleece*
later re-appeared on 'Beat Club Vol 4' (BMG Video) as does 'Heathrow
Shuffle'.

THE ORPHANAGE, San Francisco, August 1974
Interview with Tom Donahue, threading between eight live songs with the
short lived backing band Soundhole. A particularly fine version of 'Snow In
San Anselmo'.

THE LAST WALTZ, 1976
Film by Martin Scorsese, recording The Band's farewell concert. Van
Morrison sings 'Caravan', and joins in on the encore of 'I Shall Be
Released'. A soundboard tape from the original concert surfaced on the
'Friends and Other Strangers' bootleg CD, which also includes Van's duet

with Richard Manuel on 'Tura Lura Lura'.

MIDNIGHT SPECIAL, NBC 28 March 1977

Five songs, as part of a supergroup featuring the weird combination of Carlos Santana, George Benson, Dr John, Tom Scott and Etta James. The set list is equally interesting, including 'Cold Wind In August' and 'Joyous Sound'.

PROMOTIONAL APPEARANCE. MAUNKBERRY'S, Granada TV 15 June 1977

'Joyous Sound' appears again here, with 'Venice USA', 'The Eternal Kansas City' and an untitled instrumental. The band includes Dr John – again – and Mick Ronson.

WONDERLAND, Vara Studios 1977

The same band appear playing in the studio on this Dutch TV special, which also includes stock footage of Irish landscapes, not quite chiming in with a playlist of 'Baby Please Don't Go', 'The Eternal Kansas City' and 'Cold Wind In August'.

SATURDAY NIGHT LIVE, 4 November 1978

The Bobby Tench led band perform 'Wavelength' and 'Kingdom Hall' for TV, live in New York. A ten minute concert repeated since on MTV

OUR TIMES, WB promo Denver 1978

Five songs with the same band as above, a mixture of the old – 'Brown Eyed Girl' and 'Caravan' – and the new, ie 'Kingdom Hall', 'Checkin' It Out' and 'Wavelength'. Also broadcast on the Don Kirshner show, and reprised as an "official" release by dubious sources in Italy.

VAN MORRISON IN IRELAND, February 1979

Moondance/Checking It Out/Moonshine Whiskey/Tupelo Honey/Wavelength/
St Dominic's Preview/Don't Look Back/I've Been Working/Gloria/Cyprus Avenue
The band as above, in Dublin and Belfast, interspersing live music with footage of them on tour and places from Van's past, in particular some stunning shots of Cyprus Avenue. Commercially released (twice) in stereo sound, though now deleted. Directed by Michael Radford of *Il Postino* fame.
Narrowcast – 1980
Hendring – 1987

LIVE AT THE CAPITOL THEATRE, PASSAIC, NEW JERSEY 6 October 1979

Kingdom Hall/Bright Side Of The Road/Here Comes The Night/Into The Mystic/You Make Me Feel So Free/Warm Love/Call Me Up In Dreamland/It's All In The Game/Ain't Nothing You Can Do/Angeliou/Full Force

Gale/Moondance/Moonshine Whiskey/Wavelength/Tupelo Honey/I've Been
Working/Troubadours/Brown Eyed Girl/Gloria
Bootleg B/W video of a new band featuring Pee Wee Ellis, John Platania,
Pete Wingfield, and Mark Isham.

MONTREUX JAZZ FESTIVAL, 10 July 1980

Five songs form the Casino de Montreux, subsequently broadcast by TV 5
in 1988. Pee Wee Ellis excels on eight minute workouts of 'Summertime In
England' and 'Haunts Of Ancient Peace', and proceedings finish with an
(edited) 'Ballerina'. Superlative.

ROTTERDAM, 23 May 1981

'Summertime In England' is also the highlight of this Dutch TV concert
from Festival 81.

ROCKPALAST, ESSEN, 3 April 1982

Rockpalast concerts are rightly legendary because of the time and care
given to the acts chosen, almost as if they were culturally important, or
something. Compare this to current British TV, where rock is something
watched mainly by insomniacs, or those with a copy of
Radio Times, a keen eye, and a reliable video recorder. Even if you do stay
up for, say, a Neil Young And Crazy Horse concert, it is suddenly pulled, for
no given reason. End of sermon.
This is a particularly good example, recorded at the Grugahalle in Essen.
Eighteen songs with a band including Chris Michie on guitar and the
Ellis/Isham brass section. A ten minute 'Summertime In England' is a
deserved highlight. Van has already taken to his habit of nipping off stage,
and thus misses two songs here.

LATE LATE SHOW, March 1983

Van performs 'Cry For Home', live on Irish TV.

ROCKPALAST, "MIDEM" CANNES, 26 January 1984

An hour-and-a-half of music and twenty songs, in perfect sound and vision,
from the Nouveau Palace De Festival. A completely different band to two
years before, featuring Martin Drover, Richie Buckley, Kenny Craddock, Arty
McGlynn, Jerome Rimson and Terry Popple. Van himself plays lots of
keyboards. The set largely duplicates the previous German outing.
Additions include 'Inarticulate Speech Of the Heart', 'Higher Than The
World' and 'River Of Time'.

WEMBLEY STADIUM, 7 July 1984

An MTV out-take, in which Van joins in an encore of 'It's All Over Now Baby
Blue' with its composer, Bob Dylan, and a ragbag of Eric Clapton, Chrissie
Hynde, Carlos Santana and Mick Taylor.

MARY O'HARA SHOW, ITV, 19 August 1984

Performance of 'Northern Muse (Solid Ground)', on an MOR show par excellence.

CELTIC SWING promo, November 1984

Van's first commercial video for the MTV age, though it has certainly not yet killed *this* radio fanatic.

PAVILION THEATRE, GLASGOW, 15 October 1984

Van sings 'Celtic Swing' and 'Cry For Home' with the Battlefield Band, hosts of this programme for BBC Scotland.

A GRAND NIGHT OUT, 23 October 1984

Introduced by Phil Coulter, Van sings 'A Sense Of Wonder' and 'What Would I Do' as part of a celebration of sixty years of BBC broadcasts from Ulster.

OLD GREY WHISTLE TEST, BBC2 13 November 1984

Van performs 'A Sense Of Wonder' live in the studio, twice. One version appeared on New Year's Eve on a "Pick Of The Year" special. Van's band remains the same as on the second Rockpalast.

ENTERTAINMENT CENTRE, SYDNEY, Australian TV February 1985

Film of two songs from the Australian tour, recorded live for TV. 'A Sense Of Wonder' and 'Tore Down A La Rimbaud'.

THE TUBE, Channel 4, 29 March 1985

'Tore Down A La Rimbaud', 'The Master's Eyes' and 'If Only You Knew' live at the Tyne Tees studios.

SELF AID, Dublin 17 May 1986

RTE broadcast of 'Thanks For The Information', 'Here Comes The Night' and 'A Town Called Paradise', with Neil Drinkwater on keyboards added to the standard band.

CHET BAKER AT RONNIE SCOTT'S, 6 June 1986

Van sings 'Send In The Clowns'
Hendrin – 1990

WOGAN, 27 June 1986

Performs 'Ivory Tower' in front of Terry, in an update of the saying "pearls before swine".

NIMAJAZZ, Queen's University, Belfast, 13 November 1987

Van guests with the big band of the Northern Ireland Music Association, including old colleague John Wilson on drums. Six songs, including 'Listen To The Lion' and 'Haunts Of Ancient Peace'.

SATURDAY REVIEW, 15 November 1986

BBC2 interview with Mick Brown, and two songs, 'The Healing Has Begun' and 'In The Garden'.

POLYDOR PROMO VIDEO, 7 July 1987

Twenty minute interview with Bill Morrison, interspersing two performances from the Hammersmith Odeon of 'Did Ye Get Healed?' and 'The Mystery'.

AS I ROVED OUT, BELFAST, 29 October 1987

Forty Minute in concert special with The Chieftains, filmed at Balmoral Studios. Shown on RTE and the BBC in March 1988. Van sings and plays drums on four songs, 'Raglan Road', 'Star Of The County Down', 'My Lagan Love' and 'Celtic Ray'.

THE LATE LATE SHOW: TRIBUTE TO THE CHIEFTAINS, RTE March 1988

Morrison guests on 'Star Of The County Down', 'My Lagan Love' and 'Marie's Wedding', the last with Christy Moore, Gary Moore (no relation) and Paul Brady.
RTE Video – 1988

VAN THE MAN, Ulster Television, 20 April 1988

Interview and discussion, filmed at the Riverside Theatre at the University of Coleraine, and broadcast on Irish TV in July. Includes an acoustic performance with Van on guitar, Clive Culbertson on double bass and Derek Bell on piano, and conversations with Professor Bob Welch and Martin Lynch. The songs performed are 'When I Was A Cowboy', 'Foggy Mountain Top', 'A Sense Of Wonder', 'In The Garden' – collected on WPV – 'Star Of the County Down' and 'Raglan Road'. Primal stuff.

ECO ROCK, FIFE AID, ST ANDREWS 24 July 1988

'A Sense Of Wonder', 'Mairie's Wedding' and 'Cleaning Windows', recorded with a pick up band for a charity concert.
Video: Castle/Hendrin – 1990

SONGS OF INNOCENCE: VAN MORRISON AND THE CHIEFTAINS AT THE ULSTER HALL, BELFAST, 15 September 1988

Tore Down A La Rimbaud/In The Garden/Rave On, John Donne/Did Ye Get Healed?/Star Of the County Down/She Moved Through The Fair/Ta Mo Chleamhnas Deanta/I'll Tell Me Ma/Carrickfergus/Celtic Ray/Marie's Wedding/Boffyflow And Spike/Goodnight Irene/Moondance
Hour long concert broadcast on Channel 4 in March 1989. Fourteen songs, the first four with his own band – Arty McGlynn, Clive Culbertson, Dave Early, Richie Buckley and June Boyce – and special guest Derek Bell. 'Rave On, John Donne' appears on WPV. The rest is with The Chieftains, who as

this set list indicates range far wider than Irish traditional. A wonderful show.

HAVE I TOLD YOU LATELY
Polydor promo for single

THE PRINCE'S TRUST 1989 ROCK GALA,
NEC Birmingham, broadcast on ITV, with a full orchestra conducted by George Martin on 'Orangefield'.

ATHENS, 27-28 June 1989
Duet with Dylan, see *One Irish Rover*, 16 March 1991.

MONTREUX JAZZ FESTIVAL, 17 July 1989
BBC broadcast 'Vanlose Stairway', with Georgie Fame and the Dallas Jazz Orchestra.

KILLER: JERRY LEE LEWIS AT THE HAMMERSMITH ODEON, 21 November 1989
Van is interviewed, and performs two songs, 'Goodnight Irene' and 'What'd I Say', the latter of which appears on the MCA commercial video release of this tribute concert.

VAN MORRISON: THE CONCERT, Beacon Theatre NY, 30 November 1989
I Will Be There/Whenever God Shines His Light/Cleaning Windows/Orangefield/When Will I Ever Learn To Live In God/Thank God For Self Love/Raglan Road/Carrickfergus/Summertime In England/Caravan/Moondance/Fever/Star Of The County Down/In The Garden/Have I Told You Lately/Gloria/It Serves Me Right To Suffer/Boom Boom/She Moved Through The Fair
with Mose Allison and John Lee Hooker
Video: Polygram – 1990

LATE NIGHT WITH LETTERMAN, New York 1 December 1989
Ten minute appearance.

WHENEVER GOD SHINES HIS LIGHT
Polydor promo video for single.

WOGAN, BBC1 December 1989
Duet with Cliff Richard on 'Whenever God Shines His Light'.

TOP OF THE POPS, BBC1 December 1989
They repeat their joint performance.

ARENA SPECIAL: SLIM GALLIARD'S CIVILISATION
>BBC2 series, broadcast late 1989, in which Morrison jams on 'Arabian Boogie' and recites extracts from Kerouac's *On The Road* while Galliard provides a piano accompaniment.

SAN REMO FESTIVAL, 24 February 1990
>He sings 'Have I Told You Lately' to a backing track. Broadcast on Super Channel.

ROCK STEADY SPECIAL, Channel 4 February 1990
>Van and Mose Allison performing together in Bristol.

THE SHOW, BBC Northern Ireland 17 March 1990
>Four songs live at the Joker Club, Belfast.

MONTREUX JAZZ FESTIVAL, 11 July 1990

THE WALL, Berlin 21 July 1990
>Channel 4 carry live coverage of Roger Waters' multi-media event, resurrecting his gloomy Pink Floyd epic. Morrison performs two of Waters' songs, 'Comfortably Numb' and 'The Tide Is Turning'.

REAL REAL GONE, late 1990
>Polydor promo video for single.

CLEAR COOL CRYSTAL STREAMS, LWT 21 October 1990
>Melvyn Bragg's *South Bank Show* spends sixty minutes on Van Morrison and his music, on a prime time slot.

SHOWTIME: COAST TO COAST, 22 October 1990
>US TV broadcasts two songs live in a Los Angeles TV studio, with jazz maestros Herbie Hancock, Chick Corea and Larry Carlton.

THE LATE SHOW, BBC2 13 November 1990
>Three songs live in the studio.

VAN MORRISON AND TOM JONES, 14 February 1991
>Promo video for new album, with film of two songs in the studio, 'Carrying A Torch' and 'I'm Not Feeling It Anymore'.

MEAN FIDDLER, 6 March 1991
>(Officially) unreleased Polydor promo for 'I Can't Start Loving You', with The Chieftains.

CONEY ISLAND OF THE MIND, Channel 4, 12 March 1991

Half hour TV special, filmed in Wicklow and Belfast, in which Morrison meets various Irish poets.

ONE IRISH ROVER BBC2, 16 March 1991
Arena Special, also broadcast on cable in the States, featuring nineteen separate performances with the likes of The Chieftains, John Lee Hooker, Dylan and The Danish Radio Big Band, as well as Morrison's own band. 'Foreign Window' and 'One Irish Rover', with Bob Dylan strumming alongside, were filmed in Athens in June 1989.

EMA AWARDS, BBC1, 16 March 1991
Show features 'You're The One'.

CIVIC HALL, WOLVERHAMPTON, 17 January 1992
Amateur video.

SYMPHONY HALL, BIRMINGHAM, 25 September 1992
Another homemade video.

FLEADH 93, FINSBURY PARK, 12 June 1993

MUZIEKCENTRUM VREDENBURG, UTRECHT, 23 October 1993

MANCHESTER APOLLO, 4 March 1994

MONTREUX JAZZ FESTIVAL, 9 July 94

A RIVER OF SOUND, Irish TV 1995
'My Lagan Love' accompanied only by piano, in comprehensive TV history of Irish music, placed in a world context.

DAYS LIKE THIS PROMO, April 1995

PERFECT FIT PROMO, July 1995

DAVID LETTERMAN: LETTERMAN IN LONDON BBC2 17 May 1995
Van duets with Sinead O'Connor on 'Have I Told You Lately', backed by The Chieftains.

ALBUM OF THE YEAR – LIVE, 23 September 1995
Songs from 'Days Like This', featuring trumpeter Guy Barker

LATER, BBC 2 January 1996
Three songs by Morrison backed by Georgie Fame and band. Van looks both mysterious and menacing in hat, dark glasses and black suit.

ROYAL CONCERT HALL, GLASGOW, 14 January 1996
'Slim Slo Slider' brings WPV to a triumphant conclusion.

IRMAS, DUBLIN, 29 March 1996

DAVID LETTERMAN SHOW, 30 April 1996
'Moondance' reprised.

FILM SOUNDTRACKS

THE SCHOONER (dir Bill Muscally) Eire 1983. A film for RTE, with original soundtrack by Morrison, recorded at Cucumber studios.

LAMB (dir Colin Gregg). Original soundtrack composed by Morrison.

SONGS USED IN FILMS

'Astral Weeks'
SLIPSTREAM Canada 1970

'Baby Please Don't Go'
GOOD MORNING VIETNAM (dir Barry Levinson) USA 1987
WILD AT HEART (dir David Lynch) USA 1990

'Brown Eyed Girl'
SLEEPING WITH THE ENEMY, USA 1991

'Gloria'
THE OUTSIDERS (dir Francis Ford Coppola) USA 1983

'Hungry For Your Love'
AN OFFICER AND A GENTLEMAN (dir Taylor Hackford) USA 1982

'Moondance'
AN AMERICAN WEREWOLF IN LONDON (dir John Landis) USA 1982

'Slim Slo Slider':
THREE AMERICAN ALBUMS (dir Wim Wenders) West Germany 1970

'Wonderful Remark'
KING OF COMEDY (dir Martin Scorsese) USA 1983

Bibliography

BANGS, LESTER
> 'Astral Weeks', *Stranded* 1979, reprinted in *Psychotic Reactions And Carburetor Dung* Heinemann 1988 pp20-28

BONO
> 'Bono Talking With Bob Dylan And Van Morrison', *Hot Press* 24 August 1984, reprinted in *The U2 File* ed Niall Stokes, Omnibus 1985 p160

BROWN, MICK
> *American Heartbeat, Travels From Woodstock To San Jose By Song*

BURGESS, STEVE
> 'The Common One', *Dark Star* 25, December 1980

CLARKE, VICTORIA
> 'The Hardest Thinking Man In Showbiz', *Q* August 1993

CLAYSON, ALAN
> *Call Up The Groups, The Golden Age Of British Beat 1962-67* Blandford Press, Poole 1985, pp168-70
> *Beat Merchants: The Origins, History, Impact And Rock Legacy Of The 1960s British Pop Groups* Blandford 1995

CLAYTON-LEA, TONY & TAYLOR, RICHIE
> *Irish Rock* Sidgwick and Jackson 1992

COLLIS, JOHN
> *The Rock Primer* (ed) Penguin 1980 pp163, 302-3
> *Van Morrison: Inarticulate Speech Of The Heart Little*, Brown and Company 1996. Articulate and wise, with lots of original research among Van's early friends. The book seems a little rushed, and ends on a negative note, regarding Morrison's personality
> 'Van Morrison', *Rock: The Rough Guide* ed Jonathan Buckley and Mark

Ellingham, Rough Guides 1996 pp582-4

COPPLE, CYNTHIA
Van Morrison: Reliable Sources Caledonia Productions San Rafael 1973 (ed). The authorised version of Van's life, but never widely available, except to journalists

CRUIKSHANK, BEN
Into The Sunset: The Music Of Van Morrison Agenda 1996. A useful track by track guide, with short articles on key influences

DAVIES, MIKE
'Van Morrison Interview', *Nuggets* 8, Summer 1977

DENSELOW, ROBIN
When The Music's Over: The Story Of Political Pop Faber 1989, pp158, 161, 207

DENSMORE, JOHN
Riders On The Storm Bloomsbury 1991, pp74-6

DeWITT, HOWARD
The Mystic's Music Horizon Books, Freemont, California 1983

DOGGETT, PETER
'Them', *Record Collector* 149, January 1992
'Van Morrison', *Record Collector* 178-180 June – August 1994

DU NOYER, PAUL
'Blind Date', *Q*, August 1989
'The Big Man', *Q*, April 1997

FALLON, BP
'Interview', *The Guardian* 15 June 1996

FLANAGAN, BILL
'Van Morrison', *Musician* 1984, reprinted in *Written In My Soul* Omnibus 1990 pp447-20

GARRY, MAC
'One Of Them – The Astral Van Morrison', *Zigzag* 5, September 1969

GILLETT, CHARLIE
The Sound Of The City 1970, rev ed Souvenir 1983 pp408-9

GRAHAM, BILL

My Life Inside Rock And Roll, Delta 1993 Passages not in the published version later appeared in *Musician*, January 1994

GRISSIM, JOHN

Interview, *Rolling Stone* June 1972, reprinted in *Rolling Stone Interviews Vol 2*, ed Ben Fong-Torres, Warner Paperback Library NY 1973, pp74-83

HATCH, DAVID

From Blues To Rock Manchester Univ Press 1987, pp23

HEYLIN, CLINTON

The Great White Wonders: A History Of Rock Bootlegs Viking 1994 pp305-6, p327

HODGETT, TREVOR

'Them', *Record Collector* 89, January 1987

HOGG, BRIAN

'Van Morrison And Them', *Strange Things Are Happening*, September 1988

HOLDEN, STEPHEN

'St Dominic's Preview', *Rolling Stone* 31 August 1972, reprinted in *Rolling Stone Record Review II* Pocket Books, NY 1974, pp458-61

HOSKYNS, BARNEY

'100 Great Voices', *Mojo Music Guide 2*

KELLY, PAT

More Than A Song To Sing: Mystical Ideas And The Lyrics Of Van Morrison Rowan Press, Darlington 1993. Sincerity is the key word here, both Van's and the author's response to key lines of his songs, through which Kelly pursues six key themes. A fan's response, par excellence

KUREISHI, HANIF

'With Your Tongue Down My Throat', *Granta* 22, Autumn 1987, pp21-76

LANDAU, JON

'His Band And Street Choir', *Rolling Stone* 4 February 1971, reprinted in *Rolling Stone Record Review II* Pocket Books NY 1974, pp454-8

LANDY, Elliott
>   *Woodstock Vision: The Spirit Of A Generation* Continuum, NY 1994

MARCUS, Greil
>   Interview, *Rolling Stone* July 1970, reprinted in *Rolling Stone Interviews Vol II*,
>   ed Ben Fong-Torres, Warner Paperback Library NY 1973 pp57-61
>   *Mystery Train* 1975, 4th ed Penguin 1991 p153
>   'Van Morrison', *The Rolling Stone Illustrated History Of Rock 'N' Roll* ed Jim
>   Miller, Random House NY 1980 pp320-3
>   'Success And Failure In The Wilderness', New West 28 October 1980, reprinted
>   in *In The Fascist Bathroom* Viking 1993, pp146-8

MARSH, Dave
>   *Rolling Stone Record Guide* (ed), Random House, NY 1979 pp256-7
>   *The Heart Of Rock And Soul: The 1001 Greatest Singles Ever Made*

MARTIN, Gavin
>   'Poetry, Punks And Pawns' *Record Hunter*, April 1991

MAY, Chris & PHILLIPS, Tim
>   *British Beat* Socion Books 1974

MORRISON, Van
>   *The Songs Of Van Morrison* Wise 1971 Anthology Wise 1992. Words and
>   music for 26 songs

O'CONNOR, Nuala
>   *Bringing It All Back Home; The Influence Of Irish Music* BBC 1991, pp126-8

PALMER, Myles
>   'The Lion Of Caledonia' *Let It Rock* January 1973

POWER, Vincent
>   *Send 'Em Home* Sweating Kildanore Press 1990

PRENDERGAST, Mark
>   *Irish Rock: Roots, Personalities, Directions* O'Brien Press, Dublin 1987 pp113-142

REBENNACK, Mac
>   *Under A Hoodoo Moon; The Life Of The Night Tripper* St Martin's Press, New
>   York 1994 pp224-5

REYNOLDS, Simon & PRESS, Joy

The Sex Revolts: Gender, Rebellion And Rock 'N' Roll Serpent's Tail 1995 pp168-170

ROCCA, Michelle

'Pillow Talk', *Mojo* 100, August 1995

ROGAN, Johnny

Van Morrison Proteus 1984. Written with all the meticulous detail that one would expect, but a sour book, which devalues Van's music because of his public persona
'Van Morrison', *Record Collector* 57, May 1984

SALEWICZ, Chris

'Van Morrison, The Hermit Of Holland Park', *Q* January 1987

SARLIN, Bob

'Van Morrison – Belfast Cowboy', *Turn It Up! (I Can't Hear The Words)* Simon and Schuster 1973 pp89-104

SINCLAIR, David

Rock On CD: The Essential Guide Kyle Cathie 1992 pp221-4

SMITH, Joe

Off The Record: An Oral History Of Popular Music Sidgwick and Jackson 1989, pp270-272

STAMBLER, Irwin

Encyclopedia Of Pop, Rock & Soul St James Press 1977 pp359-60

TAME, David

Beethoven And The Spiritual Path Quest

TOBLER, John

'Van Morrison Out Of The Mystic', *Zigzag* 36
100 Great Albums Of The Sixties Little Brown 1994, p78

TRAUM, Happy

Interview, *Rolling Stone* 9 July 1970, reprinted in *The Rolling Stone Interviews 1967-1980* ed Peter Hebst, St Martin's Press, NY 1981 pp100-106

TURNER, Steve

Hungry For Heaven; Rock And Roll And The Search For Redemption 1988, rev ed Hodder 1995, pp123-8
Van Morrison: Too Late To Stop Now Bloomsbury 1993. The best overall survey of Van's career, sympathetically written and profusely illustrated.

WILD, DAVID
Interview, *Rolling Stone* 9 August 1990

WYATT, ROBERT
'The Record That Changed My Life', *Q* June 1995

YORKE, RITCHIE
Van Morrison: Into the Music Charisma/Futura 1975 The only book so far to receive the approval of the singer, though perhaps it is over reverential as a result. Fascinating all the same, and long out of print

Individual reviews from which I have quoted are referred to individually in the text. I can supply any further details on request.

FANZINES

Into The Music 1-9, ed Donal Caine

The Van Morrison Newsletter 1-10, ed Stephen McGinn

Wavelength, ed Simon Gee
PO Box 80, Winsford, Cheshire CW7 4ES, wavelength@netcentral.co.uk
Wavelength is one of the most comprehensive, readable and devoted as any fanzine going, although its production levels really lift it out of that category. It contains a wealth of information and detail. Simon Gee currently planning a complete listing of all the setlists of as many Van Morrison concerts as can be retrieved from the memories or tape recorders of its readers.

BOOKS IN PROGRESS

Gerald Dawe: *The Burning Ground – The Making Of A Musician*
Patrick Humphries: *Complete Guide To The Music Of Van Morrison*
(due March 1997)
Michelle Rocca: *Conversations With Van Morrison*

Brian Hinton's literary reviews and poems appear regularly in the magazine Tears In The Fence. For further details contact David Gabby, 38 Hod View, Stourpaine, Blandford Forum, Dorset DT11 8TN